THIS ABILITY

Dedication

To my Mother and Father, Virgilia and William Cotter, my Uncle Msgr. Theodore Mooney, my Brothers and Sisters, my Husband Mark Badger and our Son Bill for their love and devotion.

This Ability
An International Legal Analysis of Disability Discrimination

ANNE-MARIE MOONEY COTTER

ASHGATE

Published by
Ashgate Publishing Limited
Gower House
Croft Road
Aldershot
Hampshire GU11 3HR
England

Ashgate Publishing Company
Suite 420
101 Cherry Street
Burlington, VT 05401-4405
USA

Ashgate website: http://www.ashgate.com

British Library Cataloguing in Publication Data
Cotter, Anne-Marie Mooney
   This ability : an international legal analysis of
   disability discrimination
   1. Discrimination against people with disabilities - Law
   and legislation - Cross-cultural studies 2. People with
   disabilities - Legal status, laws, etc. - Cross-cultural
   studies
   I. Title
   346'.013

Library of Congress Cataloging-in-Publication Data
Cotter, Anne-Marie Mooney.
   This ability : an international legal analysis of disability discrimination / by Anne-
Marie Mooney Cotter.
      p. cm.
   Includes bibliographical references and index.
   ISBN: 978-0-7546-4913-7 (hardback)
   1. Discrimination against people with disabilities--Law and legislation 2. People
with disabilities--Legal status, laws, etc. I. Title

   K637.C68 2007
   342.08'7--dc22

2006034018

ISBN: 978-0-7546-4913-7

Printed and bound in Great Britain by Antony Rowe Ltd, Chippenham, Wiltshire.

Contents

Biography

Dr. Anne-Marie Mooney Cotter, Esq. is a Montrealer, fluent in both English and French. She earned her Bachelor's degree from McGill University at age 18, her Juris Doctor law degree from one of the leading civil rights institutions Howard University School of Law, and her Doctorate degree (Ph.D.) from Concordia University, where she specialized in Political Economy International Law, particularly on the issue of equality. Her work experience has been extensive, Chief Advisor and later Administrative Law Judge appointed by the Prime Minister to the Veterans Review and Appeals Tribunal in Canada; Supervising Attorney and later Executive Director for the Legal Services Corporation in the United States; National Director for an environmental network in Canada; Faculty for Business Law at the Law School, Law Society of Ireland; Associate at the law firm of Blake Cassels and Graydon L.L.P. with a secondment as in-house counsel with Agrium Inc. in Canada; and Attorney with the Disability Law Center of Alaska. She is also a gold medallist in figure skating. Dr. Cotter is the wife of Mark Badger and the proud mother of Bill.

Chapter 1

Introduction to This Ability

> So we come here today to dramatize a shameful condition. In a sense we've come to our nation's capital to cash a check. When the architects of our republic wrote the magnificent words of the Constitution and the Declaration of Independence, they were signing a promissory note to which every (human) was to fall heir. This note was the promise that all ... would be guaranteed the unalienable rights of life, liberty, and the pursuit of happiness .... A check which has come back marked insufficient funds. We refuse to believe that there are insufficient funds in the great vaults of opportunity of this nation. And so we've come to cash this check, a check that will give us upon demand the riches of freedom and the security of justice.[1]

In our universal quest for justice and specifically disability discrimination, we may learn from the immortal words of one of the greatest civil rights leaders and human rights activists Dr. Martin Luther King Jr. This book, *This Ability*, focuses on the goal of disability equality, and the importance of the law and legislation to combat discrimination. The aim of this book is to better understand the issue of inequality and to improve the likelihood of achieving disability equality in the future and ending disability inequality. *This Ability* examines the primary role of legislation, which has an impact on the court process, as well as the primary role of the judicial system, which has an impact on the fight for disability equality. This is the third book in a series of books on discrimination law. Other titles in the series are '*Gender Injustice*' dealing with gender discrimination, and '*Race Matters*' dealing with race discrimination. A similar approach and structure is used throughout the series to illustrate comparisons and contradictions in discrimination law.

Fundamental rights are rights which either are inherent in a person by natural law or are instituted in the citizen by the State. The ascending view of the natural law of divine origin over human law involves moral expectations in human beings through a social contract, which includes minimum moral rights of which one may not be deprived by government or society. The competing view is that courts operating under the Constitution can enforce only those guarantees which are expressed. Thus, legislation has an impact on the court system and on society as a whole. Internationally and nationally, attempts have been made to improve the situation of those with a disability and outlaw discrimination through acceptance and accommodation.

In looking at the relationship between 'This Ability' and the law, the book deals comprehensively with the issue of disability discrimination throughout its chapters: Chapter 1 introduces the reader to the core area of disability inequality;

Chapter 2 covers disability inequality in human relations around the world; Chapter 3 looks at the United Nations; Chapters 4 and 5 examine disability inequality in Australia and New Zealand, and Africa and South Africa, respectively; Chapters 6 and 7 examine disability inequality in Canada, Mexico and the United States, and the North American situation with the North American Free Trade Agreement regarding disability inequality, respectively; Chapters 8 and 9 examine disability inequality in the United Kingdom and Ireland, and the European situation with the European Union Treaty regarding disability inequality, respectively; and Chapter 10 concludes this overview of disability inequality.

The globalization process and the various economic agreements have a direct impact on people's lives as key players in the labor market today. This study seeks to comparatively analyze legislation impacting disability equality in various countries internationally. It also examines the two most important trade agreements of our day, namely the North American Free Trade Agreement and the European Union Treaty in a historical and compelling analysis of equality. Although an important trade agreement with implications for labor, the North American Free Trade Agreement has a different system from the European system in that it has no overseeing court with jurisdiction over the respective countries. Further, the provisions for non-discrimination in the labor process are contained in a separate document, the North American Agreement on Labor Cooperation. On the other hand, the European Union Treaty takes a different approach, by directly providing for non-discrimination, as well as an overseeing court, the European Court of Justice, and the treaty is made part of the domestic law of every Member State, weakening past discriminatory laws and judgments. Further, the European process actively implements disability equality by way of European Union legislation.

North America, as the new world with its image of freedom and equality, is considered to have made great strides in civil rights. However, the American philosophy of survival of the fittest and the pursuit of materialism have slowed down the process. With the advent of the European Union, the coming together of nations has had a very positive influence on the enforcement of human rights, much more so than that of North America, because of the unique European approach.

All parties must cooperate, and governments need to work with businesses, trade unions and society as a whole, and together they can create an environment where all humans can participate at all levels of political life and decision-making. Indeed, combating disability inequality and achieving disability equality requires a strong 'This Ability' focus in constitutional, legal, judicial and electoral frameworks for all humans to be actively involved at the national and international levels.

According to liberal democracy, the rule of law is the foundation stone for the conduct of institutions. *This Ability* offers a defence of the notion that social reform is possible and plausible through key institutions, which include the legal system and its use of the law. For liberal democracy, the legislative system is the core for the governance of society in the way it functions toward social equality of opportunity. It is clear that if we reform our legislation and our laws, then there will be a change in the institutions of society and their functioning, which will be a major step forward in societal reform.

The law is of central importance in the debate for change from disability inequality to disability equality. Actionable and enforceable rights are legal norms, which represent social facts demarcating areas of action linked with universalized freedom.[2] Law is a powerful tool, which can and must be used to better society. Associated with command, duty and sanction, and emanating from a determined source, law is a rule of conduct enforced by sanctions, and administered by a determinate locus of power concentrated in a sovereign or a surrogate, the court. Therefore, the justice system and the courts play a vital role in enforcing the law.

Legitimacy has subjective guarantees of internalization with the acceptance and belief in authority, and objective guarantees of enforcement with the expectation of reactions to the behavior.[3] Therefore, law must recognize equally all members of society, including those with a disability, in order for it to be effective. Further, in order for a law to be seen as legitimate from society's point of view and accepted by the people, in general to be followed, a process of inclusive interaction by all affected must first be realized. When creating laws, this means that input from various groups, including all humans and especially those with a disability, is critical.

Thus, laws have two components, namely, facts, which stabilize expectations and sustain the order of freedom, and norms, which provide a claim of approval by everyone. Law makes possible highly artificial communities whose integration is based simultaneously on the threat of internal sanctions and the supposition of a rationally motivated agreement.[4] Discrimination and injustice can be undercut through the effective use of both the law and the courts.

The facticity of the enforcement of law is intertwined with the legitimacy of a genesis of law that claims to be rational, because it guarantees liberty. Laws can go a long way in forbidding inequality and providing for equality; where one ends the other begins. There are two ranks of law, namely ordinary law of legislation, administration and adjudication, and higher constitutional law affecting rights and liberties, which government must respect and protect. The latter encompasses the constitutions of the various nations as interpreted by the supreme courts. Law holds its legitimacy and validity by virtue of its coercive potential, its rational claim of acceptance as right. It is procedurally constructed to claim agreement by all citizens in a discursive process purported to be open to all equally for legitimacy and a presumption of fair results. The legitimate legal order is found in its reflexive process. Therefore, we must all believe that equality is a good and necessary thing, which is essential to the very growth of society.

Thus, conflict resolution is a process of reasoned agreement where, firstly, members assume the same meanings by the same words; secondly, members are rationally accountable for their actions; and thirdly, mutually acceptable resolutions can be reached so that supporting arguments justify the confidence in the notion that the truth in justice will not be proven false.[5] Disenchantment with the law and the legal process only serves to undermine the stabilization of communities. By legitimizing the legal process and holding up the ideals of equality in the fight against disability discrimination, the law and the courts can bring about change.

All humans have had to fight in the formulation of laws and in the enforcement of equality in the courts. Class rests on economic determination and historical change, like disability. Inequality in the distribution of private property among different classes of people has been a characteristic of society. The ruling class loathes that which it is not, that which is foreign to it, and this has traditionally been those with a disability. The patriarchal system has freely fashioned laws and adjusted society to suit those in power, and this has traditionally been white Anglo-Saxon Protestant men.

Physical and mental attributes, opportunities and relationships are socially constructed and are learned through socialization processes. They are context and time-specific but changeable, since the physical and the mental determine what is expected, allowed and valued in a given situation. In most societies, there are differences and inequalities between humans in the assignment of responsibilities, undertaking of activities, access to and control over resources, and decision-making opportunities, with disability part of the broader sociocultural context. There are important criteria for analysis, including disability, race, gender, poverty and class, and age, and hence all these can, alone or combined, amount to discrimination.

The concept of equality is the ignoring of difference between individuals for a particular purpose in a particular context, or the deliberate indifference to specified differences in the acknowledgement of the existence of difference. It is important to note that assimilation is not equality. The notion of rights and of equality should be bound to the notion of justice and fairness. Legal freedom and rights must be seen as relationships not possessions, as doing, not having. While injustice involves a constraint of freedom and a violation of human dignity through a process of oppression and domination, justice involves the institutional conditions necessary for the development and exercise of individual capacities for collective communication and cooperation.[6] Discrimination is the withholding from the oppressed and subordinated what enables them to exercise private and public autonomy. The struggle must be continued to bring about psychological, sociological and institutional changes to allow all members of the human race to feel equal and to recognize one another as being so. Solidarity and cooperation are required for universal and global equality.

Though humans are mortal and civilizations come and go, from Biblical times to our days, there has been a fixed pivot for the thoughts of all generations and for men of all continents, namely the equal dignity inherent in the human personality.[7] Even Pope John XXIII described the United Nations Declaration of Human Rights in his 1963 Encyclical *Pacem in Terris*, as 'one of the most important acts of the United Nations' and as 'a step towards the politico-judicial organization of the world community'; 'In social life, every right conferred on man by nature creates in others (individuals and collectivities) a duty, that of recognizing and respecting that right'.[8] Further, Pope John Paul II described the importance of work and of just remuneration in his 1981 Encyclical *Laborem Exercens*:

Work bears a particular mark of ... humanity, the mark of a person operating within a community of persons .... While work, in all its many senses, is an obligation, that is to say a duty, it is also a source of rights on the part of the worker. These rights must be examined in the broad context of human rights as a whole, which are connatural with man, and many of which are proclaimed by various international organisations and increasingly guaranteed by the individual States for their citizens. Respect for this broad range of human rights constitutes the fundamental condition for peace in the modern world: peace both within individual countries and societies and in international relations .... The human rights that flow from work are part of the broader context of those fundamental rights of the person .... The key problem of social ethic...is that of just remuneration for work done .... Hence, in every case, a just wage is the concrete means of verifying the justice of the whole socio-economic system and, in any case, of checking that it is functioning justly.[9]

An improvement in equality of opportunity is sought rather than a utopian state of equality. No one should misunderstand this. Clearly, oppression exists. Rather, this book *This Ability* seeks to add to the list of inequalities to be considered, and does not rule out other forms of injustices besides disability inequality. Generalities are not presumed nor are they made here, for this would detract from the very purpose of this book, to bring to the forefront of discussion the reality of injustice, not to create further injustice.

Notes

[1]   King Jr., Dr. Martin Luther, *March on Washington*, 1963.
[2]   Habermas, Jurgen, *Between Facts and Norms*, 1998, p.xii.
[3]   Fried, Morton, *The Evolution of Political Society*, 1967, p.23.
[4]   Habermas, Jurgen, *Between Facts and Norms*, 1998, p.8.
[5]   *Ibid.*, at p.xv.
[6]   Habermas, Jurgen, *Between Facts and Norms*, 1998, p.419.
[7]   Cassin, René, *From the Ten Commandments to the Rights of Man*, France, 1969.
[8]   Pope John XXIII, *Pacem in Terris*, Rome, 1963.
[9]   Pope John Paul II, *Laborem Exercens*, Rome, 1981.

References

Cassin, René (1969), *From the Ten Commandments to the Rights of Man*, France.
Fried, Morton (1967), *The Evolution of Political Society*, Random House, New York.
Habermas, Jurgen (1998), *Between Facts and Norms*, MIT Press, Massachusetts.
King Jr., Dr. Martin Luther (1963), *March on Washington*.
Pope John XXIII (1963), *Pacem in Terris*, Rome.
Pope John Paul II (1981), *Laborem Exercens*, Rome.

Chapter 2

This Ability in Disability Discrimination

Introduction

This chapter will begin by examining this ability generally, and will go on to examine this ability specifically, looking at the World Program of Action Concerning Disabled Persons and Standard Rules on the Equalization of Opportunities for Persons with Disabilities. All human rights, civil, cultural, economic, political and social, including the right to development, are universal, indivisible, interdependent and interrelated. Governments and others must not only refrain from violating human rights, but must work actively to promote and protect these rights. Human rights issues of discrimination continue to mar progress towards empowerment where those with a disability continue to be over-represented among the poor and face systemic barriers that prevent them from accessing the opportunities created for the achievement of equality.

This Ability Generally

There is considerable ambiguity in the general literature on disability discrimination about whether anti-discrimination law is primarily intended to protect people whose work performance 'productivity' is not limited or only trivially limited, by their condition, or whether people who are substantially limited in what they can do are also seen as potential beneficiaries of the law.[1] This ambiguity reflects different conceptions of equality. There are two broad conceptions: equality of opportunity and equality of results. Equality of opportunity is oriented towards individual merit, in the sense that it aims for equality in the opportunities of individuals to work and be paid, in accordance with their abilities. This conception is most relevant to disabled people whose productivity is unimpaired and whose opportunities are currently limited by stigma and stereotyping. By contrast, a conception oriented to equality of results, envisaging elements of redistribution and positive action, would appear to offer more to those who have substantial limitations. These two conceptions are clear alternatives, and imply different definitions of disability. The individual merit approach suggests that the definition should encompass minor impairments, medical conditions which are not substantially limiting in their effect on a person's activities and perceived disabilities. The equality of results approach suggests a definition nearer in conception to those found in social policy, which would target a different group of people with substantial limitations.

Within the equal opportunities/individual merit approach can be found a spectrum of tests for discrimination. At one end of the spectrum, there is the 'equality as mere rationality', where arbitrary and unreasonable behaviour is deemed discriminatory, but justifications for discrimination are accepted at face value. At the other end of the spectrum, there is the 'equality as fairness', where justifications are examined critically, the possibility of indirect discrimination is recognised, and burdens of proof may be shifted. Many argue that reasonable accommodation for disabled people comes within an 'equality as fairness' conception of the scope of anti-discrimination law, while others see accommodation as a form of positive action. There is a third conception of equality which goes beyond the individual merit approach but avoids the explicitly redistributive language of equality of results, the 'radical equality of opportunity', which argues for institutional and structural changes to remove the barriers to equal participation for disabled people. It involves the creation of positive duties on employers to promote equality, by reviewing employment practices and workplace organization.

Officials often consider a range of factors, such as the person's age, education and work history. An employment officer seeking to help a disabled person into work may consider such factors along with considerations arising from the person's medical condition and limitations, and may take a view about whether the costs of accommodation in a particular job are reasonable and comparable with the costs that would arise in other possible jobs. Existing employees are, implicitly or explicitly, given the right to accommodation in their existing job or with the same employer. The question of whether the person is sufficiently disabled in general life activities that accommodation would be needed in any job is not necessarily considered. The first step is to see whether the person can resume his previous job with adaptations and adjustments. Possible job changes and re-training with the same employer are considered next. If these steps do not lead to a resumption of employment, other job options are considered. The establishment of rights to reasonable accommodation for existing employees can be understood as arising from the established corpus of laws and practices governing employers' obligations to their employees.

However, building disability rights on the existing corpus of employee rights has the important limitation that the rights created are confined to those in employment. While many people who face late-onset disabilities may be protected by such measures, those seeking access to employment do not benefit. From this perspective, one purpose of a definition of disability is to establish a standard for specifying who has rights under antidiscrimination legislation which is common to both existing and prospective employees, and avoids setting different standards for 'insiders' and 'outsiders'. This is a laudable ideal, but it comes up against a very basic problem about the fair allocation of costs across employers. The difficulty for a job-seeker is that no employer has any particular or special duty towards him, relative to other employers. Where the costs of accommodation are significant, some public or social financing structure provides the most direct and effective method of spreading burdens.[2]

Prejudice is, as the name implies, the process of pre-judging something. In general, it implies coming to a judgment on the subject before learning where the preponderance of the evidence actually lies, or formation of a judgment without direct experience. When applied to social groups, prejudice generally refers to existing biases toward the members of such groups, often based on social stereotypes, and at its most extreme, becomes denying groups benefits and rights unjustly or, conversely, unfairly showing unwarranted favor towards others. It may be a matter of early education; those taught that certain attitudes are the correct ones may form opinions without weighing the evidence on both sides of a given question. Many prejudicial behaviors are picked up at a young age by children emulating their elders' way of thinking and speaking, with no malice intended on the child's part. Overall, prejudice has been termed an adaptive behavior by sociologists.

In terms of discrimination, to discriminate is to make a distinction. Commonplace forms of invidious discrimination include distinctions by disability, race, skin color, ethnicity, nationality, gender, marital status, religion, age, and socio-economic class. Invidious discrimination classifies people into different groups in which group members receive distinct and typically unequal treatments and rights without rational justification. Expectations and obligations of group members are also biased by invidious discrimination. If the justification is rational, then the discrimination is not invidious. By virtue of establishing nationalism, as opposed to globalism, every government has formalized and supported discrimination. However, many governments have attempted to control discrimination through civil rights legislation, equal opportunity laws and institutionalized policies of affirmative action.

Affirmative action or positive discrimination is a policy or a program providing access to systems for people of a minority group who have traditionally been discriminated against, with the aim of creating a more egalitarian society. This consists of access to education, employment, health care or social welfare. The terms affirmative action and positive discrimination originate in law, where it is common for lawyers to speak of affirmative or positive remedies that command the wrongdoer to do something. In contrast, negative remedies command the wrongdoer to not do something or to stop doing something. In employment, affirmative action may also be known as employment equity or preferential hiring. In this context affirmative action requires that institutions increase hiring and promotion of candidates of mandated groups. Affirmative action originally began as a government remedy for past government and social injustices. Affirmative action exists to change the distribution of jobs, education, wealth, or other things, based on certain characteristics.

Supporters of affirmative action argue that affirmative action policies counteract a systemic discrimination by providing a balancing force. A certain group may be less proportionately represented in an area, often employment or education, due predominantly, in the view of proponents, to past or ongoing discrimination against members of the group. The theory is that a simple adoption of meritocratic principles along the lines of disability-blindness would not suffice to change the situation: regardless of overt principles, people already in positions of power were likely to hire people they already knew, and people from similar backgrounds; also, ostensible measures of merit might well be biased toward the same groups who were already empowered. In such a circumstance, proponents believe government action giving members of the group preferential treatment is necessary in order to achieve a proportionate distribution.

From its outset, affirmative action was seen as a transitional strategy, with the intent that in a period, variously estimated from a generation to a century, the effects of past discrimination would be sufficiently countered that such a strategy would no longer be necessary: the power elite would reflect the demographics of society at large. Though affirmative action in the United States is primarily associated with racial issues, the American Civil Rights Movement originally gave as its purpose the correction of a history of oppression against all working-class and low-income people, and people with a disability should figure prominently among its beneficiaries. A written affirmative action plan must include goals and timetables for achieving full utilization of those with a disability, in quotas based on an analysis of the current workforce compared to the availability in the general labor pool of those with a disability.

Opponents of affirmative action regard it as demeaning to members of disabled groups, in that affirmative action wrongly sends a condescending message that they are not capable enough to be considered on their own merits. Critics often object to the use of quotas in affirmative action. Quotas are illegal in the United States, except when a judge issues an order for a specific institution to make up for extreme past discrimination. There is dispute over whether this *de jure* illegality prevents *de facto* quotas, and attempts have been made to show that these goals are not quotas. However, some believe eradicating affirmative action will further deepen economic disparity between groups.

Affirmative action in the United States was originally conceived as a means to compensate African Americans for centuries of slavery, as newly granted legal equality was considered insufficient to redress African American grievances. However, the initiative quickly ballooned to encompass various other groups that had never suffered from slavery. Thus the original justification, which the potential victims of affirmative action were initially compelled to accept, has been abandoned. Supporters of affirmative action argue that it benefits society as a whole; given that affirmative action is effective, creating a diverse culture increases the quality of the society.

Free market libertarians believe any form of unjustified discrimination is likely to lead to inefficiencies, and that a rational person would therefore be unlikely to seek to discriminate one way or another and should therefore be free to decide who to select. Therefore, libertarians generally do not advocate anti-discrimination laws, as they reportedly distort the situation. They believe that inefficient, overregulated, non-competitive industries enable unjustified discrimination, as said industries need not compete and hire on credentials relevant to the job. In terms of policy, libertarians favor repealing all affirmative action legislation and regulation, so that the government has no official stance on the practice, leaving the decision to uphold and maintain such a policy up to the individual institutions.

Equal opportunity refers to the idea that all people should start out in life from the same platform, in that all should have equal opportunities in life, regardless of where they were born or who their parents were. Egalitarianism is the moral doctrine that equality ought to prevail throughout society, and according to legal egalitarianism, everyone ought to be considered equal under the law. The United States Declaration of Independence included moral and legal egalitarianism. Because 'all men are created equal', the State is under an obligation to treat each person equally under the law. Originally this statement excluded women, slaves and other minority groups, such those with a disability, but over time this kind of egalitarianism has won wide adherence and is a core component of modern civil rights policies.

This Ability Specifically

While the significance of national and regional particularities and various historical, cultural and religious backgrounds must be borne in mind, it is the duty of States, regardless of their political, economic and cultural systems, to promote and protect human rights and fundamental freedoms of all people. The implementation of these principles of equality, including through national laws, strategies, policies, programs and development priorities, is the sovereign responsibility of each State, in conformity with human rights and fundamental freedoms. The significance of and full respect for various disabled, religious, philosophical and ethical values, and cultural and racial backgrounds of individuals and communities should contribute to the full enjoyment of human rights, in order to achieve equality, development and peace.

There must be immediate and concerted action by all to create a peaceful, just and humane world based on human rights and fundamental freedoms, including the principle of equality for all people of all ages and from all walks of life, and to this end, broad-based and sustained economic growth in the context of sustainable development is necessary to sustain social development and social justice. Success will require a strong commitment on the part of governments, international organizations and institutions at all levels. It will also require adequate mobilization of resources from multilateral, bilateral and private sources for the advancement of all humans for strengthening the capacity of national, sub-regional, regional and international institutions; a commitment to equal rights, equal responsibilities and equal opportunities for the equal participation of all regardless of disability in all national, regional and international bodies in the policy-making processes; and the establishing or strengthening of mechanisms at all levels for accountability to the world's population in general.

As globalization continues to influence economic opportunities worldwide, its effects remain uneven, creating both risks and opportunities for different groups. For many, globalization has intensified existing inequalities and insecurities, often translating into the loss of livelihoods, labor rights, and social benefits. Member States of the United Nations have endorsed the Millennium Development Goals of halving extreme poverty by 2015 and of achieving equality.

Social movements are fuelling increased global networking, civil society activism, and consumer awareness. Organizations and networks are taking on issues of social justice and equal rights to influence economic policies and decisions at the micro, meso and macro levels.

Even with economic growth, conditions can arise which can aggravate social inequality and marginalization. Hence, it is indispensable to search for new alternatives that ensure that all members of society benefit from economic growth based on a holistic approach to all aspects of development: equality between the people, social justice, conservation and protection of the environment, sustainability, solidarity, participation and cooperation, peace and respect for human rights. The rapid process of adjustment due to downsizing in sectors has also led to increased unemployment and underemployment. Structural adjustment programs have not been successfully designed to minimize their negative effects on vulnerable and disadvantaged groups, nor to assure positive effects on those groups by preventing their marginalization in society.

Multilateral trade negotiations underscore the increasing interdependence of national economies, as well as the importance of trade liberalization and access to open dynamic markets. Therefore, only a new era of international cooperation among peoples based on a spirit of partnership within an equitable international social and economic environment, along with a radical transformation of the relationship to one of full and equal partnership will enable the world to meet the challenges of the twenty-first century. Interestingly, the growing strength of the non-governmental sector has become a driving force for change. Non-governmental organizations (NGOs) have played an important advocacy role in advancing legislation or mechanisms to ensure the promotion of all people, and have become catalysts for new approaches to development.

Actions to be taken at the national and international levels by governments, the United Nations' system, international and regional organizations, including international financial institutions, the private sector, non-governmental organizations (NGOs) and other actors of civil society, include the creation and maintenance of a non-discriminatory, as well as a disability sensitive legal environment through review of legislation with a view to striving to remove discriminatory provisions. Problems continue to persist in addressing the challenges of inequalities, empowerment, poverty eradication, and advancement of all. Vast political, economic and ecological crises, systematic or *de facto* discrimination, violations of and failure to protect human rights and fundamental freedoms, and ingrained prejudicial attitudes towards different groups are impediments to equality. It will be critical for the international community to demonstrate a new commitment for the future to inspire a new generation to work together for a more just society. The advancement of all and the achievement of disability equality are a matter of human rights and a condition for social justice.

World Program of Action Concerning Disabled Persons

The United Nations' World Program of Action Concerning Disabled Persons was formulated on 22 November 1983. The Preamble of the World Program of Action Concerning Disabled Persons states:

> The General Assembly,
>
> Recalling its resolutions 32/133 of 16 December 1977 and 34/154 of 17 December 1979, by which it appealed to Member States to make generous voluntary contributions to the International Year of Disabled Persons,
>
> Recalling also its resolution 36/77 of 8 December 1981, by which it welcomed the contributions made by Governments and private sources to the United Nations Trust Fund for the International Year of Disabled Persons and appealed for further voluntary contributions which would facilitate the follow-up to the Year,
>
> Deeply concerned that no less than five hundred million persons are estimated to suffer from disability of one form or another, of whom four hundred million are estimated to be in developing countries,
>
> Convinced that the International Year of Disabled Persons gave a genuine and meaningful impetus to activities related to the equalization of opportunities for disabled persons, as well as prevention and rehabilitation at all levels,
>
> Noting the emergence of organizations of disabled persons in all parts of the world and their positive influence on the image and condition of persons with a disability,
>
> Desirous of ensuring effective follow-up to the International Year of Disabled Persons and aware that, if this is to be achieved, Member States, organs, organizations and agencies of the United Nations system, non-governmental organizations and organizations of disabled persons must therefore be encouraged to continue the activities already undertaken and to initiate new programs and activities,
>
> Stressing that the primary responsibility for promoting effective measures for the prevention of disability, rehabilitation and the realization of the goals of 'full participation' of disabled persons in social life and development and of 'equality' rests with individual countries and that international action should be directed towards assisting and supporting national efforts in this regard, such as consultative services in designing national plans and programs in the field of disability prevention, rehabilitation and the equalization of opportunities for persons with disabilities,
>
> Reiterating its appreciation to the Advisory Committee for the International Year of Disabled Persons for its work, in particular for its contribution to the formulation of the World Program of Action concerning Disabled Persons,

Recalling its resolution 37/52 of 3 December 1982, by which it adopted the World Program of Action concerning Disabled Persons, which, in paragraph 157, states that the Trust Fund established by the General Assembly for the International Year of Disabled Persons should be used to meet requests for assistance from developing countries and organizations of disabled persons and to further the implementation of the World Program of Action, and, in paragraph 158, indicates that, in general, there is a need to increase the flow of resources to developing countries to implement the objectives of the World Program of Action, that, therefore, the Secretary-General should explore new ways and means of raising funds and take the necessary follow-up measures for mobilizing resources, and that voluntary contributions from Governments and from private sources should be encouraged,

Recalling further its resolution 37/53 of 3 December 1982, by which it proclaimed the period 1983-1992 United Nations Decade of Disabled Persons as a long-term plan of action, on the understanding that no additional resources from the United Nations system would be needed for this purpose, and encouraged Member States to utilize this period as one of the means to implement the World Program of Action concerning Disabled Persons,

Concerned that developing countries are experiencing increasing difficulties in mobilizing adequate resources for meeting pressing needs in the field of disability prevention, rehabilitation and equalization of opportunities for the millions of persons with disabilities, in the face of pressing demands from other high-priority sectors concerned with basic needs,

Convinced that the United Nations Decade of Disabled Persons should give a strong impetus to the implementation of the World Program of Action concerning Disabled Persons and to a broader understanding of its importance,

Noting Economic and Social Council resolution 1983/19 of 26 May 1983, in which the Secretary-General was requested to monitor and support the implementation of the World Program of Action concerning Disabled Persons by enlisting extrabudgetary resources,

Noting with great appreciation the many generous voluntary contributions and pledges already made by Governments, organizations and individuals,

Noting also with appreciation the report of the Secretary-General on the results achieved so far by the United Nations Trust Fund for the International Year of Disabled Persons during the Year and its follow-up activities,

Recognizing that the Trust Fund is an important instrument for the implementation of the World Program of Action concerning Disabled Persons,

1.   Recognizes the desirability of the continuation of the United Nations Trust Fund for the International Year of Disabled Persons throughout the United Nations Decade of Disabled Persons for the benefit of disabled persons, particularly those in developing countries;

2. Decides that the Trust Fund should continue its activities pending a report by the Secretary-General to the General Assembly at its thirty-ninth session, which should include recommendations for the further implementation of the World Program of Action concerning Disabled Persons, the funding of such activities by voluntary contributions, the possible terms of reference of a trust fund for the United Nations Decade of Disabled Persons, the implementation of the provisions contained in Assembly resolution 36/77 concerning the organization of support services for technical co-operation in favour of disabled persons, as well as the organization of task forces mentioned in Assembly resolution 37/53;

3. Stresses the need for the administration of the Trust Fund to continue to be carried out as an integral part of the substantive responsibilities for disability matters discharged by the Secretariat;

4. Recommends that the resources of the Trust Fund should be geared, within the framework of the United Nations Decade of Disabled Persons, towards the implementation of the World Program of Action concerning Disabled Persons and towards helping persons with disabilities to organize themselves, towards assisting in implementing support and consultative services for technical co-operation and inter-organizational task forces, as mentioned in resolutions 36/77 and 37/53, and towards strengthening the activities of the regional commissions in the field of disability prevention and the advancement of persons with disabilities;

5. Requests the Secretary-General to take the necessary steps to strengthen the Trust Fund and, to this effect, to enlist extra budgetary resources as indicated in paragraph 158 of the World Program of Action concerning Disabled Persons;

6. Appeals to Governments and private sources for continuing generous voluntary contributions to the Trust Fund;

7. Calls upon all Member States, all non-governmental organizations concerned and organizations of disabled persons and calls also upon all organs, organizations and agencies of the United Nations system, through a reallocation of existing resources, to continue to ensure the early implementation of the World Program of Action concerning Disabled Persons;

8. Requests the Secretary-General to include in his reports to the General Assembly on the implementation of the World Program of Action concerning Disabled Persons a section on the activities of the Trust Fund.[3]

More than 500 million people in the world are disabled as a consequence of mental, physical or sensory impairment. They are entitled to the same rights as all other human beings and to equal opportunities. Too often their lives are handicapped by physical and social barriers in society which hamper their full participation. Because of this, millions of children and adults in all parts of the world often face a life that is segregated and debased.

Everywhere, however, the ultimate responsibility for remedying the conditions, that lead to impairment and for dealing with the consequences of disability rests with Governments. This does not weaken the responsibility of society in general, or of individuals, or of organizations. Governments should take the lead in awakening the consciousness of populations regarding the gains to be derived by individuals and society from the inclusion of disabled persons in every area of social, economic and political life. Governments must also ensure that people who are made dependent by severe disability have an opportunity to achieve a standard of living equal to that of their fellow citizens. Non-governmental organizations can assist Governments by formulating needs, suggesting suitable solutions and providing services complementary to those provided by Governments.

Sharing of financial and material resources by all sections of the population could be of major significance to disabled persons by resulting in expanded community services and improved economic opportunities. Much disability could be prevented through measures taken against malnutrition, environmental pollution, poor hygiene, inadequate prenatal and postnatal care, water-borne diseases and accidents of all types. The international community could make a major breakthrough against disabilities caused by poliomyelitis, tetanus, whooping-cough and diphtheria, and to a lesser extent tuberculosis, through a world-wide expansion of programs of immunization.

The objectives and purpose of the World Program of Action concerning Disabled Persons is to promote effective measures for prevention of disability, rehabilitation and the realization of the goals of 'full participation' of disabled persons in social life and development, and of 'equality'. This means opportunities equal to those of the whole population and an equal share in the improvement in living conditions resulting from social and economic development. These concepts apply with the same scope and with the same urgency to all countries, regardless of their level of development.

In many countries, the prerequisites for achieving the purposes of the Program are economic and social development, extended services provided to the whole population in the humanitarian area, the redistribution of resources and income and an improvement in the living standards of the population. It is necessary to use every effort to prevent wars leading to devastation, catastrophe and poverty, hunger, suffering, diseases and mass disability of people, and therefore to adopt measures at all levels to strengthen international peace and security, to settle all international disputes by peaceful means and to eliminate all forms of discrimination in countries where they still exist. It would also be desirable to recommend to all States' Members of the United Nations that they maximize the use of their resources for peaceful purposes, including prevention of disability and satisfaction of the needs of disabled persons. All forms of technical assistance that help developing countries to move towards these objectives can support the implementation of the Program. It is essential that all nations should include in their general development plans immediate measures for the prevention of disability, for the rehabilitation of disabled persons and for the equalization of opportunities.

The following distinction is made by the World Health Organization, in the context of health experience, between impairment, disability and handicap: 'Impairment' means any loss or abnormality of psychological, physiological, or anatomical structure or function; 'Disability' means any restriction or lack resulting from an impairment of ability to perform an activity in the manner or within the range considered normal for a human being; 'Handicap' means a disadvantage for a given individual, resulting from an impairment or disability, which limits or prevents the fulfillment of a role that is normal, depending on age, sex, social and cultural factors, for that individual. Handicap is therefore a function of the relationship between disabled persons and their environment. It occurs when they encounter cultural, physical or social barriers that prevent their access to the various systems of society that are available to other citizens. Thus, handicap is the loss or limitation of opportunities to take part in the life of the community on an equal level with others. Disabled people do not form a homogeneous group. The mentally ill and the mentally retarded, the visually, hearing and speech impaired, and those with restricted mobility or with so-called 'medical disabilities' all encounter different barriers, of different kinds, which have to be overcome in different ways. The following definitions are developed from that perspective.

The relevant terms of action proposed in the World Program are defined as prevention, rehabilitation and equalization of opportunities. 'Prevention' means measures aimed at preventing the onset of mental, physical and sensory impairments, primary prevention or at preventing impairment, when it has occurred, from having negative physical, psychological and social consequences. 'Rehabilitation' means a goal-oriented and time-limited process aimed at enabling an impaired person to reach an optimum mental, physical and/or social functional level, thus providing her or him with the tools to change her or his own life. It can involve measures intended to compensate for a loss of function or a functional limitation and other measures intended to facilitate social adjustment or readjustment. 'Equalization of opportunities' means the process through which the general system of society, such as the physical and cultural environment, housing and transportation, social and health services, educational and work opportunities, cultural and social life, including sports and recreational facilities, are made accessible to all.

In terms of rehabilitation efforts, emphasis should be placed on the abilities of the individual, whose integrity and dignity must be respected. The normal development and maturation process of disabled children should be given the maximum attention. The capacities of disabled adults to perform work and other activities should be utilized. Important resources for rehabilitation exist in the families of disabled persons and in their communities. In helping disabled persons, every effort should be made to keep their families together, to enable them to live in their own communities and to support family and community groups who are working with this objective. In planning rehabilitation and supportive programs, it is essential to take into account the customs and structures of the family and community and to promote their abilities to respond to the needs of the disabled individual.

Rehabilitation usually includes the following types of services: Early detection, diagnosis and intervention; Medical care and treatment; Social, psychological and other types of counseling and assistance; Training in self-care activities, including mobility, communication and daily living skills, with special provisions as needed, for the hearing impaired, the visually impaired and the mentally retarded; Provision of technical and mobility aids and other devices; Specialized education services; Vocational rehabilitation services, including vocational guidance, vocational training, placement in open or sheltered employment; and Follow-up.

Services for disabled persons should be provided within the existing social, health, education and labour structures of society. These include all levels of health care; primary, secondary and higher education, general programs of vocational training and placement in employment; and measures of social security and social services. Rehabilitation services are aimed at facilitating the participation of disabled persons in regular community services and activities. Rehabilitation should take place in the natural environment, supported by community-based services and specialized institutions. Large institutions should be avoided. Specialized institutions, where necessary, should be organized so as to ensure an early and lasting integration of disabled persons into society.

Rehabilitation programs should make it possible for disabled persons to take part in designing and organizing the services that they and their families consider necessary. Procedures for the participation of disabled persons in the decision-making relating to their rehabilitation should be provided for within the system. When people such as the severely mentally disabled may not be able to represent themselves adequately in decisions affecting their lives, family members or legally designated agents should take part in planning and decision-making. Efforts should be increased to develop rehabilitation services integrated in other services and make them more readily available. These should not rely on imported costly equipment, raw material and technology. The transfer of technology among nations should be enhanced and should concentrate on methods that are functional and relate to prevailing conditions.

In terms of equalization of opportunities, to achieve the goals of 'full participation and equality', rehabilitation measures aimed at the disabled individual are not sufficient. Experience shows that it is largely the environment that determines the effect of an impairment or a disability on a person's daily life. A person is handicapped when he or she is denied the opportunities generally available in the community that are necessary for the fundamental elements of living, including family life, education, employment, housing, financial and personal security, participation in social and political groups, religious activity, intimate and sexual relationships, access to public facilities, freedom of movement and the general style of daily living.

Societies sometimes cater only to people who are in full possession of all their physical and mental faculties. They have to recognize the fact that, despite preventive efforts, there will always be a number of people with impairments and disabilities, and that societies have to identify and remove obstacles to their full participation. Thus, whenever pedagogically possible, education should take place in the ordinary school system, work be provided through open employment and housing be made available as to the population in general. It is the duty of every Government to ensure that the benefits of development programs also reach disabled citizens. Measures to this effect should be incorporated into the general planning process and the administrative structure of every society. Extra services which disabled persons might need should, as far as possible, be part of the general services of a country. Anyone in charge of any kind of enterprise should make it accessible to people with disabilities. This applies to public agencies at various levels, to Non-Governmental Organizations (NGOs), to firms and to private individuals. It also applies to the international level. People with permanent disabilities who are in need of community support services, aids and equipment to enable them to live as normally as possible both at home and in the community should have access to such services. Those who live with such disabled persons and help them in their daily activities should themselves receive support to enable them to have adequate rest and relaxation and an opportunity to take care of their own needs

The principle of equal rights for the disabled and non-disabled implies that the needs of each and every individual are of equal importance, that these needs must be made the basis for the planning of societies, and that all resources must be employed in such a way as to ensure, for every individual, equal opportunity for participation. Disability policies should ensure the access of the disabled to all community services. As disabled persons have equal rights, they also have equal obligations. It is their duty to take part in the building of society. Societies must raise the level of expectation as far as disabled persons are concerned, and in so doing mobilize their full resources for social change. This means, among other things, that young disabled persons should be provided with career and vocational opportunities – not early retirement pensions or public assistance.

Persons with disabilities should be expected to fulfill their role in society and meet their obligations as adults. The image of disabled persons depends on social attitudes based on different factors that may be the greatest barrier to participation and equality. We see the disability, shown by the white cane, crutches, hearing aids and wheelchairs, but not the person. What is required is to focus on the ability, not on the disability of disabled persons.

All over the world, disabled persons have started to unite in organizations as advocates for their own rights to influence decision-makers in Governments and all sectors of society. The role of these organizations includes providing a voice of their own, identifying needs, expressing views on priorities, evaluating services and advocating change and public awareness. As a vehicle of self-development, these organizations provide the opportunity to develop skills in the negotiation process, organizational abilities, mutual support, information-sharing and often vocational skills and opportunities. In view of their vital importance in the process of participation, it is imperative that their development be encouraged. Mentally handicapped people are now beginning to demand a voice of their own and insisting on their right to take part in decision-making and discussion. Even those with limited communication skills have shown themselves able to express their point of view. In this respect, they have much to learn from the self-advocacy movement of persons with other disabilities. This development should be encouraged.

Information should be prepared and disseminated to improve the situation of disabled persons. The cooperation of all public media should be sought to bring about presentations that will promote an understanding of the rights of disabled persons aimed at the public and the persons with disabilities themselves, and that will avoid reinforcing traditional stereotypes and prejudices.

In terms of employment, many persons with disabilities are denied employment or given only menial and poorly remunerated jobs. This is true even though it can be demonstrated that with proper assessment, training and placement, the great majority of disabled persons can perform a large range of tasks in accordance with prevailing work norms. In times of unemployment and economic distress, disabled persons are usually the first to be discharged and the last to be hired. In some industrialized countries experiencing the effects of economic recession, the rate of unemployment among disabled job-seekers is double that of able-bodied applicants for jobs. In many countries various programs have been developed and measures taken to create jobs for disabled persons. These include sheltered and production workshops, sheltered enclaves, designated positions, quota schemes, subsidies for employers who train and subsequently engage disabled workers, cooperatives of and for the disabled, etc. The actual number of disabled workers employed in either regular or special establishments is far below the number of employable disabled workers. The wider application of ergonomic principles leads to adaptation of the workplace, tools, machinery and equipment at relatively little cost and helps widen employment opportunities for the disabled.

Many disabled persons, particularly in the developing countries, live in rural areas. When the family economy is based on agriculture or other rural occupations and when the traditional extended family exists, it may be possible for most disabled persons to be given some useful tasks to perform. As more families move from rural areas to urban centres, as agriculture becomes more mechanized and commercialized, as money transactions replace barter systems and as the institution of the extended family disintegrates, the vocational plight of disabled persons becomes more severe. For those living in urban slums, competition for employment is heavy, and other economically productive activity is scarce. Many disabled persons in such areas suffer from enforced inactivity and become dependent; others must resort to begging.

In terms of National Action, the World Program of Action is designed for all nations. The time-span for its implementation and the choice of items to be implemented as a priority will, however, vary from nation to nation depending on the existing situation and their resource constraints, levels of socio-economic development, cultural traditions, and their capacity to formulate and implement the actions envisaged in the Program. National Governments bear the ultimate responsibility for the implementation of the measures recommended in this section. Owing, however, to constitutional differences between countries, both local authorities and other bodies within the public and private sectors will be called upon to implement the national measures contained in the World Program of Action.

Member States should urgently initiate national long-term programs to achieve the objectives of the World Program of Action; such programs should be an integral component of the nation's general policy for socio-economic development. Matters concerning disabled persons should be treated within the appropriate general context and not separately. Each ministry or other body within the public or private sector responsible for, or working within, a specific sector should be responsible for those matters related to disabled persons which fall within its area of competence. Governments should establish a focal point (for example, a national commission, committee or similar body) to look into and follow the activities related to the World Program of Action of various ministries, of other government agencies and of non-governmental organizations. Any mechanism set up should involve all parties concerned, including organizations of disabled persons. The body should have access to decision makers at the highest level.

To implement the World Program of Action, it is necessary for Member States: To plan, organize and finance activities at each level; To create, through legislation, the necessary legal bases and authority for measures to achieve the objectives; To ensure opportunities by eliminating barriers to full participation; To provide rehabilitation services by giving social, nutritional, medical, educational and vocational assistance and technical aids to disabled persons; To establish or mobilize relevant public and private organizations; To support the establishment and growth of organizations of disabled persons; To prepare and disseminate information relevant to the issues of the World Program of Action among all elements of the population, including persons with disabilities and their families; To promote public education to ensure a broad understanding of the key issues of the World Program of Action and its implementation; To facilitate research on matters related to the World Program of Action; To promote technical assistance and cooperation related to the World Program of Action; and To facilitate the participation of disabled persons and their organizations in decisions related to the World Program of Action.

In terms of disability and a new international order, the transfer of resources and technology from developed to developing countries as envisaged within the framework of the new international economic order, as well as other provisions for strengthening the economies of developing nations, would, if implemented, be of benefit to the people of these countries, including the disabled. Improvement of economic conditions in the developing countries, particularly their rural areas, would provide new employment opportunities for disabled persons and needed resources to support measures for prevention, re-habilitation and the equalization of opportunities. The transfer of appropriate technology, if properly managed, could lead to the development of industries specializing in the mass production of devices and aids for dealing with the effects of physical, mental or sensory impairments.

The International Development Strategy for the Third United Nations Development Decade urges that particular efforts should be made to integrate the disabled in the development process and that effective measures for prevention, rehabilitation and equalization of opportunities are therefore essential. Positive action to this end would be part of the more general effort to mobilize all human resources for development. Changes in the international economic order will have to go hand in hand with domestic changes aimed at achieving full participation by disadvantaged population groups.

In terms of the participation of disabled persons in decision-making, Member States should increase their assistance to organizations of disabled persons and help them organize and coordinate the representation of the interests and concerns of disabled persons. Member States should actively seek out and encourage in every possible way the development of organizations composed of or representing disabled persons. Such organizations, in whose membership and governing bodies disabled persons, or in some cases relatives, have a decisive influence, exist in many countries. Many of them have not the means to assert themselves and fight for their rights. Member States should establish direct contacts with such organizations and provide channels for them to influence government policies and decisions in all areas that concern them Member States should give the necessary financial support to organizations of disabled persons for this purpose. Organizations and other bodies at all levels should ensure that disabled persons can participate in their activities to the fullest extent possible.

In terms of human rights, In order to achieve the theme of the International Year of Disabled Persons, 'Full participation and equality', it is strongly urged that the United Nations system make all its facilities totally barrier-free, ensure that communication is fully available to sensorially impaired persons and adopt an affirmative action plan that includes administrative policies and practices to encourage the employment of disabled persons in the entire United Nations system.

In considering the status of disabled persons with respect to human rights, priority should be placed on the use of United Nations covenants and other instruments, as well as those of other international organizations within the United Nations system that protect the rights of all persons. This principle is consistent with the theme of the International Year of Disabled Persons, 'Full participation and equality'. Specifically, organizations and bodies involved in the United Nations system responsible for the preparation and administration of international agreements, covenants and other instruments that might have a direct or indirect impact on disabled people should ensure that such instruments fully take into account the situation of persons who are disabled.

The States parties to the International Covenants on Human Rights should pay due attention, in their reports, to the application of the Covenants to the situation of disabled persons. The working group of the Economic and Social Council entrusted with the examination of reports under the International Covenant on Economic, Social and Cultural Rights and the Commission on Human Rights, which has the function of examining reports under the International Covenant on Civil and Political Rights, should pay due attention to this aspect of the reports.

Particular conditions may exist which inhibit the ability of disabled persons to exercise the human rights and freedoms recognized as universal to all mankind. Consideration should be given by the United Nations Commission on Human Rights to such conditions. The Commission on Human Rights should continue to consider methods of achieving international cooperation for the implementation of internationally recognized basic rights for all, including disabled persons.

Standard Rules on the Equalization of Opportunities for Persons with Disabilities, General Assembly Resolution 48/96 of 20 December 1993

The United Nations' Standard Rules on the Equalization of Opportunities for Persons with Disabilities was adopted by General Assembly Resolution 48/96 on 20 December 1993. The Standard Rules represent a strong moral and political commitment of Governments to take action to attain equalization of opportunities for persons with disabilities. For people with disabilities, the enumerated current needs are:

1. There are persons with disabilities in all parts of the world and at all levels in every society. The number of persons with disabilities in the world is large and is growing.

2. Both the causes and the consequences of disability vary throughout the world. Those variations are the result of different socio-economic circumstances and of the different provisions that States make for the well-being of their citizens.

3. Present disability policy is the result of developments over the past 200 years. In many ways it reflects the general living conditions and social and economic policies of different times. In the disability field, however, there are also many specific circumstances that have influenced the living conditions of persons with disabilities. Ignorance, neglect, superstition and fear are social factors that throughout the history of disability have isolated persons with disabilities and delayed their development.

4. Over the years disability policy developed from elementary care at institutions to education for children with disabilities and rehabilitation for persons who became disabled during adult life. Through education and rehabilitation, persons with disabilities became more active and a driving force in the further development of disability policy. Organizations of persons with disabilities, their families and advocates were formed, which advocated better conditions for persons with disabilities. After the Second World War the concepts of integration and normalization were introduced, which reflected a growing awareness of the capabilities of persons with disabilities.

5. Towards the end of the 1960s organizations of persons with disabilities in some countries started to formulate a new concept of disability. That new concept indicated the close connection between the limitation experienced by individuals with disabilities, the design and structure of their environments and the attitude of the general population. At the same time the problems of disability in developing countries were more and more highlighted. In some of those countries the

percentage of the population with disabilities was estimated to be very high and, for the most part, persons with disabilities were extremely poor.[4]

Previous international action includes:

6. The rights of persons with disabilities have been the subject of much attention in the United Nations and other international organizations over a long period of time. The most important outcome of the International Year of Disabled Persons, 1981, was the World Program of Action concerning Disabled Persons, adopted by the General Assembly by its resolution 37/52 of 3 December 1982. The Year and the World Program of Action provided a strong impetus for progress in the field. They both emphasized the right of persons with disabilities to the same opportunities as other citizens and to an equal share in the improvements in living conditions resulting from economic and social development. There also, for the first time, handicap was defined as a function of the relationship between persons with disabilities and their environment.

7. The Global Meeting of Experts to Review the Implementation of the World Program of Action concerning Disabled Persons at the Mid-Point of the United Nations Decade of Disabled Persons was held at Stockholm in 1987. It was suggested at the Meeting that a guiding philosophy should be developed to indicate the priorities for action in the years ahead. The basis of that philosophy should be the recognition of the rights of persons with disabilities.

8. Consequently, the Meeting recommended that the General Assembly convene a special conference to draft an international convention on the elimination of all forms of discrimination against persons with disabilities, to be ratified by States by the end of the Decade.

9. A draft outline of the convention was prepared by Italy and presented to the General Assembly at its forty-second session. Further presentations concerning a draft convention were made by Sweden at the forty-fourth session of the Assembly. However, on both occasions, no consensus could be reached on the suitability of such a convention. In the opinion of many representatives, existing human rights documents seemed to guarantee persons with disabilities the same rights as other persons.[5]

The effort towards standard rules encompasses:

10. Guided by the deliberations in the General Assembly, the Economic and Social Council, at its first regular session of 1990, finally agreed to concentrate on the elaboration of an international instrument of a different kind. By its resolution 1990/26 of 24 May 1990, the Council authorized the Commission for Social Development to consider, at its thirty-second session, the establishment of an ad hoc open-ended working group of government experts, funded by voluntary contributions, to elaborate standard rules on the equalization of opportunities for disabled children, youth and adults, in close collaboration with the specialized agencies, other intergovernmental bodies and non-governmental organizations, especially organizations of disabled persons. The Council also requested the Commission to finalize the text of those rules for consideration in 1993 and for submission to the General Assembly at its forty-eighth session.

11. The subsequent discussions in the Third Committee of the General Assembly at the forty-fifth session showed that there was wide support for the new initiative to elaborate standard rules on the equalization of opportunities for persons with disabilities.

12. At the thirty-second session of the Commission for Social Development, the initiative for standard rules received the support of a large number of representatives and discussions led to the adoption of resolution 32/2 of 20 February 1991, in which the Commission decided to establish an ad hoc open-ended working group in accordance with Economic and Social Council resolution 1990/26.[6]

The stated purpose and content of the Standard Rules on the Equalization of Opportunities for Persons with Disabilities are:

13. The Standard Rules on the Equalization of Opportunities for Persons with Disabilities have been developed on the basis of the experience gained during the United Nations Decade of Disabled Persons (1983-1992). The International Bill of Human Rights, comprising the Universal Declaration of Human Rights, the International Covenant on Economic, Social and Cultural Rights and the International Covenant on Civil and Political Rights, the Convention on the Rights of the Child and the Convention on the Elimination of All Forms of Discrimination against Women, as well as the World Program of Action concerning Disabled Persons, constitute the political and moral foundation for the Rules.

14. Although the Rules are not compulsory, they can become international customary rules when they are applied by a great number of States with the intention of respecting a rule in international law. They imply a strong moral and political commitment on behalf of States to take action for the equalization of opportunities for persons with disabilities. Important principles for responsibility, action and cooperation are indicated. Areas of decisive importance for the quality of life and for the achievement of full participation and equality are pointed out. The Rules offer an instrument for policy-making and action to persons with disabilities and their organizations. They provide a basis for technical and economic cooperation among States, the United Nations and other international organizations.

15. The purpose of the Rules is to ensure that girls, boys, women and men with disabilities, as members of their societies, may exercise the same rights and obligations as others. In all societies of the world there are still obstacles preventing persons with disabilities from exercising their rights and freedoms and making it difficult for them to participate fully in the activities of their societies. It is the responsibility of States to take appropriate action to remove such obstacles. Persons with disabilities and their organizations should play an active role as partners in this process. The equalization of opportunities for persons with disabilities is an essential contribution in the general and worldwide effort to mobilize human resources. Special attention may need to be directed towards groups such as women, children, the elderly, the poor, migrant workers, persons with dual or multiple disabilities, indigenous people and ethnic minorities. In

addition, there are a large number of refugees with disabilities who have special needs requiring attention.[7]

The fundamental concepts in disability policy are:

16. The concepts set out below appear throughout the Rules. They are essentially built on the concepts in the World Program of Action concerning Disabled Persons. In some cases they reflect the development that has taken place during the United Nations Decade of Disabled Persons.[8]

Disability and handicap are defined:

17. The term 'disability' summarizes a great number of different functional limitations occurring in any population in any country of the world. People may be disabled by physical, intellectual or sensory impairment, medical conditions or mental illness. Such impairments, conditions or illnesses may be permanent or transitory in nature.

18. The term 'handicap' means the loss or limitation of opportunities to take part in the life of the community on an equal level with others. It describes the encounter between the person with a disability and the environment. The purpose of this term is to emphasize the focus on the shortcomings in the environment and in many organized activities in society, for example, information, communication and education, which prevent persons with disabilities from participating on equal terms.

19. The use of the two terms 'disability' and 'handicap', as defined in paragraphs 17 and 18 above, should be seen in the light of modern disability history. During the 1970s there was a strong reaction among representatives of organizations of persons with disabilities and professionals in the field of disability against the terminology of the time. The terms 'disability' and 'handicap' were often used in an unclear and confusing way, which gave poor guidance for policy-making and for political action. The terminology reflected a medical and diagnostic approach, which ignored the imperfections and deficiencies of the surrounding society.

20. In 1980, the World Health Organization adopted an international classification of impairments, disabilities and handicaps, which suggested a more precise and at the same time relativistic approach. The International Classification of Impairments, Disabilities, and Handicaps makes a clear distinction between 'impairment', 'disability' and 'handicap'. It has been extensively used in areas such as rehabilitation, education, statistics, policy, legislation, demography, sociology, economics and anthropology. Some users have expressed concern that the Classification, in its definition of the term 'handicap', may still be considered too medical and too centred on the individual, and may not adequately clarify the interaction between societal conditions or expectations and the abilities of the individual. Those concerns, and others expressed by users during the 12 years since its publication, will be addressed in forthcoming revisions of the Classification.

21. As a result of experience gained in the implementation of the World Program of Action and of the general discussion that took place during the United Nations

Decade of Disabled Persons, there was a deepening of knowledge and extension of understanding concerning disability issues and the terminology used. Current terminology recognizes the necessity of addressing both the individual needs (such as rehabilitation and technical aids) and the shortcomings of the society (various obstacles for participation).[9]

Prevention includes:

22. The term 'prevention' means action aimed at preventing the occurrence of physical, intellectual, psychiatric or sensory impairments (primary prevention) or at preventing impairments from causing a permanent functional limitation or disability (secondary prevention). Prevention may include many different types of action, such as primary health care, prenatal and postnatal care, education in nutrition, immunization campaigns against communicable diseases, measures to control endemic diseases, safety regulations, programs for the prevention of accidents in different environments, including adaptation of workplaces to prevent occupational disabilities and diseases, and prevention of disability resulting from pollution of the environment or armed conflict.[10]

Rehabilitation includes:

23. The term 'rehabilitation' refers to a process aimed at enabling persons with disabilities to reach and maintain their optimal physical, sensory, intellectual, psychiatric and/or social functional levels, thus providing them with the tools to change their lives towards a higher level of independence. Rehabilitation may include measures to provide and/or restore functions, or compensate for the loss or absence of a function or for a functional limitation. The rehabilitation process does not involve initial medical care. It includes a wide range of measures and activities from more basic and general rehabilitation to goal-oriented activities, for instance vocational rehabilitation.[11]

Importantly, equalization of opportunities are:

24. The term 'equalization of opportunities' means the process through which the various systems of society and the environment, such as services, activities, information and documentation, are made available to all, particularly to persons with disabilities.

25. The principle of equal rights implies that the needs of each and every individual are of equal importance, that those needs must be made the basis for the planning of societies and that all resources must be employed in such a way as to ensure that every individual has equal opportunity for participation.

26. Persons with disabilities are members of society and have the right to remain within their local communities. They should receive the support they need within the ordinary structures of education, health, employment and social services.

27. As persons with disabilities achieve equal rights, they should also have equal obligations. As those rights are being achieved, societies should raise their expectations of persons with disabilities. As part of the process of equal

opportunities, provision should be made to assist persons with disabilities to assume their full responsibility as members of society.[12]

The Preamble of the Standard Rules outlines:

States,

Mindful of the pledge made, under the Charter of the United Nations, to take joint and separate action in cooperation with the Organization to promote higher standards of living, full employment, and conditions of economic and social progress and development,

Reaffirming the commitment to human rights and fundamental freedoms, social justice and the dignity and worth of the human person proclaimed in the Charter,

Recalling in particular the international standards on human rights, which have been laid down in the Universal Declaration of Human Rights, the International Covenant on Economic, Social and Cultural Rights and the International Covenant on Civil and Political Rights,

Underlining that those instruments proclaim that the rights recognized therein should be ensured equally to all individuals without discrimination,

Recalling the Convention on the Rights of the Child, which prohibits discrimination on the basis of disability and requires special measures to ensure the rights of children with disabilities, and the International Convention on the Protection of the Rights of All Migrant Workers and Members of Their Families, which provides for some protective measures against disability,

Recalling also the provisions in the Convention on the Elimination of All Forms of Discrimination against Women to ensure the rights of girls and women with disabilities,

Having regard to the Declaration on the Rights of Disabled Persons, the Declaration on the Rights of Mentally Retarded Persons, the Declaration on Social Progress and Development, the Principles for the Protection of Persons with Mental Illness and for the Improvement of Mental Health Care and other relevant instruments adopted by the General Assembly,

Also having regard to the relevant conventions and recommendations adopted by the International Labour Organisation, with particular reference to participation in employment without discrimination for persons with disabilities,

Mindful of the relevant recommendations and work of the United Nations Educational, Scientific and Cultural Organization, in particular the World Declaration on Education for All, the World Health Organization, the United Nations Children's Fund and other concerned organizations,

Having regard to the commitment made by States concerning the protection of the environment,

Mindful of the devastation caused by armed conflict and deploring the use of scarce resources in the production of weapons,

Recognizing that the World Program of Action concerning Disabled Persons and the definition therein of equalization of opportunities represent earnest ambitions on the part of the international community to render those various international instruments and recommendations of practical and concrete significance,

Acknowledging that the objective of the United Nations Decade of Disabled Persons (1983-1992) to implement the World Program of Action is still valid and requires urgent and continued action,

Recalling that the World Program of Action is based on concepts that are equally valid in developing and industrialized countries,

Convinced that intensified efforts are needed to achieve the full and equal enjoyment of human rights and participation in society by persons with disabilities,

Re-emphasizing that persons with disabilities, and their parents, guardians, advocates and organizations, must be active partners with States in the planning and implementation of all measures affecting their civil, political, economic, social and cultural rights,

In pursuance of Economic and Social Council resolution 1990/26, and basing themselves on the specific measures required for the attainment by persons with disabilities of equality with others, enumerated in detail in the World Program of Action,

Have adopted the Standard Rules on the Equalization of Opportunities for Persons with Disabilities outlined below, in order:

(a) To stress that all action in the field of disability presupposes adequate knowledge and experience of the conditions and special needs of persons with disabilities;

(b) To emphasize that the process through which every aspect of societal organization is made accessible to all is a basic objective of socio-economic development;

(c) To outline crucial aspects of social policies in the field of disability, including, as appropriate, the active encouragement of technical and economic cooperation;

(d) To provide models for the political decision-making process required for the attainment of equal opportunities, bearing in mind the widely differing technical and economic levels, the fact that the process must reflect keen understanding of the cultural context within which it takes place and the crucial role of persons with disabilities in it;

(e) To propose national mechanisms for close collaboration among States, the organs of the United Nations system, other intergovernmental bodies and organizations of persons with disabilities;

(f) To propose an effective machinery for monitoring the process by which States seek to attain the equalization of opportunities for persons with disabilities.[13]

In terms of I. Preconditions for equal participation, Rule 1, Awareness-raising, enumerates the responsibilities:

States should take action to raise awareness in society about persons with disabilities, their rights, their needs, their potential and their contribution.

1. States should ensure that responsible authorities distribute up-to-date information on available programs and services to persons with disabilities, their families, professionals in the field and the general public. Information to persons with disabilities should be presented in accessible form.

2. States should initiate and support information campaigns concerning persons with disabilities and disability policies, conveying the message that persons with disabilities are citizens with the same rights and obligations as others, thus justifying measures to remove all obstacles to full participation.

3. States should encourage the portrayal of persons with disabilities by the mass media in a positive way; organizations of persons with disabilities should be consulted on this matter.

4. States should ensure that public education programs reflect in all their aspects the principle of full participation and equality.

5. States should invite persons with disabilities and their families and organizations to participate in public education programs concerning disability matters.

6. States should encourage enterprises in the private sector to include disability issues in all aspects of their activity.

7. States should initiate and promote programs aimed at raising the level of awareness of persons with disabilities concerning their rights and potential. Increased self-reliance and empowerment will assist persons with disabilities to take advantage of the opportunities available to them.

8. Awareness-raising should be an important part of the education of children with disabilities and in rehabilitation programs. Persons with disabilities could also assist one another in awareness-raising through the activities of their own organizations.

9. Awareness-raising should be part of the education of all children and should be a component of teacher-training courses and training of all professionals.[14]

Rule 2, Medical care, mentions:

> States should ensure the provision of effective medical care to persons with disabilities.
>
> 1. States should work towards the provision of programs run by multidisciplinary teams of professionals for early detection, assessment and treatment of impairment. This could prevent, reduce or eliminate disabling effects. Such programs should ensure the full participation of persons with disabilities and their families at the individual level, and of organizations of persons with disabilities at the planning and evaluation level.
>
> 2. Local community workers should be trained to participate in areas such as early detection of impairments, the provision of primary assistance and referral to appropriate services.
>
> 3. States should ensure that persons with disabilities, particularly infants and children, are provided with the same level of medical care within the same system as other members of society.
>
> 4. States should ensure that all medical and paramedical personnel are adequately trained and equipped to give medical care to persons with disabilities and that they have access to relevant treatment methods and technology.
>
> 5. States should ensure that medical, paramedical and related personnel are adequately trained so that they do not give inappropriate advice to parents, thus restricting options for their children. This training should be an ongoing process and should be based on the latest information available.
>
> 6. States should ensure that persons with disabilities are provided with any regular treatment and medicines they may need to preserve or improve their level of functioning.[15]

Rule 3, Rehabilitation, is listed as a fundamental concept in disability policy:

> States should ensure the provision of rehabilitation services to persons with disabilities in order for them to reach and sustain their optimum level of independence and functioning.
>
> 1. States should develop national rehabilitation programs for all groups of persons with disabilities. Such programs should be based on the actual individual needs of persons with disabilities and on the principles of full participation and equality.
>
> 2. Such programs should include a wide range of activities, such as basic skills training to improve or compensate for an affected function, counselling of persons with disabilities and their families, developing self-reliance, and occasional services such as assessment and guidance.
>
> 3. All persons with disabilities, including persons with severe and/or multiple disabilities, who require rehabilitation should have access to it.

4. Persons with disabilities and their families should be able to participate in the design and organization of rehabilitation services concerning themselves.

5. All rehabilitation services should be available in the local community where the person with disabilities lives. However, in some instances, in order to attain a certain training objective, special time-limited rehabilitation courses may be organized, where appropriate, in residential form.

6. Persons with disabilities and their families should be encouraged to involve themselves in rehabilitation, for instance as trained teachers, instructors or counsellors.

7. States should draw upon the expertise of organizations of persons with disabilities when formulating or evaluating rehabilitation programs.[16]

Rule 4, Support services, notes:

States should ensure the development and supply of support services, including assistive devices for persons with disabilities, to assist them to increase their level of independence in their daily living and to exercise their rights.

1. States should ensure the provision of assistive devices and equipment, personal assistance and interpreter services, according to the needs of persons with disabilities, as important measures to achieve the equalization of opportunities.

2. States should support the development, production, distribution and servicing of assistive devices and equipment and the dissemination of knowledge about them.

3. To achieve this, generally available technical know-how should be utilized. In States where high-technology industry is available, it should be fully utilized to improve the standard and effectiveness of assistive devices and equipment. It is important to stimulate the development and production of simple and inexpensive devices, using local material and local production facilities when possible. Persons with disabilities themselves could be involved in the production of those devices.

4. States should recognize that all persons with disabilities who need assistive devices should have access to them as appropriate, including financial accessibility. This may mean that assistive devices and equipment should be provided free of charge or at such a low price that persons with disabilities or their families can afford to buy them.

5. In rehabilitation programs for the provision of assistive devices and equipment, States should consider the special requirements of girls and boys with disabilities concerning the design, durability and age-appropriateness of assistive devices and equipment.

6. States should support the development and provision of personal assistance programs and interpretation services, especially for persons with severe and/or multiple disabilities. Such programs would increase the level of participation of persons with disabilities in everyday life at home, at work, in school and during leisure-time activities.

7. Personal assistance programs should be designed in such a way that the persons with disabilities using the programs have a decisive influence on the way in which the programs are delivered.[17]

In terms of II. Target areas for equal participation, Rule 5, Accessibility, is mentioned as a key factor:

> States should recognize the overall importance of accessibility in the process of the equalization of opportunities in all spheres of society. For persons with disabilities of any kind, States should (a) introduce programs of action to make the physical environment accessible; and (b) undertake measures to provide access to information and communication.
>
> (a) Access to the physical environment
>
> 1. States should initiate measures to remove the obstacles to participation in the physical environment. Such measures should be to develop standards and guidelines and to consider enacting legislation to ensure accessibility to various areas in society, such as housing, buildings, public transport services and other means of transportation, streets and other outdoor environments.
>
> 2. States should ensure that architects, construction engineers and others who are professionally involved in the design and construction of the physical environment have access to adequate information on disability policy and measures to achieve accessibility.
>
> 3. Accessibility requirements should be included in the design and construction of the physical environment from the beginning of the designing process.
>
> 4. Organizations of persons with disabilities should be consulted when standards and norms for accessibility are being developed. They should also be involved locally from the initial planning stage when public construction projects are being designed, thus ensuring maximum accessibility.
>
> (b) Access to information and communication
>
> 5. Persons with disabilities and, where appropriate, their families and advocates should have access to full information on diagnosis, rights and available services and programs, at all stages. Such information should be presented in forms accessible to persons with disabilities.
>
> 6. States should develop strategies to make information services and documentation accessible for different groups of persons with disabilities. Braille, tape services, large print and other appropriate technologies should be used to provide access to written information and documentation for persons with visual impairments. Similarly, appropriate technologies should be used to provide access to spoken information for persons with auditory impairments or comprehension difficulties.
>
> 7. Consideration should be given to the use of sign language in the education of deaf children, in their families and communities. Sign language interpretation

services should also be provided to facilitate the communication between deaf persons and others.

8. Consideration should also be given to the needs of people with other communication disabilities.

9. States should encourage the media, especially television, radio and newspapers, to make their services accessible.

10. States should ensure that new computerized information and service systems offered to the general public are either made initially accessible or are adapted to be made accessible to persons with disabilities.

11. Organizations of persons with disabilities should be consulted when measures to make information services accessible are being developed.[18]

Rule 6, Education, is stressed:

States should recognize the principle of equal primary, secondary and tertiary educational opportunities for children, youth and adults with disabilities, in integrated settings. They should ensure that the education of persons with disabilities is an integral part of the educational system.

1. General educational authorities are responsible for the education of persons with disabilities in integrated settings. Education for persons with disabilities should form an integral part of national educational planning, curriculum development and school organization.

2. Education in mainstream schools presupposes the provision of interpreter and other appropriate support services. Adequate accessibility and support services, designed to meet the needs of persons with different disabilities, should be provided.

3. Parent groups and organizations of persons with disabilities should be involved in the education process at all levels.

4. In States where education is compulsory it should be provided to girls and boys with all kinds and all levels of disabilities, including the most severe.

5. Special attention should be given in the following areas:

(a) Very young children with disabilities;

(b) Pre-school children with disabilities;

(c) Adults with disabilities, particularly women.

6. To accommodate educational provisions for persons with disabilities in the mainstream, States should:

(a) Have a clearly stated policy, understood and accepted at the school level and by the wider community;

(b) Allow for curriculum flexibility, addition and adaptation;

(c) Provide for quality materials, ongoing teacher training and support teachers.

7. Integrated education and community-based programs should be seen as complementary approaches in providing cost-effective education and training for persons with disabilities. National community-based programs should encourage communities to use and develop their resources to provide local education to persons with disabilities.

8. In situations where the general school system does not yet adequately meet the needs of all persons with disabilities, special education may be considered. It should be aimed at preparing students for education in the general school system. The quality of such education should reflect the same standards and ambitions as general education and should be closely linked to it. At a minimum, students with disabilities should be afforded the same portion of educational resources as students without disabilities. States should aim for the gradual integration of special education services into mainstream education. It is acknowledged that in some instances special education may currently be considered to be the most appropriate form of education for some students with disabilities.

9. Owing to the particular communication needs of deaf and deaf/blind persons, their education may be more suitably provided in schools for such persons or special classes and units in mainstream schools. At the initial stage, in particular, special attention needs to be focused on culturally sensitive instruction that will result in effective communication skills and maximum independence for people who are deaf or deaf/blind.[19]

Rule 7, Employment, is of vital concern:

States should recognize the principle that persons with disabilities must be empowered to exercise their human rights, particularly in the field of employment. In both rural and urban areas they must have equal opportunities for productive and gainful employment in the labour market.

1. Laws and regulations in the employment field must not discriminate against persons with disabilities and must not raise obstacles to their employment.

2. States should actively support the integration of persons with disabilities into open employment. This active support could occur through a variety of measures, such as vocational training, incentive-oriented quota schemes, reserved or designated employment, loans or grants for small business, exclusive contracts or priority production rights, tax concessions, contract compliance or other technical or financial assistance to enterprises employing workers with disabilities. States should also encourage employers to make reasonable adjustments to accommodate persons with disabilities.

3. States' action programs should include:

(a) Measures to design and adapt workplaces and work premises in such a way that they become accessible to persons with different disabilities;

(b) Support for the use of new technologies and the development and production of assistive devices, tools and equipment and measures to facilitate access to such devices and equipment for persons with disabilities to enable them to gain and maintain employment;

(c) Provision of appropriate training and placement and ongoing support such as personal assistance and interpreter services.

4. States should initiate and support public awareness-raising campaigns designed to overcome negative attitudes and prejudices concerning workers with disabilities.

5. In their capacity as employers, States should create favourable conditions for the employment of persons with disabilities in the public sector.

6. States, workers' organizations and employers should cooperate to ensure equitable recruitment and promotion policies, employment conditions, rates of pay, measures to improve the work environment in order to prevent injuries and impairments and measures for the rehabilitation of employees who have sustained employment-related injuries.

7. The aim should always be for persons with disabilities to obtain employment in the open labour market. For persons with disabilities whose needs cannot be met in open employment, small units of sheltered or supported employment may be an alternative. It is important that the quality of such programs be assessed in terms of their relevance and sufficiency in providing opportunities for persons with disabilities to gain employment in the labour market.

8. Measures should be taken to include persons with disabilities in training and employment programs in the private and informal sectors.

9. States, workers' organizations and employers should cooperate with organizations of persons with disabilities concerning all measures to create training and employment opportunities, including flexible hours, part-time work, job-sharing, self-employment and attendant care for persons with disabilities.[20]

Rule 8, Income maintenance and social security are important areas:

States are responsible for the provision of social security and income maintenance for persons with disabilities.

1. States should ensure the provision of adequate income support to persons with disabilities who, owing to disability or disability-related factors, have temporarily lost or received a reduction in their income or have been denied employment opportunities. States should ensure that the provision of support takes into account the costs frequently incurred by persons with disabilities and their families as a result of the disability.

2. In countries where social security, social insurance or other social welfare schemes exist or are being developed for the general population, States should ensure that such systems do not exclude or discriminate against persons with disabilities.

3. States should also ensure the provision of income support and social security protection to individuals who undertake the care of a person with a disability.

4. Social security systems should include incentives to restore the income-earning capacity of persons with disabilities. Such systems should provide or contribute to the organization, development and financing of vocational training. They should also assist with placement services.

5. Social security programs should also provide incentives for persons with disabilities to seek employment in order to establish or re-establish their income-earning capacity.

6. Income support should be maintained as long as the disabling conditions remain in a manner that does not discourage persons with disabilities from seeking employment. It should only be reduced or terminated when persons with disabilities achieve adequate and secure income.

7. States, in countries where social security is to a large extent provided by the private sector, should encourage local communities, welfare organizations and families to develop self-help measures and incentives for employment or employment-related activities for persons with disabilities.[21]

Rule 9, Family life and personal integrity are maintained:

States should promote the full participation of persons with disabilities in family life. They should promote their right to personal integrity and ensure that laws do not discriminate against persons with disabilities with respect to sexual relationships, marriage and parenthood.

1. Persons with disabilities should be enabled to live with their families. States should encourage the inclusion in family counselling of appropriate modules regarding disability and its effects on family life. Respite-care and attendant-care services should be made available to families which include a person with disabilities. States should remove all unnecessary obstacles to persons who want to foster or adopt a child or adult with disabilities.

2. Persons with disabilities must not be denied the opportunity to experience their sexuality, have sexual relationships and experience parenthood. Taking into account that persons with disabilities may experience difficulties in getting married and setting up a family, States should encourage the availability of appropriate counselling. Persons with disabilities must have the same access as others to family-planning methods, as well as to information in accessible form on the sexual functioning of their bodies.

3. States should promote measures to change negative attitudes towards marriage, sexuality and parenthood of persons with disabilities, especially of girls and

women with disabilities, which still prevail in society. The media should be encouraged to play an important role in removing such negative attitudes.

4. Persons with disabilities and their families need to be fully informed about taking precautions against sexual and other forms of abuse. Persons with disabilities are particularly vulnerable to abuse in the family, community or institutions and need to be educated on how to avoid the occurrence of abuse, recognize when abuse has occurred and report on such acts.[22]

Rule 10, Culture is a unifying value:

States will ensure that persons with disabilities are integrated into and can participate in cultural activities on an equal basis.

1. States should ensure that persons with disabilities have the opportunity to utilize their creative, artistic and intellectual potential, not only for their own benefit, but also for the enrichment of their community, be they in urban or rural areas. Examples of such activities are dance, music, literature, theatre, plastic arts, painting and sculpture. Particularly in developing countries, emphasis should be placed on traditional and contemporary art forms, such as puppetry, recitation and story-telling.

2. States should promote the accessibility to and availability of places for cultural performances and services, such as theatres, museums, cinemas and libraries, to persons with disabilities.

3. States should initiate the development and use of special technical arrangements to make literature, films and theatre accessible to persons with disabilities.[23]

Rule 11, Recreation and sports are stressed:

States will take measures to ensure that persons with disabilities have equal opportunities for recreation and sports.

1. States should initiate measures to make places for recreation and sports, hotels, beaches, sports arenas, gym halls, etc., accessible to persons with disabilities. Such measures should encompass support for staff in recreation and sports programs, including projects to develop methods of accessibility, and participation, information and training programs.

2. Tourist authorities, travel agencies, hotels, voluntary organizations and others involved in organizing recreational activities or travel opportunities should offer their services to all, taking into account the special needs of persons with disabilities. Suitable training should be provided to assist that process.

3. Sports organizations should be encouraged to develop opportunities for participation by persons with disabilities in sports activities. In some cases, accessibility measures could be enough to open up opportunities for participation. In other cases, special arrangements or special games would be needed. States should support the participation of persons with disabilities in national and international events.

4. Persons with disabilities participating in sports activities should have access to instruction and training of the same quality as other participants.

5. Organizers of sports and recreation should consult with organizations of persons with disabilities when developing their services for persons with disabilities.[24]

Rule 12, Religion is emphasized:

States will encourage measures for equal participation by persons with disabilities in the religious life of their communities.

1. States should encourage, in consultation with religious authorities, measures to eliminate discrimination and make religious activities accessible to persons with disabilities.

2. States should encourage the distribution of information on disability matters to religious institutions and organizations. States should also encourage religious authorities to include information on disability policies in the training for religious professions, as well as in religious education programs.

3. They should also encourage the accessibility of religious literature to persons with sensory impairments.

4. States and/or religious organizations should consult with organizations of persons with disabilities when developing measures for equal participation in religious activities.[25]

In terms of III. Implementation measures, Rule 13, Information and research are stressed for disability rights:

States assume the ultimate responsibility for the collection and dissemination of information on the living conditions of persons with disabilities and promote comprehensive research on all aspects, including obstacles that affect the lives of persons with disabilities.

1. States should, at regular intervals, collect gender-specific statistics and other information concerning the living conditions of persons with disabilities. Such data collection could be conducted in conjunction with national censuses and household surveys and could be undertaken in close collaboration, inter alia , with universities, research institutes and organizations of persons with disabilities. The data collection should include questions on programs and services and their use.

2. States should consider establishing a data bank on disability, which would include statistics on available services and programs as well as on the different groups of persons with disabilities. They should bear in mind the need to protect individual privacy and personal integrity.

3. States should initiate and support programs of research on social, economic and participation issues that affect the lives of persons with disabilities and their families. Such research should include studies on the causes, types and

frequencies of disabilities, the availability and efficacy of existing programs and the need for development and evaluation of services and support measures.

4. States should develop and adopt terminology and criteria for the conduct of national surveys, in cooperation with organizations of persons with disabilities.

5. States should facilitate the participation of persons with disabilities in data collection and research. To undertake such research States should particularly encourage the recruitment of qualified persons with disabilities.

6. States should support the exchange of research findings and experiences.

7. States should take measures to disseminate information and knowledge on disability to all political and administration levels within national, regional and local spheres.[26]

Rule 14, Policy-making and planning are noted as crucial:

States will ensure that disability aspects are included in all relevant policy-making and national planning.

1. States should initiate and plan adequate policies for persons with disabilities at the national level, and stimulate and support action at regional and local levels.

2. States should involve organizations of persons with disabilities in all decision-making relating to plans and programs concerning persons with disabilities or affecting their economic and social status.

3. The needs and concerns of persons with disabilities should be incorporated into general development plans and not be treated separately.

4. The ultimate responsibility of States for the situation of persons with disabilities does not relieve others of their responsibility. Anyone in charge of services, activities or the provision of information in society should be encouraged to accept responsibility for making such programs available to persons with disabilities.

5. States should facilitate the development by local communities of programs and measures for persons with disabilities. One way of doing this could be to develop manuals or check-lists and provide training programs for local staff.[27]

Rule 15, Legislation, is of vital importance to ensure disability equality:

States have a responsibility to create the legal bases for measures to achieve the objectives of full participation and equality for persons with disabilities.

1. National legislation, embodying the rights and obligations of citizens, should include the rights and obligations of persons with disabilities. States are under an obligation to enable persons with disabilities to exercise their rights, including their human, civil and political rights, on an equal basis with other citizens. States must ensure that organizations of persons with disabilities are involved in the

development of national legislation concerning the rights of persons with disabilities, as well as in the ongoing evaluation of that legislation.

2. Legislative action may be needed to remove conditions that may adversely affect the lives of persons with disabilities, including harassment and victimization. Any discriminatory provisions against persons with disabilities must be eliminated. National legislation should provide for appropriate sanctions in case of violations of the principles of non-discrimination.

3. National legislation concerning persons with disabilities may appear in two different forms. The rights and obligations may be incorporated in general legislation or contained in special legislation. Special legislation for persons with disabilities may be established in several ways:

(a) By enacting separate legislation, dealing exclusively with disability matters;

(b) By including disability matters within legislation on particular topics;

(c) By mentioning persons with disabilities specifically in the texts that serve to interpret existing legislation.

A combination of those different approaches might be desirable. Affirmative action provisions may also be considered.

4. States may consider establishing formal statutory complaints mechanisms in order to protect the interests of persons with disabilities.[28]

Rule 16, Economic policies are important for advancement:

States have the financial responsibility for national programs and measures to create equal opportunities for persons with disabilities.

1. States should include disability matters in the regular budgets of all national, regional and local government bodies.

2. States, non-governmental organizations and other interested bodies should interact to determine the most effective ways of supporting projects and measures relevant to persons with disabilities.

3. States should consider the use of economic measures (loans, tax exemptions, earmarked grants, special funds, and so on) to stimulate and support equal participation by persons with disabilities in society.

4. In many States it may be advisable to establish a disability development fund, which could support various pilot projects and self-help programs at the grass-roots level.[29]

Rule 17, Coordination of work is stressed:

> States are responsible for the establishment and strengthening of national coordinating committees, or similar bodies, to serve as a national focal point on disability matters.
>
> 1. The national coordinating committee or similar bodies should be permanent and based on legal as well as appropriate administrative regulation.
>
> 2. A combination of representatives of private and public organizations is most likely to achieve an intersectoral and multidisciplinary composition. Representatives could be drawn from concerned government ministries, organizations of persons with disabilities and non-governmental organizations.
>
> 3. Organizations of persons with disabilities should have considerable influence in the national coordinating committee in order to ensure proper feedback of their concerns.
>
> 4. The national coordinating committee should be provided with sufficient autonomy and resources to fulfil its responsibilities in relation to its decision-making capacities. It should report to the highest governmental level.[30]

Rule 18, Organizations of persons with disabilities are central to disability rights:

> States should recognize the right of the organizations of persons with disabilities to represent persons with disabilities at national, regional and local levels. States should also recognize the advisory role of organizations of persons with disabilities in decision-making on disability matters.
>
> 1. States should encourage and support economically and in other ways the formation and strengthening of organizations of persons with disabilities, family members and/or advocates. States should recognize that those organizations have a role to play in the development of disability policy.
>
> 2. States should establish ongoing communication with organizations of persons with disabilities and ensure their participation in the development of government policies.
>
> 3. The role of organizations of persons with disabilities could be to identify needs and priorities, to participate in the planning, implementation and evaluation of services and measures concerning the lives of persons with disabilities, and to contribute to public awareness and to advocate change.
>
> 4. As instruments of self-help, organizations of persons with disabilities provide and promote opportunities for the development of skills in various fields, mutual support among members and information sharing.
>
> 5. Organizations of persons with disabilities could perform their advisory role in many different ways such as having permanent representation on boards of government-funded agencies, serving on public commissions and providing expert knowledge on different projects.

6. The advisory role of organizations of persons with disabilities should be ongoing in order to develop and deepen the exchange of views and information between the State and the organizations.

7. Organizations should be permanently represented on the national coordinating committee or similar bodies.

8. The role of local organizations of persons with disabilities should be developed and strengthened to ensure that they influence matters at the community level.[31]

Rule 19, Personnel training is important for advancement:

States are responsible for ensuring the adequate training of personnel, at all levels, involved in the planning and provision of programs and services concerning persons with disabilities.

1. States should ensure that all authorities providing services in the disability field give adequate training to their personnel.

2. In the training of professionals in the disability field, as well as in the provision of information on disability in general training programs, the principle of full participation and equality should be appropriately reflected.

3. States should develop training programs in consultation with organizations of persons with disabilities, and persons with disabilities should be involved as teachers, instructors or advisers in staff training programs.

4. The training of community workers is of great strategic importance, particularly in developing countries. It should involve persons with disabilities and include the development of appropriate values, competence and technologies as well as skills which can be practised by persons with disabilities, their parents, families and members of the community.[32]

Rule 20, National monitoring and evaluation of disability programs in the implementation of the Rules are crucial to disability equality:

States are responsible for the continuous monitoring and evaluation of the implementation of national programs and services concerning the equalization of opportunities for persons with disabilities.

1. States should periodically and systematically evaluate national disability programs and disseminate both the bases and the results of the evaluations.

2. States should develop and adopt terminology and criteria for the evaluation of disability-related programs and services.

3. Such criteria and terminology should be developed in close cooperation with organizations of persons with disabilities from the earliest conceptual and planning stages.

4. States should participate in international cooperation in order to develop common standards for national evaluation in the disability field. States should encourage national coordinating committees to participate also.

5. The evaluation of various programs in the disability field should be built in at the planning stage, so that the overall efficacy in fulfilling their policy objectives can be evaluated.[33]

Rule 21, Technical and economic cooperation is noted:

States, both industrialized and developing, have the responsibility to cooperate in and take measures for the improvement of the living conditions of persons with disabilities in developing countries.

1. Measures to achieve the equalization of opportunities of persons with disabilities, including refugees with disabilities, should be integrated into general development programs.

2. Such measures must be integrated into all forms of technical and economic cooperation, bilateral and multilateral, governmental and non-governmental. States should bring up disability issues in discussions on such cooperation with their counterparts.

3. When planning and reviewing programs of technical and economic cooperation, special attention should be given to the effects of such programs on the situation of persons with disabilities. It is of the utmost importance that persons with disabilities and their organizations are consulted on any development projects designed for persons with disabilities. They should be directly involved in the development, implementation and evaluation of such projects.

4. Priority areas for technical and economic cooperation should include:

(a) The development of human resources through the development of skills, abilities and potentials of persons with disabilities and the initiation of employment-generating activities for and of persons with disabilities.

(b) The development and dissemination of appropriate disability-related technologies and know-how.

5. States are also encouraged to support the formation and strengthening of organizations of persons with disabilities.

6. States should take measures to improve the knowledge of disability issues among staff involved at all levels in the administration of technical and economic cooperation programs.[34]

Rule 22, International cooperation is needed for global progress toward disability equality:

States will participate actively in international cooperation concerning policies for the equalization of opportunities for persons with disabilities.

1. Within the United Nations, the specialized agencies and other concerned intergovernmental organizations, States should participate in the development of disability policy.

2. Whenever appropriate, States should introduce disability aspects in general negotiations concerning standards, information exchange, development programs, etc.

3. States should encourage and support the exchange of knowledge and experience among:

(a) Non-governmental organizations concerned with disability issues;

(b) Research institutions and individual researchers involved in disability issues;

(c) Representatives of field programs and of professional groups in the disability field;

(d) Organizations of persons with disabilities;

(e) National coordinating committees.

4. States should ensure that the United Nations and the specialized agencies, as well as all intergovernmental and interparliamentary bodies, at global and regional levels, include in their work the global and regional organizations of persons with disabilities.[35]

In terms of IV. Monitoring mechanism:

1. The purpose of a monitoring mechanism is to further the effective implementation of the Rules. It will assist each State in assessing its level of implementation of the Rules and in measuring its progress. The monitoring should identify obstacles and suggest suitable measures that would contribute to the successful implementation of the Rules. The monitoring mechanism will recognize the economic, social and cultural features existing in individual States. An important element should also be the provision of advisory services and the exchange of experience and information between States.

2. The Rules shall be monitored within the framework of the sessions of the Commission for Social Development. A Special Rapporteur with relevant and extensive experience in disability issues and international organizations shall be appointed, if necessary, funded by extrabudgetary resources, for three years to monitor the implementation of the Rules.

3. International organizations of persons with disabilities having consultative status with the Economic and Social Council and organizations representing persons with disabilities who have not yet formed their own organizations should be invited to create among themselves a panel of experts, on which organizations of persons with disabilities shall have a majority, taking into account the different kinds of disabilities and necessary equitable geographical distribution, to be consulted by the Special Rapporteur and, when appropriate, by the Secretariat.

4. The panel of experts will be encouraged by the Special Rapporteur to review, advise and provide feedback and suggestions on the promotion, implementation and monitoring of the Rules.

5. The Special Rapporteur shall send a set of questions to States, entities within the United Nations system, and intergovernmental and non-governmental organizations, including organizations of persons with disabilities. The set of questions should address implementation plans for the Rules in States. The questions should be selective in nature and cover a number of specific rules for in-depth evaluation. In preparing the questions the Special Rapporteur should consult with the panel of experts and the Secretariat.

6. The Special Rapporteur shall seek to establish a direct dialogue not only with States but also with local non-governmental organizations, seeking their views and comments on any information intended to be included in the reports. The Special Rapporteur shall provide advisory services on the implementation and monitoring of the Rules and assistance in the preparation of replies to the sets of questions.

7. The Department for Policy Coordination and Sustainable Development of the Secretariat, as the United Nations focal point on disability issues, the United Nations Development Program and other entities and mechanisms within the United Nations system, such as the regional commissions and specialized agencies and inter-agency meetings, shall cooperate with the Special Rapporteur in the implementation and monitoring of the Rules at the national level.

8. The Special Rapporteur, assisted by the Secretariat, shall prepare reports for submission to the Commission for Social Development at its thirty-fourth and thirty-fifth sessions. In preparing such reports, the Rapporteur should consult with the panel of experts.

9. States should encourage national coordinating committees or similar bodies to participate in implementation and monitoring. As the focal points on disability matters at the national level, they should be encouraged to establish procedures to coordinate the monitoring of the Rules. Organizations of persons with disabilities should be encouraged to be actively involved in the monitoring of the process at all levels.

10. Should extrabudgetary resources be identified, one or more positions of interregional adviser on the Rules should be created to provide direct services to States, including:

(a) The organization of national and regional training seminars on the content of the Rules;

(b) The development of guidelines to assist in strategies for implementation of the Rules;

(c) Dissemination of information about best practices concerning implementation of the Rules.

11. At its thirty-fourth session, the Commission for Social Development should establish an open-ended working group to examine the Special Rapporteur's report and make recommendations on how to improve the application of the Rules. In examining the Special Rapporteur's report, the Commission, through its open-ended working group, shall consult international organizations of persons with disabilities and specialized agencies, in accordance with rules 71 and 76 of the rules of procedure of the functional commissions of the Economic and Social Council.

12. At its session following the end of the Special Rapporteur's mandate, the Commission should examine the possibility of either renewing that mandate, appointing a new Special Rapporteur or considering another monitoring mechanism, and should make appropriate recommendations to the Economic and Social Council.

13. States should be encouraged to contribute to the United Nations Voluntary Fund on Disability in order to further the implementation of the Rules.[36]

Overall, the International Day of Disabled Persons is part of a worldwide celebration that occurs on December 3rd of each year. It involves disability organizations, individuals with a disability, businesses, federal, state and local governments and community organizations in events to celebrate and acknowledge the experience and ability of people with a disability, by increasing their efforts to achieve equality and inclusion for people with disabilities in all areas of our society.

Conclusion

In order to achieve this ability and protect human rights, it is necessary for States to avoid, as far as possible, resorting to reservations of international agreements, and to ensure that no reservation is incompatible with the object and purpose of the Convention or is otherwise incompatible with international treaty law. The full enjoyment of equal rights is undermined by the discrepancies between some national legislation, and international law and international instruments on human rights. Overly complex administrative procedures, lack of awareness within the judicial process and inadequate monitoring of the violation of human rights, coupled with the underrepresentation of disabled groups in justice systems, insufficient information on existing rights, and persistent attitudes and practices perpetuate *de facto* and *de jure* inequality, which is also exacerbated by the lack of enforcement of civil, penal, labor and commercial laws or codes, or administrative rules and regulations intended to ensure the full enjoyment of human rights and fundamental freedoms.

Notes

[1]   European Union Commission, Directorate-General for Employment and Social Affairs, *Definition of Disability in Europe, A Comparative Analysis, Social security and social integration*, 2002.

[2]   *Ibid.*

[3]   United Nations, World Program of Action Concerning Disabled Persons, at the Preamble.

[4]   United Nations, Standard Rules on the Equalization of Opportunities for Persons with Disabilities, at Articles 1-5.

[5]   *Ibid.*, at Articles 6 - 9.

[6]   *Ibid.*, at Articles 10 - 12.

[7]   *Ibid.*, at Articles 13 – 15.

[8]   *Ibid.*, at Article 16.

[9]   *Ibid.*, at Articles 17 – 21.

[10]   *Ibid.*, at Article 22.

[11]   *Ibid.*, at Article 23.

[12]   *Ibid.*, at Articles 24 – 27.

[13]   *Ibid.*, at the Preamble.

[14]   *Ibid.*, at I. Preconditions for equal participation, Rule 1.

[15]   *Ibid.*, at I. Preconditions for equal participation, Rule 2.

[16]   *Ibid.*, at I. Preconditions for equal participation, Rule 3.

[17]   *Ibid.*, at I. Preconditions for equal participation, Rule 4.

[18]   *Ibid.*, at II. Target areas for equal participation, Rule 5.

[19]   *Ibid.*, at II. Target areas for equal participation, Rule 6.

[20]   *Ibid.*, at II. Target areas for equal participation, Rule 7.

[21]   *Ibid.*, at II. Target areas for equal participation, Rule 8.

[22]   *Ibid.*, at II. Target areas for equal participation, Rule 9.

[23]   *Ibid.*, at II. Target areas for equal participation, Rule 10.

[24]   *Ibid.*, at II. Target areas for equal participation, Rule 11.

[25]   *Ibid.*, at II. Target areas for equal participation, Rule 12.

[26]   *Ibid.*, at III. Implementation measures, Rule 13.

[27]   *Ibid.*, at III. Implementation measures, Rule 14.

[28]   *Ibid.*, at III. Implementation measures, Rule 15.

[29]   *Ibid.*, at III. Implementation measures, Rule 16.

[30]   *Ibid.*, at III. Implementation measures, Rule 17.

[31]   *Ibid.*, at III. Implementation measures, Rule 18.

[32]   *Ibid.*, at III. Implementation measures, Rule 19.

[33]   *Ibid.*, at III. Implementation measures, Rule 20.

[34]   *Ibid.*, at III. Implementation measures, Rule 21.

[35]   *Ibid.*, at III. Implementation measures, Rule 22.

[36]   *Ibid.*, at IV. Monitoring mechanism.

References

European Union Commission, Directorate-General for Employment and Social Affairs, *Definition of Disability in Europe, A Comparative Analysis, Social Security and Social Integration*, 2002.

United Nations Standard Rules on the Equalization of Opportunities for Persons with Disabilities, Adopted by General Assembly Resolution 48/96.

United Nations, World Program of Action Concerning Disabled Persons.

Chapter 3

This Ability in the United Nations

Introduction

This chapter will examine this ability in the United Nations. It will look at the important United Nations' legislation dealing with disability discrimination in the fight for disability equality, namely the Universal Declaration of Human Rights; the Charter of the United Nations; the Statute of the International Court of Justice; the Equal Remuneration Convention (ILO No. 100); the Discrimination (Employment and Occupation) Convention (ILO No. 111); the Employment Policy Convention (ILO No. 122); the International Covenant on Civil and Political Rights; the Optional Protocol to the International Covenant on Civil and Political Rights; the International Covenant on Economic, Social and Cultural Rights; the Declaration on the Rights of Mentally Retarded Persons, General Assembly Resolution 2856 (XXVI) of 20 December 1971; the Declaration on the Rights of Disabled Persons, General Assembly Resolution 3447 (XXX) of 9 December 1975; the Principles for the protection of persons with mental illness and the improvement of mental health care, General Assembly Resolution 46/119 of 17 December 1991; and for minorities with a disability, the International Convention on the Elimination of All Forms of Racial Discrimination, and for women with a disability, the Convention on the Elimination of All Forms of Discrimination against Women and the Optional Protocol to the Convention on the Elimination of All Forms of Discrimination against Women.

Through the work of the United Nations, international laws have been developed that require countries to work towards the elimination of all forms of disability discrimination. These international laws, called treaties or conventions, which operate like a contract, apply throughout the world. When a country becomes a Party to a convention, it is bound to act in accordance with the rules contained in that convention. In addition to international treaties and conventions, there are several international declarations which express the international community's aspirations to eliminate disability discrimination. The declarations are statements of principles, which are developed through the United Nations or other international bodies. These international declarations differ from treaties, because they do not always impose binding international legal obligations. However, these declarations are morally binding and have much influence over countries in setting acceptable standards of human rights protections.

This Ability

Universal Declaration of Human Rights

The Universal Declaration of Human Rights was adopted by the United Nations on 10 December 1948. The Preamble of the Universal Declaration of Human Rights states:

> Whereas recognition of the inherent dignity and of the equal and inalienable rights of all members of the human family is the foundation of freedom, justice and peace in the world,
>
> Whereas disregard and contempt for human rights have resulted in barbarous acts which have outraged the conscience of mankind, and the advent of a world in which human beings shall enjoy freedom of speech and belief and freedom from fear and want has been proclaimed as the highest aspiration of the common people,
>
> Whereas it is essential, if man is not to be compelled to have recourse, as a last resort, to rebellion against tyranny and oppression, that human rights should be protected by the rule of law,
>
> Whereas it is essential to promote the development of friendly relations between nations,
>
> Whereas the peoples of the United Nations have in the Charter reaffirmed their faith in fundamental human rights, in the dignity and worth of the human person and in the equal rights of men and women and have determined to promote social progress and better standards of life in larger freedom,
>
> Whereas Member States have pledged themselves to achieve, in co-operation with the United Nations, the promotion of universal respect for and observance of human rights and fundamental freedoms,
>
> Whereas a common understanding of these rights and freedoms is of the greatest importance for the full realization of this pledge.
>
> The General Assembly of the United Nations proclaims:
>
> THIS UNIVERSAL DECLARATION OF HUMAN RIGHTS as a common standard of achievement for all peoples and all nations, to the end that every individual and every organ of society, keeping this Declaration constantly in mind, shall strive by teaching and education to promote respect for these rights and freedoms and by progressive measures, national and international, to secure their universal and effective recognition and observance, both among the peoples of Member States themselves and among the peoples of territories under their jurisdiction.[1]

Internationally, the fundamental concept of human rights is one which human beings have striven both to suppress and promote. Article 1 recognizes human beings as free and equal:

1. All human beings are born free and equal in dignity and rights. They are endowed with reason and conscience and should act towards one another in a spirit of brotherhood. [2]

In the fight for disability equality, Article 2 is a helpful tool, since it holds that:

2. Everyone is entitled to all the rights and freedoms set forth in this Declaration, without distinction of any kind, such as race, color, sex, language, religion, political or other opinion, national or social origin, property, birth or other status. [3]

Equality before the law without discrimination, important for disability equality, is guaranteed in Article 7:

7. All are equal before the law and are entitled without any discrimination to equal protection of the law. All are entitled to equal protection against any discrimination in violation of this Declaration and against any incitement to such discrimination. [4]

In the effort to redress discriminatory action, Article 8 establishes that everyone has the right to an effective remedy by the competent national tribunals for acts violating the fundamental rights granted him by the constitution or by law.[5]

Employment rights, including equal pay for equal work, are protected under Article 23:

23. (1) Everyone has the right to work, to free choice of employment, to just and favorable conditions of work and to protection against unemployment.

(2) Everyone, without any discrimination, has the right to equal pay for equal work.

(3) Everyone who works has the right to just and favorable remuneration ensuring for himself and his family an existence worthy of human dignity, and supplemented, if necessary, by other means of social protection.

(4) Everyone has the right to form and to join trade unions for the protection of his interests.[6]

The right to education as a means of enhancement and advancement is established in Article 26, which holds that everyone has the right to education, in that education shall be free, at least in the elementary and fundamental stages, and elementary education shall be compulsory. Technical and professional education shall be made generally available and higher education shall be equally accessible to all on the basis of merit. Further, education shall be directed to the full development of the human personality and to the strengthening of respect for human rights and fundamental freedoms; it shall promote understanding, tolerance and friendship among all nations, racial or religious groups, and shall further the activities of the United Nations for the maintenance of peace.[7]

The Universal Declaration of Human Rights of 1948 was codified into two Covenants, which the General Assembly adopted on 16 December 1966, and they are the International Covenant on Civil and Political Rights and the International Covenant on Economic, Social and Cultural Rights. Described as the 'International Bill of Human Rights', the Covenants along with the Optional Protocols are landmarks in the efforts of the international community to promote human rights.

Charter of the United Nations

The Preamble of the Charter of the United Nations, signed on 26 June 1945, states:

WE THE PEOPLES OF THE UNITED NATIONS DETERMINED

to save succeeding generations from the scourge of war, which twice in our lifetime has brought untold sorrow to mankind, and
to reaffirm faith in fundamental human rights, in the dignity and worth of the human person, in the equal rights of men and women and of nations large and small, and
to establish conditions under which justice and respect for the obligations arising from treaties and other sources of international law can be maintained, and
to promote social progress and better standards of life in larger freedom,

AND FOR THESE ENDS

to practice tolerance and live together in peace with one another as good neighbours, and
to unite our strength to maintain international peace and security, and
to ensure, by the acceptance of principles and the institution of methods, that armed force shall not be used, save in the common interest, and
to employ international machinery for the promotion of the economic and social advancement of all peoples,

HAVE RESOLVED TO COMBINE OUR EFFORTS TO ACCOMPLISH THESE AIMS

Accordingly, our respective Governments, through representatives assembled in the city of San Francisco, who have exhibited their full powers found to be in good and due form, have agreed to the present Charter of the United Nations and do hereby establish an international organization to be known as the United Nations.[8]

The purposes of the United Nations as outlined in Article 1 are to maintain international peace and security, and to that end to take effective collective measures for the prevention and removal of threats to the peace, and for the suppression of acts of aggression or other breaches of the peace, and to bring about by peaceful means, and in conformity with the principles of justice and international law, adjustment or settlement of international disputes or situations which might lead to a breach of the peace; to develop friendly relations among nations based on respect for the principle of equal rights and self-determination of peoples, and to take other appropriate measures to strengthen universal peace; to achieve international cooperation in solving international problems of an economic, social, cultural, or humanitarian character, and in promoting and encouraging respect for human rights and for fundamental freedoms for all without distinction; and to be a center for harmonizing the actions of nations in the attainment of these common ends. [9]

In terms of international economic and social cooperation, Article 55 guarantees equal rights in employment without distinction:

> 55. With a view to the creation of conditions of stability and well-being which are necessary for peaceful and friendly relations among nations based on respect for the principle of equal rights and self-determination of peoples, the United Nations shall promote:
> a. higher standards of living, full employment, and conditions of economic and social progress and development;
> b. solutions of international economic, social, health, and related problems; and international cultural and educational cooperation; and
> c. universal respect for, and observance of, human rights and fundamental freedoms for all without distinction as to race, sex, language, or religion.[10]

Importantly, the International Court of Justice (ICJ) is established under Article 92 as the principal judicial organ of the United Nations, functioning in accordance with the Statute of the Permanent Court of International Justice.[11] Article 94 binds Member States in their compliance with the decisions of the ICJ in that each Member of the United Nations undertakes to comply with the decision of the International Court of Justice in any case to which it is a party; and if any party to a case fails to perform the obligations incumbent upon it under a judgment rendered by the Court, the other party may have recourse to the Security Council, which may, if it deems necessary, make recommendations or decide upon measures to be taken to give effect to the judgment.[12]

Further, Article 95 holds that nothing in the present Charter shall prevent Members of the United Nations from entrusting the solution of their differences to other tribunals by virtue of agreements already in existence or which may be concluded in the future.[13] By virtue of Article 96, the General Assembly, the Security Council, and other organs of the United Nations and specialized agencies may request the International Court of Justice to give an advisory opinion on any legal question.[14]

Statute of the International Court of Justice

Article 1 of the Statute of the International Court of Justice, signed on 26 June 1945, holds that the International Court of Justice (ICJ), established by the Charter of the United Nations as the principal judicial organ of the United Nations, shall be constituted and shall function in accordance with the provisions of the present Statute.[15] By virtue of Article 34, only States may be parties in cases before the Court which, subject to and in conformity with its Rules, may request of public international organizations information relevant to cases before it, and shall receive such information presented by such organizations on their own initiative.[16]

Jurisdiction of the Court is established under Article 36 as comprising all cases which the parties refer to it and all matters specially provided for in the Charter of the United Nations or in treaties and conventions in force. Further, the States Parties to the present Statute may at any time declare that they recognize as compulsory *ipso facto* and without special agreement, in relation to any other State accepting the same obligation, the jurisdiction of the Court in all legal disputes concerning the interpretation of a treaty; any question of international law; the existence of any fact which, if established, would constitute a breach of an international obligation; and the nature or extent of the reparation to be made for the breach of an international obligation.[17]

As to the application of choice of law, Article 38 maintains that the Court, whose function is to decide in accordance with international law such disputes as are submitted to it, shall apply international conventions, whether general or particular, establishing rules expressly recognized by the contesting States; international custom, as evidence of a general practice accepted as law; the general principles of law recognized by civilized nations; and judicial decisions and the teachings of the most highly qualified publicists of the various nations, as subsidiary means for the determination of rules of law.[18]

Equal Remuneration Convention (ILO No. 100)

According to the Equal Remuneration Convention (ILO No. 100) of 9 June 1951, the term 'remuneration' is defined in Article 1 as the ordinary, basic or minimum wage or salary and any additional emoluments whatsoever payable directly or indirectly, whether in cash or in kind, by the employer to the worker and arising out of the worker's employment.[19]

Different methods for equality are envisioned in Article 2

> 2.1. Each Member shall, by means appropriate to the methods in operation for determining rates of remuneration, promote and, in so far as is consistent with such methods, ensure the application to all workers of the principle of equal remuneration for… workers for work of equal value.

> 2. This principle may be applied by means of:

>> (a) National laws or regulations;
>> (b) Legally established or recognised machinery for wage determination;
>> (c) Collective agreements between employers and workers; or
>> (d) A combination of these various means.[20]

Further, objective methods of appraisal are ensured in Article 3:

> 3.1. Where such action will assist in giving effect to the provisions of this Convention, measures shall be taken to promote objective appraisal of jobs on the basis of the work to be performed.

2. The methods to be followed in this appraisal may be decided upon by the authorities responsible for the determination of rates of remuneration, or, where such rates are determined by collective agreements, by the parties thereto.[21]

Discrimination (Employment and Occupation) Convention (ILO No. 111)

The General Conference of the International Labor Organisation, convened at Geneva, adopted on 5 July 1958 the Discrimination (Employment and Occupation) Convention (ILO No. 111), which entered into force on 15 June 1960. The Preamble of the Discrimination (Employment and Occupation) Convention states:

> Having decided upon the adoption of certain proposals with regard to discrimination in the field of employment and occupation, and
>
> Having determined that these proposals shall take the form of an international Convention, and Considering that the Declaration of Philadelphia affirms that all human beings, irrespective of race, creed or sex, have the right to pursue both their material well-being and their spiritual development in conditions of freedom and dignity, of economic security and equal opportunity, and
>
> Considering further that discrimination constitutes a violation of rights enunciated by the Universal Declaration of Human Rights.[22]

The word discrimination is defined in Article I:

> 1. For the purpose of this Convention the term 'discrimination' includes:
>
> (a) Any distinction, exclusion or preference made on the basis of race, color, sex, religion, political opinion, national extraction or social origin, which has the effect of nullifying or impairing equality of opportunity or treatment in employment or occupation;
>
> 2. Any distinction, exclusion or preference in respect of a particular job based on the inherent requirements thereof shall not be deemed to be discrimination.
>
> 3. For the purpose of this Convention the terms 'employment' and 'occupation' include access to vocational training, access to employment and to particular occupations, and terms and conditions of employment.[23]

Member commitment to equality of opportunity and treatment is contained in Article 2:

> 2. Each Member for which this Convention is in force undertakes to declare and pursue a national policy designed to promote, by methods appropriate to national conditions and practice, equality of opportunity and treatment in respect of employment and occupation, with a view to eliminating any discrimination in respect thereof.[24]

Further, Article 3 specifically enunciates Member responsibilities:

> 3. Each Member for which this Convention is in force undertakes, by methods appropriate to national conditions and practice:
>
> (a) To seek the co-operation of employers' and workers' organizations and other appropriate bodies in promoting the acceptance and observance of this policy;
>
> (b) To enact such legislation and to promote such educational programs as may be calculated to secure the acceptance and observance of the policy;
>
> (c) To repeal any statutory provisions and modify any administrative instructions or practices which are inconsistent with the policy;
>
> (d) To pursue the policy in respect of employment under the direct control of a national authority;
>
> (e) To ensure observance of the policy in activities of vocational guidance, vocational training and placement services under the direction of a national authority;
>
> (f) To indicate in its annual reports on the application of the Convention the action taken in pursuance of the policy and the results secured by such action.[25]

Special measures are provided for in Article 5:

> 5. 1. Special measures of protection or assistance provided in other Conventions or Recommendations adopted by the International Labor Conference shall not be deemed to be discrimination.
>
> 2. Any Member may, after consultation with representative employers' and workers' organizations, where such exist, determine that other special measures designed to meet the particular requirements of persons who, for reasons such as sex, age, disablement, family responsibilities or social or cultural status, are generally recognized to require special protection or assistance, shall not be deemed to be discrimination.[26]

Employment Policy Convention (ILO No. 122)

The General Conference of the International Labor Organization, convened in Geneva, adopted on 9 July 1964 the Employment Policy Convention (ILO No. 122), which entered into force on 9 July 1965. The Preamble of the Employment Policy Convention (ILO No. 122) states:

> Considering that the Declaration of Philadelphia recognizes the solemn obligation of the International Labor Organization to further among the nations of the world programs which will achieve full employment and the raising of standards of living, and that the Preamble to the Constitution of the International Labor

Organization provides for the prevention of unemployment and the provision of an adequate living wage, and

Considering further that under the terms of the Declaration of Philadelphia it is the responsibility of the International Labor Organization to examine and consider the bearing of economic and financial policies upon employment policy in the light of the fundamental objective that 'all human beings, irrespective of race, creed or sex, have the right to pursue both their material well-being and their spiritual development in conditions of freedom and dignity, of economic security and equal opportunity', and

Considering that the Universal Declaration of Human Rights provides that 'everyone has the right to work, to free choice of employment, to just and favorable conditions of work and to protection against unemployment'.[27]

A commitment to full, productive and freely chosen employment is envisioned in Article 1:

1. With a view to stimulating economic growth and development, raising levels of living, meeting manpower requirements and overcoming unemployment and under-employment, each Member shall declare and pursue, as a major goal, an active policy designed to promote full, productive and freely chosen employment.

2. The said policy shall aim at ensuring that:

(a) There is work for all who are available for and seeking work;

(b) Such work is as productive as possible;

(c) There is freedom of choice of employment and the fullest possible opportunity for each worker to qualify for, and to use his skills and endowments in, a job for which he is well suited, irrespective of race, color, sex, religion, political opinion, national extraction or social origin.

3. The said policy shall take due account of the stage and level of economic development and the mutual relationships between employment objectives and other economic and social objectives, and shall be pursued by methods that are appropriate to national conditions and practices.[28]

National conditions are taken into account in the carrying out of the policy:

2. Each Member shall, by such methods and to such extent as may be appropriate under national conditions:

(a) Decide on and keep under review, within the framework of a coordinated economic and social policy, the measures to be adopted for attaining the objectives specified in article 1;

(b) Take such steps as may be needed, including when appropriate the establishment of programs, for the application of these measures.[29]

A consultation process is envisioned in Article 3 for the implementation of the Employment Policy Convention:

> 3. In the application of this Convention, representatives of the persons affected by the measures to be taken, and in particular representatives of employers and workers, shall be consulted concerning employment policies, with a view to taking fully into account their experience and views and securing their full co-operation in formulating and enlisting support for such policies.[30]

International Covenant on Civil and Political Rights (ICCPR)

The International Covenant on Civil and Political Rights was adopted and opened for signature, ratification and accession by the United Nations General Assembly in resolution 2200A (XXI) of 16 December 1966, and entered into force on 23 March 1976.[31] The Covenant is divided into six parts: Part I reaffirms the right of self-determination; Part II formulates general obligations by States Parties, notably to implement the Covenant through legislative and other measures, to provide effective remedies to victims and to ensure equality, and it restricts the possibility of derogation; Part III outlines the general civil and political rights, including the right to life, the prohibition of torture, the right to liberty and security of person, the right to freedom of movement, the right to a fair hearing, the right to privacy, the right to freedom of religion, freedom of expression, freedom of peaceful assembly, the right to family life, the rights of children to special protection, the right to participate in the conduct of public affairs, the overarching right to equal treatment, and the special rights of persons belonging to ethnic, religious and linguistic minorities; Part IV regulates the election of members of the Human Rights Committee, the State reporting procedure and the interstate complaints mechanism; Part V stipulates that nothing in the Covenant shall be interpreted as impairing the inherent right of all peoples to fully enjoy and to utilize their natural resources; and Part VI provides that the Covenant shall extend to all parts of federal States and sets out the amendment procedure. The Covenant is not subject to denunciation.

In the Preamble of the Covenant on Civil and Political Rights, the States Parties to the present Covenant undertake the agreement:

> Considering that, in accordance with the principles proclaimed in the Charter of the United Nations, recognition of the inherent dignity and of the equal and inalienable rights of all members of the human family is the foundation of freedom, justice and peace in the world,
>
> Recognizing that these rights derive from the inherent dignity of the human person,
>
> Recognizing that, in accordance with the Universal Declaration of Human Rights, the ideal of free human beings enjoying civil and political freedom and freedom from fear and want can only be achieved if conditions are created whereby

everyone may enjoy his civil and political rights, as well as his economic, social and cultural rights,

Considering the obligation of States under the Charter of the United Nations to promote universal respect for, and observance of, human rights and freedoms,

Realizing that the individual, having duties to other individuals and to the community to which he belongs, is under a responsibility to strive for the promotion and observance of the rights recognized in the present Covenant.[32]

The obligations of Member States are established in Article 2 without distinction in that:

Each State Party to the present Covenant undertakes to respect and to ensure to all individuals within its territory and subject to its jurisdiction the rights recognized in the present Covenant, without distinction of any kind, such as race, color, sex, language, religion, political or other opinion, national or social origin, property, birth or other status.[33]

Further, where not already provided for by existing legislative or other measures, each State Party to the present Covenant undertakes to take the necessary steps in accordance with its constitutional processes and with the provisions of the present Covenant, to adopt such legislative or other measures as may be necessary to give effect to the rights recognized in the present Covenant; and each State Party to the present Covenant undertakes to ensure that any person whose rights or freedoms as herein recognized are violated shall have an effective remedy, notwithstanding that the violation has been committed by persons acting in an official capacity; to ensure that any person claiming such a remedy shall have his rights thereto determined by competent judicial, administrative or legislative authorities, or by any other competent authority provided for by the legal system of the State, and to develop the possibilities of judicial remedy; and to ensure that the competent authorities shall enforce such remedies when granted.

Equality before the law, important for disability equality, is guaranteed under Article 26:

26. All persons are equal before the law and are entitled without any discrimination to the equal protection of the law. In this respect, the law shall prohibit any discrimination and guarantee to all persons equal and effective protection against discrimination on any ground such as race, color, sex, language, religion, political or other opinion, national or social origin, property, birth or other status.[34]

It prohibits discrimination in law or in fact in any field regulated by public authorities and its scope is not limited to civil and political rights, so that it can be used to challenge discriminatory laws whether or not they relate to civil and political rights.

Article 28 establishes the Human Rights Committee, consisting of eighteen members, carrying out the functions provided.[35] Additionally, the submission of reports in compliance with the Covenant is required in Article 40 and Article 45. Under Article 40, the States Parties to the present Covenant undertake to submit reports on the measures they have adopted which give effect to the rights recognized herein and on the progress made in the enjoyment of those rights within one year of the entry into force of the present Covenant for the States Parties concerned; and thereafter whenever the Committee so requests. Reports shall indicate the factors and difficulties, if any, affecting the implementation of the present Covenant. The Committee shall study the reports submitted by the States Parties to the present Covenant, and shall transmit its reports, and such general comments as it may consider appropriate, to the States Parties.[36] Under Article 45, the Committee shall submit to the General Assembly of the United Nations, through the Economic and Social council, an annual report on its activities.[37]

The Human Rights Committee monitors implementation by States Parties in a variety of ways, and initial and periodic reports are examined by the plenary, which formulates concluding observations with concrete recommendations. In order to assist States Parties in preparing reports, the Committee has formulated 28 general comments, which constitute a commentary on the provisions of the Covenant, and in advance of the examination of a report, the Committee forwards a list of issues to the State Party concerned. The list is prepared by the members and takes into consideration information received from other United Nations organs and specialized agencies as well as from non-governmental organizations (NGOs).

Other procedures of recourse are permitted under Article 44, which states that the provisions for the implementation of the present Covenant shall apply without prejudice to the procedures prescribed in the field of human rights by or under the constituent instruments and the conventions of the United Nations and of the specialized agencies and shall not prevent the States Parties to the present Covenant from having recourse to other procedures for settling a dispute in accordance with general or special international agreements in force between them.[38]

Optional Protocol to the International Covenant on Civil and Political Rights

The Optional Protocol to the International Covenant on Civil and Political Rights (ICCPR) of 16 December 1966 allows individuals, whose countries are party to the ICCPR and the protocol, who claim their rights under the ICCPR have been violated, and who have exhausted all domestic remedies, to submit written communications to the UN Human Rights Committee. States Parties to the ICCPR undertake to ensure that all enjoy all the civil and political rights in the Covenant on a basis of equality.

The Preamble of the Optional Protocol to the International Covenant on Civil and Political Rights states:

> The States Parties to the present Protocol,
>
> Considering that in order further to achieve the purposes of the International Covenant on Civil and Political Rights (hereinafter referred to as the Covenant)

and the implementation of its provisions it would be appropriate to enable the Human Rights Committee set up in part IV of the Covenant (hereinafter referred to as the Committee) to receive and consider, as provided in the present Protocol, communications from individuals claiming to be victims of violations of any of the rights set forth in the Covenant.[39]

Article I empowers the Committee to hear claims of violations:

1. A State Party to the Covenant that becomes a Party to the present Protocol recognizes the competence of the Committee to receive and consider communications from individuals subject to its jurisdiction who claim to be victims of a violation by that State Party of any of the rights set forth in the Covenant. No communication shall be received by the Committee if it concerns a State Party to the Covenant which is not a Party to the present Protocol.[40]

Further, Article 2 preserves people's rights to redress:

2. Subject to the provisions of article 1, individuals who claim that any of their rights enumerated in the Covenant have been violated and who have exhausted all available domestic remedies may submit a written communication to the Committee for consideration.[41]

International Covenant on Economic, Social and Cultural Rights (ICESCR)

The International Covenant on Economic, Social and Cultural Rights was adopted and opened for signature, ratification and accession by General Assembly resolution 2200A (XXI) of 16 December 1966, and entered into force 16 January 1976.[42] Economic, social and cultural rights are designed to ensure the protection of people as full persons, based on a perspective in which people can enjoy rights, freedoms and social justice. In a world where, according to the United Nations Development Program (UNDP), 'a fifth of the developing world's population goes hungry every night, a quarter lacks access to even a basic necessity like safe drinking water, and a third lives in a state of abject poverty at such a margin of human existence that words simply fail to describe it',[43] the importance of renewed attention and commitment to the full realization of economic, social and cultural rights is self-evident with such marginalization. Despite significant progress since the establishment of the United Nations in addressing problems of human deprivation, well over 1 billion people live in circumstances of extreme poverty, homelessness, hunger and malnutrition, unemployment, illiteracy and chronic ill-health. More than 1.5 billion people lack access to clean drinking water and sanitation, and some 500 million children do not have access to even primary education, with more than 1 billion adults not able to read and write.

In the Preamble of the International Covenant on Economic, Social and Cultural Rights, the States Parties to the present Covenant undertake the agreement:

Considering that, in accordance with the principles proclaimed in the Charter of the United Nations, recognition of the inherent dignity and of the equal and inalienable rights of all the members of the human family is the foundation of freedom, justice and peace in world,

Recognizing that these rights derive from the inherent dignity of the human person,

Recognizing that, in accordance with the Universal Declaration of Human Rights, the ideal of free human beings enjoying freedom from fear and want can only be achieved if conditions are created whereby everyone may enjoy his economic, social and cultural rights, as well as his civil and political rights and freedom,

Realizing that the individual, having duties to other individuals and to the community to which he belongs, is under a responsibility to strive for the promotion and observance of the rights recognized in the present Covenant.[44]

Member States' obligations are outlined in Article 2, which holds that each State Party to the present Covenant undertakes to take steps, individually and through international assistance and cooperation, especially economic and technical, to the maximum of its available resources, with a view to achieving progressively the full realization of the rights recognized in the present Covenant by all appropriate means, including particularly the adoption of legislative measures. Further, the States Parties to present Covenant undertake to guarantee that the rights enunciated in the present Covenant will be exercised without discrimination of any kind as to race, color, sex, language, religion, political or other opinion, national or social origin, property, birth or other status.[45]

Employment rights under Article 6 establishes that the States Parties to the present Covenant recognize the right to work, which includes the right of everyone to the opportunity to gain his living by work which he freely chooses or accepts, and will take appropriate steps to safeguard this right. Further, the steps to be taken by a State Party to the present Covenant to achieve the full realization of this right shall include technical and vocational guidance and training programs, policies and techniques to achieve steady economic, social and cultural development, and full and productive employment under conditions safeguarding fundamental political and economic freedoms to the individual.

Article 7 is an important guarantee for equal rights in terms of equal pay and access to employment:

7. The States to the present Covenant recognize the right of everyone to the enjoyment of just and favorable conditions of work which ensure, in particular:
(1) Remuneration which provides all workers, as a minimum, with:
    1. Fair wages and equal remuneration for work of equal value without distinction of any kind, … with equal pay for equal work;
    2. A decent living for themselves and their families in accordance with the provisions of the present Covenant;
(2) Safe and healthy working conditions;
(3) Equal opportunity for everyone to be promoted in his employment to an appropriate higher level, subject to no considerations other than those of seniority and competence;

(4) Rest, leisure and reasonable limitation of working hours and periodic holidays with pay, as well as remuneration for public holidays.[46]

Article 13 guarantees the right to education for the enhancement of the person in that the States Parties to the present Covenant recognize the right of everyone to education. They agree that education shall be directed to the full development of the human personality and the sense of its dignity, and shall strengthen the respect for human rights and fundamental freedoms. They further agree that education shall enable all persons to participate effectively in a free society, promote understanding, tolerance and friendship among all nations and all racial, ethnic or religious groups, and further the activities of the United Nations for the maintenance of peace.[47]

Compliance by States Parties with their obligations under the Covenant and the level of implementation of the rights and duties in question is monitored by the Committee on Economic, Social and Cultural Rights, which submits annual reports on its activities to the Economic and Social Council. The Committee works on the basis of many sources of information, including reports submitted by States Parties and information from United Nations specialized agencies, including the International Labour Organisation, the United Nations Educational, Scientific and Cultural Organization, the World Health Organization, the Food and Agriculture Organization of the United Nations, the World Bank, and the International Monetary Fund. In addition, information is submitted from the United Nations Development Program, the Office of the United Nations High Commissioner for Refugees, and the United Nations Centre for Human Settlements (Habitat). It also makes use of information from other United Nations treaty bodies, from national non-governmental and community-based organizations working in States which have ratified the Covenant, and from international human rights and other non-governmental organizations (NGOs).

Of all the basic human rights standards, the International Covenant on Economic, Social and Cultural Rights provides one of the most important international legal frameworks for protecting basic human rights. The Covenant contains significant international legal provisions establishing economic, social and cultural rights, including rights relating to work in just and favorable conditions, social protection, an adequate standard of living, the highest attainable standards of physical and mental health, education, and enjoyment of the benefits of cultural freedom and scientific progress. In the fight against discrimination, it also provides for the right of self-determination; the right to work; the right to just and favorable conditions of work; the right to form and join trade unions; the right to social security and social insurance; protection and assistance to the family; the right to adequate standard of living; the right to the highest attainable standard of physical and mental health; the right to education; the right to take part in cultural life; and the right to enjoy the benefits of scientific progress.

Declaration on the Rights of Mentally Retarded Persons, General Assembly Resolution 2856 (XXVI) of 20 December 1971

The Declaration on the Rights of Mentally Retarded Persons was adopted by United Nations General Assembly Resolution 2856 (XXVI) on 20 December 1971. The Preamble states:

> The General Assembly,
>
> Mindful of the pledge of the States Members of the United Nations under the Charter to take joint and separate action in co-operation with the Organization to promote higher standards of living, full employment and conditions of economic and social progress and development,
>
> Reaffirming faith in human rights and fundamental freedoms and in the principles of peace, of the dignity and worth of the human person and of social justice proclaimed in the Charter,
>
> Recalling the principles of the Universal Declaration of Human Rights, the International Covenants on Human Rights, the Declaration of the Rights of the Child and the standards already set for social progress in the constitutions, conventions, recommendations and resolutions of the International Labour Organisation, the United Nations Educational, Scientific and Cultural Organization, the World Health Organization, the United Nations Children's Fund and other organizations concerned,
>
> Emphasizing that the Declaration on Social Progress and Development has proclaimed the necessity of protecting the rights and assuring the welfare and rehabilitation of the physically and mentally disadvantaged,
>
> Bearing in mind the necessity of assisting mentally retarded persons to develop their abilities in various fields of activities and of promoting their integration as far as possible in normal life,
>
> Aware that certain countries, at their present stage of development, can devote only limited efforts to this end,
>
> Proclaims this Declaration on the Rights of Mentally Retarded Persons and calls for national and international action to ensure that it will be used as a common basis and frame of reference for the protection of these rights.[48]

1. The mentally retarded person has, to the maximum degree of feasibility, the same rights as other human beings.

2. The mentally retarded person has a right to proper medical care and physical therapy and to such education, training, rehabilitation and guidance as will enable him to develop his ability and maximum potential.

3. The mentally retarded person has a right to economic security and to a decent standard of living. He has a right to perform productive work or to engage in any other meaningful occupation to the fullest possible extent of his capabilities.

4. Whenever possible, the mentally retarded person should live with his own family or with foster parents and participate in different forms of community life. The family with which he lives should receive assistance. If care in an institution becomes necessary, it should be provided in surroundings and other circumstances as close as possible to those of normal life.

5. The mentally retarded person has a right to a qualified guardian when this is required to protect his personal well-being and interests.

6. The mentally retarded person has a right to protection from exploitation, abuse and degrading treatment. If prosecuted for any offence, he shall have a right to due process of law with full recognition being given to his degree of mental responsibility.

7. Whenever mentally retarded persons are unable, because of the severity of their handicap, to exercise all their rights in a meaningful way or it should become necessary to restrict or deny some or all of these rights, the procedure used for that restriction or denial of rights must contain proper legal safeguards against every form of abuse. This procedure must be based on an evaluation of the social capability of the mentally retarded person by qualified experts and must be subject to periodic review and to the right of appeal to higher authorities.[49]

Declaration on the Rights of Disabled Persons, General Assembly Resolution 3447 (XXX) of 9 December 1975

The Declaration on the Rights of Disabled Persons was adopted by United Nations General Assembly Resolution 3447 (XXX) on 9 December 1975. The Preamble states:

> The General Assembly,
>
> Mindful of the pledge made by Member States, under the Charter of the United Nations to take joint and separate action in co-operation with the Organization to promote higher standards of living, full employment and conditions of economic and social progress and development,
>
> Reaffirming its faith in human rights and fundamental freedoms and in the principles of peace, of the dignity and worth of the human person and of social justice proclaimed in the Charter,
>
> Recalling the principles of the Universal Declaration of Human Rights, the International Covenants on Human Rights, the Declaration of the Rights of the Child and the Declaration on the Rights of Mentally Retarded Persons, as well as

the standards already set for social progress in the constitutions, conventions, recommendations and resolutions of the International Labour Organisation, the United Nations Educational, Scientific and Cultural Organization, the World Health Organization, the United Nations Children's Fund and other organizations concerned,

Recalling also Economic and Social Council resolution 1921 (LVIII) of 6 May 1975 on the prevention of disability and the rehabilitation of disabled persons,

Emphasizing that the Declaration on Social Progress and Development has proclaimed the necessity of protecting the rights and assuring the welfare and rehabilitation of the physically and mentally disadvantaged,

Bearing in mind the necessity of preventing physical and mental disabilities and of assisting disabled persons to develop their abilities in the most varied fields of activities and of promoting their integration as far as possible in normal life,

Aware that certain countries, at their present stage of development, can devote only limited efforts to this end,

Proclaims this Declaration on the Rights of Disabled Persons and calls for national and international action to ensure that it will be used as a common basis and frame of reference for the protection of these rights.[50]

1. The term 'disabled person' means any person unable to ensure by himself or herself, wholly or partly, the necessities of a normal individual and/or social life, as a result of deficiency, either congenital or not, in his or her physical or mental capabilities.

2. Disabled persons shall enjoy all the rights set forth in this Declaration. These rights shall be granted to all disabled persons without any exception whatsoever and without distinction or discrimination on the basis of race, colour, sex, language, religion, political or other opinions, national or social origin, state of wealth, birth or any other situation applying either to the disabled person himself or herself or to his or her family.

3. Disabled persons have the inherent right to respect for their human dignity. Disabled persons, whatever the origin, nature and seriousness of their handicaps and disabilities, have the same fundamental rights as their fellow-citizens of the same age, which implies first and foremost the right to enjoy a decent life, as normal and full as possible.

4. Disabled persons have the same civil and political rights as other human beings; paragraph 7 of the Declaration on the Rights of Mentally Retarded Persons applies to any possible limitation or suppression of those rights for mentally disabled persons.

5. Disabled persons are entitled to the measures designed to enable them to become as self-reliant as possible.

6. Disabled persons have the right to medical, psychological and functional treatment, including prosthetic and orthetic appliances, to medical and social rehabilitation, education, vocational training and rehabilitation, aid, counselling, placement services and other services which will enable them to develop their capabilities and skills to the maximum and will hasten the processes of their social integration or reintegration.

7. Disabled persons have the right to economic and social security and to a decent level of living. They have the right, according to their capabilities, to secure and retain employment or to engage in a useful, productive and remunerative occupation and to join trade unions.

8. Disabled persons are entitled to have their special needs taken into consideration at all stages of economic and social planning.

9. Disabled persons have the right to live with their families or with foster parents and to participate in all social, creative or recreational activities. No disabled person shall be subjected, as far as his or her residence is concerned, to differential treatment other than that required by his or her condition or by the improvement which he or she may derive therefrom. If the stay of a disabled person in a specialized establishment is indispensable, the environment and living conditions therein shall be as close as possible to those of the normal life of a person of his or her age.

10. Disabled persons shall be protected against all exploitation, all regulations and all treatment of a discriminatory, abusive or degrading nature.

11. Disabled persons shall be able to avail themselves of qualified legal aid when such aid proves indispensable for the protection of their persons and property. If judicial proceedings are instituted against them, the legal procedure applied shall take their physical and mental condition fully into account.[51]

Principles for the Protection of Persons with Mental Illness and the Improvement of Mental Health Care, General Assembly Resolution 46/119 of 17 December 1991

The Principles for the Protection of Persons with Mental Illness and the Improvement of Mental Health Care was adopted by United Nations General Assembly Resolution 46/119 on 17 December 1991. The Preamble states:

These Principles shall be applied without discrimination of any kind such as on grounds of disability, race, colour, sex, language, religion, political or other opinion, national, ethnic or social origin, legal or social status, age, property or birth.

General limitation clause

The exercise of the rights set forth in these Principles may be subject only to such limitations as are prescribed by law and are necessary to protect the health or safety of the person concerned or of others, or otherwise to protect public safety, order, health or morals or the fundamental rights and freedoms of others.[52]

Principle 1 concerns Fundamental freedoms and basic rights:

1. All persons have the right to the best available mental health care, which shall be part of the health and social care system.

2. All persons with a mental illness, or who are being treated as such persons, shall be treated with humanity and respect for the inherent dignity of the human person.

3. All persons with a mental illness, or who are being treated as such persons, have the right to protection from economic, sexual and other forms of exploitation, physical or other abuse and degrading treatment.

4. There shall be no discrimination on the grounds of mental illness. 'Discrimination' means any distinction, exclusion or preference that has the effect of nullifying or impairing equal enjoyment of rights. Special measures solely to protect the rights, or secure the advancement, of persons with mental illness shall not be deemed to be discriminatory. Discrimination does not include any distinction, exclusion or preference undertaken in accordance with the provisions of these Principles and necessary to protect the human rights of a person with a mental illness or of other individuals.

5. Every person with a mental illness shall have the right to exercise all civil, political, economic, social and cultural rights as recognized in the Universal Declaration of Human Rights, the International Covenant on Economic, Social and Cultural Rights, the International Covenant on Civil and Political Rights, and in other relevant instruments, such as the Declaration on the Rights of Disabled Persons and the Body of Principles for the Protection of All Persons under Any Form of Detention or Imprisonment.

6. Any decision that, by reason of his or her mental illness, a person lacks legal capacity, and any decision that, in consequence of such incapacity, a personal representative shall be appointed, shall be made only after a fair hearing by an independent and impartial tribunal established by domestic law. The person whose capacity is at issue shall be entitled to be represented by a counsel. If the person whose capacity is at issue does not himself or herself secure such representation, it shall be made available without payment by that person to the extent that he or she does not have sufficient means to pay for it. The counsel shall not in the same proceedings represent a mental health facility or its personnel and shall not also represent a member of the family of the person whose capacity is at issue unless the tribunal is satisfied that there is no conflict of interest. Decisions regarding capacity and the need for a personal representative shall be reviewed at reasonable intervals prescribed by domestic law. The person whose capacity is at issue, his or her personal representative, if any, and any other interested person shall have the right to appeal to a higher court against any such decision.

7. Where a court or other competent tribunal finds that a person with mental illness is unable to manage his or her own affairs, measures shall be taken, so far

as is necessary and appropriate to that person's condition, to ensure the protection of his or her interest.[53]

Principle 2 stresses the Protection of minors:

Special care should be given within the purposes of these Principles and within the context of domestic law relating to the protection of minors to protect the rights of minors, including, if necessary, the appointment of a personal representative other than a family member.[54]

Principle 3 stresses the importance of Life in the community:

Every person with a mental illness shall have the right to live and work, as far as possible, in the community.[55]

Principle 4 looks at the Determination of mental illness:

1. A determination that a person has a mental illness shall be made in accordance with internationally accepted medical standards.

2. A determination of mental illness shall never be made on the basis of political, economic or social status, or membership of a cultural, racial or religious group, or any other reason not directly relevant to mental health status.

3. Family or professional conflict, or non-conformity with moral, social, cultural or political values or religious beliefs prevailing in a person's community, shall never be a determining factor in diagnosing mental illness.

4. A background of past treatment or hospitalization as a patient shall not of itself justify any present or future determination of mental illness.

5. No person or authority shall classify a person as having, or otherwise indicate that a person has, a mental illness except for purposes directly relating to mental illness or the consequences of mental illness.[56]

Principle 5 provides a safeguard against Medical examinations:

No person shall be compelled to undergo medical examination with a view to determining whether or not he or she has a mental illness except in accordance with a procedure authorized by domestic law.[57]

Principle 6 guards the ethical principle of Confidentiality:

The right of confidentiality of information concerning all persons to whom these Principles apply shall be respected.[58]

Principle 7 stresses the Role of community and culture:

1. Every patient shall have the right to be treated and cared for, as far as possible, in the community in which he or she lives.

2. Where treatment takes place in a mental health facility, a patient shall have the right, whenever possible, to be treated near his or her home or the home of his or her relatives or friends and shall have the right to return to the community as soon as possible.

3. Every patient shall have the right to treatment suited to his or her cultural background.[59]

Principle 8 emphasizes Standards of care:

1. Every patient shall have the right to receive such health and social care as is appropriate to his or her health needs, and is entitled to care and treatment in accordance with the same standards as other ill persons.

2. Every patient shall be protected from harm, including unjustified medication, abuse by other patients, staff or others or other acts causing mental distress or physical discomfort.[60]

Principle 9 examines Treatments:

1. Every patient shall have the right to be treated in the least restrictive environment and with the least restrictive or intrusive treatment appropriate to the patient's health needs and the need to protect the physical safety of others.

2. The treatment and care of every patient shall be based on an individually prescribed plan, discussed with the patient, reviewed regularly, revised as necessary and provided by qualified professional staff.

3. Mental health care shall always be provided in accordance with applicable standards of ethics for mental health practitioners, including internationally accepted standards such as the Principles of Medical Ethics adopted by the United Nations General Assembly. Mental health knowledge and skills shall never be abused.

4. The treatment of every patient shall be directed towards preserving and enhancing personal autonomy.[61]

Principle 10 looks at Medication:

1. Medication shall meet the best health needs of the patient, shall be given to a patient only for therapeutic or diagnostic purposes and shall never be administered as a punishment or for the convenience of others. Subject to the provisions of paragraph 15 of Principle 11, mental health practitioners shall only administer medication of known or demonstrated efficacy.

2. All medication shall be prescribed by a mental health practitioner authorized by law and shall be recorded in the patient's records.[62]

Principle 11 stresses the important issue of Consent to treatment:

1. No treatment shall be given to a patient without his or her informed consent, except as provided for in paragraphs 6, 7, 8, 13 and 15 below.

2. Informed consent is consent obtained freely, without threats or improper inducements, after appropriate disclosure to the patient of adequate and understandable information in a form and language understood by the patient on:

(a) The diagnostic assessment;

(b) The purpose, method, likely duration and expected benefit of the proposed treatment;

(c) Alternative modes of treatment, including those less intrusive; and

(d) Possible pain or discomfort, risks and side-effects of the proposed treatment.

3. A patient may request the presence of a person or persons of the patient's choosing during the procedure for granting consent.

4. A patient has the right to refuse or stop treatment, except as provided for in paragraphs 6, 7, 8, 13 and 15 below. The consequences of refusing or stopping treatment must be explained to the patient.

5. A patient shall never be invited or induced to waive the right to informed consent. If the patient should seek to do so, it shall be explained to the patient that the treatment cannot be given without informed consent.

6. Except as provided in paragraphs 7, 8, 12, 13, 14 and 15 below, a proposed plan of treatment may be given to a patient without a patient's informed consent if the following conditions are satisfied:

(a) The patient is, at the relevant time, held as an involuntary patient;

(b) An independent authority, having in its possession all relevant information, including the information specified in paragraph 2 above, is satisfied that, at the relevant time, the patient lacks the capacity to give or withhold informed consent to the proposed plan of treatment or, if domestic legislation so provides, that, having regard to the patient's own safety or the safety of others, the patient unreasonably withholds such consent; and

(c) The independent authority is satisfied that the proposed plan of treatment is in the best interest of the patient's health needs.

7. Paragraph 6 above does not apply to a patient with a personal representative empowered by law to consent to treatment for the patient; but, except as provided in paragraphs 12, 13, 14 and 15 below, treatment may be given to such a patient without his or her informed consent if the personal representative, having been given the information described in paragraph 2 above, consents on the patient's behalf.

8. Except as provided in paragraphs 12, 13, 14 and 15 below, treatment may also be given to any patient without the patient's informed consent if a qualified mental health practitioner authorized by law determines that it is urgently necessary in order to prevent immediate or imminent harm to the patient or to other persons. Such treatment shall not be prolonged beyond the period that is strictly necessary for this purpose.

9. Where any treatment is authorized without the patient's informed consent, every effort shall nevertheless be made to inform the patient about the nature of the treatment and any possible alternatives and to involve the patient as far as practicable in the development of the treatment plan.

10. All treatment shall be immediately recorded in the patient's medical records, with an indication of whether involuntary or voluntary.

11. Physical restraint or involuntary seclusion of a patient shall not be employed except in accordance with the officially approved procedures of the mental health facility and only when it is the only means available to prevent immediate or imminent harm to the patient or others. It shall not be prolonged beyond the period which is strictly necessary for this purpose. All instances of physical restraint or involuntary seclusion, the reasons for them and their nature and extent shall be recorded in the patient's medical record. A patient who is restrained or secluded shall be kept under humane conditions and be under the care and close and regular supervision of qualified members of the staff. A personal representative, if any and if relevant, shall be given prompt notice of any physical restraint or involuntary seclusion of the patient.

12. Sterilization shall never be carried out as a treatment for mental illness.

13. A major medical or surgical procedure may be carried out on a person with mental illness only where it is permitted by domestic law, where it is considered that it would best serve the health needs of the patient and where the patient gives informed consent, except that, where the patient is unable to give informed consent, the procedure shall be authorized only after independent review.

14. Psychosurgery and other intrusive and irreversible treatments for mental illness shall never be carried out on a patient who is an involuntary patient in a mental health facility and, to the extent that domestic law permits them to be carried out, they may be carried out on any other patient only where the patient has given informed consent and an independent external body has satisfied itself that there is genuine informed consent and that the treatment best serves the health needs of the patient.

15. Clinical trials and experimental treatment shall never be carried out on any patient without informed consent, except that a patient who is unable to give informed consent may be admitted to a clinical trial or given experimental treatment, but only with the approval of a competent, independent review body specifically constituted for this purpose.

16. In the cases specified in paragraphs 6, 7, 8, 13, 14 and 15 above, the patient or his or her personal representative, or any interested person, shall have the right to

appeal to a judicial or other independent authority concerning any treatment given to him or her.[63]

Principle 12 stresses Notice of rights:

> 1. A patient in a mental health facility shall be informed as soon as possible after admission, in a form and a language which the patient understands, of all his or her rights in accordance with these Principles and under domestic law, which information shall include an explanation of those rights and how to exercise them.
>
> 2. If and for so long as a patient is unable to understand such information, the rights of the patient shall be communicated to the personal representative, if any and if appropriate, and to the person or persons best able to represent the patient's interests and willing to do so.
>
> 3. A patient who has the necessary capacity has the right to nominate a person who should be informed on his or her behalf, as well as a person to represent his or her interests to the authorities of the facility.[64]

Principle 13 looks at Rights and conditions in mental health facilities:

> 1. Every patient in a mental health facility shall, in particular, have the right to full respect for his or her:
>
> (a) Recognition everywhere as a person before the law;
>
> (b) Privacy;
>
> (c) Freedom of communication, which includes freedom to communicate with other persons in the facility; freedom to send and receive uncensored private communications; freedom to receive, in private, visits from a counsel or personal representative and, at all reasonable times, from other visitors; and freedom of access to postal and telephone services and to newspapers, radio and television;
>
> (d) Freedom of religion or belief.
>
> 2. The environment and living conditions in mental health facilities shall be as close as possible to those of the normal life of persons of similar age and in particular shall include:
>
> (a) Facilities for recreational and leisure activities;
>
> (b) Facilities for education;
>
> (c) Facilities to purchase or receive items for daily living, recreation and communication;
>
> (d) Facilities, and encouragement to use such facilities, for a patient's engagement in active occupation suited to his or her social and cultural background, and for appropriate vocational rehabilitation measures to promote reintegration in the community. These measures should include vocational guidance, vocational

training and placement services to enable patients to secure or retain employment in the community.

3. In no circumstances shall a patient be subject to forced labour. Within the limits compatible with the needs of the patient and with the requirements of institutional administration, a patient shall be able to choose the type of work he or she wishes to perform.

4. The labour of a patient in a mental health facility shall not be exploited. Every such patient shall have the right to receive the same remuneration for any work which he or she does as would, according to domestic law or custom, be paid for such work to a non-patient. Every such patient shall, in any event, have the right to receive a fair share of any remuneration which is paid to the mental health facility for his or her work.[65]

Principle 14 notes Resources for mental health facilities:

1. A mental health facility shall have access to the same level of resources as any other health establishment, and in particular:

(a) Qualified medical and other appropriate professional staff in sufficient numbers and with adequate space to provide each patient with privacy and a programme of appropriate and active therapy;

(b) Diagnostic and therapeutic equipment for the patient;

(c) Appropriate professional care; and

(d) Adequate, regular and comprehensive treatment, including supplies of medication.

2. Every mental health facility shall be inspected by the competent authorities with sufficient frequency to ensure that the conditions, treatment and care of patients comply with these Principles.[66]

Principle 15 looks at Admission principles:

1. Where a person needs treatment in a mental health facility, every effort shall be made to avoid involuntary admission.

2. Access to a mental health facility shall be administered in the same way as access to any other facility for any other illness.

3. Every patient not admitted involuntarily shall have the right to leave the mental health facility at any time unless the criteria for his or her retention as an involuntary patient, as set forth in Principle 16, apply, and he or she shall be informed of that right.[67]

Principle 16 looks further at Involuntary admission:

1. A person may (a) be admitted involuntarily to a mental health facility as a patient; or (b) having already been admitted voluntarily as a patient, be retained as an involuntary patient in the mental health facility if, and only if, a qualified mental health practitioner authorized by law for that purpose determines, in accordance with Principle 4, that that person has a mental illness and considers:

(a) That, because of that mental illness, there is a serious likelihood of immediate or imminent harm to that person or to other persons; or

(b) That, in the case of a person whose mental illness is severe and whose judgement is impaired, failure to admit or retain that person is likely to lead to a serious deterioration in his or her condition or will prevent the giving of appropriate treatment that can only be given by admission to a mental health facility in accordance with the principle of the least restrictive alternative.

In the case referred to in subparagraph (b), a second such mental health practitioner, independent of the first, should be consulted where possible. If such consultation takes place, the involuntary admission or retention may not take place unless the second mental health practitioner concurs.

2. Involuntary admission or retention shall initially be for a short period as specified by domestic law for observation and preliminary treatment pending review of the admission or retention by the review body. The grounds of the admission shall be communicated to the patient without delay and the fact of the admission and the grounds for it shall also be communicated promptly and in detail to the review body, to the patient's personal representative, if any, and, unless the patient objects, to the patient's family.

3. A mental health facility may receive involuntarily admitted patients only if the facility has been designated to do so by a competent authority prescribed by domestic law.[68]

Principle 17 stresses the role of a Review body:

1. The review body shall be a judicial or other independent and impartial body established by domestic law and functioning in accordance with procedures laid down by domestic law. It shall, in formulating its decisions, have the assistance of one or more qualified and independent mental health practitioners and take their advice into account.

2. The review body's initial review, as required by paragraph 2 of Principle 16, of a decision to admit or retain a person as an involuntary patient shall take place as soon as possible after that decision and shall be conducted in accordance with simple and expeditious procedures as specified by domestic law.

3. The review body shall periodically review the cases of involuntary patients at reasonable intervals as specified by domestic law.

4. An involuntary patient may apply to the review body for release or voluntary status, at reasonable intervals as specified by domestic law.

5. At each review, the review body shall consider whether the criteria for involuntary admission set out in paragraph 1 of Principle 16 are still satisfied, and, if not, the patient shall be discharged as an involuntary patient.

6. If at any time the mental health practitioner responsible for the case is satisfied that the conditions for the retention of a person as an involuntary patient are no longer satisfied, he or she shall order the discharge of that person as such a patient.

7. A patient or his personal representative or any interested person shall have the right to appeal to a higher court against a decision that the patient be admitted to, or be retained in, a mental health facility.[69]

Principle 18 looks at Procedural safeguards:

1. The patient shall be entitled to choose and appoint a counsel to represent the patient as such, including representation in any complaint procedure or appeal. If the patient does not secure such services, a counsel shall be made available without payment by the patient to the extent that the patient lacks sufficient means to pay.

2. The patient shall also be entitled to the assistance, if necessary, of the services of an interpreter. Where such services are necessary and the patient does not secure them, they shall be made available without payment by the patient to the extent that the patient lacks sufficient means to pay.

3. The patient and the patient's counsel may request and produce at any hearing an independent mental health report and any other reports and oral, written and other evidence that are relevant and admissible.

4. Copies of the patient's records and any reports and documents to be submitted shall be given to the patient and to the patient's counsel, except in special cases where it is determined that a specific disclosure to the patient would cause serious harm to the patient's health or put at risk the safety of others. As domestic law may provide, any document not given to the patient should, when this can be done in confidence, be given to the patient's personal representative and counsel. When any part of a document is withheld from a patient, the patient or the patient's counsel, if any, shall receive notice of the withholding and the reasons for it and shall be subject to judicial review.

5. The patient and the patient's personal representative and counsel shall be entitled to attend, participate and be heard personally in any hearing.

6. If the patient or the patient's personal representative or counsel requests that a particular person be present at a hearing, that person shall be admitted unless it is determined that the person's presence could cause serious harm to the patient's health or put at risk the safety of others.

7. Any decision whether the hearing or any part of it shall be in public or in private and may be publicly reported shall give full consideration to the patient's own wishes, to the need to respect the privacy of the patient and of other persons

and to the need to prevent serious harm to the patient's health or to avoid putting at risk the safety of others.

8. The decision arising out of the hearing and the reasons for it shall be expressed in writing. Copies shall be given to the patient and his or her personal representative and counsel. In deciding whether the decision shall be published in whole or in part, full consideration shall be given to the patient's own wishes, to the need to respect his or her privacy and that of other persons, to the public interest in the open administration of justice and to the need to prevent serious harm to the patient's health or to avoid putting at risk the safety of others.[70]

Principle 21 protects the right to Complaints:

Every patient and former patient shall have the right to make a complaint through procedures as specified by domestic law.[71]

Principle 22 provides for Monitoring and remedies:

States shall ensure that appropriate mechanisms are in force to promote compliance with these Principles, for the inspection of mental health facilities, for the submission, investigation and resolution of complaints and for the institution of appropriate disciplinary or judicial proceedings for professional misconduct or violation of the rights of a patient.[72]

Principle 23 notes Implementation:

1. States should implement these Principles through appropriate legislative, judicial, administrative, educational and other measures, which they shall review periodically.

2. States shall make these Principles widely known by appropriate and active means.[73]

International Convention on the Elimination of All Forms of Racial Discrimination (ICEAFRD)

Important for minorities with a disability, the International Convention on the Elimination of All Forms of Racial Discrimination was adopted on 21 December 1965.[74] The Convention was the first human rights instrument to establish an international monitoring system and was also revolutionary in its provision of national measures toward the advancement of specific racial or ethnic groups. The Convention is especially important for minorities with a disability who suffer double discrimination due to both disability and race. The Convention defines and condemns racial discrimination, and commits States to change national laws and policies, which create or perpetuate racial discrimination. It was the first human rights instrument to establish an international monitoring system and was also revolutionary in its provision of national measures toward the advancement of specific racial or ethnic groups. One of the main objectives of the Convention is to promote racial equality, and as such, the Convention not only aims to achieve *de jure* racial equality but also *de facto* equality, which allows the various ethnic, racial and national groups to enjoy the same social development. Furthermore, the Convention recognizes that certain racial or ethnic groups, such as those with a disability, may need special protection or may need to be assisted by special measures in order to achieve adequate development, and the Convention provides that such special measures shall not be considered racial discrimination as long as they are not continued after the objectives for which they were taken have been achieved.

Article 1(1) defines racial discrimination:

1(1) In this Convention, the term 'racial discrimination' shall mean any distinction, exclusion, restriction or preference based on race, color, descent, or national or ethnic origin which has the purpose or effect of nullifying or impairing the recognition, enjoyment or exercise, on an equal footing, of human rights and fundamental freedoms in the political, economic, social, cultural or any other field of public life. (2) This Convention shall not apply to distinctions, exclusions, restrictions or preferences made by a State Party to this Convention between citizens and non-citizens.[75]

Affirmative action programs by way of special measures are covered under Article 1(3):

1(3) Special measures taken for the sole purpose of securing adequate advancement of certain racial or ethnic groups or individuals requiring such protection as may be necessary in order to ensure such groups or individuals equal enjoyment or exercise of human rights and fundamental freedoms shall not be deemed racial discrimination, provided, however, that such measures do not, as a consequence, lead to the maintenance of separate rights for different racial groups and that they shall not be continued after the objectives for which they were taken have been achieved.[76]

Convention on the Elimination of All Forms of Discrimination against Women (CEDAW)

Important for women with a disability, the Convention on the Elimination of All Forms of Discrimination against Women (CEDAW) was adopted on 18 December 1979.[77] It is the most comprehensive treaty specifically on the human rights of women, establishing legally binding obligations to end discrimination. The Convention is especially important for women with a disability who suffer double discrimination due to both disability and gender. Described as the 'International Bill of Rights for Women', the Convention provides for equality between women and men in the enjoyment of civil, political, economic, social and cultural rights. Discrimination against women is to be eliminated through legal, policy and programmatic measures, and through temporary special measures to accelerate women's equality, which are defined as non-discriminatory. States Parties are required to end all forms of discrimination against women and to ensure their equality with men in political and public life with regard to nationality, education, employment, health, and economic and social benefits. The Convention obliges States Parties to modify the social and cultural patterns of conduct of men and women, in order to eliminate prejudices and customs and all other practices, which are based on the idea of the inferiority or superiority of either of the sexes or on stereotyped roles for men and women.

Discrimination against women is defined in Article 1 as to mean any distinction, exclusion or restriction made on the basis of sex which has the effect or purpose of impairing or nullifying the recognition, enjoyment or exercise by women, irrespective of their marital status, on a basis of equality of men and women, of human rights and fundamental freedoms in the political, economic, social, cultural, civil or any other field.[78] Article 4 contains an affirmative action strategy in that adoption by States Parties of temporary special measures aimed at accelerating *de facto* equality between men and women shall not be considered discrimination as defined in the present Convention, but shall in no way entail as a consequence the maintenance of unequal or separate standards; these measures shall be discontinued when the objectives of equality of opportunity and treatment have been achieved. Further, adoption by States Parties of special measures, including those measures contained in the present Convention, aimed at protecting maternity shall not be considered discriminatory.[79]

Crucially, Article 11(1) guarantees employment rights for women in terms of access to employment and equal pay:

> 11(1). States Parties shall take all appropriate measures to eliminate discrimination against women in the field of employment in order to ensure, on a basis of equality of men and women, the same rights, in particular:
> (a) The right to work as an inalienable right of all human beings;
> (b) The right to the same employment opportunities, including the application of the same criteria for selection in matters of employment;
> (c) The right to free choice of profession and employment, the right to promotion, job security and all benefits and conditions of service and the right to receive vocational training and retraining, including apprenticeships, advanced vocational training and recurrent training;
> (d) The right to equal remuneration, including benefits, and to equal treatment in respect of work of equal value, as well as equality of treatment in the evaluation of the quality of work;
> (e) The right to social security, particularly in cases of retirement, unemployment, sickness, invalidity and old age and other incapacity to work, as well as the right to paid leave;
> (f) The right to protection of health and to safety in working conditions, including the safeguarding of the function of reproduction.[80]

The important concept of equality before the law is guaranteed in Article 15:

> 15(1). States Parties shall accord to women equality with men before the law.
> (2). States Parties shall accord to women, in civil matters, a legal capacity identical to that of men and the same opportunities to exercise that capacity. In particular, they shall give women equal rights to conclude contracts and to

administer property and shall treat them equally in all stages of procedure in courts and tribunals.

(3). States Parties agree that all contracts and all other private instruments of any kind with a legal effect which is directed at restricting the legal capacity of women shall be deemed null and void.[81]

Optional Protocol to the Convention on the Elimination of All Forms of Discrimination against Women

The Optional Protocol to the Convention on the Elimination of All Forms of Discrimination Against Women (CEDAW) was adopted by the United Nations Commission on the Status of Women on 10 December 1999.[82] Essentially, an optional protocol is an additional enforcement mechanism for the original convention. The motivation behind the development of an Optional Protocol for CEDAW was to bring CEDAW itself on an equal footing with other international human rights instruments, enhancing its enforcement mechanisms. However, the Optional Protocol has provided an opportunity to strengthen the weak enforcement ability of CEDAW. The objective of the Optional Protocol is to allow individuals or groups of individuals such as women with a disability who have exhausted national remedies to petition the Committee directly about alleged violations of the Convention by their governments. By the Optional Protocol, States Parties undertake to make the Convention and the Protocol widely known and to facilitate access to information about the views and recommendations of the Committee.

Overall, the International Day of Disabled Persons each year aims to promote an understanding of disability issues and mobilize support for the dignity, rights and well-being of persons with disabilities. It also seeks to increase awareness of gains to be derived from the integration of disabled persons in every aspect of political, social, economic and cultural life. The observance of the Day focuses on giving a voice to the human experiences of disabled persons. The voice of persons with disabilities is seldom heard in the mainstream media. When persons with disabilities are portrayed, they are either stereotyped or presented as an inspiration for 'overcoming' a disability. Observance of the Day should therefore be used to offer an opportunity for persons with disabilities to speak for themselves. The theme of the Day is based on the goal of full participation and equality of persons with disabilities in social life and development, established by the World Programme of Action concerning Disabled Persons, adopted by the General Assembly in 1982. Since the adoption of the World Programme of Action, initiatives have been taken to realize its goals worldwide.

Much needs to be done inside and outside the United Nations. Awareness and information about the situation of persons with disabilities is critical if full participation and equality are to be achieved. The media is a key partner in the process of empowering persons with disabilities, in addressing discrimination, prejudice and ignorance, and in ending stereotypical portrayals of persons with disabilities. Non-governmental organizations also have a vital role to play in building understanding among society as a whole, on issues as diverse as the impact of landmines, the importance of educating disabled children, and the need to utilize information and communications technologies to empower disabled people.

Conclusion

On the international level, attempts have been made to provide legislatively for equality to end disability discrimination. Historically, people with a disability have had no input in the Constitution and the laws of the land. In recycling discrimination, 'the stream always tries to return to its habitual course'.[83] However, international law has made great strides to work toward this ability and overcome disability discrimination.

Notes

[1] United Nations, Universal Declaration of Human Rights, at the Preamble.
[2] *Ibid.*, at Article 1.
[3] *Ibid.*, at Article 3.
[4] *Ibid.*, at Article 7.
[5] *Ibid.*, at Article 8.
[6] *Ibid.*, at Article 23.
[7] *Ibid.*, at Article 26.
[8] United Nations, Charter of the United Nations, at the Preamble.
[9] *Ibid.*, at Article 1.
[10] *Ibid.*, at Article 55.
[11] *Ibid.*, at Article 92.
[12] *Ibid.*, at Article 94.
[13] *Ibid.*, at Article 95.
[14] *Ibid.*, at Article 96.
[15] United Nations, Statute of the International Court of Justice, at Article 1.
[16] *Ibid.*, at Article 34.
[17] *Ibid.*, at Article 36.
[18] *Ibid.*, at Article 38.
[19] United Nations, Equal Remuneration Convention (ILO No. 100), at Article 1.
[20] *Ibid.*, at Article 2.
[21] *Ibid.*, at Article 3.
[22] United Nations, Discrimination (Employment and Occupation) Convention (ILO No. 111), at the Preamble.
[23] *Ibid.*, at Article 1.
[24] *Ibid.*, at Article 2.
[25] *Ibid.*, at Article 3.
[26] *Ibid.*, at Article 5.
[27] United Nations, Employment Policy Convention (ILO No. 122), at the Preamble.
[28] *Ibid.*, at Article 1.
[29] *Ibid.*, at Article 2.
[30] *Ibid.*, at Article 3.
[31] United Nations, International Covenant on Civil and Political Rights.

32 *Ibid.*, at the Preamble.
33 *Ibid.*, at Article 2.
34 *Ibid.*, at Article 26.
35 *Ibid.*, at Article 28.
36 *Ibid.*, at Article 40.
37 *Ibid.*, at Article 45.
38 *Ibid.*, at Article 44.
39 United Nations, Optional Protocol to the International Covenant on Civil and Political Rights, at the Preamble.
40 *Ibid.*, at Article 1.
41 *Ibid.*, at Article 2.
42 United Nations, International Covenant on Economic, Social and Cultural Rights.
43 United Nations Development Program, *Human Development Report*, Oxford University Press, Oxford, 1994, p.2.
44 United Nations, International Covenant on Economic, Social and Cultural Rights, at the Preamble.
45 *Ibid.*, at Article 2.
46 *Ibid.*, at Article 7.
47 *Ibid.*, at Article 13.
48 United Nations, Declaration on the Rights of Mentally Retarded Persons, at the Preamble.
49 United Nations, Declaration on the Rights of Mentally Retarded Persons.
50 United Nations, Declaration on the Rights of Disabled Persons, at the Preamble.
51 United Nations, Declaration on the Rights of Disabled Persons.
52 United Nations, Principles for the Protection of Persons with Mental Illness and the Improvement of Mental Health Care, at the Preamble.
53 *Ibid.*, at Principle 1.
54 *Ibid.*, at Principle 2.
55 *Ibid.*, at Principle 3.
56 *Ibid.*, at Principle 4.
57 *Ibid.*, at Principle 5.
58 *Ibid.*, at Principle 6.
59 *Ibid.*, at Principle 7.
60 *Ibid.*, at Principle 8.
61 *Ibid.*, at Principle 9.
62 *Ibid.*, at Principle 10.
63 *Ibid.*, at Principle 11.
64 *Ibid.*, at Principle 12.
65 *Ibid.*, at Principle 13.
66 *Ibid.*, at Principle 14.
67 *Ibid.*, at Principle 15.
68 *Ibid.*, at Principle 16.
69 *Ibid.*, at Principle 17.
70 *Ibid.*, at principle 18.
71 *Ibid.*, at Principle 21.
72 *Ibid.*, at Principle 22.
73 *Ibid.*, at Principle 23.
74 United Nations, International Convention on the Elimination of All Forms of Racial Discrimination.
75 *Ibid.*, at Article 1(1).

76   *Ibid.*, at Article 1(3)
77   United Nations, Convention on the Elimination of All Forms of Discrimination against Women.
78   *Ibid.*, at Article 1.
79   *Ibid.*, at Article 4.
80   *Ibid.*, at Article 11(1).
81   *Ibid.*, at Article 15.
82   United Nations, Optional Protocol to the Convention on the Elimination of All Forms of Discrimination against Women.
83   Canadian Advisory Council on the Status of Women, *Feminist Guide to the Canadian Constitution*, Ottawa, 1992, at p.57.

References

Canadian Advisory Council on the Status of Women (1992), *Feminist Guide to the Canadian Constitution*, Ottawa.

United Nations, Charter of the United Nations, 1945.

United Nations, Convention on the Elimination of all Forms of Discrimination Against Women, 1979.

United Nations, Declaration on the Rights of Disabled Persons, 1975.

United Nations, Declaration on the Rights of Mentally Retarded Persons, 1971.

United Nations Development Program (1994), *Human Development Report*, Oxford University Press, Oxford.

United Nations, Discrimination (Employment and Occupation) Convention (ILO No. 111), 1958.

United Nations, Employment Policy Convention (ILO No. 122), 1964.

United Nations, Equal Remuneration Convention (ILO No. 100), 1951.

United Nations, International Convention on the Elimination of All Forms of Racial Discrimination, 1965.

United Nations, International Covenant on Civil and Political Rights, 1966.

United Nations, International Covenant on Economic, Social and Cultural Rights, 1966.

United Nations, Optional Protocol to the Convention on the Elimination of All Forms of Discrimination against Women, 1999.

United Nations, Optional Protocol to the International Covenant on Civil and Political Rights, 1966.

United Nations, Principles for the Protection of Persons with Mental Illness and the Improvement of Mental Health Care, 1991.

United Nations, Statute of the International Court of Justice, 1945.

United Nations, Universal Declaration of Human Rights, 1948.

Chapter 4

This Ability in
Australia and New Zealand

Introduction

This chapter will examine this ability in Australia and New Zealand. It will initially look at the situation in Australia, examining such legislation as the Disability Discrimination Act and the Human Rights and Equal Opportunity Commission Act, as well as for minorities with a disability the Racial Discrimination Act and the Racial Hatred Act, and for women with a disability the Sex Discrimination Act. It will then look at the situation in New Zealand, examining such legislation as the Treaty of Waitangi, the Bill of Rights, and the Human Rights Act and the Human Rights Amendment Act, as well as for minorities with a disability the Race Relations Act.

Australia

Australian laws do impose an obligation on everyone to be vigilant about disability discrimination and to take action when incidents of prejudice occur, particularly where those incidents might be unlawful. Australia is a party to a number of international conventions and declarations which impose obligations to eliminate disability discrimination when ratified in Australian law, including the Universal Declaration of Human Rights. When Australia becomes a party to an international convention, the terms of the convention create binding obligations in international law. However, international laws do not automatically become a part of Australian law. The Australian government can choose to give effect to its international obligations in various forms, legislative, policy or symbolic. In Australia, they are reflected in a range of government policies and programs, and some are also incorporated in law. Australia has taken practical steps to improve access to justice and protection under the law in the pursuit of equality, and is committed to providing more accessible, low-cost alternative dispute resolution options. Australia has a regime of legislation and institutional mechanisms to protect against disability discrimination, and is committed to promoting, supporting and protecting human rights.

Concerning the National Inquiry on Employment and Disability, there are three issues of common concern to people with disability who are, or who are about to be, in the open workforce, and their actual or potential employers:
1. Information. People with a disability and employers are concerned about the

absence of easily accessible and comprehensive information that can assist in their decision making processes and support their ongoing needs; 2. Cost. People with disability are concerned about the costs of participation, and employers are concerned about the costs of employing a person with disability; and 3. Risk. People with disability and employers are concerned about the financial and personal impact of participating in the workplace, especially if a job does not work out.

It is recommended: Mapping government services and Developing up-to-date information regarding the government programs available to employers and people with disability; the relationships between various government agencies and programs, and the outcomes of those programs; Economic cost of disability to people with different disabilities participating in the open workplace, employment services assisting people with different disabilities, and large, medium and small employers of people with different disabilities; International approaches to encouraging the participation and employment of people with disability with a view to developing a more streamlined and comprehensive program of support, assistance and incentives and a whole-of-government approach; Case management model for people with disability throughout the job readiness, recruitment and retention stages of the employment process, with a view to ensuring coordination of all services and supports across all levels of government; Simplification of welfare payments and the introduction of a cost of disability allowance, which takes into account the varying needs of people with different disabilities; Simplification of welfare payments and the introduction of a cost of participation allowance, which takes into account the varying needs of people with different disabilities; Need to extend eligibility for health care concessions for people with disability, focusing on the cost of health care for people with different disabilities, the additional health costs that may be incurred because of participation in the open workplace, and the impact of health care costs on participation in the open workplace; Mobility Allowance should take into account the cost of transport to and from the workplace for people with different disabilities on an 'as needed' basis; Need to extend eligibility for transport concessions for people with disability; Workplace Modifications Scheme (WMS) to include eligibility for any employee with disability, whether or not the person is referred by a government-funded employment service or working on a full-time, part-time or casual basis, expansion of the types of modifications covered by the scheme, portability of WMS-funded equipment, increased amounts available for modifications, simplified application process, and promotion of the scheme; Tax incentives regarding employment of people with disability; Impact of occupational health and safety laws, disability discrimination laws, industrial relations laws and the interaction between those laws on employers who hire people with disability; Robust government-supported work trial schemes that benefit employers and people with disability; Measures to improve transition to work schemes, including provision of appropriate supports for other work experience, traineeship and apprenticeship schemes and public sector leadership in recruiting people with disability into work experience, traineeships and apprenticeships; Post-placement support services offered by the Commonwealth government; Creating a flexible workplace for employees with disability, with efforts with people designing family-friendly workplaces; Recruitment and support needs of people with mental illness; Better coordination, increased funding and streamlined access to work and home-based personal assistance to enable people with disability in full-time, part-time or casual employment, apprenticeships, traineeships and work experience programs access to the help they need to meet their employment or study obligations; Mandatory accessible international procurement policies for government agencies; Mandatory reporting scheme regarding employment of people with disability; National scheme of awards for best practice in furthering employment opportunities for people with disability, with a sharing of expertise with the business community; Ensure recruitment agencies have policies and practices designed to encourage hiring of people with disability; Creation of an inter-sector leadership coalition, including representatives from employers, disability groups, employment service providers and government agencies.

Disability Discrimination Act 1992

The Disability Discrimination Act 1992 prohibits discrimination on the ground of disability. The objects of the Act are outlined in Section 3:

> 3(a) to eliminate, as far as possible, discrimination against persons on the ground of disability in the areas of:
>> (i) work, accommodation, education, access to premises, clubs and sport; and
>> (ii) the provision of goods, facilities, services and land; and
>> (iii) existing laws; and
>> (iv) the administration of Commonwealth laws and programs; and
> (b) to ensure, as far as practicable, that persons with disabilities have the same rights to equality before the law as the rest of the community; and
> (c) to promote recognition and acceptance within the community of the principle that persons with disabilities have the same fundamental rights as the rest of the community.[1]

Disability discrimination is defined under Section 5:

> 5(1) For the purposes of this Act, a person (*discriminator*) discriminates against another person (*aggrieved person*) on the ground of a disability of the aggrieved person if, because of the aggrieved person's disability, the discriminator treats or proposes to treat the aggrieved person less favourably than, in circumstances that are the same or are not materially different, the discriminator treats or would treat a person without the disability.
> (2) For the purposes of subsection (1), circumstances in which a person treats or would treat another person with a disability are not materially different because of the fact that different accommodation or services may be required by the person with a disability.[2]

Indirect disability discrimination is defined under Section 6:

6.For the purposes of this Act, a person (*discriminator*) discriminates against another person (*aggrieved person*) on the ground of a disability of the aggrieved person if the discriminator requires the aggrieved person to comply with a requirement or condition:

(a) with which a substantially higher proportion of persons without the disability comply or are able to comply; and

(b) which is not reasonable having regard to the circumstances of the case; and

(c) with which the aggrieved person does not or is not able to comply.[3]

An Act done because of disability and for other reason is defined under Section 10:

10. If:

(a) an act is done for 2 or more reasons; and

(b) one of the reasons is the disability of a person (whether or not it is the dominant or a substantial reason for doing the act);

then, for the purposes of this Act, the act is taken to be done for that reason.[4]

Further, Section 11 addresses unjustifiable hardship:

11. For the purposes of this Act, in determining what constitutes unjustifiable hardship, all relevant circumstances of the particular case are to be taken into account including:

(a) the nature of the benefit or detriment likely to accrue or be suffered by any persons concerned; and

(b) the effect of the disability of a person concerned; and

(c) the financial circumstances and the estimated amount of expenditure required to be made by the person claiming unjustifiable hardship; and

(d) in the case of the provision of services, or the making available of facilities – an action plan given to the Commission....[5]

Discrimination in employment is prohibited under Section 15:

15(1) It is unlawful for an employer or a person acting or purporting to act on behalf of an employer to discriminate against a person on the ground of the other person's disability or a disability of any of that other person's associates:

(a) in the arrangements made for the purpose of determining who should be offered employment; or

(b) in determining who should be offered employment; or

(c) in the terms or conditions on which employment is offered.

(2) It is unlawful for an employer or a person acting or purporting to act on behalf of an employer to discriminate against an employee on the ground of the employee's disability or a disability of any of that employee's associates:

(a) in the terms or conditions of employment that the employer affords the employee; or

(b) by denying the employee access, or limiting the employee's access, to opportunities for promotion, transfer or training, or to any other benefits associated with employment; or
(c) by dismissing the employee; or
(d) by subjecting the employee to any other detriment.

(3) Neither paragraph (1)(a) nor (b) renders it unlawful for a person to discriminate against another person, on the ground of the other person's disability, in connection with employment to perform domestic duties on the premises on which the first-mentioned person resides.

(4) Neither paragraph (1)(b) nor (2)(c) renders unlawful discrimination by an employer against a person on the ground of the person's disability, if taking into account the person's past training, qualifications and experience relevant to the particular employment and, if the person is already employed by the employer, the person's performance as an employee, and all other relevant factors that it is reasonable to take into account, the person because of his or her disability:

(a) would be unable to carry out the inherent requirements of the particular employment; or
(b) would, in order to carry out those requirements, require services or facilities that are not required by persons without the disability and the provision of which would impose an unjustifiable hardship on the employer.[6]

Further, discrimination against contract workers is prohibited under Section 17:

17(1) It is unlawful for a principal to discriminate against a contract worker on the ground of the contract worker's disability or a disability of any of the contract worker's associates:

(a) in the terms or conditions on which the principal allows the contract worker to work; or
(b) by not allowing the contract worker to work or continue to work; or
(c) by denying the contract worker access, or limiting the contract worker's access, to any benefit associated with the work in respect of which the contract with the employer is made; or
(d) by subjecting the contract worker to any other detriment.

(2) Paragraph (1)(b) does not render it unlawful for a principal to discriminate against a contract worker on the ground of the contract worker's disability, if taking into account the contract worker's past training, qualifications and experience relevant to working as a contract worker and, if the person is already working for the principal as a contract worker, the contract worker's performance as a contract worker, and all other relevant factors that it is reasonable to take into account, the person because of the contract worker's disability:

(a) would be unable to carry out the inherent requirements of a contract worker; or
(b) would, in order to carry out those requirements, require services or facilities that are not required by persons without the disability and the provision of which would impose an unjustifiable hardship on the principal.[7]

Section 23 speaks to discrimination concerning access to premises:

23(1) It is unlawful for a person to discriminate against another person on the ground of the other person's disability or a disability of any of that other person's associates:

(a) by refusing to allow the other person access to, or the use of, any premises that the public or a section of the public is entitled or allowed to enter or use (whether for payment or not); or

(b) in the terms or conditions on which the first-mentioned person is prepared to allow the other person access to, or the use of, any such premises; or

(c) in relation to the provision of means of access to such premises; or

(d) by refusing to allow the other person the use of any facilities in such premises that the public or a section of the public is entitled or allowed to use (whether for payment or not); or

(e) in the terms or conditions on which the first-mentioned person is prepared to allow the other person the use of any such facilities; or

(f) by requiring the other person to leave such premises or cease to use such facilities.

(2) This section does not render it unlawful to discriminate against a person on the ground of the person's disability in relation to the provision of access to premises if:

(a) the premises are so designed or constructed as to be inaccessible to a person with a disability; and

(b) any alteration to the premises to provide such access would impose unjustifiable hardship on the person who would have to provide that access.[8]

Disability discrimination in accommodation is prohibited under Section 25:

25(1) It is unlawful for a person, whether as principal or agent, to discriminate against another person on the ground of the other person's disability or a disability of any of that other person's associates:

(a) by refusing the other person's application for accommodation; or
(b) in the terms or conditions on which the accommodation is offered to the other person; or
(c) by deferring the other person's application for accommodation or according to the other person a lower order of precedence in any list of applicants for that accommodation.

(2) It is unlawful for a person, whether as principal or agent, to discriminate against another person on the ground of the other person's disability or a disability of any of the other person's associates:

(a) by denying the other person access, or limiting the other person's access, to any benefit associated with accommodation occupied by the other person; or

(b) by evicting the other person from accommodation occupied by the other person; or

(c) by subjecting the other person to any other detriment in relation to accommodation occupied by the other person; or

(d) by refusing to permit the other person to make reasonable alterations to accommodation occupied by that person if:

> (i) that person has undertaken to restore the accommodation to its condition before alteration on leaving the accommodation; and
>
> (ii) in all the circumstances it is likely that the person will perform the undertaking; and
>
> (iii) in all the circumstances, the action required to restore the accommodation to its condition before alteration is reasonably practicable; and
>
> (iv) the alteration does not involve alteration of the premises of any other occupier; and
>
> (v) the alteration is at that other person's own expense.

(3) This section does not apply to or in respect of:

(a) the provision of accommodation in premises if:

> (i) the person who provides or proposes to provide the accommodation or a near relative of that person resides, and intends to continue to reside on those premises; and
>
> (ii) the accommodation provided in those premises is for no more than 3 persons other than a person referred to in subparagraph (a)(i) or near relatives of such a person; or

(b) the accommodation is provided by a charitable or other voluntary body solely for persons who have a particular disability and the person discriminated against does not have that particular disability; or

(c) the provision of accommodation in premises where special services or facilities would be required by the person with a disability and the provision of such special services or facilities would impose unjustifiable hardship on the person providing or proposing to provide the accommodation whether as principal or agent.[9]

Importantly, special measures are provided under Section 45:

45. This Part does not render it unlawful to do an act that is reasonably intended to:

(a) ensure that persons who have a disability have equal opportunities with other persons in circumstances in relation to which a provision is made by this Act; or

(b) afford persons who have a disability or a particular disability, goods or access to facilities, services or opportunities to meet their special needs in relation to:

> (i) employment, education, accommodation, clubs or sport; and
>
> (ii) the provision of goods, services, facilities or land; or
>
> (iii) the making available of facilities; or
>
> (iv) the administration of Commonwealth laws and programs; or
>
> (v) their capacity to live independently; or

(c) afford persons who have a disability or a particular disability, grants, benefits or programs, whether direct or indirect, to meet their special needs in relation to:

(i) employment, education, accommodation, clubs or sport; or

(ii) the provision of goods, services, facilities or land; or

(iii) the making available of facilities; or

(iv) the administration of Commonwealth laws and programs; or

(v) their capacity to live independently.

The functions of the Human Rights and Equal Opportunity Commission are outlined in Section 67:

67(1) The following functions are conferred on the Commission:

(c) to exercise the powers conferred on it by section 55;

(d) to report to the Minister on matters relating to the development of disability standards;

(e) to monitor the operation of such standards and report to the Minister the results of such monitoring;

(f) to receive action plans under section 64;

(g) to promote an understanding and acceptance of, and compliance with, this Act;

(h) to undertake research and educational programs, and other programs, on behalf of the Commonwealth for the purpose of promoting the objects of this Act;

(i) to examine enactments, and (when requested to do so by the Minister) proposed enactments, for the purpose of ascertaining whether the enactments or proposed enactments are, or would be, inconsistent with or contrary to the objects of this Act, and to report to the Minister the results of any such examination;

(j) on its own initiative or when requested by the Minister, to report to the Minister as to the laws that should be made by the Parliament, or action that should be taken by the Commonwealth, on matters relating to discrimination on the ground of disability;

(k) to prepare, and to publish in such manner as the Commission considers appropriate, guidelines for the avoidance of discrimination on the ground of disability;

(l) where the Commission thinks it appropriate to do so, with the leave of the court hearing the proceedings and subject to any conditions imposed by the court, to intervene in proceedings that involve issues of discrimination on the ground of disability;

(m) to do anything incidental or conducive to the performance of any of the preceding functions.

(2) The Commission is not to regard an enactment or proposed enactment as being inconsistent with or contrary to the objects of this Act for the purposes of paragraph (1)(i) because of a provision of the enactment or proposed enactment that is included for the purpose referred to in section 45.[10]

Finally, the Disability Discrimination Commissioner is named under Section 113:

113(1) There is to be a Disability Discrimination Commissioner, who is to be appointed by the Governor-General.

(2) A person is not qualified to be appointed as the Disability Discrimination Commissioner unless the Governor-General is satisfied that the person has appropriate qualifications, knowledge or experience.[11]

Further, the following legislative instruments may be relevant to disability discrimination.

Human Rights and Equal Opportunity Commission Act (HREOCA)

Important for those with a disability, the Human Rights and Equal Opportunity Commission Act 1986 (HREOCA) gives effect to such relevant international conventions and declarations as the International Covenant on Civil and Political Rights, the Declaration on the Rights of Persons Belonging to National or Ethnic, Religious or Linguistic Minorities, and the International Labor Organization Convention on Discrimination in Employment and Occupation. The Human Rights and Equal Opportunity Commission (HREOC) inquires into complaints under federal anti-discrimination law and educates the community about obligations under domestic legislation. The HREOCA enables the HREOC to investigate complaints of breaches of conventions by Commonwealth Government agencies and may also investigate complaints of racial discrimination in employment by any employer. Important for disability rights, the Federal Magistrates Court may provide substantive relief and interim relief in relation to complaints under the Disability Act, the Racial Discrimination Act, the Sex Discrimination Act, and the HREOC Act. The Federal Magistrates Court can make:

> (a) an order declaring that the respondent has committed unlawful discrimination and directing the respondent not to repeat or continue such unlawful discrimination;
>
> (b) an order requiring a respondent to perform any reasonable act or course of conduct to redress any loss or damage suffered by an applicant;
>
> (c) an order requiring a respondent to employ or reemploy an applicant;
>
> (d) an order requiring a respondent to pay to an applicant damages by way of compensation for any loss or damage suffered because of the conduct of the respondent;
>
> (e) an order requiring a respondent to vary the termination of a contract or agreement to redress any loss or damage suffered by an applicant;
>
> (f) an order declaring that it would be inappropriate for any further action to be taken in the matter.

Workplace Relations Act

The Workplace Relations Act 1996 has provisions to safeguard groups of workers.[12] The Act provides for equal remuneration for work of equal value without discrimination on the grounds of race.

Racial Discrimination Act (RDA)

Important for minorities with a disability, the Racial Discrimination Act 1975 (RDA), also known as An Act relating to the Elimination of Racial and other Discrimination, prohibits discrimination on the grounds of race, color, descent and national or ethnic origin.[13] The RDA gives effect to Australia's obligations under the International Convention on the Elimination of All Forms of Racial Discrimination. The RDA aims to ensure that all Australians can enjoy their human rights and freedoms in full equality regardless of their race, color, descent, or national or ethnic origin. The RDA applies to everyone in Australia including businesses, schools, and local, State, Territory and Commonwealth government agencies and departments. It overrides racially discriminatory legislation, making it ineffective. However, Commonwealth legislation which is racially discriminatory is not necessarily overridden by the RDA. Under the RDA, racial discrimination is unlawful whenever it impairs a person's equal enjoyment of his human rights and fundamental freedoms. In addition, the RDA has specific provisions making it unlawful to discriminate in areas such as employment, land, housing and accommodation, provision of goods and services, access to places and facilities for use by the public, advertising and joining a trade union. The RDA also makes indirect racial discrimination unlawful. In some cases, the RDA will permit special measures, which are distinctions based on race where there might be more favorable treatment for one racial group over another. It does so as a form of affirmative action, so that a group which has been traditionally denied human rights and access to rights can receive special treatment to redress the situation and to allow that group to enjoy human rights on an equal footing with the rest of the community. This form of favorable treatment is not unlawful discrimination and the special measure will be removed when equality has been achieved. Government support for special measures is not discriminatory, because the aim is to enhance the access of minority groups to justice, cultural expression and other rights and freedoms. The RDA is administered by the Human Rights and Equal Opportunity Commission (HREOC). HREOC has the responsibility for investigating complaints.

Importantly, Section 9 prohibits racial discrimination:

> 9(1) It is unlawful for a person to do any act involving a distinction, exclusion, restriction or preference based on race, color, descent or national or ethnic origin which has the purpose or effect of nullifying or impairing the recognition, enjoyment or exercise, on an equal footing, of any human right or fundamental freedom in the political, economic, social, cultural or any other field of public life.

> (1A) Where:
> (a) a person requires another person to comply with a term, condition or requirement which is not reasonable having regard to the circumstances of the case; and
> (b) the other person does not or cannot comply with the term, condition or requirement; and

(c) the requirement to comply has the purpose or effect of nullifying or impairing the recognition, enjoyment or exercise, on an equal footing, by persons of the same race, color, descent or national or ethnic origin as the other person, of any human right or fundamental freedom in the political, economic, social, cultural or any other field of public life;

the act of requiring such compliance is to be treated, for the purposes of this Part, as an act involving a distinction based on, or an act done by reason of, the other person's race, color, descent or national or ethnic origin.

(2) A reference in this section to a human right or fundamental freedom in the political, economic, social, cultural or any other field of public life includes any right of a kind referred to in Article 5 of the Convention.

(3) This section does not apply in respect of the employment, or an application for the employment, of a person on a ship or aircraft (not being an Australian ship or aircraft) if that person was engaged, or applied, for that employment outside Australia.[14]

In addition, Section 10 guarantees equality before the law:

10(1) If, by reason of, or of a provision of, a law of the Commonwealth or of a State or Territory, persons of a particular race, color or national or ethnic origin do not enjoy a right that is enjoyed by persons of another race, color or national or ethnic origin, or enjoy a right to a more limited extent than persons of another race, color or national or ethnic origin, then, notwithstanding anything in that law, persons of the first-mentioned race, color or national or ethnic origin shall, by force of this section, enjoy that right to the same extent as persons of that other race, color or national or ethnic origin.[15]

Racial Hatred Act (RHA)

Important for minorities with a disability, the Racial Hatred Act 1995 (RHA) extends the coverage of the Racial Discrimination Act (RDA) to allow people to complain about racially offensive or abusive behavior. In 1995, the RHA amended the RDA by adding in new laws specifically dealing with racial vilification. The RHA gives effect to some of Australia's obligations under the International Covenant on Civil and Political Rights and the International Convention on the Elimination of All Forms of Racial Discrimination. The RHA aims to strike a balance between two valued rights, namely the right to communicate freely and the right to live free from vilification. It covers public acts, which are done, in whole or in part, because of the race, color, or national or ethnic origin of a person or group and reasonably likely in all circumstances to offend, insult, humiliate or intimidate that person or group. In bringing a complaint under the RHA, the complainant is responsible for proving that the act was done in public, that it was done because of his ethnicity and that it was reasonably likely to offend, insult, humiliate or intimidate a reasonable person of that ethnicity. In claiming an exception, the respondent is responsible for establishing that the act was a genuine exception and that it was done reasonably and in good faith.

Sex Discrimination Act

Important for women with a disability, the Sex Discrimination Act 1984 prohibits discrimination on the grounds of gender, marital status, pregnancy, and potential pregnancy and family responsibilities, and is administered by the Sex Discrimination Commissioner under the auspices of the Human Rights & Equal Opportunity Commission (HREOC).[16]

Importantly, Section 5 deals directly with the definition of gender discrimination:

> 5(1) For the purposes of this Act, a person (in this subsection referred to as the discriminator) discriminates against another person (in this subsection referred to as the aggrieved person) on the ground of the sex of the aggrieved person if, by reason of:
> (a) the sex of the aggrieved person;
> (b) a characteristic that appertains generally to persons of the sex of the aggrieved person; or
> (c) a characteristic that is generally imputed to persons of the sex of the aggrieved person; the discriminator treats the aggrieved person less favourably than, in circumstances that are the same or are not materially different, the discriminator treats or would treat a person of the opposite sex.
> (2) For the purposes of this Act, a person (the discriminator) discriminates against another person (the aggrieved person) on the ground of the sex of the aggrieved person if the discriminator imposes, or proposes to impose, a condition, requirement or practice that has, or is likely to have, the effect of disadvantaging persons of the same sex as the aggrieved person. [17]

In terms of affirmative action, Section 7D stipulates that a person may take special measures for the purpose of achieving substantive equality between men and women; or people of different marital status; or women who are pregnant and people who are not pregnant; or women who are potentially pregnant and people who are not potentially pregnant.[18] The Act provides an important role for the HREOC in addressing the issue of gender discrimination. Its functions are defined under Section 48, namely to promote an understanding and acceptance of, and compliance with, this Act; to undertake research and educational programs, and other programs, on behalf of the Commonwealth for the purpose of promoting the objects of this Act; to examine enactments, and proposed enactments, for the purpose of ascertaining whether they are or would be inconsistent with or contrary to the objects of this Act, and to report to the Minister the results of any such examination[19]

Overall, Australia aims to bolster the efforts of all government agencies, the private sector, the community and individuals to achieve equality, through, namely advancing outcomes in areas where there is discrimination and inequality; improving outcomes for those with special needs including those with disabilities, the Indigenous population and those from a non-English speaking background; encouraging increased efforts by State/Territory and Commonwealth agencies to develop inclusive policies, programs and services; encouraging and facilitating the increased involvement of the private sector and community groups in taking responsibility for addressing discrimination and inequality.[20]

In terms of power and decision-making, the critical area of concern is inequality in the sharing of power and decision-making at all levels, with correction action to take measures to ensure equal access to and full participation in power structures and decision-making; and to increase the capacity of all humans to participate in decision-making and leadership. All peoples have a right and a responsibility to participate in the decision-making processes that shape the nation. Unless human beings are full and active participants in all spheres of public and private life, across a wide range of decision-making positions, the future will not reflect the talents, experience and aspirations of all citizens. Overall, greater diversity should be encouraged among those occupying senior decision-making positions, and opportunities should be expanded to participate in high-level positions, in order to create or strengthen national machineries and other governmental bodies; integrate neutral perspectives in legislation, public policies, programs and projects; and generate and disseminate disaggregated data and information for planning and evaluation. The participation of all humans on equal terms in political, social, economic and cultural life is essential to the progress and the well-being of society in general.

In terms of human rights, the critical area of concern is the lack of respect for and adequate promotion and protection of human rights, with corrective action, through the full implementation of all human rights instruments; ensure equality and non-discrimination under the law and in practice; and achieve legal literacy. Of particular concern is the level of access to and participation in processes relating to Australia's obligations under international instruments on human rights, including reporting and monitoring obligations. Human rights are an inalienable, integral and indivisible aspect of life, in the legislative protections and the existence of agencies to enable citizens to exercise their rights and responsibilities.[21]

Overall, in the fight for disability rights, the implementation of standards for accessible public transport, the introduction of standards for equal participation in education by students with disabilities, and progress towards improved standards for access to buildings are important areas of achievement. However, supports and services for Australians affected by mental illness and their families remain inadequate. It is a government's responsibility to create an equal playing field so that people with disabilities can compete with able-bodied Australians on equal terms. Much needs to be done to improve services and supports to assist Australians with disabilities, from young people living in aged care nursing homes for lack of anywhere else to go, to parents and schools not being provided with sufficient resources to manage behavioral issues arising from disabilities. Laws need to be changed to stamp out disability discrimination but this must be done without imposing hardships on companies. The first major review of the Disability Discrimination Act (DDA) recommended laws be strengthened to make it a duty for employers, educators and other service providers to make reasonable adjustments to cater for disabled people. The change would enable disabled people to make a formal complaint of discrimination if an employer failed to make a reasonable adjustment. The DDA does require organizations to make reasonable adjustments to eliminate discriminatory barriers. Explicit recognition of this duty is balanced by expanding the operation of the unjustifiable hardship defence. Adjustments will produce net benefits for the community without imposing undue hardship on the organizations required to make them, and will benefit not only the disabled but the whole community.

New Zealand

New Zealand has ratified international covenants, which obligate governments to ensure equal rights to enjoy all economic, social, cultural, civil and political rights. Although, international agreements do not automatically become part of New Zealand domestic law upon ratification but must be enacted into law by Parliament, jurisprudence has developed in New Zealand that recognizes the value of international agreements as tools for interpreting the legislative provisions which implement them into domestic law.

The following legislative instruments may be relevant to disability discrimination.

Treaty of Waitangi

In the late 1830s, there were approximately 125,000 Mäori in New Zealand and about 2000 settlers. More immigrants were arriving all the time though, and Captain William Hobson was sent to act for the British Crown in the negotiation of a treaty between the Crown and Mäori. The Colonial Secretary, Lord Normanby, instructed Hobson:

> All dealings with the Aborigines for their Lands must be conducted on the same principles of sincerity, justice, and good faith as must govern your transactions with them for the recognition of Her Majesty's Sovereignty in the Islands. Nor is this all. They must not be permitted to enter into any Contracts in which they might be the ignorant and unintentional authors of injuries to themselves. You will not, for example, purchase from them any Territory the retention of which by them would be essential, or highly conducive, to their own comfort, safety or subsistence. The acquisition of Land by the Crown for the future Settlement of British Subjects must be confined to such Districts as the Natives can alienate without distress or serious inconvenience to themselves. To secure the observance of this rule will be one of the first duties of their official protector.

The Preamble of the English version of the Treaty of Waitangi, which came into effect on 6 February 1840, states:

> HER MAJESTY VICTORIA Queen of the United Kingdom of Great Britain and Ireland regarding with Her Royal favor the Native Chiefs and Tribes of New Zealand and anxious to protect their just Rights and Property and to secure to them the enjoyment of Peace and Good Order has deemed it necessary in consequence of the great number of Her Majesty's Subjects who have already settled in New

Zealand and the rapid extension of Emigration both from Europe and Australia which is still in progress to constitute and appoint a functionary properly authorized to treat with the Aborigines of New Zealand for the recognition of Her Majesty's Sovereign authority over the whole or any part of those islands, Her Majesty therefore being desirous to establish a settled form of Civil Government with a view to avert the evil consequences which must result from the absence of the necessary Laws and Institutions alike to the native population and to Her subjects has been graciously pleased to empower and to authorize me William Hobson a Captain in Her Majesty's Royal Navy Consul and Lieutenant Governor of such parts of New Zealand as may be or hereafter shall be ceded to her Majesty to invite the confederated and independent Chiefs of New Zealand to concur in the following Articles and Conditions.[22]

In terms of the meaning of the Treaty, the Preamble of the English text states the British intentions were to protect Mäori interests from the encroaching British settlement; provide for British settlement; and establish a government to maintain peace and order. The Mäori text has a different emphasis, suggesting that the Queen's main promises to Mäori were to secure tribal *rangatiratanga*; and secure Mäori land ownership.

Article 1 states:

The Chiefs of the Confederation of the United Tribes of New Zealand and the separate and independent Chiefs who have not become members of the Confederation cede to Her Majesty the Queen of England absolutely and without reservation all the rights and powers of Sovereignty which the said Confederation or Individual Chiefs respectively exercise or possess, or may be supposed to exercise or to possess over their respective Territories as the sole Sovereigns thereof.[23]

In terms of the meaning of the Treaty, in the Mäori text of Article 1, Mäori gave the British a right of governance, *kawanatanga*, whereas in the English text, Mäori ceded 'sovereignty'. One of the problems that faced the original translators of the English draft of the Treaty was that 'sovereignty' in the British understanding of the word had no direct translation in the context of Mäori society. *Rangatira* (chiefs) held the autonomy and authority, *rangatiratanga*, over their own domains but there was no supreme ruler of the whole country. In the Mäori text, the translators used the inadequate term *kawanatanga*, a transliteration of the word 'governance', which was then in current use. Mäori understanding of this word came from familiar use in the New Testament of the Bible when referring to the likes of Pontious Pilate, and from their knowledge of the role of the *Kawana* or Governor of New South Wales whose jurisdiction then extended to British subjects in New Zealand. As a result, in Article 1, Mäori believe they ceded to the Queen a right of governance in return for the promise of protection, while retaining the authority they always had to manage their own affairs.

Article 2 states:

Her Majesty the Queen of England confirms and guarantees to the Chiefs and Tribes of New Zealand and to the respective families and individuals thereof the full exclusive and undisturbed possession of their Lands and Estates Forests Fisheries and other properties which they may collectively or individually possess so long as it is their wish and desire to retain the same in their possession; but the Chiefs of the United Tribes and the individual Chiefs yield to Her Majesty the exclusive right of Preemption over such lands as the proprietors thereof may be disposed to alienate at such prices as may be agreed upon between the respective Proprietors and persons appointed by Her Majesty to treat with them in that behalf.[24]

In terms of the meaning of the Treaty, the Māori text of Article 2 uses the word *rangatiratanga* in promising to uphold the authority that tribes had always had over their lands and taonga. This choice of wording emphasizes status and authority. In the English text, the Queen guaranteed to Māori the undisturbed possession of their properties, including their lands, forests, and fisheries, for as long as they wished to retain them, emphasizing property and ownership rights. Article 2 provides for land sales to be effected through the Crown. This gave the Crown the right of pre-emption in land sales. The Waitangi Tribunal, after reading the instructions for the Treaty provided by Lord Normanby, concluded that the purpose of this provision was not just to regulate settlement but to ensure that each tribe retained sufficient land for its own purposes and needs.

Article 3 states:

In consideration thereof Her Majesty the Queen of England extends to the Natives of New Zealand Her royal protection and imparts to them all the Rights and Privileges of British Subjects.
W HOBSON Lieutenant Governor.
Now therefore We the Chiefs of the Confederation of the United Tribes of New Zealand being assembled in Congress at Victoria in Waitangi and We the Separate and Independent Chiefs of New Zealand claiming authority over the Tribes and Territories which are specified after our respective names, having been made fully to understand the Provisions of the foregoing Treaty, accept and enter into the same in the full spirit and meaning thereof: in witness of which we have attached our signatures or marks at the places and the dates respectively specified.[25]

In terms of the meaning of the Treaty, in Article 3, the Crown promised to Māori the benefits of royal protection and full citizenship. This text emphasizes equality. Further, in the epilogue, the signatories acknowledge that they have entered into the full spirit of the Treaty. These words are important, for it is the principles of the Treaty, rather than the meaning of its strict terms, that the Waitangi Tribunal must determine today. In doing this, the Tribunal must have regard to cultural meanings of words, the surrounding circumstances, comments made at the time, and the parties' objectives, as far as these can be gathered from other sources.

Bill of Rights Act

Important for those with a disability, according to the Preamble of the Bill of Rights Act 1990, as amended by the Human Rights Act, the Bill of Rights aims to affirm, protect, and promote human rights and fundamental freedoms in New Zealand; and to affirm New Zealand's commitment to the International Covenant on Civil and Political Rights.[26]

Freedom from discrimination is guaranteed under Section 19:

> 19(1) Everyone has the right to freedom from discrimination on the grounds of discrimination in the Human Rights Act 1993.
> (2) Measures taken in good faith for the purpose of assisting or advancing persons or groups of persons disadvantaged because of discrimination that is unlawful by virtue of Part II of the Human Rights Act 1993 do not constitute discrimination.[27]

Remedies are contained in Section 27:

> 27(1) Every person has the right to the observance of the principles of natural justice by any tribunal or other public authority which has the power to make a determination in respect of that person's right, obligations, or interests protected or recognized by law.
> (2) Every person whose rights, obligations, or interests protected or recognized by law have been affected by a determination of any tribunal or other public authority has the right to apply, in accordance with law, for judicial review of that determination.
> (3) Every person has the right to bring civil proceedings against, and to defend civil proceedings brought by, the Crown, and to have those proceedings heard, according to law, in the same way as civil proceedings between individuals.[28]

The Bill of Rights Act aims to affirm, protect and promote human rights and fundamental freedoms in New Zealand; and to affirm New Zealand's commitment to the International Covenant on Civil and Political Rights. It applies to acts done by the legislative, executive and judicial branches of the Government, or by any person or body in the performance of any public function, power or duty conferred or imposed on that person or body by or pursuant to law.

Human Rights Act (HRA) and the Human Rights Amendment Act

Important for those with a disability, the Human Rights Act 1993 (HRA) protects New Zealanders from unlawful discrimination in a number of areas of life. The Human Rights Commission (HRC) was established by the Human Rights Commission Act 1977 (HRCA), and is empowered under the HRA to protect human rights in accordance with United Nations Covenants and Conventions. The Human Rights Amendment Act 2001 made several significant changes to the HRA, and specifically to the functions and powers of the Commission, and the way complaints of unlawful discrimination are received and resolved by the Commission. Some of the key changes to the Commission's functions and powers include: advocating and promoting respect for and appreciation of human rights in New Zealand society, and encouraging the maintenance and development of harmonious relations between individuals and the diverse groups in New Zealand society; advocating and promoting, by education and publicity, respect for, and observance of, human rights; making public statements promoting an understanding of, and compliance with, the New Zealand Bill of Rights Act 1990; developing a national plan of action, in consultation with interested parties, for the promotion and protection of human rights in New Zealand; promoting, by research, education and discussion, a better understanding of the human rights dimensions of the Treaty of Waitangi and their relationship with domestic and international human rights law; bringing civil proceedings for any breach of the Act arising out of any inquiry conducted by the Commission; applying to a court or tribunal to be appointed as intervener or as counsel, assisting the Court or Tribunal, if this will facilitate the performance of the Commission's functions relating to advocacy for, or promotion of, human rights.

Further, the functions and powers of the HRC include to encourage, by education and publicity, respect for and observance of human rights; to encourage and coordinate programs and activities in the field of human rights; to make public statements in relation to any matter affecting human rights, including statements promoting an understanding of, and compliance with, this Act; to prepare and publish, as the Commission considers appropriate, guidelines for the avoidance of acts or practices that may be inconsistent with, or contrary to, the provisions of this Act; to receive and invite representations from members of the public on any matter affecting human rights; to consult and cooperate with other persons and bodies concerned with the protection of human rights; to inquire generally into any matter, including any enactment or law, or any practice, or any procedure, whether governmental or nongovernmental, if it appears to the Commission that human rights are, or may be, infringed thereby; and to report to the Prime Minister from time to time on any matter affecting human rights, including the desirability of legislative, administrative, or other action to give better protection to human rights and to ensure better compliance with standards laid down in international instruments on human rights, the desirability of New Zealand becoming bound by any international instrument on human rights, and the implications of any proposed legislation or proposed policy of the Government that the Commission considers may affect human rights.[29] Employment remains the largest area of complaints at about 60 per cent.

Overall, the Act defines unlawful discrimination, and prohibited grounds are personal characteristics, such as disability, race or sex, and discrimination because of these characteristics is unlawful.

Important for disability rights, Section 21 defines disability discrimination under prohibited grounds for discrimination:

> 21. (1) For the purposes of this Act, the prohibited grounds of discrimination are
>
>   (h) Disability, which means
>   (i) Physical disability or impairment;
>   (ii) Physical illness;
>   (iii) Psychiatric illness;
>   (iv) Intellectual or psychological disability or impairment;

(v) Any other loss or abnormality of psychological, physiological, or anatomical structure or function;

(vi) Reliance on a guide dog, wheelchair, or other remedial means;

(vii) The presence in the body of organisms capable of causing illness.

(2) Each of the grounds specified in subsection (1) of this section is a prohibited ground of discrimination, for the purposes of this Act, if

(a) It pertains to a person or to a relative or associate of a person; and

(b) It either

(i) Currently exists or has in the past existed; or

(ii) Is suspected or assumed or believed to exist or to have existed by the person alleged to have discriminated.[30]

Further, indirect discrimination is defined in Section 65:

65. Where any conduct, practice, requirement, or condition that is not apparently in contravention of any provision of this Part of this Act has the effect of treating a person or group of persons differently on one of the prohibited grounds of discrimination in a situation where such treatment would be unlawful under any provision of this Part of this Act other than this section, that conduct, practice, condition, or requirement shall be unlawful under that provision unless the person whose conduct or practice is in issue, or who imposes the condition or requirement, establishes good reason for it.[31]

As regards discrimination in employment, Section 22(1) states:

22(1) Where an applicant for employment or an employee is qualified for work of any description, it shall be unlawful for an employer, or any person acting or purporting to act on behalf of an employer:

(a) to refuse or omit to employ the applicant on work of that description which is available; or

(b) to offer or afford the applicant or the employee less favourable terms of employment, conditions of work, superannuation or other fringe benefits, and opportunities for training, promotion, and transfer than are made available to applicants or employees of the same or substantially similar capabilities employed in the same or substantially similar circumstances on work of that description; or

(c) to terminate the employment of the employee, or subject the employee to any detriment, in circumstances in which the employment of other employees employed on work of that description would not be terminated, or in which other employees employed on work of that description would not be subjected to such detriment; or

(d) to retire the employee, or to require or cause the employee to retire or resign (applies to all (a), (b), (c) and (d)), by reason of any of the prohibited grounds of discrimination.[32]

Specifically as regards exceptions to disability, Section 29 states:

29.(1) Nothing in section 22 of this Act shall prevent different treatment based on disability where:

(a) The position is such that the person could perform the duties of the position satisfactorily only with the aid of special services or facilities and it is not reasonable to expect the employer to provide those services or facilities; or

(b) The environment in which the duties of the position are to be performed or the nature of those duties, or of some of them, is such that the person could perform those duties only with a risk of harm to that person or to others, including the risk of infecting others with an illness, and it is not reasonable to take that risk.

(2) Nothing in subsection (1) (b) of this section shall apply if the employer could, without unreasonable disruption, take reasonable measures to reduce the risk to a normal level.

(3) Nothing in section 22 of this Act shall apply to terms of employment or conditions of work that are set or varied after taking into account:

(a) Any special limitations that the disability of a person imposes on his or her capacity to carry out the work; and

(b) Any special services or facilities that are provided to enable or facilitate the carrying out of the work.[33]

Further, Section 35 outlines the general qualification on exceptions:

35. No employer shall be entitled…to accord to any person in respect of any position different treatment based on a prohibited ground of discrimination even though some of the duties of that position would fall within any of those exceptions if, with some adjustment of the activities of the employer (not being an adjustment involving unreasonable disruption of the activities of the employer), some other employee could carry out those particular duties.[34]

Measures to ensure equality are established under Section 73:

73 (1) Anything done or omitted which would otherwise constitute a breach of any of the provisions of this Part of this Act shall not constitute such a breach if:

(a) it is done or omitted in good faith for the purpose of assisting or advancing persons or groups of persons, being in each case persons against whom discrimination is unlawful by virtue of this Part of this Act; and

(b) those persons or groups need or may reasonably be supposed to need assistance or advancement in order to achieve an equal place with other members of the community. [35]

Race Relations Act

Important for minorities with a disability, the Race Relations Act 1971 guards against race discrimination in a number of areas, including employment, with Section 5 stating:

5(1) It shall be unlawful for any [person who is an] employer, or any person acting or purporting to act on behalf of any [person who is an] employer

(a) To refuse or omit to employ any person on work of any description which is available and for which that person is qualified; or

(b) To refuse or omit to offer or afford any person the same terms of employment, conditions of work, fringe benefits, and opportunities for training, promotion, and transfer as are made available for persons of the same or substantially similar qualifications employed in the same or substantially similar circumstances on work of that description; or

(c) To dismiss any person, or subject any person to any detriment, in circumstances in which other persons employed by that employer on work of that description are not or would not be dismissed or are not or would not be subjected to such detriment by reason of the color, race, or ethnic or national origins of that person....

(3) Nothing in this section shall apply in respect of the employment of any person for any purpose for which persons of a particular ethnic or national origin have or are commonly found to have a particular qualification or aptitude.[36]

Importantly, in terms of measures to ensure equality, Section 9 states:

9. Anything done or omitted which would otherwise constitute a breach of any of the provisions of sections 4 to 7 of this Act shall not constitute such a breach if

(a) It is done or omitted in good faith for the purpose of assisting or advancing persons or groups of persons, being in each case persons of a particular color, race, or ethnic or national origin; and

(b) Those groups or persons need or may reasonably be supposed to need assistance or advancement in order to achieve an equal place with other members of the community.[37]

Interestingly, in terms of racial disharmony, Section 9A states:

9A(1) It shall be unlawful for any person

(a) To publish or distribute written matter which is threatening, abusive, or insulting, or to broadcast by means of radio or television words which are threatening, abusive, or insulting; or

(b) To use in any public place..., or within the hearing of persons in any such public place, or at any meeting to which the public are invited or have access, words which are threatening, abusive, or insulting,

being matter or words likely to excite hostility or ill-will against, or bring into contempt or ridicule, any group of persons in New Zealand on the ground of the color, race, or ethnic or national origins of that group of persons.[38]

Employment Contracts Act

The Employment Contracts Act 1991 provides people with the right to take race discrimination cases to the Employment Court as a personal grievance. The complainant must choose either the Employment Contracts Act or the Human Rights Act as the forum for a complaint, and cases cannot be transferred from one jurisdiction to another.[39]

Health and Disability Commissioner Act 1994 and Code of Health & Disability Services Consumers' Rights

Under the Health and Disability Commissioner Act 1994, the Health and Disability Commissioner may investigate alleged breaches by providers, as they relate to the services and, in instances of possible discrimination by the provider, may be referred by the Commissioner to the Human Rights Commission. Further, under the auspices of the Health and Disability Commissioner, a Code of Health and Disability Services Consumers' Rights came into force on 1 July 1996.[40] It aims to promote the rights of consumers to receive services of an appropriate standard, and to facilitate the fair, simple, and speedy resolution of complaints related to these rights. In particular, Right 2 of the Code states that every consumer has the right to be free from discrimination, coercion, harassment, and sexual, financial or other exploitation.[41] Discrimination is defined in the Code as discrimination that is unlawful under the Human Rights Act 1993.[42] Exploitation includes any abuse of a position of trust, breach of a fiduciary duty, or exercise of undue influence.[43]

New Zealand Disability Strategy

Overall, the aim of the New Zealand Disability Strategy: Making a World of Difference – *Whakanui Oranga* is to eliminate disability barriers wherever they exist.[44] The barriers range from the purely physical, such as access to facilities, to the attitudinal, due to poor awareness of disability issues. Many are unable to reach their potential or participate fully in the community because of barriers they face doing things that most New Zealanders take for granted. The Strategy will guide Government action to promote a more inclusive society. It is an enduring framework which will ensure that government departments and other government agencies consider disabled people before making decisions. It will sit alongside other government programmes such as the Positive Ageing Strategy, the New Zealand Health Strategy and the Re-evaluation of Human Rights Protections in New Zealand. The Government will take the lead, but everything must be done to influence the attitudes and behaviour of society as a whole. The monitoring and reporting on the Strategy implementation is coordinated and supported by the Office for Disability Issues. All government departments are required to develop annual Disability Strategy implementation work plans with goals and actions. At the end of each year covered by the work plans, departments are required to prepare a progress report. The Minister for Disability Issues is required to report annually to Parliament on progress in implementing the Strategy.

The New Zealand Disability Strategy presents a long-term plan for changing New Zealand from a disabling to an inclusive society. It has been developed in consultation with disabled people and the wider disability sector, and reflects many individuals' experiences of disability. Disability is not something individuals have. What individuals have are impairments. They may be physical, sensory, neurological, psychiatric, intellectual or other impairments. Disability is the process which happens when one group of people create barriers by designing a world only for their way of living, taking no account of the impairments other people have. Along with other New Zealanders, disabled people aspire to a good life. However, they also face huge barriers to achieving the life that so many take for granted. These barriers are created when we build a society that takes no account of the impairments other people have. Our society is built in a way that assumes we can all see signs, read directions, hear announcements, reach buttons, have the strength to open heavy doors and have stable moods and perceptions.

Underpinning the New Zealand Disability Strategy is a vision of a fully inclusive society. New Zealand will be inclusive when people with impairments can say they live in 'A society that highly values our lives and continually enhances our full participation'. Achieving this vision will involve ensuring that disabled people have a meaningful partnership with Government, communities and support agencies, based on respect and equality. Disabled people will be integrated into community life on their own terms, their abilities will be valued, their diversity and interdependence will be recognised, and their human rights will be protected.

The New Zealand Disability Strategy is vital to the well-being of the one-in-five New Zealanders who identify that they have a long-term impairment. By implementing the Strategy, New Zealand will become a more inclusive society, eliminating the barriers to people with disabilities participating in and contributing to society. The Strategy has the vision of a society that highly values the lives and continually enhances full participation of disabled people. It provides an enduring framework to ensure that government departments and agencies consider disabled people before making decisions. In taking the lead, the Government will do everything possible to influence the attitudes and behaviour of society as a whole. By all New Zealanders considering issues facing people with disabilities and their aspirations, New Zealand can become a fully inclusive society.

Our society is built in a way that assumes that we can all move quickly from one side of the road to the other; that we can all see signs, read directions, hear announcements, reach buttons, have the strength to open heavy doors and have stable moods and perceptions. Although New Zealand has standards for accessibility, schools, workplaces, supermarkets, banks, movie theatres, marae, churches and houses are, in the main, designed and built by non-disabled people for non-disabled users.

Disability relates to the interaction between the person with the impairment and the environment. It has a lot to do with discrimination, and has a lot in common with other attitudes and behaviours such as racism and sexism that are not acceptable in our society. People and groups of people should not be judged by one particular aspect of their lives, whether it is their race, gender, age or impairment. Individual beliefs and assumptions, as well as the practices of institutions, mean that many disabled people are not able to access things that many non-disabled people take for granted. The desire to break down the barriers that cause disability is also closely linked to ideas about the human rights of people with impairments.

Vision of a non-disabling society will happen where: disabled people have a meaningful partnership with Government, communities and support agencies, based on respect and equality; we have moved forward from exclusion, tolerance and accommodation of disabled people to a fully inclusive and mutually supportive society; disabled people are integrated into community life on their own terms. This means that equal opportunities are assured but individual choices are available and respected; the abilities of disabled people are valued and not questioned; interdependence is recognised and valued, especially the important relationships between disabled people and their families, friends, whānau and other people who provide support; human rights are protected as a fundamental cornerstone of government policy and practice; the diversity of disabled people, including their cultural backgrounds, is recognised, and there is flexibility to support their differing aspirations and goals; disabled people are treated equitably, regardless of gender, age, cultural background, type of impairment or when and how the impairment was acquired; community-based services ensure that disabled people are supported to live in their own communities, and institutionalisation is eliminated; the idea that society imposes many of the disabling barriers faced by people with impairments is widely understood and, therefore, legislation, policy and other activities enhance rather than disable the lives of people with impairments; and the principles of the Treaty of Waitangi are recognised.

Because everyone comes from different backgrounds, holds different beliefs and has different needs, there is a great diversity of people who have impairments. The key common factor among people with impairments is that they face many lifelong barriers to their full participation in New Zealand society. Attitudes have been identified, through consultation, as the major barrier that operates at all levels of daily life in the general population. Attitudes and ignorance make their presence felt as stigma, prejudice and discrimination. Disability discrimination was the largest category of complaints to the Human Rights Commission. Stigma, prejudice and discrimination affect our behaviours. Sometimes the combination of attitudes and behaviours can seem to create almost insurmountable barriers, for example, whole systems or organisations can become a barrier much in the way that institutionalised racism operates.

Barriers are spread out throughout the life cycle:

As a child ...
*   For disabled children, it is hard to get the best start to their life ahead. Children's needs can put big demands, including financial pressure, on their families and whānau.

As a youth ...
*   Disabled people are much less likely to have educational qualifications than non-disabled people. Educational disadvantages lead to employment disadvantages as career opportunities become limited.

As an adult ...
*   Disabled people are much less likely to be employed. The unemployment rate for people with ongoing mental illness is very high. Half of recent complaints

to the Human Rights Commission in regard to disability related to employment.

As older ...

- Older people experience difficulties when their problems are seen as an inevitable part of ageing. Faced with this attitude, they may miss the opportunity to remain able and independent through rehabilitation, correction of health problems or provision of support services. For older disabled people, one of the biggest problems can be being denied the opportunity to remain in their familiar surroundings and 'age in place'. Even in their own homes, some can feel isolated and insecure if they have limited contact with families, friends and their community.

A whole life ...

- Despite New Zealand having strong standards for physical accessibility, access to public facilities and other buildings, such as marae, is poor. On top of that, most public transport is not independently accessible, and car modifications are expensive. As a group, disabled people are likely to have lower incomes and fewer financial and family resources than the general population. This economic disadvantage is compounded by the financial cost of disability. The earning potential of families with disabled children can be curtailed by their need to provide support for their children or live and work in areas where they can access family or professional support.

The Government recognises that a lot of work is required to remove the barriers to participation faced by disabled people and create a fully inclusive society. As part of the New Zealand Disability Strategy, 15 Objectives and detailed Actions to achieve this have been developed. Government departments are expected to develop annual New Zealand Disability Strategy implementation work plans that spell out what work they are doing to implement the Strategy. Government initiatives that will benefit disabled people, such as the New Zealand Positive Ageing Strategy, the New Zealand Health Strategy, the Mäori Health Strategy and the Pacific Health and Disability Action Plan, will complement the New Zealand Disability Strategy. The decisions that territorial authorities and non-departmental public bodies make also have a significant impact on the lives of disabled people. It is important that territorial authorities and other public bodies support and assist with implementing the New Zealand Disability Strategy, and ways of making this happen need to be considered in discussions. The Minister for Disability Issues will report to Parliament annually on progress in implementing the Strategy and full reviews of progress will be conducted after five and ten years.

In looking at the Government's Objectives, in order to advance New Zealand towards a fully inclusive society, the Strategy includes 15 Objectives, underpinned by detailed Actions:

Objective 1: Encourage and educate for a non-disabling society: Encourage the emergence of a non-disabling society that respects and highly values the lives of disabled people and supports inclusive communities. Actions to be taken include: Develop national and locally-based anti-discrimination programmes; Recognise that it is disabled people who are experts on their own experience; Recognise and honour the achievements of disabled people; Include the perspectives of disabled people in ethical and bioethical debates; and encourage ongoing debate on disability issues.

Objective 2: Ensure rights for disabled people: Uphold and promote the rights of disabled people. Actions to be taken include: Provide information for everyone about the rights of disabled people; Provide education to ensure that disabled people understand their rights, recognise discrimination and are able to be self-advocates; Educate agencies responsible for supporting children and families about the rights and abilities of disabled parents; Review Human Rights legislation to ensure the ongoing enhancement and strengthening of the rights of disabled people; Investigate, and if appropriate support, development of a United Nations convention on the rights of disabled people; Investigate the level of access that disabled people have to independent advocacy, and address any shortfall in service provision; Evaluate New Zealand's performance on the rights of disabled people and Consider disabled people whenever New Zealand's performance is being evaluated against international human rights obligations; for example, the Convention on the Elimination of All Forms of Discrimination Against Women, and United Nations Convention on the Rights of the Child.

Objective 3: Provide the best education for disabled people: Improve education so that all children, youth and adult learners will have equal opportunities to learn and develop in their local, regular educational centres. Actions to be taken: Ensure that no child is denied access to their local, regular school because of their impairment; Support the development of effective communication by providing access to education in New Zealand Sign Language, communication technologies and human aids; Ensure that teachers and other educators understand the learning needs of disabled people; Ensure that disabled students, families, teachers and other educators have equitable access to the resources available to meet their needs; Facilitate opportunities for disabled students to make contact with their disabled peers in other schools; Improve schools' responsiveness to and accountability for the needs of disabled students; Promote appropriate and effective inclusive educational settings that will meet individual educational needs; and Improve post-compulsory education options for disabled people, including: promoting best practice, providing career guidance, increasing lifelong opportunities for learning and better aligning financial support with educational opportunities.

Objective 4: Provide opportunities in employment and economic development for disabled people: Enable disabled people to work in the open labour market, in accordance with human rights principles, and maintain an adequate income. Actions to be taken: In terms of Planning and training for entering employment,

Provide education and training opportunities to increase the individual capacity of disabled people to move into employment; Enable disabled people to lead the development of their own training and employment goals, and to participate in the development of support options to achieve those goals; Educate employers about the abilities of disabled people; Provide information about career options, ways to generate income, and assistance available for disabled people; Investigate longer-term incentives to increase training, employment and development opportunities for disabled people; Ensure a smooth transition from school to work; and Investigate the requirements of the International Labour Organisation Convention on Vocational Rehabilitation and Employment, with a view to ratification. In terms of Employment and economic development, Encourage the development of a range of employment options recognising the diverse needs of disabled people; Ensure disabled people have the same employment conditions, rights and entitlements as everyone else has, including minimum wage provisions for work of comparable productivity; Make communication services, resources and flexible workplace options available; Operate equal employment opportunity and affirmative action policies in the public sector; Investigate a legislative framework for equal employment opportunities across the public and private sectors; Ensure disabled people have access to economic development initiatives; Encourage staff and service organisations, such as unions, to appoint or elect disabled people as delegates and members of their executives; Ensure that the needs of disabled people are taken into account in developing more flexible income support benefits, to make access to work and training easier; and Review income support provisions to ensure they provide an adequate standard of living.

Objective 5: Foster leadership by disabled people: Acknowledge the experience of disability as a form of specialised knowledge and strengthen the leadership of disabled people. Actions to be taken: Encourage disabled people to take part in decision-making as service users, as staff in the delivery of services, and in the governance, management, planning and evaluation within all services that disabled people access; Assist self-help initiatives, service provision and advocacy organisations run by disabled people for disabled people; Model the inclusion of disabled people in leadership roles within government departments, in order to encourage leadership by disabled people within all organisations; Support the establishment of a leadership development and mentoring programme for disabled people; Establish a register of disabled people for government appointments; and Make information available to disabled people and their advocacy organisations about how to influence government policy.

Objective 6: Foster an aware and responsive public service: Ensure that government agencies, publicly funded services and publicly accountable bodies are aware of and responsive to disabled people. Actions to be taken: Develop mechanisms to ensure that all government policy and legislation is consistent with the objectives of the New Zealand Disability Strategy; Adapt public sector training to ensure that service development and service delivery are consistent with the New Zealand Disability Strategy; Ensure that all government agencies treat disabled people with dignity and respect; Improve the quality of information available, including where to go for more information, the services available and how to access them; Make all information and communication methods offered to the general public available in formats appropriate to the different needs of disabled people; Ensure the locations and buildings of all government agencies and public services are accessible; and Work with territorial authorities to develop ways they can support the New Zealand Disability Strategy.

Objective 7: Create long-term support systems centred on the individual: Create a quality assessment and service delivery system that is centred on disabled people, ensures their participation in assessment and service delivery, has invisible borders and is easy to access. Actions to be taken: Ensure that overarching processes, eligibility criteria and allocation of resources are nationally consistent, but that individual needs are treated flexibly; Ensure that government agencies, publicly funded services and publicly accountable bodies co-operate to ensure that the disabled person is at the centre of service delivery; Investigate the development of a holistic approach to assessment and service provision, that applies across agencies and funding sources; Develop and maintain effective rehabilitation services; Encourage equity of funding and service provision for people with similar needs, regardless of the cause of their impairment; Identify unmet need and develop affordable solutions to fill these gaps; Improve timeliness of service provision; Develop a highly skilled workforce to support disabled people; and Ensure that disability services do not perpetuate the myth that disabled people are ill, while recognising that disabled people do need access to health services without discrimination.

Objective 8: Support quality living in the community for disabled people: Provide opportunities for disabled people to have their own homes and lives in the community. Actions to be taken: in terms of living in the community, Increase opportunities for disabled people to live in the community with choice of affordable, quality housing; Support disabled people living in rural areas to remain in their own communities by improving their access to services; Support the development of independent communication for disabled people; and Ensure disabled people are able to access appropriate health services within their community; In terms of moving around the community, Require all new scheduled public transport to be accessible in order to phase out inaccessible public transport; Encourage the development of accessible routes to connect buildings, public spaces and transport systems; and Develop nationally consistent access to passenger services where there is no accessible public transport.

Objective 9: Support lifestyle choices, recreation and culture for disabled people: Create and support lifestyle choices for disabled people within the community and promote access to recreation and cultural opportunities. Actions to be taken: Support disabled people in making their own choices about their relationships, sexuality and reproductive potential; Provide opportunities for disabled people to create, perform and develop their own arts, and to access arts activities; Educate arts administrators/organisations and other recreational and sporting organisations about disability issues and inclusion; and Support the development of arts, recreational and sports projects, including those run by and for disabled people.

Objective 10: Collect and use relevant information about disabled people and disability issues: Improve the quality of relevant disability information collected, analysed and used, including regular national surveys of activity limitation. Actions to be taken: Ensure that guidelines for research funding take into account the need for research on disability issues, include disabled people in the development and monitoring of the disability research agenda, and enable disabled people to put forward their own experiences in the context of the research; Collect relevant and useful information about disability through all relevant surveys to inform the research programme; Use disability research, and analyse disability data to contribute to policy work, service development and monitoring; Undertake research focusing on disability issues for Mäori and Pacific peoples; Make disability research information available to disabled people in culturally appropriate and accessible formats; Adopt ethical and procedural standards for disability research projects; and Appoint disabled people as members of ethics committees.

Objective 11: Promote participation of disabled Mäori: Promote opportunities for disabled Mäori to participate in their communities and access disability services, since disabled Mäori should receive an equitable level of resource that is delivered in a culturally appropriate way. Actions to be taken: Build the capacity of disabled Mäori through the equitable allocation of resources within the context of Mäori development frameworks; Establish more disability support services designed and provided by Mäori for Mäori; Ensure mainstream providers of disability services are accessible to and culturally appropriate for disabled Mäori and their whänau; Train more Mäori disability service provider professionals and increase the advisory capacity of Mäori; Ensure that Government funded or sponsored marae-based initiatives meet the access requirements of disabled people, and encourage all other marae-based initiatives also to meet those requirements; Support training and development of trilingual interpreters for Deaf people; and Ensure Te Puni Kökiri undertakes a leadership role in promoting the participation of disabled Mäori.

Objective 12: Promote participation of disabled Pacific peoples: Promote opportunities for disabled Pacific peoples to participate in their communities and access disability services, since disabled Pacific peoples should receive an equitable level of resource that is delivered in a culturally appropriate way. Actions to be taken: Increase access to, and quality of, both Pacific and mainstream service providers that deliver disability services to disabled Pacific peoples, their families and communities; Support disability workforce development and training for Pacific peoples, by training Pacific peoples as providers of disability information and services for their local communities; Encourage Pacific communities to consider disability issues and perspectives and further their own understanding of disability through the development of community-based plans for disability issues; Support training and development of trilingual interpreters for Deaf people; and Ensure the Ministry of Pacific Island Affairs undertakes a leadership role in promoting the participation of disabled Pacific peoples.

Objective 13: Enable disabled children and youth to lead full and active lives: Disabled children and youth should enjoy full and active lives, in conditions that prepare them for adulthood and which ensure their dignity, affirm their right to a good future and to participate in education, relationships, leisure, work and political processes, recognise their emerging identities as individuals and reinforce their sense of self, promote self-reliance, recognise their important links with family, friends and school, and facilitate their active participation in the community. Actions to be taken: Ensure all agencies that support children, youth and families work collaboratively to ensure that their services are accessible, appropriate and welcoming to disabled children, youth and their families; Ensure that the Youth Development Strategy recognises the needs of disabled children and youth; Conduct anti-discrimination and education campaigns that are age-appropriate and effective; Establish a process for including advice from disabled people on disability issues for children and youth within relevant government agencies and Commissioners' offices; Provide access for disabled children, youth and their families to child, youth and family-focused support, education, health care services, rehabilitation services, recreation opportunities and training; Improve support for disabled children and youth during transition between early childhood education, primary school, secondary school, tertiary education and employment; Introduce ways of involving disabled children and youth in decision-making and giving them greater control over their lives; Develop a range of accommodation options so that disabled young people can live independently; Provide and evaluate educational initiatives about sexuality, safety and relationships for disabled children and youth; and Ensure the Ministry of Youth Affairs and Ministry of Social Policy undertake a leadership role in promoting the participation of disabled children and youth.

Objective 14: Promote participation of disabled women in order to improve their quality of life: Improve opportunities for disabled women to participate in their communities, access appropriate disability services, and improve their quality of life. Actions to be taken: Promote women's rights and provide opportunities for disabled women to achieve the same level of economic wellbeing and educational attainment as men; Provide equitable, appropriate and welcoming access to services; Support disabled women to live independent and secure lives in the environment and with the people of their choosing; Ensure that criteria and considerations for the health and reproduction-related treatment of disabled women are the same as for non-disabled women; Include the perspectives of disabled women in the development of all strategies; and Ensure the Ministry of Women's

Affairs undertakes a leadership role in promoting the participation of disabled women, to improve their quality of life.

Objective 15: Value families, whänau and people providing ongoing support: Acknowledge and support the roles, responsibilities and issues facing family, whänau and those who support disabled people. Actions to be taken: Ensure needs assessment processes are holistic and take account of the needs of families/whänau as well as the disabled person; Improve the support and choices for those who support disabled people; Provide education and information for families with disabled family members; Ensure that, where appropriate, the family, whänau and those who support disabled people are given an opportunity to have input into decisions affecting their disabled family member; Develop a resource kit for professionals on when and how to interact with families/whänau of disabled people; Work actively to ensure that families, whänau and those who support disabled people can be involved in policy and service development and delivery, and in monitoring and evaluation processes where appropriate; Encourage debate around responsibility for caring, payment for caring and how to further recognise and value the caring role; and Provide families and those who support disabled people with information that is accurate, accessible and easily found.[45]

Conclusion

Despite strong legislative provisions both in Australia and New Zealand, there is still progress to be made to achieve this ability, equal outcomes and opportunities for all. Disability equality and the rights contained within legislation rely on the overall legal system, as well as cultural attitudes for implementation and enforcement. However, gaps do exist in the coverage of legislation, and in the manner by which it is enforced. Taking concrete action to advance human rights and support opportunity and choice require a concerted effort across the whole of government, in addition to the important ongoing role of specialist human rights monitoring and complaints mechanisms.

Notes

[1] Disability Discrimination Act, Australia, at Section 3.
[2] *Ibid.*, at Section 5.
[3] *Ibid.*, at Section 6.
[4] *Ibid.*, at Section 10.
[5] *Ibid.*, at Section 11.
[6] *Ibid.*, at Section 15.
[7] *Ibid.*, at Section 17.
[8] *Ibid.*, at Section 23.
[9] *Ibid.*, at Section 25.
[10] *Ibid.*, at Section 67.
[11] *Ibid.*, at Section 113.

12   Workplace Relations Act, Australia.
13   Racial Discrimination Act, Australia.
14   *Ibid.*, at Section 9.
15   *Ibid.*, at Section 10.
16   Sex Discrimination Act, Australia, at Section 3.
17   *Ibid.*, at Section 5.
18   *Ibid.*, at Section 7D.
19   *Ibid.*, at Section 48.
20   Government of Australia, *Australia's Beijing Plus Five Action Plan 2001~2005*.
21   *Ibid.*
22   Treaty of Waitangi, New Zealand, at the Preamble.
23   *Ibid.*, at Article 1.
24   *Ibid.*, at Article 2.
25   *Ibid.*, at Article 3.
26   Bill of Rights Act, New Zealand, at the Preamble.
27   *Ibid.*, at Section 19.
28   *Ibid.*, at Section 27.
29   Human Rights Act, New Zealand, at Section 5(1).
30   *Ibid.*, at Section 21.
31   *Ibid.*, at Section 65.
32   *Ibid.*, at Section 22(1).
33   *Ibid.*, at Section 29.
34   *Ibid.*, at Section 35.
35   *Ibid.*, at Section 73.
36   Race Relations Act, New Zealand., at Section 5.
37   *Ibid.*, at Section 9.
38   *Ibid.*, at Section 9A.
39   Employment Contracts Act, New Zealand.
40   Health and Disability Commissioner Act and Code of Health & Disability Services Consumers' Rights, New Zealand.
41   *Ibid.*, at Right 2.
42   *Ibid.*
43   *Ibid.*
44   Ministry of Health, New Zealand, Making a World of Difference, Whakanui Oranga, Minister for Disability Issues, 2001.
45   *Ibid.*

References

Bill of Rights Act, New Zealand, 1990.
Disability Discrimination Act, Australia, 1992.
Employment Contracts Act, New Zealand.
Government of Australia, *Australia's Beijing Plus Five Action Plan 2001~2005*.
Health and Disability Commissioner Act 1994 and Code of Health & Disability Services Consumers' Rights, New Zealand.
Human Rights Act, New Zealand.
Ministry of Health, New Zealand, Making a World of Difference, Whakanui Oranga, Minister for Disability Issues, 2001.

Race Relations Act, New Zealand.
Racial Discrimination Act, Australia.
Sex Discrimination Act, Australia.
Treaty of Waitangi, New Zealand,
Workplace Relations Act, Australia.

Chapter 5

This Ability in
Africa and South Africa

Introduction

This chapter will examine this ability in the continent of Africa, and in South Africa. It will initially look at the situation in Africa, examining such legislation as the Charter of the Organization of African Unity, the African Charter on Human and Peoples' Rights and the Protocol of the African Charter on Human and Peoples' Rights, and for women with a disability, the Protocol on Rights of Women in Africa. It will then go on to look at the situation in South Africa, examining such legislation as the Interim Constitution Schedule 4 and the Constitution, the Employment Equity Act, and the Promotion of Equality and Prevention of Unfair Discrimination Act.

Africa

Africa is not a single uniform entity. Within Africa, there is much diversity, in terms of disability, culture, gender relations, geography, society, family, economy, and natural resources. There is not one formula that can be applied in every case, and every community has to make its individual needs heard. In addition, Africa is not static. It is a continent in flux and is rapidly undergoing fundamental changes, namely the growth of urban populations, deterioration of the environment and increasing desertification, deterioration of living standards, growing dependency on world markets, increasing numbers of young people and children, and civil strife and conflict. Development policies, plans and programs must be flexible to react and respond to these changes.

      The knowledge, attitudes and practices of the general African population towards disability and disabled people have some components historically accumulated and based on the cultural and institutional heritage from the past.[1] This is especially so among populations where a majority live in traditional ways, a lesser proportion are in transition, and a small, powerful minority are considered 'modern'.

      Disability-related Non-Governmental Organizations (NGOs) are classifiable according to their objectives, sources of finance and locus of control, with some overlap: Service providers, which include foreign Christian missions and Indigenous Churches, with some groups having a medical and preventive focus and others a welfare, education or employment orientation; Foreign aid organizations, with some having general development aims and incidentally support disability projects, or aim for all their aided projects to be disability-friendly, or some being country-to-country, or some specializing in health, education or childhood, or some having a specific disability focus and campaign position; Personnel providers, which have sent therapists and special educators to Africa; In-country fundraising organizations, developing particular disability projects; National Organizations, focusing initially on welfare, service provision and fundraising, with some evolution towards advocacy and rights campaigning; and Other Groupings, with people with double or triple 'disadvantages' beginning to coalesce, such as 'black and disabled' or 'woman and disabled'. However, many disabled people such as those who are also rural, elderly or from an ethnic minority, remain with very little representation in any forum.

Disability service developments during the past several decades seem to have been dominated by the disparate trends and methods of various European countries funding them. Such developments, imported from countries with much stronger economies and longer histories of universal primary education, child-centred education, and educational research, have seldom been culturally or conceptually appropriate to the countries in which they have taken place. Setting current efforts against a century or more of previous development is intended to bring more realistic perspectives. In fact, much of the earlier development was also done by Europeans with African assistants, but the Europeans mostly lived for a substantial period of time in the country where development was happening. They also made plans that were often culturally inappropriate, but at least they had to implement their own plans, and thereby could learn something by which further developments could be made more appropriate. There has been a long period for potential interaction between African and European notions of welfare provisions, the development of institutions, and the adaptation of education for children with special needs.[2]

Overall, in terms of trade and its impact on disability in Africa, in 2000, the United States Congress passed the African Growth and Opportunity Act (AGOA), which eliminated US duties on textile imports from eligible sub-Saharan countries.[3] However, to ensure long-term benefits from better access to American markets, African countries must diversify their economies, investing in the infrastructure and education that attract higher-tech companies. Further, a new round of global trade negotiations, dubbed the Doha Development Round, began in 2002, with the negotiations focused on agriculture. Africa's main goals are to substantially reduce or eliminate all tariffs on agricultural products, including quota duties; substantially reduce or eliminate tariff escalation; simplify complex tariffs by converting all tariffs to an *ad valorem* or fixed percentage of a product's value; substantially reduce or eliminate market-distorting export subsidies and domestic support; and recognize the special needs of the world's least developed countries.

In addition, the New Partnership for Africa's Development (NEPAD) is a pledge by all of Africa's leaders to eradicate poverty and move towards sustainable growth and development. The partnership focuses on African ownership of the development process and seeks to reinvigorate the continent in all areas of human activity. Through the partnership, African leaders have agreed to promote the role of different groups in social and economic development; promote and protect democracy and human rights by developing standards for accountability, transparency, and participatory governance; restore and maintain macroeconomic stability; implement transparent legal and regulatory frameworks; revitalize and extend education, technical training, and health care services; and promote the development of infrastructure, agriculture, agroprocessing, and manufacturing to meet the needs of export and domestic markets and local employment. NEPAD draws Africa's attention to the seriousness of the continent's economic challenges, the potential for addressing them and the challenge of mobilizing support. The main strategies proposed include pursuing equality in education, business, and public service; developing education and human resources at all levels, and in particular increasing the role of information and communication technology in education and training, inducing a 'brain gain' for Africa and eliminating disparities in education; and increasing domestic resource mobilization and accelerating foreign investment; creating a conducive environment for private sector activities, with an emphasis on domestic entrepreneurs.

African countries adopted the Dakar/Ngor Declaration in 1992 as the African common position to the International Conference on Population and Development (ICPD). It was recognized that population and development are inextricably linked, and that empowering and meeting people's needs for education and health, including reproductive health, are necessary for both individual advancement and balanced development. For population and sustainable development in Africa, a key measure must be the promotion of access to equitable distribution of resources. Further, there needs to be a mix of macroeconomic and structural policies and programs for enhancing investment, growth, poverty reduction and social development; infrastructure improvement and institutional support services policies; and policies aimed at strengthening grassroots institutions and local participation. The ICPD+5 Program of Action recommended a set of interdependent quantitative goals and objectives, which included universal access to primary education, with special attention to closing the gap in primary and secondary school education; universal access to primary health care; universal access to a full range of comprehensive reproductive health care services, including family planning; reductions in infant, child and maternal morbidity and mortality; and increased life expectancy.

Charter of the Organization of African Unity

The heads of African states and governments assembled in the City of Addis Ababa, Ethiopia, and on 25 May 1963 signed the Charter of the Organization of African Unity, which entered into force on 13 September 1963. The Preamble of the Charter of the Organization of African Unity states:

> Convinced that it is the inalienable right of all people to control their own destiny,
>
> Conscious of the fact that freedom, equality, justice and dignity are essential

objectives for the achievement of the legitimate aspirations of the African peoples,

Conscious of our responsibility to harness the natural and human resources of our continent for the total advancement of our peoples in all spheres of human endeavor,

Inspired by a common determination to promote understanding among our peoples and cooperation among our states in response to the aspirations of our peoples for brother-hood and solidarity, in a larger unity transcending ethnic and national differences,

Convinced that, in order to translate this determination into a dynamic force in the cause of human progress, conditions for peace and security must be established and maintained,

Determined to safeguard and consolidate the hard-won independence as well as the sovereignty and territorial integrity of our states, and to fight against neo-colonialism in all its forms,

Dedicated to the general progress of Africa,

Persuaded that the Charter of the United Nations and the Universal Declaration of Human Rights, to the Principles of which we reaffirm our adherence, provide a solid foundation for peaceful and positive cooperation among States,

Desirous that all African States should henceforth unite so that the welfare and well-being of their peoples can be assured,

Resolved to reinforce the links between our states by establishing and strengthening common institutions.[4]

Article I establishes the Organization of African Unity:

I.1. The High Contracting Parties do by the present Charter establish an Organization to be known as the ORGANIZATION OF AFRICAN UNITY.

2. The Organization shall include the Continental African States, Madagascar and other Islands surrounding Africa.[5]

Its purposes are outlined in Article II:

II. 1. The Organization shall have the following purposes:

(a) To promote the unity and solidarity of the African States;

(b) To coordinate and intensify their cooperation and efforts to achieve a better life for the peoples of Africa;

(c) To defend their sovereignty, their territorial integrity and independence;

(d) To eradicate all forms of colonialism from Africa; and

(e) To promote international cooperation, having due regard to the Charter of the United Nations and the Universal Declaration of Human Rights.

2. To these ends, the Member States shall coordinate and harmonize their general policies, especially in the following fields:

(a) Political and diplomatic cooperation;

(b) Economic cooperation, including transport and communications;

(c) Educational and cultural cooperation;

(d) Health, sanitation and nutritional cooperation;

(e) Scientific and technical cooperation; and

(f) Cooperation for defense and security.[6]

The various institutions are outlined in Article VII:

VII. The Organization shall accomplish its purposes through the following principal institutions:

1. The Assembly of Heads of State and Government.

2. The Council of Ministers.

3. The General Secretariat.

4. The Commission of Mediation, Conciliation and Arbitration.[7]

The Assembly of Heads of State and Government is contained in Article VIII:

VIII. The Assembly of Heads of State and Government shall be the supreme organ of the Organization. It shall, subject to the provisions of this Charter, discuss matters of common concern to Africa with a view to coordinating and harmonizing the general policy of the Organization. It may in addition review the structure, functions and acts of all the organs and any specialized agencies which may be created in accordance with the present Charter.[8]

The Council of Ministers is contained in Article XII:

XII. 1. The Council of Ministers shall consist of Foreign Ministers or other Ministers as are designated by the Governments of Member States.

2. The Council of Ministers shall meet at least twice a year. When requested by any Member State and approved by two-thirds of all Member States, it shall meet in extraordinary session.[9]

The General Secretariat is contained in Article XVI:

XVI. There shall be a Secretary-General of the Organization, who shall be appointed by the Assembly of Heads of State and Government. The Secretary-General shall direct the affairs of the Secretariat.[10]

The Commission of Mediation, Conciliation and Arbitration is contained in Article XIX:

XIX. Member States pledge to settle all disputes among themselves by peaceful means and, to this end decide to establish a Commission of Mediation, Conciliation and Arbitration, the composition of which and condition of service shall be defined by a separate Protocol to be approved by the Assembly of Heads of State and Government. Said Protocol shall be regarded as forming an integral part of the present Charter.[11]

The Specialized Commission is contained in Article XX:

XX. The Assembly shall establish such Specialized Commissions as it may, deem necessary, including the following:

1. Economic and Social Commission.

2. Educational, Scientific, Cultural and Health Commission.

3. Defense Commission.[12]

African Charter on Human and Peoples' Rights

The African Charter on Human and Peoples' Rights was adopted by the Eighteenth Assembly of Heads of State and Government on 27 June 1981 in Nairobi, Kenya. The Preamble of the African Charter on Human and Peoples' Rights states:

The African States members of the Organization of African Unity, parties to the present Convention entitled African Charter on Human and Peoples' Rights,

Considering the Charter of the Organization of African Unity, which stipulates that 'freedom, equality, justice and dignity are essential objectives for the achievement of the legitimate aspirations of the African peoples';

Reaffirming the pledge they solemnly made in Article 2 of the said Charter to eradicate all forms of colonialism from Africa, to coordinate and intensify their cooperation and efforts to achieve a better life for the peoples of Africa and to promote international cooperation having due regard to the Charter of the United Nations and the Universal Declaration of Human Rights;

Taking into consideration the virtues of their historical tradition and the values of African civilization which should inspire and characterize their reflection on the concept of human and peoples' rights;

Recognizing on the one hand, that fundamental human rights stem from the attitudes of human beings, which justifies their international protection, and on the other hand that the reality and respect of peoples' rights should necessarily guarantee human rights;

Considering that the enjoyment of rights and freedoms also implies the performance of duties on the part of everyone;

Convinced that it is henceforth essential to pay particular attention to the right to development and that civil and political rights cannot be dissociated from economic, social and cultural rights in their conception as well as universality and that the satisfaction of economic, social and cultural rights is a guarantee for the enjoyment of civil and political rights;

Conscious of their duty to achieve the total liberation of Africa, the peoples of which are still struggling for their dignity and genuine independence, and undertaking to eliminate colonialism, neo-colonialism, apartheid, zionism and to dismantle aggressive foreign military bases and all forms of discrimination, language, religion or political opinions;

Reaffirming their adherence to the principles of human and peoples' rights and freedoms contained in the declarations, conventions and other instruments adopted by the Organization of African Unity, the Movement of Non-Aligned Countries and the United Nations;

Firmly convinced of their duty to promote and protect human and peoples' rights and freedoms and taking into account the importance traditionally attached to these rights and freedoms in Africa.[13]

In terms of rights and duties and specifically human and peoples' Rights, Article 1 states:

The Member States of the Organization of African Unity, parties to the present Charter shall recognize the rights, duties and freedoms enshrined in the Charter and shall undertake to adopt legislative or other measures to give effect to them.[14]

Important for disability rights, Article 2 protects against discrimination:

Every individual shall be entitled to the enjoyment of the rights and freedoms recognized and guaranteed in the present Charter without distinction of any kind such as race, ethnic group, color, sex, language, religion, political or any other opinion, national and social origin, fortune, birth or any status.[15]

Further, Article 3 guarantees equal protection of the law:

Every individual shall be equal before the law.

Every individual shall be entitled to equal protection of the law.[16]

Also important for disability rights, the concept of equality is guaranteed in Article 19:

All peoples shall be equal; they shall enjoy the same respect and shall have the same rights. Nothing shall justify the domination of a people by another.[17]

Article 5 upholds the dignity of the human person:

> Every individual shall have the right to the respect of the dignity inherent in a human being and to the recognition of his legal status. All forms of exploitation and degradation of man, particularly slavery, slave trade, torture, cruel, inhuman or degrading punishment and treatment shall be prohibited.[18]

In looking at the importance of the courts in safeguarding rights, Article 7 establishes that:

> 7.1. Every individual shall have the right to have his cause heard. This comprises: (a) the right to an appeal to competent national organs against acts of violating his fundamental rights as recognized and guaranteed by conventions, laws, regulations and customs in force; (b) the right to be presumed innocent until proved guilty by a competent court or tribunal; (c) the right to defence, including the right to be defended by counsel of his choice; (d) the right to be tried within a reasonable time by an impartial court or tribunal. 2. No one may be condemned for an act or omission which did not constitute a legally punishable offence at the time it was committed. No penalty may be inflicted for an offence for which no provision was made at the time it was committed. Punishment is personal and can be imposed only on the offender.[19]

Employment rights and equal pay for equal work are guaranteed in Article 15:

> Every individual shall have the right to work under equitable and satisfactory conditions, and shall receive equal pay for equal work.[20]

The right to education for advancement and the importance of community are recognized in Article 17:

> Every individual shall have the right to education.
>
> Every individual may freely take part in the cultural life of his community.
>
> The promotion and protection of morals and traditional values recognized by the community shall be the duty of the State.[21]

Article 20 upholds self-determination of people:

> All peoples shall have the right to existence. They shall have the unquestionable and inalienable right to self-determination. They shall freely determine their political status and shall pursue their economic and social development according to the policy they have freely chosen.
>
> Colonized or oppressed peoples shall have the right to free themselves from the bonds of domination by resorting to any means recognized by the international community.
>
> All peoples shall have the right to the assistance of the State Parties to the present Charter in their liberation struggle against foreign domination, be it political,

economic or cultural.[22]

Cultural development of the heritage of mankind is recognized in Article 22:

> All peoples shall have the right to their economic, social and cultural development with due regard to their freedom and identity and in the equal enjoyment of the common heritage of mankind.

> States shall have the duty, individually or collectively, to ensure the exercise of the right to development.[23]

The paramount role of the Courts is guaranteed in Article 26:

> State Parties to the present Charter shall have the duty to guarantee the independence of the Courts and shall allow the establishment and improvement of appropriate national institutions entrusted with the promotion and protection of the rights and freedoms guaranteed by the present Charter.[24]

Duties of individuals towards one another are established in Article 27:

> Every individual shall have duties towards his family and society, the State and other legally recognized communities and the international community.

> The rights and freedoms of each individual shall be exercised with due regard to the rights of others, collective security, morality and common interest.[25]

Further, important for disability rights, respect and tolerance without discrimination are espoused in Article 28:

> Every individual shall have the duty to respect and consider his fellow beings without discrimination, and to maintain relations aimed at promoting, safeguarding and reinforcing mutual respect and tolerance.[26]

In Article 29, the individual shall also have the duty, among other things:

> To serve his national community by placing his physical and intellectual abilities at its service;

> To preserve and strengthen positive African cultural values in his relations with other members of the society, in the spirit of tolerance, dialogue and consultation and, in general, to contribute to the promotion of the moral well being of society.[27]

The African Commission on Human and Peoples' Right is established under Article 30:

> An African Commission on Human and Peoples' Rights, hereinafter called 'the Commission', shall be established within the Organization of African Unity to promote human and peoples' rights and ensure their protection in Africa.[28]

The mandate of the Commission is contained in Article 45:

> The functions of the Commission shall be:

> To promote human and peoples' rights and in particular:

>> to collect documents, undertake studies and researches on African problems in the field of human and peoples' rights, organize seminars, symposia and conferences, disseminate information, encourage national and local institutions concerned with human and peoples' rights and, should the case arise, give its views or make recommendations to Governments.

>> to formulate and lay down principles and rules aimed at solving legal problems relating to human and peoples' rights and fundamental freedoms upon which African Governments may base their legislation.

>> cooperate with other African and international institutions concerned with the promotion and protection of human and peoples' rights.

> Ensure the protection of human and peoples' rights under conditions laid down by the present Charter.

> Interpret all the provisions of the present Charter at the request of a State Party, an institution of the OAU or an African Organization recognized by the OAU.

> Perform any other tasks which may be entrusted to it by the Assembly of Heads of State and Government.[29]

The procedure of the Commission is contained in Article 46:

> The Commission may resort to any appropriate method of investigation; it may hear from the Secretary General of the Organization of African Unity or any other person capable of enlightening it.[30]

Communications from States are envisioned in Article 47:

> If a State Party to the present Charter has good reasons to believe that another State Party to this Charter has violated the provisions of the Charter, it may draw, by written communication, the attention of that State to the matter. This Communication shall also be addressed to the Secretary General of the OAU and to the Chairman of the Commission. Within three months of the receipt of the Communication, the State to which the Communication is addressed shall give the enquiring State, written explanation or statement elucidating the matter. This should include as much as possible, relevant information relating to the laws and rules of procedure applied and applicable and the redress already given or course of action available.[31]

Further, Article 48 provides for submissions to the Commission:

> If within three months from the date on which the original communication is received by the State to which it is addressed, the issue is not settled to the satisfaction of the two States involved through bilateral negotiation or by any other peaceful procedure, either State shall have the right to submit the matter to the Commission through the Chairman and shall notify the other States involved.[32]

So too under Article 49:

> Notwithstanding the provisions of Article 47, if a State Party to the present Charter considers that another State Party has violated the provisions of the Charter, it may refer the matter directly to the Commission by addressing a communication to the Chairman, to the Secretary General of the Organization of African unity and the State concerned.[33]

Exhaustion of remedies is recognized under Article 50:

> The Commission can only deal with a matter submitted to it after making sure that all local remedies, if they exist, have been exhausted, unless it is obvious to the Commission that the procedure of achieving these remedies would be unduly prolonged.[34]

A report issued by the Commission is entailed in Article 52:

> After having obtained from the States concerned and from other sources all the information it deems necessary and after having tried all appropriate means to reach an amicable solution based on the respect of human and peoples' rights, the Commission shall prepare, within a reasonable period of time from the notification referred to in Article 48, a report to the States concerned and communicated to the Assembly of Heads of State and Government.[35]

In terms of Applicable Principles, Article 60 states:

> The Commission shall draw inspiration from international law on human and peoples' rights, particularly from the provisions of various African instruments on Human and Peoples' Rights, the Charter of the United Nations, the Charter of the Organization of African Unity, the Universal Declaration of Human Rights, other instruments adopted by the United Nations and by African countries in the field of Human and Peoples' Rights, as well as from the provisions of various instruments adopted within the Specialized Agencies of the United Nations of which the Parties to the present Charter are members.[36]

Further, Article 61 holds:

> The Commission shall also take into consideration, as subsidiary measures to determine the principles of law, other general or special international conventions, laying down rules expressly recognized by Member States of the Organization of African Unity, African practices consistent with international norms on Human and Peoples' Rights, customs generally accepted as law, general principles of law

recognized by African States as well as legal precedents and doctrine.[37]

Protocol to the African Charter on Human and Peoples' Rights on the Establishment of an African Court on Human and Peoples' Rights

The Preamble of the Protocol to the African Charter on Human and Peoples' Rights on the Establishment of an African Court on Human and Peoples' Rights 2003 states:

> The Member States of the Organization of African Unity hereinafter referred to as the OAU, States Parties to the African Charter on Human and Peoples' Rights,
>
> Considering that the Charter of the Organization of African Unity recognizes that freedom, equality, justice, peace and dignity are essential objectives for the achievement of the legitimate aspirations of the African Peoples;
>
> Noting that the African Charter on Human and Peoples' Rights reaffirms adherence to the principles of Human and Peoples' Rights, freedoms and duties contained in the declarations, conventions and other instruments adopted by the Organization of African Unity, and other international organizations;
>
> Recognizing that the two-fold objective of the African Commission on Human and Peoples' Rights is to ensure on the one hand promotion and on the other protection of Human and Peoples' Rights, freedom and duties;
>
> Recognizing further, the efforts of the African Charter on Human and Peoples' Rights in the promotion and protection of Human and Peoples' Rights since its inception in 1987;
>
> Firmly convinced that the attainment of the objectives of the African Charter on Human and Peoples' Rights requires the establishment of an African Court on Human and Peoples' Rights to complement and reinforce the functions of the African Commission on Human and Peoples' Rights.[38]

An African Court of Human and Peoples' Rights, important for disability rights, is established under Article 1:

> There shall be established within the Organization of African Unity an African Court of Human and Peoples' Rights hereinafter referred to as 'the Court', the organization, jurisdiction and functioning of which shall be governed by the present Protocol.[39]

The relationship between the Court and the Commission is enunciated under Article 2:

> The Court shall, bearing in mind the provisions of this Protocol, complement the protective mandate of the African Commission on Human and Peoples' Rights hereinafter referred to as 'the Commission', conferred upon it by the African Charter on Human and Peoples' Rights, hereinafter referred to as 'the Charter'.[40]

The Jurisdiction of the Court is established under Article 3:

The jurisdiction of the Court shall extend to all cases and disputes submitted to it concerning the interpretation and application of the Charter, this Protocol and any other relevant Human Rights instrument ratified by the States concerned. In the event of a dispute as to whether the Court has jurisdiction, the Court shall decide.[41]

The Court may issue advisory opinions as outlined under Article 4:

At the request of a Member State of the OAU, the OAU, any of its organs, or any African organization recognized by the OAU, the Court may provide an opinion on any legal matter relating to the Charter or any other relevant human rights instruments, provided that the subject matter of the opinion is not related to a matter being examined by the Commission. The Court shall give reasons for its advisory opinions provided that every judge shall be entitled to deliver a separate of dissenting decision.[42]

Access to the Court is established under Article 5:

The following are entitled to submit cases to the Court:

The Commission

The State Party, which had lodged a complaint to the Commission

The State Party against which the complaint has been lodged at the Commission

The State Party whose citizen is a victim of human rights violation

African intergovernmental organizations

When a State Party has an interest in a case, it may submit a request to the Court to be permitted to join.

The Court may entitle relevant non-governmental organizations (NGOs) with observer status before the Commission, and individuals to institute cases directly before it ....[43]

The issue of admissibility of cases is examined in Article 6:

The Court, when deciding on the admissibility of a case instituted under Article 5 ... of this Protocol, may request the opinion of the Commission which shall give it as soon as possible.

The Court shall rule on the admissibility of cases taking into account the provisions of Article 56 of the Charter.

The Court may consider cases or transfer them to the Commission.[44]

Article 7 establishes the Sources of Law:

The Court shall apply the provision of the Charter and any other relevant human rights instruments ratified by the States concerned.[45]

The independence of the Court is underlined in Article 17:

The independence of the judges shall be fully ensured in accordance with international law.

No judge may hear any case in which the same judge has previously taken part as agent, counsel or advocate for one of the parties or as a member of a national or international court or a commission of enquiry or in any other capacity. Any doubt on this point shall be settled by decision of the Court.[46]

Evidence is outlined under Article 26:

The Court shall hear submissions by all parties and if deemed necessary, hold an enquiry. The States concerned shall assist by providing relevant facilities for the efficient handling of the case.

The Court may receive written and oral evidence including expert testimony and shall make its decision on the basis of such evidence.[47]

Findings of the Court are provided for under Article 27:

If the Court finds that there has been violation of a human or peoples' rights, it shall make appropriate orders to remedy the violation, including the payment of fair compensation or reparation.

In cases of extreme gravity and urgency, and when necessary to avoid irreparable harm to persons, the Court shall adopt such provisional measures as it deems necessary.[48]

Finally, the Judgment of Court is underlined under Article 28:

The Court shall render its judgment within ninety (90) days of having completed its deliberations.

The judgment of the Court decided by majority shall be final and not subject to appeal.

Without prejudice to sub-Article 2 …, the Court may review its decision in the light of new evidence under conditions to be set out in the Rules of Procedure.

The Court may interpret its own decision.

The judgment of the Court shall be read in open court, due notice having been given to the parties.

Reasons shall be given for the judgment of the Court.

> If the judgment of the court does not represent, in whole or in part, the unanimous decision of the judges, any judge shall be entitled to deliver a separate or dissenting opinion.[49]

Importantly, Article 30 provides for the execution of judgment:

> The States Parties to the present Protocol undertake to comply with the judgment in any case to which they are parties within the time stipulated by the Court and to guarantee its execution.[50]

Protocol on Rights of Women in Africa

Important for women with a disability, in the Preamble to the Protocol on Rights of Women in Africa 2003, the State Parties to the Protocol on the Rights of Women in Africa undertake the agreement:

> CONSIDERING that Article 66 of the African Charter on Human and Peoples' Rights provides for special protocols or agreements, if necessary, to supplement the provisions of the African Charter, and that the OAU Assembly of Heads of State and Government meeting in its Thirty-first Ordinary Session in Addis Ababa, Ethiopia, in June 1995, endorsed by resolution AHG/Res.240 (XXXI) the recommendation of the African Commission on Human and Peoples' Rights to elaborate a Protocol on the Rights of Women in Africa;

> CONSIDERING that Article 2 of the African Charter on Human and Peoples' Rights enshrines the principle of non-discrimination on the grounds of race, ethnic group, color, sex, language, religion, political or any other opinion, national and social origin, fortune, birth or other status;

> FURTHER CONSIDERING that Article 18 of the African Charter on Human and Peoples' Rights calls on all Member States to eliminate every discrimination against women and to ensure the protection of the rights of women as stipulated in international declarations and conventions;

> NOTING that Articles 60 and 61 of the African Charter on Human and Peoples' Rights recognize regional and international human rights instruments and African practices consistent with international norms on human and peoples' rights as being important reference points for the application and interpretation of the African Charter;

> RECALLING that women's rights have been recognized and guaranteed in all international human rights instruments, notably the Universal Declaration of Human Rights, the International Covenant on Civil and Political Rights, the International Covenant on Economic, Social and Cultural Rights, the Convention on the Elimination of All Forms of Discrimination Against Women and all other international conventions and covenants relating to the rights of women as being inalienable, interdependent and indivisible human rights;

NOTING that women's rights and women's essential role in development have been reaffirmed in the United Nations Plans of Action on the Environment and Development in 1992, on Human Rights in 1993, on Population and Development in 1994 and on Social Development in 1995;

FURTHER NOTING that the Plans of Action adopted in Dakar and in Beijing call on all Member States of the United Nations, which have made a solemn commitment to implement them, to take concrete steps to give greater attention to the human rights of women in order to eliminate all forms of discrimination and of gender-based violence against women;

BEARING IN MIND related Resolutions, Declarations, Recommendations, Decisions and other Conventions aimed at eliminating all forms of discrimination and at promoting equality between men and women;

CONCERNED that despite the ratification of the African Charter on Human and Peoples' Rights and other international human rights instruments by the majority of Member States, and their solemn commitment to eliminate all forms of discrimination and harmful practices against women, women in Africa still continue to be victims of discrimination and harmful practices;

FIRMLY CONVINCED that any practice that hinders or endangers the normal growth and affects the physical, emotional and psychological development of women and girls should be condemned and eliminated, and DETERMINED to ensure that the rights of women are protected in order to enable them to enjoy fully all their human rights.[51]

Article 1 defines 'Discrimination against women' to mean any distinction, exclusion or restriction based on sex, or any differential treatment whose objective or effects compromise or destroy the recognition, enjoyment or the exercise by women, regardless of their marital status, of human rights and fundamental freedoms in all spheres of life.[52] Further, 'Harmful Practices (HPs)' means all behavior, attitudes and practices which negatively affect the fundamental rights of women and girls, such as their right to life, health and bodily integrity.[53]

Importantly, Article 2(1) is paramount in the fight for the elimination of discrimination against women:

2(1) State Parties shall combat all forms of discrimination against women through appropriate legislative measures. In this regard they shall:
  i.   include in their national constitutions and other legislative instruments the principle of equality between men and women and ensure its effective application;
  ii.   enact and effectively implement appropriate national legislative measures to prohibit all forms of harmful practices which endanger the health and general well-being of women and girls;
  iii. integrate a gender perspective in their policy decisions, legislation, development plans, activities and all other spheres of life;
  iv.   take positive action in those areas where discrimination against women in law and in fact continues to exist.[54]

In looking at the important concern of economic and social welfare rights, Article 13 is paramount for equal rights:

13. State Parties shall guarantee women equal opportunities to work. In this respect, they shall:

i. promote equality in access to employment;

ii. promote the right to equal remuneration for jobs of equal value for men and women;

iii. ensure transparency in employment and dismissal relating to women in order to address issues of sexual harassment in the workplace;

iv. allow women freedom to choose their occupation, and protect them from exploitation by their employers;

v. create conditions to promote and support the occupations and economic activities dominated by women, in particular, within the informal sector;

vi. encourage the establishment of a system of protection and social insurance for women working in the informal sector;

vii. introduce a minimum age of work and prohibit children below that age from working, and prohibit the exploitation of children, especially the girl-child;

viii. take the necessary measures to recognize the economic value of the work of women in the home;

ix. guarantee adequate pre and post-natal maternity leave;

x. ensure equality in taxation for men and women;

xi. recognize the right of salaried women to the same allowances and entitlements as those granted to salaried men for their spouses and children;

xii. recognize motherhood and the upbringing of children as a social function for which the State, the private sector and both parents must take responsibility.[55]

Importantly, special protection of women with disabilities is ensured under Article 23:

23. The States Parties undertake to:

a. ensure the protection of women with disabilities and take specific measures commensurate with their physical, economic and social needs to facilitate their access to employment, professional and vocational training as well as their participation in decision-making;

b. ensure the right of women with disabilities to freedom from violence, including sexual abuse, discrimination based on disability and the right to be treated with dignity.[56]

South Africa

One of the greatest hurdles disabled people face when trying to access mainstream programs is negative attitudes. It is these attitudes that lead to the social exclusion and marginalization of people with disabilities.[57] According to the latest statistics,

the following divisions have been made from a population figure of 40,583,573:
Sight disabled 1,091,022; Hearing disabled 383,408; Physically disabled 55,774;
Mentally handicapped 192,554; with a Total 1,722,758. In other words, 4.3
percent of the South African population is disabled. However, only 0.26 percent of
disabled people in South Africa are formally employed. Of the total number of
disabled people aged 15 years or older, 88 percent were economically inactive and
unemployed, but looking for work, compared with 63 percent of the rest of the
population. Overall, 19 percent of White disabled people are employed in full-time
positions compared with Africans at 6 percent, Colored at 4 percent and Indians at
9 percent. The employment rate for disabled women is 11 percent compared with
15 percent for disabled men, and 80 percent of disabled women are economically
inactive compared with 74 percent disabled men. Of those who became disabled
before the age of 2, a mere 7 percent are employed and 87 percent are
economically inactive, compared with those who became disabled after 19 years,
17 percent are employed and 71 percent are economically inactive. Disabled
people face serious barriers to employment.[58]

The reality in South Africa is that people with disabilities still face
unacceptable social and economic exclusion. Disabled people are
disproportionately among the poorest of the poor and more likely than their able-
bodied peers to be uneducated, unemployed or under-employed.[59] The realities of
life are grim for South Africa's disabled people, particularly among the African
community, with a high unemployment rate among the disabled. Better education
and rehabilitation services seemed to have an impact on a person's ability to find
employment but in this regard coloured and African disabled people are more
disadvantaged than Indian and white disabled people.

The social grant system and the delivery of public services to disabled
people requires radical transformation in terms of administration and distribution
and must be contextualized within a wider poverty-eradication and disability
empowerment strategy. Programs for the disabled must be monitored and properly
evaluated. The way to combat discrimination is neither to deny its existence or its
systemic roots, nor to trivialise its impact. Those who deny it must be challenged
because it is such denial that potentially entrenches inherited inequalities. We need
to strengthen and in some cases purify the capacity of the democratic institutions to
deal with the barriers that perpetuate social exclusion and discrimination on the
grounds of disability. Educational programs that popularise a rights-based
approach to addressing discrimination should be developed for civil society but
also for disabled people. An integrated disability development approach must link
prevention, rehabilitation and social safety nets with empowerment strategies and
changes in attitudes.

It is necessary to address discrimination and inequality in its many
institutional and social forms. This includes changing the skewed distribution of
resources through the equitable distribution of State funds, a program of black
economic empowerment, including women's economic empowerment, affirmative
action, land reform and social development. It requires the transformation, in terms
of composition, culture and focus, of institutions such as the judiciary, public
service, private sector, academia and parastatals. Essential to this are programs to

promote multi-culturalism, multi-lingualism and tolerance in all our educational institutions and other important sites of social development. There is a need to focus on the ability and not the disability. It is clear that much needs to be done to ensure that more peoples with disabilities rightfully enjoy their constitutional rights.[60]

Interim Constitution Schedule 4

The Constitutional Principles for the Republic of South Africa are contained in Schedule 4 of the Interim Constitution (Act 200 of 1993). Important for disability rights, Article I guarantees equality:

> I. The Constitution of South Africa shall provide for the establishment of one sovereign state, a common South African citizenship and a democratic system of government committed to achieving equality between men and women and people of all races.[61]

Article II also guarantees fundamental rights, freedoms and civil liberties by holding that everyone shall enjoy all universally accepted fundamental rights, freedoms and civil liberties, which shall be provided for and protected by entrenched and justiciable provisions in the Constitution.[62] Further, Article IV is the Supremacy clause, which states that the Constitution shall be the supreme law of the land; it shall be binding on all organs of state at all levels of government.[63]

Important for disability rights, the prohibition against discrimination and the promotion of equality are contained within Article III:

> III. The Constitution shall prohibit racial, gender and all other forms of discrimination and shall promote racial and gender equality and national unity.[64]

Further, the fundamental guarantee of equality of all before the law is contained in Article V:

> V. The legal system shall ensure the equality of all before the law and an equitable legal process. Equality before the law includes laws, programs or activities that have as their object the amelioration of the conditions of the disadvantaged, including those disadvantaged on the grounds of race, color or gender.[65]

The separation of powers for objectivity and accountability is contained in Article VI, which establishes that there shall be a separation of powers between the legislature, executive and judiciary, with appropriate checks and balances to ensure accountability, responsiveness and openness.[66] Further, the important role of the judiciary is outlined in Article VII, by holding that the judiciary shall be appropriately qualified, independent and impartial, and shall have the power and jurisdiction to safeguard and enforce the Constitution and all fundamental rights.[67]

Constitution of South Africa

The Constitution of the Republic of South Africa 1996 was first adopted by the Constitutional Assembly on 8 May 1996 (Act 108 of 1996), and was signed into law on 10 December 1996. As an integration of ideas from ordinary citizens, civil society and political parties represented in and outside of the Constitutional Assembly, the Constitution of South Africa represents the collective wisdom of the South African people and has been arrived at by general agreement. The objective in this process was to ensure that the final Constitution be legitimate, credible and accepted by all South Africans.

The Preamble of the Constitution reads:

> We, the people of South Africa,
> Recognize the injustices of our past;
> Honour those who suffered for justice and freedom in our land;
> Respect those who have worked to build and develop our country; and
> Believe that South Africa belongs to all who live in it, united in our diversity.
> We therefore, through our freely elected representatives, adopt this Constitution as the supreme law of the Republic so as to
> Heal the divisions of the past and establish a society based on democratic values, social justice and fundamental human rights;
> Lay the foundations for a democratic and open society in which government is based on the will of the people and every citizen is equally protected by law;
> Improve the quality of life of all citizens and free the potential of each person; and
> Build a united and democratic South Africa able to take its rightful place as a sovereign state in the family of nations.
> May God protect our people.
> Nkosi Sikelel' iAfrika. Morena boloka setjhaba sa heso.
> God seën Suid-Afrika. God bless South Africa.
> Mudzimu fhatutshedza Afurika. Hosi katekisa Afrika.[68]

The Founding Provisions of the Republic of South Africa are found in Section 1 of the Constitution, which stresses equality and the advancement of human rights, by stating that the Republic of South Africa is one, sovereign, democratic state founded on the following values: human dignity, the achievement of equality and the advancement of human rights and freedoms; non-racialism and non-sexism; and the supremacy of the constitution and the rule of law.[69]

The Supremacy Clause is found in Section 2 of the Constitution, which holds that this Constitution is the supreme law of the Republic; law or conduct inconsistent with it is invalid, and the obligations imposed by it must be fulfilled.[70] Important for disability rights, the right to equality is espoused in Section 3, which states that all citizens are equally entitled to the rights, privileges and benefits of citizenship; and equally subject to the duties and responsibilities of citizenship.[71]

Chapter 2 of the Constitution enumerates the Bill of Rights for South Africa. Section 7 states:

7(1) This Bill of Rights is a cornerstone of democracy in South Africa. It enshrines the rights of all people in our country and affirms the democratic values of human dignity, equality and freedom.

(2) The state must respect, protect, promote and fulfil the rights in the Bill of Rights.

(3) The rights in the Bill of Rights are subject to the limitations contained or referred to in Section 36, or elsewhere in the Bill.[72]

Application and jurisdiction of the Bill of Rights are outlined in Section 8:

8(1) The Bill of Rights applies to all law, and binds the legislature, the executive, the judiciary and all organs of state.

(2) A provision of the Bill of Rights binds a natural or a juristic person if, and to the extent that, it is applicable, taking into account the nature of the right and the nature of any duty imposed by the right.

(3) When applying a provision of the Bill of Rights to a natural or juristic person in terms of subsection (2), a court:

a.   in order to give effect to a right in the Bill, must apply, or if necessary develop, the common law to the extent that legislation does not give effect to that right; and

b.   may develop rules of the common law to limit the right, provided that the limitation is in accordance with Section 36(1).

(4) A juristic person is entitled to the rights in the Bill of Rights to the extent required by the nature of the rights and the nature of that juristic person.[73]

In terms of disability equality, Section 9 goes on to outline and guarantee the important concept of equal protection:

9(1) Everyone is equal before the law and has the right to equal protection and benefit of the law.

(2) Equality includes the full and equal enjoyment of all rights and freedoms. To promote the achievement of equality, legislative and other measures designed to protect or advance persons, or categories of persons, disadvantaged by unfair discrimination may be taken.

(3) The state may not unfairly discriminate directly or indirectly against anyone on one or more grounds, including race, gender, sex, pregnancy, marital status, ethnic or social origin, color, sexual orientation, age, disability, religion, conscience, belief, culture, language and birth.

(4) No person may unfairly discriminate directly or indirectly against anyone on one or more grounds in terms of subsection (3). National legislation must be enacted to prevent or prohibit unfair discrimination.

(5) Discrimination on one or more of the grounds listed in subsection (3) is unfair unless it is established that the discrimination is fair.[74]

On human dignity, Section 10 states that everyone has inherent dignity and the right to have their dignity respected and protected.[75] Further, in the interpretation of the Bill of Rights, Section 39 states the importance of human dignity and equality:

39(1) When interpreting the Bill of Rights, a court, tribunal or forum:
a.   must promote the values that underlie an open and democratic society based on human dignity, equality and freedom;
b.   must consider international law; and
c.   may consider foreign law.
(2) When interpreting any legislation, and when developing the common law or customary law, every court, tribunal or forum must promote the spirit, purport and objects of the Bill of Rights.
(3) The Bill of Rights does not deny the existence of any other rights or freedoms that are recognized or conferred by common law, customary law or legislation, to the extent that they are consistent with the Bill.[76]

In safeguarding the right to employment under the principle of freedom of trade, occupation and profession, important for disability rights, Section 22 states that every citizen has the right to choose their trade, occupation or profession freely. The practice of a trade, occupation or profession may be regulated by law.[77] In terms of labor relations, Section 23 establishes that everyone has the right to fair labor practices. Every worker has the right to form and join a trade union; to participate in the activities and programs of a trade union; and to strike.[78]

In looking at the important right to education as a way of betterment, Section 29 states that everyone has the right to a basic education, including adult basic education; and to further education, which the state, through reasonable measures, must make progressively available and accessible.[79]

In guaranteeing the right to administrative action, Section 33 states that everyone has the right to administrative action that is lawful, reasonable and procedurally fair.[80] Further, the right to access to the courts is outlined in Section 34, which holds that everyone has the right to have any dispute that can be resolved by the application of law decided in a fair public hearing before a court or, where appropriate, another independent and impartial tribunal or forum.[81]

The Constitution also goes on to provide for a limitation of rights under Section 36(1), which provides that the rights in the Bill of Rights may be limited only in terms of law of general application to the extent that the limitation is reasonable and justifiable in an open and democratic society based on human dignity, equality and freedom, taking into account all relevant factors, including the nature of the right; the importance of the purpose of the limitation; the nature and extent of the limitation; the relation between the limitation and its purpose; and less restrictive means to achieve the purpose.[82]

In order to guarantee rights enumerated under the Constitution, Section 38 ensures the enforcement of such rights, by holding that anyone listed in this Article has the right to approach a competent court, alleging that a right in the Bill of Rights has been infringed or threatened, and the court may grant appropriate relief, including a declaration of rights. The persons who may approach a court are anyone acting in their own interest; anyone acting on behalf of another person who cannot act in their own name; anyone acting as a member of, or in the interest of, a group or class of persons; anyone acting in the public interest; and an association acting in the interest of its members.[83]

The powers of the courts in constitutional matters are outlined in Section 172(1), which holds that when deciding a constitutional matter within its power, a court must declare that any law or conduct that is inconsistent with the Constitution is invalid to the extent of its inconsistency; and may make any order that is just and equitable, including an order limiting the retrospective effect of the declaration of invalidity; and an order suspending the declaration of invalidity for any period and on any conditions, to allow the competent authority to correct the defect.[84]

Under the establishment and governing principles, Section 181 lists several important institutions mandated to strengthen constitutional democracy, namely the Public Protector; the Human Rights Commission; the Commission for the Promotion and Protection of the Rights of Cultural, Religious and Linguistic Communities; the Auditor-General; and the Electoral Commission.[85] The functions of the Human Rights Commission, are listed under Section 184, which states that it must promote respect for human rights and a culture of human rights; promote the protection, development and attainment of human rights; and monitor and assess the observance of human rights in the Republic. Further, the Human Rights Commission has the powers, as regulated by national legislation, necessary to perform its functions, including the power to investigate and to report on the observance of human rights; to take steps to secure appropriate redress where human rights have been violated; and to carry out research; and to educate.[86]

Employment Equity Act

The Preamble of the Employment Equity Act 1998, an Act to provide for employment equity and to provide for matters incidental thereto, states:

> Recognizing
>
>> that as a result of apartheid and other discriminatory laws and practices, there are disparities in employment, occupation and income within the national labor market; and that those disparities create such pronounced disadvantages for certain categories of people that they cannot be redressed simply by repealing discriminatory laws,
>
> Therefore, in order to
>
>> promote the constitutional right of equality and the exercise of true democracy; eliminate unfair discrimination in employment; ensure the implementation of employment equity to redress the effects of discrimination; achieve a diverse workforce broadly representative of our people; promote economic development and efficiency in the workforce; and give effect to the obligations of the Republic as a member of the International Labor Organization.[87]

Important for disability rights, the purpose of the Act is defined in Section 2 as to achieve equity in the workplace by promoting equal opportunity and fair treatment in employment through the elimination of unfair discrimination; and implementing affirmative action measures to redress the disadvantages in employment experienced by designated groups, in order to ensure their equitable representation in all occupational categories and levels in the workforce.[88]

According to Section 3, the Act must be interpreted in compliance with the Constitution so as to give effect to its purpose; taking into account any relevant code of good practice issued in terms of this Act or any other employment law; and in compliance with the international law obligations of the Republic, in particular those contained in the Discrimination (Employment and Occupation) Convention (No. 111) 1958.[89]

The elimination and the prohibition of unfair discrimination for those with a disability are called for in Sections 5 and 6(1) respectively:

> 5. Every employer must take steps to promote equal opportunity in the workplace by eliminating unfair discrimination in any employment policy or practice.[90]

> 6(1) No person may unfairly discriminate, directly or indirectly, against an employee, in any employment policy or practice, on one or more grounds, including race, gender, sex, pregnancy, marital status, family responsibility, ethnic or social origin, color, sexual orientation, age, disability, religion, HIV status, conscience, belief, political opinion, culture, language and birth.[91]

Article 6(2) allows for affirmative action programs and bona fide occupational qualifications:

> 6(2) It is not unfair discrimination to:
> a. take affirmative action measures consistent with the purpose of this Act; or
> b. distinguish, exclude or prefer any person on the basis of an inherent requirement of a job.[92]

Further, Section 15 goes on to outline affirmative action measures which are permitted:

> 15(1) Affirmative action measures are measures designed to ensure that suitably qualified people from designated groups have equal employment opportunities and are equitably represented in all occupational categories and levels in the workforce of a designated employer.
> (2) Affirmative action measures implemented by a designated employer must include:
> a. measures to identify and eliminate employment barriers, including unfair discrimination, which adversely affect people from designated groups;
> b. measures designed to further diversity in the workplace based on equal dignity and respect of all people;
> c. making reasonable accommodation for people from designated groups in order to ensure that they enjoy equal opportunities and are equitably represented in the workforce of a designated employer;
> d. subject to subsection (3), measures to:

     i.   ensure the equitable representation of suitably qualified people from designated groups in all occupational categories and levels in the workforce; and

    ii.   retain and develop people from designated groups and to implement appropriate training measures, including measures in terms of an Act of Parliament providing for skills development.

(3) The measures referred to in subsection (2)(d) include preferential treatment and numerical goals, but exclude quotas.[93]

According to the burden of proof outlined in Section 11, whenever unfair discrimination is alleged in terms of this Act, the employer against whom the allegation is made must establish that it is fair.[94]

To combat discrimination, Section 20 outlines the requirement of an employment equity plan:

20(1) A designated employer must prepare and implement an employment equity plan which will achieve reasonable progress towards employment equity in that employer's workforce.

(2) An employment equity plan prepared in terms of subsection (1) must state:
    a.   the objectives to be achieved for each year of the plan;
    b.   the affirmative action measures to be implemented as required by subsection 15(2);
    c.   where underrepresentation of people from designated groups has been identified by the analysis, the numerical goals to achieve the equitable representation of suitably qualified people from designated groups within each occupational category and level in the workforce, the timetable within which this is to be achieved, and the strategies intended to achieve those goals;
    d.   the timetable for each year of the plan for the achievement of goals and objectives other than numerical goals;
    e.   the duration of the plan, which may not be shorter than one year or longer than five years;
    f.   the procedures that will be used to monitor and evaluate the implementation of the plan and whether reasonable progress is being made towards implementing employment equity;
    g.   the internal procedures to resolve any dispute about the interpretation or implementation of the plan;
    h.   the persons in the workforce, including senior managers, responsible for monitoring and implementing the plan; and
    i.   any other prescribed matter.[95]

The functions of the Commission for Employment Equity are enumerated in Section 30:

30(1) The Commission advises the Minister on:
    a.   codes of good practice issued by the Minister;
    b.   regulations made by the Minister; and
    c.   policy and any other matter concerning this Act.

(2) In addition to the functions in subsection (1) the Commission may:
  a.   make awards recognizing achievements of employers in furthering the purpose of this Act;
  b.   research and report to the Minister on any matter relating to the application of this Act, including appropriate and well-researched norms and benchmarks for the setting of numerical goals in various sectors; and
  c.   perform any other prescribed function.[96]

Under Section 35, a labor inspector acting in terms of this Act has the authority to enter, question and inspect as provided.[97] Further, Section 36 holds that a labor inspector must request and obtain a written undertaking from a designated employer to comply within a specified period, if the inspector has reasonable grounds to believe that the employer has failed to consult with employees; conduct an analysis; prepare and implement an employment equity plan; submit and publish its annual report; prepare a successive employment equity plan; assign responsibility to a senior manager; inform its employees; or keep records.[98] According to Section 37, a labor inspector may issue a compliance order to a designated employer if that employer has failed to act.[99] Finally, under Section 40, a designated employer may appeal to the Labor Court against a compliance order of the Director-General within 21 days after receiving that order.[100]

In terms of a Code of Good Practice, according to the Employment Equity Act, the process of developing a plan has three sequential phases: planning, development, and implementation and monitoring. The planning phase of the process should include assignment of responsibility and accountability to one or more senior managers; a communication, awareness and training program; consultation with relevant stakeholders; an analysis of existing employment policies, procedures, and practices; an analysis of the existing workforce profile; an analysis of relevant demographic information; and the development of meaningful benchmark comparisons. The development phase should include objectives set; corrective measures formulated; time frames established; the plan drawn up; resources identified and allocated for the implementation of the plan; and the plan communicated. The implementation and monitoring phase should include implementation; monitoring and evaluating progress; reviewing the plan; and reporting on progress.

In order to identify any barriers that may be responsible for the underrepresentation or under-utilization of employees from designated groups, including disability groups, a review of all employment policies, practices, procedures, and of the working environment should be undertaken of employment policy or practices, such as recruitment, selection, pre-employment testing, and induction that could be biased, inappropriate, or unaffirming; practices related to succession and experience planning, and related promotions and transfers to establish whether designated groups are excluded or adversely impacted; utilization and job assignments to establish whether designated groups are able meaningfully to participate and contribute; current training and development methodologies and strategies; remuneration structures and practices such as equal remuneration for work of equal value; employee benefits related to retirement, risk, and medical aid to establish whether designated groups have equal access; disciplinary practices which may have a disproportionately adverse effect on designated groups that may not be justified; the number and nature of dismissals, voluntary terminations and retrenchments of employees from designated groups that may indicate internal or external equity-related factors contributing to such terminations; and corporate culture which may be characterized by exclusionary social and other practices. All practices should be assessed in terms of cross-group fairness. The review should take into account more subtle or indirect forms of discrimination and stereotyping, which could result in certain groups of people not being employed in particular jobs, or which could preclude people from being promoted.

Affirmative action measures should be developed in terms of appointing members from designated groups for transparent and unbiased recruitment strategies; increasing the pool of available candidates; training, promoting and retaining people from designated groups; ensuring that members of designated groups are appointed in such positions that they are able meaningfully to participate in corporate decision-making processes; and transforming the corporate culture of the past in a way that affirms diversity in the workplace and harnesses the potential of all employees.

Promotion of Equality and Prevention of Unfair Discrimination Act

The Preamble of the Promotion of Equality and Prevention of Unfair Discrimination Act 2000 states:

> The consolidation of democracy in our country requires the eradication of social and economic inequalities, especially those that are systematic in nature, which were generated in our history by colonialism, apartheid and patriarchy, and which brought pain and suffering to the great majority of our people …;
> The Constitution provides for the enactment of national legislation to prevent or prohibit unfair discrimination and to promote the achievement of equality;
> This implies the advancement, special legal and other measures, of historically disadvantaged individuals, communities and social groups who were dispossessed of their land and resources, deprived of their human dignity and who continue to endure the consequences;
> This Act endeavours to facilitate the transition to a democratic society, united in its diversity, marked by human relations that are caring and compassionate, and guided by the principles of equality, fairness, equity, social progress, justice human dignity and freedom.[101]

Under Chapter 1, the objects of the Act are to enact legislation required by Section 9 of the Constitution; to give effect to the letter and spirit of the Constitution, in particular the equal enjoyment of all rights and freedoms by every person, the promotion of equality, the values of equality contained in Section 1 of the Constitution, the prevention of unfair discrimination and protection of human dignity as contemplated in Sections 9 and 10 of the Constitution, and the prohibition of advocacy of hatred based on race, ethnicity, gender or religion, that constitutes incitement to cause harm; to provide for measures to facilitate the eradication of unfair discrimination, hate speech and harassment, particularly on the grounds of disability, race and gender; and to provide for procedures for the determination of circumstances under which discrimination is unfair.[102]

Further, 'prohibited grounds' including disability are defined under Section 1 as:

> (a) race, gender, sex, pregnancy, marital status, ethnic or social origin, color, sexual orientation, age, disability, religion, conscience, belief, culture, language and birth; or
> (b) any other ground where discrimination based on that other ground:
>> (i) causes or perpetuates systematic disadvantaged:
>> (ii) undermines human dignity; or
>> (iii) adversely affects the equal enjoyment of a person's rights and freedoms in a serious manner that is comparable to discrimination on a ground in paragraph (a).[103]

The objects of the Act are enumerated in Section 2, and include disability:

> 2. The objects of this Act are:
> (a) to enact legislation required by section 9 of the Constitution;
> (b) to give effect to the letter and spirit of the Constitution, in particular:
>> (i) the equal enjoyment of all rights and freedoms by every person;
>> (ii) the promotion of equality;
>> (iii) the values of non-racialism and non-sexism contained in section 1 of the Constitution;
>> (iv) the prevention of unfair discrimination and protection of human dignity as contemplated in sections 9 and 10 of the Constitution;
>> (v) the prohibition of advocacy of hatred, based on race, ethnicity, gender or religion, that constitutes incitement to cause harm as contemplated in
>> section 16(2)(c) of the Constitution and section 12 of this Act;
> (c) to provide for measures to facilitate the eradication of unfair discrimination, hate speech and harassment, particularly on the grounds of race, gender and disability;
> (d) to provide for procedures for the determination of circumstances under which discrimination is unfair;
> (e) to provide for measures to educate the public and raise public awareness on the importance of promoting equality and overcoming unfair discrimination, hate speech and harassment;
> (f) to provide remedies for victims of unfair discrimination, hate speech and harassment and persons whose right to equality has been infringed;
> (g) to set out measures to advance persons disadvantaged by unfair discrimination;
> (h) to facilitate further compliance with international law obligations including treaty obligations in terms of, amongst others, the Convention on the Elimination of All Forms of Racial Discrimination and the Convention on the Elimination of All Forms of Discrimination against Women.[104]

Further, the guiding principles are contained in Section 4:

> 4. (1) In the adjudication of any proceedings which are instituted in terms of or under this Act, the following principles should apply:
>> (a) The expeditious and informal processing of cases, which facilitate participation by the parties to the proceedings;
>> (b) access to justice to all persons in relevant judicial and other dispute resolution forums;
>> (c) the use of rules of procedure…and criteria to facilitate participation;
>> (d) the use of corrective or restorative measures in conjunction with measures of a deterrent nature;
>> (e) the development of special skills and capacity for persons applying this Act in order to ensure effective implementation and administration thereof.
>
> (2) In the application of this Act the following should be recognised and taken into account:
>> (a) The existence of systemic discrimination and inequalities, particularly in respect of race, gender and disability in all spheres of life as a result of past and present unfair discrimination, brought about by colonialism, the apartheid system and patriarchy; and
>> (b) the need to take measures at all levels to eliminate such discrimination and inequalities.[105]

It is understood that by virtue of Section 5, the Act binds the State and all persons, [106] and by virtue of Section 6 neither the State nor any person may unfairly discriminate against any person.[107]

Importantly, prohibition of unfair discrimination on the ground of disability is guaranteed in Section 9:

> 9. Subject to section 6, no person may unfairly discriminate against any person on the ground of disability, including—
>> (a) denying or removing from any person who has a disability, any supporting or enabling facility necessary for their functioning in society;
>> (b) contravening the code of practice or regulations of the South African Bureau of Standards that govern environmental accessibility;
>> (c) failing to eliminate obstacles that unfairly limit or restrict persons with disabilities from enjoying equal opportunities or failing to take steps to reasonably accommodate the needs of such persons.[108]

In terms of the burden of proof in disability discrimination cases, Section 13 stipulates:

> 13(1) If the complainant makes out a prima facie case of discrimination:
>> (a) the respondent must prove, in the facts before the court, that the discrimination did not take place as alleged; or
>> (b) the respondent must prove that the conduct is not based on one or more of the prohibited grounds.
>
> (2) If the discrimination did take place:

(a) on a ground in paragraph (a) of the definition of 'prohibited grounds' ... then it is unfair, unless the respondent proves that the discrimination is fair;

(b) on a ground in paragraph (b) of the definition of 'prohibited grounds', then it is unfair –

(i) if one or more of the conditions set out in paragraph (b) of the definition of 'prohibited grounds' is established; and

(ii) unless the respondent proves that the discrimination is fair.[109]

Section 14 establishes the determination of fairness or unfairness:

14(1) It is not unfair discrimination to take measures designed to protect or advance persons or categories of persons disadvantaged by unfair discrimination or the members of such groups or categories of persons.

(2) In determining whether the respondent has proved that the discrimination is fair, the following must be taken into account:

(a) The context;

(b) the factors referred to in subsection (3);

(c) whether the discrimination reasonably and justifiably differentiates between persons according to objectively determinable criteria, intrinsic to the activity concerned.

(3) The factors referred to in subsection (2)(b) include the following:

(a) Whether the discrimination impairs or is likely to impair human dignity;

(b) the impact or likely impact of the discrimination on the complainant;

(c) the position of the complainant in society and whether he or she suffers from patterns of disadvantage or belongs to a group that suffers from patterns of disadvantage;

(d) the nature and extent of the discrimination;

(e) whether the discrimination is systematic in nature;

(f) whether the discrimination has a legitimate purpose;

(g) whether and to what extent the discrimination achieves its purpose;

(h) whether there are less restrictive and less disadvantageous means to achieve the purpose;

(i) whether and to what extent the respondent has taken such steps as being reasonable in the circumstances to:

(i) address the disadvantage which arises from or is related to one or more of the prohibited grounds; or

(ii) accommodate diversity.[110]

Importantly, according to Section 25, the State has a duty to promote equality and, as such, the State must, where necessary with the assistance of the relevant constitutional institutions, develop awareness of fundamental rights in order to promote a climate of understanding, mutual respect and equality; take measures to develop and implement programs in order to promote equality; and where necessary or appropriate develop action plans to address any unfair discrimination, hate speech or harassment. It must also enact further legislation that seeks to promote equality and to establish a legislative framework in line with the objectives of this Act; develop codes of practice as contemplated in this Act in order to promote equality; develop guidelines, including codes in respect of reasonable accommodation; provide assistance, advice and training on issues of equality; develop appropriate internal mechanisms to deal with complaints of unfair discrimination, hate speech or harassment; and conduct information campaigns to popularize this Act.[111]

Special measures to promote equality with regard to disability are contained in Section 28:

> 28. (1) If it is proved in the prosecution of any offence that unfair discrimination on the grounds of race, gender or disability played a part in the commission of the offence, this must be regarded as an aggravating circumstance for purposes of sentence.
>
> (2) The South African Human Rights Commission must, in its report referred to in section 15 of the Human Rights Commission Act, 1994 (Act No. 54 of 1994), include an assessment on the extent to which unfair discrimination on the grounds of race, gender and disability persists in the Republic, the effects thereof and recommendations on how best to address the problems.
>
> (3)(a) The State, institutions performing public functions and all persons have a duty and responsibility, in particular to:
>> (i) eliminate discrimination on the grounds of race, gender and disability;
>> (ii) promote equality in respect of race, gender and disability.
>
> (b) In carrying out the duties and responsibilities referred to in paragraph *(a)*, the State, institutions performing public functions and, where appropriate and relevant, juristic and non-juristic entities, must:
>> (i) audit laws, policies and practices with a view to eliminating all discriminatory aspects thereof;
>> (ii) enact appropriate laws, develop progressive policies and initiate codes of practice in order to eliminate discrimination on the grounds of race, gender and disability;
>> (iii) adopt viable action plans for the promotion and achievement of equality in respect of race, gender and disability; and
>> (iv) give priority to the elimination of unfair discrimination and the promotion of equality in respect of race, gender and disability.[112]

Conclusion

In terms of this ability issues of equality in Africa, African states should share experiences on best practices in order to complement each other so as to ensure effective disability mainstreaming; continue to ensure that disability issues are integrated in all development programs and plans; develop common indicators for monitoring disability issues at regional levels; and encourage and support the initiation and coordination of periodical conference/seminars on disability and development in relation to population issues. Indeed, a renewal of commitment to disability equality is overdue in Africa, where there is a great disparity in the level of human rights protection available to its inhabitants. Almost all African countries have constitutions or civil codes that prohibit discrimination. However, the level of protection varies from nation to nation. Entrenched attitudes and practices, as well as limited resources, limit the practical effect.

Notes

[1]   Miles, M., *History of Educational & Social Responses to Disability in Anglophone Eastern & Southern Africa*, 2001.
[2]   *Ibid.*
[3]   Economic Commission for Africa, *Economic Report on Africa*, 2002.
[4]   Charter of the Organization of African Unity, at the Preamble.
[5]   *Ibid.*, at Article I.
[6]   *Ibid.*, at Article II.
[7]   *Ibid.*, at Article VII.
[8]   *Ibid.*, at Article VIII.
[9]   *Ibid.*, at Article XII.
[10]   *Ibid.*, at Article XVI.
[11]   *Ibid.*, at Article XIX.
[12]   *Ibid.*, at Article XX.
[13]   African Charter on Human and Peoples' Rights.
[14]   *Ibid.*, at Article 1.
[15]   *Ibid.*, at Article 2.
[16]   *Ibid.*, at Article 3.
[17]   *Ibid.*, at Article 19.
[18]   *Ibid.*, at Article 5.
[19]   *Ibid.*, at Article 7.
[20]   *Ibid.*, at Article 15.
[21]   *Ibid.*, at Article 17.
[22]   *Ibid.*, at Article 20.
[23]   *Ibid.*, at Article 22.
[24]   *Ibid.*, at Article 26.
[25]   *Ibid.*, at Article 27.
[26]   *Ibid.*, at Article 28.
[27]   *Ibid.*, at Article 29.
[28]   *Ibid.*, at Article 30.
[29]   *Ibid.*, at Article 45.
[30]   *Ibid.*, at Article 46.
[31]   *Ibid.*, at Article 47.
[32]   *Ibid.*, at Article 48.
[33]   *Ibid.*, at Article 49.
[34]   *Ibid.*, at Article 50.
[35]   *Ibid.*, at Article 52.
[36]   *Ibid.*, at Article 60.
[37]   *Ibid.*, at Article 61.
[38]   Protocol to the African Charter on Human and Peoples' Rights on the Establishment of an African Court on Human and Peoples' Rights, at the Preamble.
[39]   *Ibid.*, at Article 1.
[40]   *Ibid.*, at Article 2.
[41]   *Ibid.*, at Article 3.
[42]   *Ibid.*, at Article 4.

43 *Ibid.*, at Article 5.
44 *Ibid.*, at Article 6.
45 *Ibid.*, at Article 7.
46 *Ibid.*, at Article 17.
47 *Ibid.*, at Article 26.
48 *Ibid.*, at Article 27.
49 *Ibid.*, at Article 28.
50 *Ibid.*, at Article 30.
51 Protocol on the Rights of Women in Africa, at the Preamble.
52 *Ibid.*, at Article 1.
53 *Ibid.*, at Article 1.
54 *Ibid.*, at Article 2(1).
55 *Ibid.*, at Article 13.
56 *Ibid*, at Article 26.
57 South Africa, *White Paper on Integrated National Disability Strategy*, 1997.
58 Statistics South Africa.
59 Vuyiswa McClain, Charlotte, *Democracy & Disability in South Africa: Still Three Nations*.
60 *Ibid.*
61 Interim Constitution of South Africa, Schedule 4, Article I.
62 *Ibid.*, at Article II.
63 *Ibid.*, at Article IV.
64 *Ibid.*, at Article III.
65 *Ibid.*, at Article V.
66 *Ibid.*, at Article VI.
67 *Ibid.*, at Article VII.
68 Constitution of South Africa, at the Preamble.
69 *Ibid.*, at Section 1.
70 *Ibid.*, at Section 2.
71 *Ibid.*, at Section 3.
72 *Ibid.*, at Section 7.
73 *Ibid.*, at Section 8.
74 *Ibid.*, at Section 9.
75 *Ibid.*, at Section 10.
76 *Ibid.*, at Section 39.
77 *Ibid.*, at Section 22.
78 *Ibid.*, at Section 23.
79 *Ibid.*, at Section 29.
80 *Ibid.*, at Section 33.
81 *Ibid.*, at Section 34.
82 *Ibid.*, at Section 36(1).
83 *Ibid.*, at Section 38.
84 *Ibid.*, at Section 172(1).
85 *Ibid.*, at Section 181.
86 *Ibid.*, at Section 184.
87 Employment Equity Act, South Africa, at the Preamble.
88 *Ibid.*, at Section 2.
89 *Ibid.*, at Section 3.
90 *Ibid.*, at Section 5.
91 *Ibid.*, at Section 6(1).

[92]   *Ibid.*, at Section 6(2).
[93]   *Ibid.*, at Section 15.
[94]   *Ibid.*, at Section 11.
[95]   *Ibid.*, at Section 20.
[96]   *Ibid.*, at Section 30.
[97]   *Ibid.*, at Section 35.
[98]   *Ibid.*, at Section 36.
[99]   *Ibid.*, at Section 37.
[100]   *Ibid.*, at Section 40.
[101]   Promotion of Equality and Prevention of Unfair Discrimination Act, South Africa, at the Preamble.
[102]   *Ibid.*, at Chapter 1.
[103]   *Ibid.*, at Section 1.
[104]   *Ibid.*, at Section 2.
[105]   *Ibid.*, at Section 4.
[106]   *Ibid.*, at Section 5.
[107]   *Ibid.*, at Section 6.
[108]   *Ibid.*, at Section 9.
[109]   *Ibid.*, at Section 13.
[110]   *Ibid.*, at Section 14.
[111]   *Ibid.*, at Section 25.
[112]   *Ibid.*, at Section 28.

References

African Charter on Human and Peoples' Rights.

Charter of the Organization of African Unity.

Constitution of South Africa.

Economic Commission for Africa (2002), *Economic Report on Africa*.

Employment Equity Act, South Africa.

Interim Constitution of South Africa, Schedule 4.

Miles, M., *History of Educational & Social Responses to Disability in Anglophone Eastern & Southern Africa*, 2001.

Promotion of Equality and Prevention of Unfair Discrimination Act, South Africa, South Africa, 2000.

Protocol on the Rights of Women in Africa.

Protocol to the African Charter on Human and Peoples' Rights on the Establishment of an African Court on Human and Peoples' Rights.

South Africa, *White Paper on Integrated National Disability Strategy*, 1997.

Statistics South Africa.

Vuyiswa McClain, Charlotte, *Democracy & Disability in South Africa: Still Three Nations*.

Chapter 6

This Ability in
Canada, Mexico and the United States

Introduction

This chapter will examine this ability in Canada, the United States, and minimally Mexico. It will review disability discrimination legislation, including the Constitution, as well as other important legislation. The British model of government, which has influenced greatly the Canadian structure, sees the legislature making the laws and the judiciary applying them.[1] Parliamentary supremacy is not founded on democratic ideals, but rather a narrow power struggle representing property. However, the US model sees judicial activism and the judicial power as fundamentally legislative in character. Royal power is displaced and overthrown, but class power remains, with the upper class combining the popular republican form of government with the protection of property. Although neighbors, Canada and the United States have had separate histories and thus have undergone very different paths, with some rights having more of an impact in one country than the other.

Canada

Canada is a relatively young nation, founded officially by Confederation in 1867. While present Canada endorses multiculturalism, it is a country founded on the tale of 'two solitudes', English and French or Anglophone and Francophone, which lies at the heart of many a legal debate. While Canada is an officially bilingual country composed of ten provinces and three territories, it is important to note that the province of Quebec remains officially unilingually Francophone.

Canadian Constitution

The Canadian Constitution, which includes the Canadian Charter of Rights and Freedoms, was proclaimed into force and entrenched on 17 April 1982.[2] It is made up of three separate documents: the British North America Act and its various amendments, the Constitution Act and its amending formula, and the Canadian Charter of Rights and Freedoms, which encompasses Articles 1 to 34 inclusively. Section 32 of the Charter provides for its application to the Parliament and government of Canada, as well as to the legislature and government of each province.[3] The purpose of the Canadian Charter of Rights and Freedoms is to protect and safeguard the rights and freedoms enumerated, and to contain governmental action within reasonable limits. The supremacy of the Constitution is contained in Section 52(1) of the Constitution Act:

> 52(1) The Constitution of Canada is the supreme law of Canada and any law that is inconsistent with the provisions of the Constitution is, to the extent of the inconsistency, of no force or effect.[4]

Section 32 provides for its application to the Parliament and government of Canada, as well as to the legislature and government of each province.[5] The purpose of the Canadian Constitution was to protect and safeguard the rights and freedoms enumerated, and to contain governmental action within reasonable limits.

Fundamental Freedoms These are protected under Section 2 of the Charter, which states:

> 2. Everyone has the following fundamental freedoms:
> (a)   freedom of conscience and religion;
> (b)   freedom of thought, belief, opinion and expression, including freedom of the press and other means of communication;
> (c)   freedom of peaceful assembly; and
> (d)   freedom of association.[6]

Multiculturalism and Aboriginal Rights Section 27 provides:

> 27. This Charter shall be interpreted in a manner consistent with the preservation and enhancement of the multicultural heritage of Canadians.[7]

In terms of protection of native people's rights within the Constitution, Section 35(1) and (2), entitled 'Rights of the Aboriginal Peoples of Canada', states:

> 35(1) The existing aboriginal and treaty rights of the aboriginal peoples of Canada are hereby recognized and affirmed.
> (2) In this Act, 'aboriginal peoples of Canada' includes the Indian, Inuit and Métis peoples of Canada.[8]

Civil Rights Important for those with a disability, the Charter guarantees equality of rights, and also deals with affirmative action programs to help reverse the discrimination process. Section 15 came into effect on 17 April 1985 after a three-year implemented delay and states:

> 15(1) Every individual is equal before and under the law and has the right to the equal protection and equal benefit of the law without discrimination and, in particular, without discrimination based on race, national or ethnic origin, colour, religion, sex, age or mental or physical disability.
>
> (2) Subsection (1) does not preclude any law, program or activity that has as its object the amelioration of conditions of disadvantaged individuals or groups

including those that are disadvantaged because of race, national or ethnic origin, colour, religion, sex, age or mental or physical disability.[9]

Further, the Charter implements equality through Section 28, which states:

> 28. Notwithstanding anything in this Charter, the rights and freedoms referred to in it are guaranteed equally to male and female persons.[10]

This provision cannot be overridden by legislation or act of Parliament.

Provisions in Denial of Rights Section 33 of the Charter is the infamous 'notwithstanding' clause, allowing the Canadian provinces to opt out of the Constitution for successive and infinite five-year periods. It provides:

> 33. Parliament or the legislature of a province may expressly declare in an act of Parliament or of the legislature ... that the act or a provision thereof shall operate notwithstanding a provision included in ... Section ... 15 of this Charter.[11]

The Canadian Constitution extends power to judges to review legislative action on the basis of congruence with protected values in the Charter, and treats the judicial branch of government as a partner with the legislative and executive branches, in determining the rights of citizens. However, Section 33, the overriding clause, will ensure that legislatures rather than judges have the final say on important matters of public policy, so that laws offensive to certain provisions of the Charter may be upheld.

Section 1 of the Charter is also an overriding clause and states:

> 1. The Canadian Charter of Rights and Freedoms set out is subject only to such reasonable limits prescribed by law as can be demonstrably justified in a free and democratic society.[12]

Thus, fundamental freedoms, as well as legal and equality rights, can be subjected to this notwithstanding clause. Remarkably, the right against disability discrimination is not absolute. The Canadian Charter of Rights and Freedoms may be used to strengthen inequalities, by weighing in on the side of power, and undermine popular movements.

In terms of the burden of proof, Section 1 of the Charter has two functions: first, it guarantees the rights and freedoms set out in the provisions which follow it; and second, it states explicitly the exclusive justificatory criteria, outside of Section 33 of the Charter, against which limitations on those rights and freedoms may be measured. The onus of proving that a limitation on any Charter right is reasonable and demonstrably justified in a free and democratic society rests upon the party seeking to uphold the limitation. Limits on constitutionally guaranteed rights are clearly exceptions to the general guarantee. The presumption is that Charter rights are guaranteed unless the party invoking Section 1 can bring itself within the exceptional criteria justifying their being limited. The standard of proof under Section 1 is a preponderance of probabilities. Proof beyond a reasonable doubt would be unduly onerous on the party seeking to limit the right, because concepts such as 'reasonableness', 'justifiability' and 'free and democratic society' are not amenable to such a standard. Nevertheless, the preponderance of probability test must be applied rigorously. The Supreme Court of Canada uses the purposive approach to interpret the Charter, whereby the underlying purpose of the legislative provision and the nature of the interest are identified. A two-step procedure is utilized to see whether the limit of the Charter contained in Section 1 can uphold an infringement of a right. Two questions are asked: (1) has the right been violated?; and (2) can the violation be justified under Section 1? The burden of proof is such that the onus of establishing a prima facie infringement of the Charter is on the person alleging it, while the onus of justifying a reasonable limit on the protected right is on the party invoking Section 1. Two criteria must be satisfied in order to come within Section 1 of the Charter: (1) the objective of the limiting measure must be sufficiently important, and the concerns must be pressing and substantial to justify overriding a constitutionally protected right; and (2) the means must be reasonable and demonstrably justified according to a proportionality test, which balances the interests of society against those of individuals. There are three components to the test: (1) the measure must be carefully designed to achieve the stated objective, and must not be arbitrary, unfair or irrational; (2) the measure should impair the right as little as possible; and (3) proportionality must exist between the effect of the limiting measure and its objectives (*Regina v. Oakes*, [1986] 1 SCR 103).[13]

Canadian Bill of Rights

In addition to the Canadian Constitution, there is the Canadian Bill of Rights.

Fundamental Freedoms The Bill of Rights in Section 1 outlines the human rights and fundamental freedoms guaranteed. It states:

> 1. It is hereby recognized and declared that in Canada there have existed and shall continue to exist without discrimination by reason of race, national origin, colour, religion or sex, the following human rights and fundamental freedoms, namely,
> (a)   the right of the individual to life, liberty, security of the person and enjoyment of property and the right not to be deprived thereof except by due process of law;
> (b)   the right of the individual to equality before the law and the protection of the law;
> (c)   freedom of religion;
> (d)   freedom of speech;
> (e)   freedom of assembly and of association; and
> (f)   freedom of the press.[14]

Canadian Human Rights Act (CHRA)

The Canadian Human Rights Act (CHRA) was implemented and came into force on 1 March 1978. It has been very influential for those seeking relief from human rights abuses and discrimination through a channel other than the traditional court system, namely the Canadian Human Rights Tribunal (CHRT). The Act implements a complaint process through a commission, which assumes that systemic discrimination does not exist but for a few cases. It differs from a proactive approach, which places an obligation on the employer to determine if systemic wage discrimination exists and to remedy it within a time frame. The Canadian Human Rights Commission (CHRC) administers the CHRA, in trying to ensure the principles of equal opportunity and non-discrimination within federal jurisdiction, that is the federal public service and federally regulated employers. The CHRA features a 'duty of accommodation' which requires employers to address the needs of people who are protected under the CHRA, including persons with disabilities, and creates a smaller, permanent human rights tribunal, which will improve the tribunal's ability to hear and make decisions about cases effectively and efficiently.

Disability is defined under Section 25:

> 25. 'Disability' means any previous or existing mental or physical disability and includes disfigurement and previous or existing dependence on alcohol or a drug.[15]

Further, important for those with a disability, the purpose of the CHRA is outlined in Section 2:

> 2. The purpose of this Act is to extend the laws in Canada to give effect, within the purview of matters coming within the legislative authority of Parliament, to the principle that all individuals should have an opportunity equal with other individuals to make for themselves the lives that they are able and wish to have and to have their needs accommodated, consistent with their duties and obligations as members of society, without being hindered in or prevented from doing so by discriminatory practices based on race, national or ethnic origin, colour, religion, age, sex, sexual orientation, marital status, family status, disability or conviction for an offence for which a pardon has been granted.[16]

In addition, Section 3 (1) states:

> 3(1). For all purposes of this Act, race, national or ethnic origin, colour, religion, age, sex, marital status, family status, disability and conviction for which a pardon has been granted are prohibited grounds of discrimination.[17]

Sections 7 and 10 go on to enumerate what is considered to be discriminatory:

> 7. It is a discriminatory practice, directly or indirectly:
> (a)   to refuse to employ or continue to employ any individual, or

(b)   in the course of employment, to differentiate adversely in relation to an employee, on a prohibited ground of discrimination. [1976~77, c.33, s.7.3][18]

10.   It is a discriminatory practice for an employer, employee organization or organization of employers:

(a)   to establish or pursue a policy or practice, or

(b)   to enter into an agreement affecting recruitment, referral, hiring, promotion, training, apprenticeship, transfer or any other matter relating to employment or prospective employment, that deprives or tends to deprive an individual or class of individuals of any employment opportunities on a prohibited ground of discrimination. [1976~77, c.33, s.l0; 1980~81~82~83, c.143, s.5.][19]

Under Section 11, it is discriminatory directly or indirectly to refuse to employ or, in the course of employment, to differentiate adversely against an employee in recruitment, referral, hiring, promotion, training or transfer policies:

11(2) In assessing the value of work performed by employees employed in the same establishment, the criterion to be applied is the composite of the skill, effort and responsibility required in the performance of the work and the conditions under which the work is performed.[20]

Further, Section 15(1) allows for a bona fide occupational exception:

15(1) It is not a discriminatory practice if
(a) any refusal, exclusion, expulsion, suspension, limitation, specification or preference in relation to any employment is established by an employer to be based on a *bona fide* occupational requirement.[21]

However, special programs, including for those with a disability, are allowed under Section 16, which states:

16. It is not a discriminatory practice for a person to adopt or carry out a special program, plan or arrangement designed to prevent disadvantages that are likely to be suffered by, or to eliminate or reduce disadvantages that are suffered by, any group of individuals when those disadvantages would be or are based on or related to the race, national or ethnic origin, colour, religion, age, sex, marital status, family status or disability of members of that group, by improving opportunities respecting goods, services, facilities, accommodation or employment in relation to that group.[22]

Further, Section 17 outlines a disability plan:

17. (1) A person who proposes to implement a plan for adapting any services, facilities, premises, equipment or operations to meet the needs of persons arising from a disability may apply to the Canadian Human Rights Commission for approval of the plan.

(2) The Commission may, by written notice to a person making an application pursuant to subsection (1), approve the plan if the Commission is satisfied that the plan is appropriate for meeting the needs of persons arising from a disability.[23]

Finally, Section 48(1) establishes the Canadian Human Rights Tribunal.[24]

The CHRA looks at comparable worth, applying the same wages where respective work is shown to be equal in value through a combination of skill, effort, responsibility and working conditions. It thereby makes comparisons between dissimilar jobs. It is a discriminatory practice to establish different wages, so that if people do work of equal value in the same establishment then they must be paid equally. Discriminatory practices for wage inequities include segregated employment, exclusion of those categorically from the existing evaluation system, under-valuation of certain positions, fewer promotion opportunities, senior rules disadvantaging some groups, and discriminatory transfers, promotion and layoffs.[25] Discrimination includes practices or attitudes, whether by design or impact, which have the effect of limiting the individual's right to the opportunities generally available, because of attributes such as disability rather than actual characteristics. There are, however, some reasonable factors to permit a pay difference, such as periodic pay increases for length of service or working in remote locations. The CHRC only has jurisdiction over the federal public service and federally regulated employers in the quest for equal pay for work of equal value. One drawback to the federal law is that it is limited to comparisons within the same establishment.

However, in terms of the onus of proof with respect to a complaint under the Act, the burden and order of proof in discrimination cases involving refusal of employment appears clear and constant through all Canadian jurisdictions: a complainant must first establish a prima facie case of discrimination; once that is done the burden shifts to the respondent to provide a reasonable explanation for the otherwise discriminatory behavior. Thereafter, assuming the employer has provided an explanation, the complainant has the eventual burden of showing that the explanation provided was merely 'pretext' and that the true motivation behind the employer's actions was in fact discriminatory (*Basi v. Canadian National Railway* (1984), 9 CHRR 4. D/5029, 5037 (CHRTribunal)).[26]

In an employment complaint, the Commission usually establishes a prima facie case by proving: (1) that the complainant was qualified for the particular employment; (2) that the complainant was not hired; and (3) that someone no better qualified but lacking the distinguishing feature which is the gravamen of the human rights complaint subsequently obtained the position. If these elements are proved, there is an evidentiary onus on the respondent to provide an explanation of events equally consistent with the conclusion that discrimination on the basis prohibited by the Code is not the correct explanation of what occurred (*Shakes v. Rex Pak Ltd.* (1982), 3 CHRR D/1001, 1002).[27] Should the respondent provide evidence of a non-discriminatory reason for refusing to employ the complainant, then the Complainant and the Commission can still establish that the reason advanced for non-employment is in fact a pretext, and that discrimination on an unlawful ground was one of the operative reasons for the respondent's actions (*Blake v. Ministry of Correctional Services and Mimico Correctional Institute*

(1984), 5 CHRR D/2417 (Ontario)).[28] The ultimate onus of proof to establish the complaint on a balance of probabilities lies with the Complainant and the Commission. Discrimination can be established by direct evidence or by circumstantial evidence, which is evidence that is consistent with the fact that is sought to be proven and inconsistent with any other rational conclusion. It is not necessary to find that the respondent intended to discriminate against the complainant. It is sufficient to establish the complaint if it is found, on the balance of probabilities, that the respondent in fact discriminated against the Complainant on one of the grounds alleged in their complaint (*Ontario Human Rights Commission v. Simpsons-Sears Ltd.*, [1985] SCR 536, 547).[29]

There are three essential steps in developing a special program: to identify as problems, areas within the organization in which the labor force is unrepresentative; to determine how the problems relate to organization policies, practices and procedures, both formal and informal; and to formulate solutions that aim to remove existing barriers and to forward equitable representation. The criteria that indicate the need for a special program are: observable absence of members of certain groups in particular job categories or in the organization as a whole; existence of particularly high unemployment rates among certain groups; internal complaints and grievances from employees; external complaints by individuals or groups; inability of the organization to recruit or retain employees in terms of high turnover; and complaints filed with the CHRC alleging discriminatory practices. The primary objective of a special program is to increase the representiveness of the organization's labor force in some specific way. In setting objectives specific to the organization, the following factors must be considered: objectives should be quantitative, namely targets or goals; objectives should aim to correct underutilization or overconcentration where they occur in an organization; objectives must be specific as to target group and should also specify job category and geographical area; objectives must be attainable within specific and reasonable timeframes. A special program is intended to be a temporary measure that should never outlive the identified problem of disadvantage, although the achievement of objectives will result in permanent organizational changes; objectives should realistically reflect the ability of the organization to respond to change; objectives must take into consideration the continuing rights of individuals, especially employees, not belonging to designated target groups; and objectives will be framed with care to be sensitive to the feelings and expectations of staff, including members of the target groups.

Canada Employment Equity Act

Important for those with a disability, the purpose of the Canada Employment Equity Act 1995, as outlined in Section 2, is to achieve equality in the workplace so that no person shall be denied employment opportunities or benefits for reasons unrelated to ability and, in the fulfilment of that goal, to correct the conditions of disadvantage in employment experienced by members of visible minorities, aboriginal peoples, women and persons with disabilities, and by giving effect to the principle that employment equity means more than treating persons in the same way but also requires special measures and the accommodation of differences.[30] The Employment Equity Act covers the federal government, including the public service and crown corporations, as well as federally-regulated private sector employers with 100 or more employees, and addresses four designated groups: persons with disabilities, women, Aboriginal peoples and visible minorities. The Canadian Human Rights Commission is responsible for enforcing the obligations of employers to implement employment equity.

Section 5 establishes a duty of employers:

> 5. Every employer shall implement employment equity by
> (*a*) identifying and eliminating employment barriers against persons in designated groups that result from the employer's employment systems, policies and practices that are not authorized by law; and
> (*b*) instituting such positive policies and practices and making such reasonable accommodations as will ensure that persons in designated groups achieve a degree of representation in each occupational group in the employer's workforce that reflects their representation in
> (i) the Canadian workforce, or
> (ii) those segments of the Canadian workforce that are identifiable by qualification, eligibility or geography and from which the employer may reasonably be expected to draw employees.[31]

Further, Section 6 states that the obligation to implement employment equity does not require an employer to take a particular measure to implement employment equity where the taking of that measure would cause undue hardship to the employer; to hire or promote unqualified persons; with respect to the public sector, to hire or promote persons without basing the hiring or promotion on selection according to merit in cases where the Public Service Employment Act requires that hiring or promotion be based on selection according to merit; or to create new positions in its workforce.[32]

Section 10 provides for the implementation of an employment equity plan:

> 10. (1) The employer shall prepare an employment equity plan that
> (*a*) specifies the positive policies and practices that are to be instituted by the employer in the short term for the hiring, training, promotion and retention of persons in designated groups and for the making of reasonable accommodations for those persons, to correct the underrepresentation of those persons identified by the analysis ...;
> (*b*) specifies the measures to be taken by the employer in the short term for the elimination of any employment barriers identified by the review ...;
> (*c*) establishes a timetable for the implementation of the matters referred to in paragraphs (*a*) and (*b*);
> (*d*) where underrepresentation has been identified by the analysis, establishes short term numerical goals for the hiring and promotion of persons in designated groups in order to increase their representation in each occupational group in the workforce in which underrepresentation has been identified and sets out measures to be taken in each year to meet those goals;

(*e*) sets out the employer's longer term goals for increasing the representation of persons in designated groups in the employer's workforce and the employer's strategy for achieving those goals; and

(*f*) provides for any other matter that may be prescribed.[33]

Under Section 29, a Tribunal may, in the same manner and to the same extent as a superior court of record, summon and enforce the attendance of witnesses and compel them to give oral and written evidence on oath and to produce such documents and things as the Tribunal considers necessary for a full review; administer oaths; and receive and accept such evidence and other information, whether on oath or by affidavit or otherwise, as the Tribunal sees fit, whether or not that evidence or information would be admissible in a court of law.[34]

Overall, Canada has gradually evolved a framework of legislation to protect the rights of persons with disabilities which are within the jurisdiction of the Government of Canada. The Framework to Improve the Social Union for Canadians reflects 'the fundamental values of Canadians, equality, respect for diversity, fairness, individual dignity and responsibility, and mutual aid and our responsibilities for one another', encompassing the following principles: All Canadians are equal and it is important to promote equality of opportunity for all Canadians; Governments have a responsibility to meet the needs of Canadians and to ensure access for all, wherever they live or move in Canada, to essential social programs and services of reasonably comparable quality; provide appropriate assistance to those in need; and promote the full and active participation of all Canadians in Canada's social and economic life; and Governments have a responsibility to sustain social programs and services. Further, a Federal Task Force was established to look at the appropriate role for the Federal Government in the area of disability issues.[35]

In terms of citizenship, the concept offers a sense of belonging in one's country and gives each individual the right to participate in society and in its economic and political systems. It confers the protection of the State within Canada and abroad, while requiring individuals to obey this country's laws. In terms of a more complete set of rights, popular conceptions of citizenship incorporate an increasingly complete set of rights. From 'civil rights' such as freedom of speech, thought and faith, citizenship came to include 'political rights' as expressed by the right to hold office or to vote. Most recently, twentieth century citizenship is understood to comprise not only these but also 'social and economic rights'. These are the level of well-being and security that are required to exist in a society. They represent a commitment that there will be no internal 'borders' and that all those who call a particular country home can participate fully in the life of the community. Section 15 of the Charter has become a touchstone for people with disabilities. However, as we have seen, the Charter has its limits.

Social and economic rights as a set of guiding principles are more a result of a consensus in society than they are the outcome of constitutional protections. The consensus that the federal government had an obligation to address these rights formed the basis for the social programs established during the three decades after the Second World War. It was the rationale for the introduction of the original programs in the 1950s and 1960s that made provision for pensions for people with disabilities, and later for the Canada Assistance Plan, which provided many of the disability-related supports and services that they require to participate in the life of their community. Conceived as a matter of right, the arguments that were used to build support for these income, education and health initiatives rested on the requirement of the federal government to provide leadership and to acknowledge the rights of Canadian citizens to have access to inclusive social and economic measures. These initiatives can be seen as the complement to equalization measures that have been put in place to deal with regional inequities. As a result, citizenship has come to be understood as a commitment, by governments and particularly the Government, that individuals will not be discriminated against or marginalized. It is also a commitment to provide, in an equitable way, high quality accessible services from sea to sea to sea.

In terms of inclusion, the principle of inclusiveness implied in Canadian citizenship gives the Government a base for its approach to today's requirements. The federal government should promote the equality commitments contained in the international and national instruments that underpin full citizenship. It should also support programs and policies that help all Canadians participate effectively in the economic and social mainstream. The Government should concern itself with ways to minimize or eliminate additional disadvantages of costs and lack of mobility that Canadian citizens face because they have disabilities. This means that every government program should incorporate the individual and particular needs of persons with disabilities in the very core of its design.

At the same time, the additional disadvantages that result from disabilities cannot always be accommodated in each and every mainstream program. Where this is the case, a complementary measure, designed to mesh with the generic program, can be put in place to ensure that no one is denied the opportunity to participate just because of disability. An initial program design that accommodates people with disabilities and that links to other programs will have a reasonable cost and might save money. The Government should acknowledge and act on its responsibility for citizens with disabilities to ensure equality and to promote their full inclusion and participation in the life of the country. Given its own significant role in ensuring a broadly based Canadian citizenship, the Government should establish a pan-Canadian approach to disability issues, that builds disability considerations into mainstream policies and programs in all areas. Where mainstream programs cannot completely eliminate the additional disadvantage of men and women with disabilities, this process must identify complementary action that enables them to benefit fully from mainstream programs. It should include in these discussions clear statements of values, principles and objectives which fully include people with disabilities in Canadian society.

The Government should demonstrate its commitment to consistent action and accountability by taking action at the political level to put in place a 'disability lens' for use by all ministers and members of the Government when they are taking decisions, which would include an assessment of the effect on people with disabilities in all relevant items that are submitted to Government. Further, in terms of government programs, it should demonstrate its commitment to consistent action and accountability by deciding that relevant government programs must set aside funds to promote accessibility for people with disabilities. An accountability mechanism is needed to ensure reconciliation between the needs of Canadians with disabilities with changing programs, policies and laws, and to ensure that the change process continues apace. There are advantages and disadvantages with any approach to keeping government accountable for its actions. The Government should demonstrate its commitment to consistent action and accountability by establishing an accountability mechanism to analyze social spending and all federal activities in support of disability and to monitor and report on checks and balances throughout the federal system.

Importantly, the disability policy framework suggested for government action must address problems in Canada's laws and regulations. Historical stereotypes and prejudices persist in some federal laws, characterizing people with disabilities as dependent, incapable and in need of charity. This depiction must be replaced with a model of equality that promotes the right to full participation in society; an entitlement to adequate supports to live in the community; the right to choice and control over one's life; and the right to dignity, respect, autonomy and self-determination. The framework must also ensure that existing and proposed laws do not create additional disadvantages for Canadians with disabilities. Out-of-date laws and programs reflect a belief that the needs of people with disabilities could be handled through income-support programs, institutional care, and programs, policies, laws and regulations that would 'protect' them. The Canadian Charter of Rights and Freedoms and the Canadian Human Rights Act prohibit discrimination based on mental or physical disability. Federal laws and policies, indeed all government activity, must follow the principles and values set out in the Charter.   It is essential for the principles and values in the Charter to be applied in a more effective way to new laws, regulations, policies, programs and procedures as they are developed; and existing laws, regulations, policies, programs and procedures that put Canadians with disabilities at a disadvantage, before these are challenged in the courts. While the federal government aims for and expects that its laws will not discriminate in their intent or effect, the reality is that, while many laws do not actively discriminate against Canadians with disabilities, their effects are discriminatory.   In terms of the legislative review process, the Government needs to establish an ongoing strategy and process to review laws, regulations, policies, practices and rules to remove barriers to full participation and ensure the equality of people with disabilities. This process can be used to apply a disability-based analysis to new policy, program and legislative initiatives and to plan for a comprehensive review of existing ones.

Canada's labor market is evolving. New types of jobs are appearing in the workplace as others disappear. Governments are trying to respond to these changes and are working to ensure that all Canadians can participate in the new economy. At the same time, the federal, provincial and territorial governments are reorganizing responsibilities for training and other programs and services related to the labor market. People with disabilities, who have been marginalized in the past, must be included in all planning for new and existing labor market programming at all levels if they are to become part of Canada's economic mainstream. Work is important, and is among the top concerns of Canadians with disabilities. It is important for the dignity of individuals, the dignity of work, the sense of accomplishment it brings them, its value to the community and to society, and the way it contributes to a sense of belonging. The tangible benefits of income, learning, and participating in the goals of an enterprise give us a sense of control over our destiny. Work is fundamental to one's sense of well-being and to citizenship. While Canada's skilled workforce is at the centre of the competitive advantage in the world, it is not capitalizing on the potential of a large segment of the working age population. At the same time, despite the struggle to create employment programs and supports that respond to the needs of workers with disabilities, and of some potential employers, there remain significant barriers to employment for Canadians with disabilities. The environments of the Canadian workplace and the economic system have a greater impact on the extent to which people with disabilities become employed or find themselves out of the workforce than does the nature of any individual's particular disabilities. Working age women and men with disabilities face attitudinal, systemic and physical barriers that make it difficult for them to prepare for, find, get and keep jobs. While quotas are not the answer, fairness is. It must be acknowledged that many of the barriers to employment and independence are the result of policies, regulations, guidelines and administration that simply ignore the individual circumstances of women and men with disabilities. Additional investments required to address these barriers will be worthwhile. Experience and research have shown that many Canadians with disabilities are ready to join the workforce and await only the necessary preparation and opportunity.

In terms of an inclusive labor market, a vision of an inclusive labor market is one in which programs and services are designed in consultation with people with disabilities, in which employers hire individuals on the basis of their skills and abilities, and accommodating different ways to get work done happens as a matter of course in the workplace. Inclusiveness should be a matter of 'business as usual'. The ideal world would be one in which 'mainstream' labor market programs fully accommodated the needs of people with disabilities and provided for additional complementary programs for these Canadians where necessary. The Government must work to make its mainstream employment and related programs fully accessible to people with disabilities. The Government should put in place operational, administrative and evaluative mechanisms to ensure that the labor market needs of people with disabilities are served by programs and services for which it retains or shares responsibility. It should provide appropriate supports to local managers to help them include people with disabilities among their clients and ensure that local managers are aware that they will be measured or evaluated on their ability to serve people with disabilities. A secure income is fundamental to the ability to enjoy the rights of citizenship. Without a secure income, an individual cannot satisfy the most basic living needs. This is especially true for some people who cannot work because of severe disabilities, and those who face significant barriers to workforce participation. Canadian citizenship implies that the federal government will be involved in ensuring and protecting the right of people with disabilities to a secure income. The Federal government was the first Canadian government to make a disability income available. It has been said that the best form of income support is a job. While a secure income gives us access to the basic necessities of life, a job gives us a sense of purpose and a sense of belonging.

Living with a disability almost always entails additional costs. These costs, which vary significantly from one individual to another, are currently paid for by the public system, by a private insurer, or by the person who has a disability. A person with a disability may need to cover the cost of a special diet or nutritional supplements. There are extra costs to make one's home accessible, or for personal supports and services, technical aids and devices, and the intangible costs associated with daily living that are greater because of disability. These are the costs of disability. The Government should recognize that measures that deal with the costs of disability need to be separated from measures that provide income to persons with disabilities. It should work with the provinces to deal with the direct costs of disability in order to identify key elements that could be funded through a pan-Canadian program; to devise new approaches to ensuring that disability-related supports are in place consistent with economic participation and citizenship; and to identify the transitional financing issues that need to be addressed through federal-provincial collaboration.

Sometimes a whisper has a more profound impact than a shout. For the last several years, Canadians with disabilities have quietly stated their case for action that recognizes and promotes their full and equal participation in the life of their country. While their arguments have been listened to at the political level and by governments, there has been a growing gap between saying and doing. Individuals with disabilities spoke forcefully about the conditions that they believe are essential:

They want a country that demonstrates vision and leadership; common principles and values for disability issues.

They want a country that ensures that people with disabilities have input into policy, programs and decision making; that takes a holistic approach to disability issues, spanning issues related to income, employment education and other areas of life; that recognizes the importance of sharing information to achieve this end.

They want a country that makes it possible for all to achieve a decent standard of living, and to contribute to the standard of living of all; that addresses the social causes of disadvantages related to disability.

They want a country that adopts a common approach to disability issues in all jurisdictions but that is sensitive to individual differences and needs; that guarantees access to similar disability-related supports in all regions, and that holds governments accountable to ensure that this is so.

They want a country that makes disability program arrangements secure and predictable; that ensures that core funding and other financial support are available for disability-related organizations.

They want a country that uses legal and other carrots and sticks to promote social and economic equity and equality of outcomes.

People were equally clear about how they felt current circumstances limited their inclusion in Canadian life no matter where they lived.

They pointed to barriers that they face in trying to participate in the country's social and economic life:

They expressed fear that current attitudes of support for leaner and meaner' governments, the shift to private responsibility, and a growing burden on those who provide services, will lead to greater inequities.

They spoke of poverty, a state that too many knew only too well.

They spoke of barriers to their mobility in this Canada because disability issues generally and services in particular, are the responsibility of many separate governments and organizations.

They lamented public ignorance about disability and the inadequate support for disability organizations that could help effect changes.

They said they were looking for leadership, for a sense that governments and particularly the Government of Canada have a vision of what should be.

They said that they were excluded from decisions about things that affect them and they pointed out that society often seems to blame individuals for the consequences of disability instead of looking for the causes of inequity in the social environment.

As people brought these issues to our attention, they urged the Government to act on the recommendations of previous reports, and expressed complete frustration that worthwhile action had been postponed for no apparent reason. People told us in three blunt words: Just do it![36]

Mexico

Constitución Política de los Estados Unidos Mexicanos

The equality of all persons before the law is guaranteed by the Constitución Política de los Estados Unidos Mexicanos, the Political Constitution of the United Mexican States.[37] Article 1 establishes that all individuals shall enjoy the guarantees set down by the Constitution, which may not be restricted or suspended, except in those cases and conditions established therein.[38] In terms of equality in employment, Article 123(7) establishes that equal work performed in the same post, with the same hours worked and conditions of efficiency shall also be remunerated with the same salary.[39]

Ley Federal de Trabajo

The entitlement to equal opportunities is set down in Article 3 and Article 164 of the Ley Federal de Trabajo (LFT), the Federal Labor Law.[40] Article 1 states that no discrimination may be established between workers.[41] Article 86 establishes that equal work performed in the same post, with the same hours worked and conditions of efficiency shall also be remunerated with the same salary.[42] Although there is no unemployment insurance per se, Articles 50 and 52 of the LFT establish an obligation on the part of employers to pay compensation to unfairly dismissed workers, who also have the option to be reinstated to the same job.[43] If the worker is discharged without justification, and his employment is for a specified period, the worker is entitled to receive a severance payment equal to the wages received for half of the time of work with the same employer. For those workers with more than one year of service, severance payment is equal to six months' wages for the first year of service plus 20 days' wages for each additional year of service. For workers with labor contracts of unspecified duration, severance payment is equal to three months' wages, and they would also have the right to receive wages for the period between the day of dismissal and the day the severance compensation is paid. If a worker asks to be reinstated and the employer refuses, he has the right to receive 20 days-wages for each year of service in addition to the above.

Ley del Seguro Social

In terms of retirement income and health benefits, the social security system administered by the IMSS covers a broad range of social insurance, including work risks, illness and maternity, disability and life, retirement and dismissal due to old age, and nursery facilities for children, as well as other social benefits. The system is financed by premiums paid by employers, employees and by contributions by the federal government. Premiums paid by the employer are equal to 8.5 per cent of insurable earnings plus 13.9 per cent of the minimum wage in the Distrito Federal for illness and maternity insurance plus a variable portion for work risks insurance. Employees' premiums are equal to two per cent of their insurable earnings. In the case of workers receiving the minimum wage, employers are obliged to pay the entire premium, according to Article 36.[44] As of July 1997, contributions for the retirement insurance scheme are administered by means of individual accounts handled by private companies known as Administradores de Fondos para el Retiro de los Trabajadores (AFORES), Worker Retirement Fund Administrators.

United States of America

Declaration of Independence

The concepts of equality and good government, found in the US judicial system, were equally important principles to the Founding Fathers of the United States. The Declaration of Independence 1776, the bedrock of the United States' jurisprudence system, was enshrined on 4 July 1776. It fundamentally states:

> We hold these truths to be self-evident, that all men are created equal; that they are endowed by their Creator with certain unalienable rights; that among these are

life, liberty and the pursuit of happiness. That, to secure these rights, governments are instituted among men, deriving their just powers from the consent of the governed; that whenever any form of government becomes destructive of these ends, it is the right of the people to alter or to abolish it, and to institute a new government, laying its foundation on such principles, and organize its powers in such form, as to them shall seem most likely to effect their safety and happiness.[45]

Federalist Papers

Influential thinkers, such as Jefferson, Madison and Jay, believed in a national government and a Bill of Rights, which they outlined in the Federalist Papers 1787~88. Government is seen as essential to the security of liberty, with every citizen ceding some rights for the protection thereof. The diversities in the faculties of men are recognized as where property rights originate. The objective of government is to secure the public good and private rights against the danger of factions, with the most common source of faction being the unequal distribution of property. The purpose of the Union is the common defence of the members, so that the means are proportionate to the ends. Government must act before the public, and must be derived from the body of society. The Constitution is founded on the assent and ratification of the people, and every man who loves liberty must cherish the attachment to the Union and preserve it. Among the three branches of government, the Judicial branch is considered the least dangerous to the political rights of the Constitution. The Executive branch dispenses the honors and holds the sword, the Legislative branch controls the purse and prescribes the rules to regulate duties and rights, and the Judiciary has no influence over the sword or the purse, needing the aid of the Executive for the efficacy of judgments. Oppression can proceed from the Courts, but liberty will not be endangered if the branches are separate. The Constitution is the fundamental law of the land. 'We, the people of the United States, to secure the blessings of liberty to ourselves and our prosperity, do ordain and establish this Constitution for the United States of America'. As a recognition of popular rights, the judgments of many unite into one, with the voluntary consent of a whole people.[46]

The Federalist Papers give us an important insight into the making of the Constitution, showing us early on the concept of equality of man and the formation of one government out of many people. The importance of the Judiciary must not be overlooked, as it is a major contributor of policy through its judgments, often itself influencing the sword, the Executive, and the purse, the Legislative. American constitutionalism is the product of the revolutionary movement in political thought of Hobbes, the parent of the modern American political process.[47] The chief purpose of political institutions is the management of social conflict. According to Hobbes, the only source of public authority is the private need of independently situated political actors, with a prior right to act based on self-defined standards of conscience and interest. If used wisely, the Constitution can serve to remedy past injustices of disability discrimination.

United States Constitution

Fundamental Freedoms The First Amendment to the Constitution, enacted in 1791, guarantees the freedoms of religion and expression. It states:

> Amendment I
> Congress shall make no law respecting an establishment of religion, or prohibiting the free exercise thereof; or abridging the freedom of speech, or of the press; or the right of the people peaceably to assemble, and to petition the government for a redress of grievances.[48]

Civil Rights Important for those with a disability, the Fifth and Fourteenth Amendments of the Constitution, enacted in 1791 and 1868 respectively, are of paramount importance in the fight for human rights. With the due process clause of the Fifth Amendment including an equal protection component, the Fifth and Fourteenth Amendments provide due process of law and equal protection to citizens from federal and state actions, respectively. They thus prohibit government from invidious discrimination. The clauses state:

> Amendment V
> No person shall ... be deprived of life, liberty, or property, without due process of law ....[49]

> Amendment XIV
> 1.   No state shall make or enforce any law which shall abridge the privileges or immunities of citizens of the United States; nor shall any state deprive any person of life, liberty, or property, without due process of law; nor deny to any person within its jurisdiction the equal protection of the laws.[50]

The 39th Article of the Magna Carta of 1215 is a foundation for the Fifth and Fourteenth Amendments of the American Constitution regarding due process and the rights of life, liberty and property. The Magna Carta states:

> No free man shall be taken or imprisoned or dispossessed, or outlawed or banished, or in any way destroyed, nor will we go upon him nor send upon him, except by the legal judgement of his peers or by the law of the land.[51]

Further, the Thirteenth Amendment, enacted in 1865, was the initial step in ending a great injustice in the United States, which had lasted for centuries, namely slavery. It states:

> Amendment XIII
> 1. Neither slavery nor involuntary servitude, except as a punishment for crime whereof the party shall have been duly convicted, shall exist within the United States, or any place subject to their jurisdiction.[52]

The American Founding Fathers designed the United States Constitution to be a set of broad guidelines established by free and intelligent men for the government of free and intelligent people for successive generations. It has survived for over two hundred years due to the common sense of the American people, the prudence of their representatives, and the calculated wisdom of its judicial interpreters, the Supreme Court of the United States.[53] Chief Justice Marshall said of the Constitution, 'It was intended to endure for ages to come and consequentially to be adapted to the various crises of human affairs' (*McCullough v. Maryland*, 4 Wheaton 415 (1819)).[54] It was a common opinion that each branch of government in matters pertaining to itself be the final judge of its own powers. However, it was the function of the judiciary, and especially the Supreme Court, to construe in the last resort the meaning of the Constitution, with its opinion final and binding. Justice Hughes stated, 'We are under a Constitution but the Constitution is what the judges say it is'. The United States Constitution, through Article 6(2) known as the Supremacy Clause, is the supreme law of the land:

> 6(2) This Constitution, and the Laws of the United States which shall be made in Pursuance thereof; and all Treaties made, or which shall be made, under the Authority of the United States, shall be the supreme Law of the Land; and the Judges in every State shall be bound thereby, any Thing in the Constitution or Laws of any State to the Contrary notwithstanding.[55]

The seminal case of *Marbury v. Madison*, 1 Cranch 137 (1803), brought forth the important principles that (1) the Constitution is the supreme law of the land; (2) the powers granted to various branches of government are limited; and (3) the sole and essential function of the Court is to determine which law should prevail in conflict of laws.[56]

In a dynamic society, the creativity of judges is important for the development of law and the adaptability of the Constitution to the needs of modern society, according to the Realist Theory. Courts are the best means for recognizing social change, in order to focus social attitudes on unachieved goals and assist in their attainment through a decision-making process of judgments and thus policy-making, according to the Free Legal Decision Sociological Jurisprudence Theory.[57] History has a record of the past and provides the Court with a reservoir of social wisdom and political insight. It points out the evils against which the great constitutional clauses were designed as remedies. The adjudicative process depends on a delicate symbiotic relationship, whereby the Court must know us better than we know ourselves, acting as a voice of the spirit to remind us of our better selves.[58] It provides a stimulus and quickens moral education. However, the roots of the Supreme Court's decisions must be already in the nation. The aspirations voiced by the Court must be those the community is willing not only to avow but in the end to live by. For the power of the great constitutional decisions rests upon the accuracy of the Court's perceptions of this kind of common will and upon its ability ultimately to command a consensus. The rule of law, the capacity to command free assent, is the substitute for power.[59] Law is the fabric of a free society, organized with a minimum of force and a maximum of reason, in an ideal sense of right and justice. A neutral government, with its various branches, serves only as a participant in the inhumanities of its citizens.

In terms of the burden of proof, the United States Supreme Court examines the legislative purpose of the governmental action alleged to be contrary to existing legislation. The cause of action is examined to see whether a Plaintiff is a member of a class, which as a matter of law can invoke the power of the court. The equal protection clause and the due process clause of the Constitutional Amendments confer a constitutional right to be free from discrimination, which does not serve an important government objective or is not substantially related to the achievement of the objective (*Davis v. Passman*, 442 US 228 (1979)).[60] Importantly, in terms of the burden of proof, over the years, in examining court challenges, the United States Supreme Court has developed three different levels of review and accompanying burden of proof, depending upon the type of action brought in a legal proceeding. The Court will first examine the legislative purpose of the governmental action alleged to be contrary to the constitutional amendments, and the plaintiff's burden to prove his case will then come into play. The three levels of review are: (1) the minimum rationality level applied to see the rational basis for the means to the ends; (2) the heightened scrutiny level where the defendant government must show that the restriction has a substantial relationship to an important government interest, applied in quasi-suspect classifications, such as gender discrimination cases; and (3) most importantly, the strict scrutiny level where the defendant government must show a compelling interest for the restriction, a hard burden to meet, applied in suspect classifications affecting fundamental rights, such as racial discrimination cases. Thus, the concept of the burden of proof is an important element in court cases. In the fight for equal rights without regard to disability, it is true that those with a disability have achieved some gains. However, some would say disability, like race, should be considered suspect and thus be subject to the highest level of review of strict scrutiny. Until such time, those with a disability may wish to argue cases not only on the basis of disability discrimination but more importantly on the basis of gender or, even more, race discrimination in order to fall under the highest level strict scrutiny standard.

Although, the American Constitution is the paramount tool for redressing wrongs, the judicial system in the United States has seen the use of two acts, the Equal Pay Act and the Civil Rights Act as alternatives to the Constitution, with the latter having been the most successful in guarding against discrimination.

Equal Pay Act

Important for women with a disability, the Equal Pay Act 1963 established that it was unlawful for an employer to pay unequal wages for equal work based on a discriminatory distinction.[61] An exception was made where there was a system of (1) seniority; (2) merit; (3) earnings based on quantity or quality of production; or (4) something other than gender. Section 16 of the Equal Pay Act states:

16. No employer having employees ... shall discriminate, within any establishment ... between employees on the basis of sex by paying wages to employees in such establishment at a rate less than the rate at which he pays wages to employees of the opposite sex in such establishment for equal work on jobs the performance of which requires equal skill, effort and responsibility, and which are performed under similar working conditions except where such payment is made pursuant to 1) a seniority system, 2) a merit system, 3) a system which measures earnings by quantity or quality of product or 4) a differential based on any other factor other than sex.[62]

The Equal Pay Act only includes jobs that are very much alike or closely related, considered virtually or substantially identical (*Brennan v. City Stores*, 479 F.2d. 235 (1973)).[63] Jobs though not identical can be considered equal for Equal Pay Act standards, if there is only an insubstantial difference in skill, effort and responsibility (*Murphy v. Miller Brewer Co.*, 307 F.Supp. 829 (1969)).[64] For the Equal Pay Act, there is discrimination when there is a different wage rate for equal work, that is work which requires equal skill, effort and responsibility under similar working conditions (*Corning Glass v. Brennan*, 417 US 188 (1974)).[65] Equal protection is violated only by intentional discrimination, and a different impact standing alone is not enough. Further, there is no legal duty to undo the effects of previous discrimination (*American Nurses' Association v. State of Illinois*, 783 F.2d. 716 (1986)).[66] In terms of the burden of proof, therefore, the plaintiff has the burden of establishing that equal pay for equal work was not received. Then, the defendant must show the different wages were based on seniority, merit, a quantitative or qualitative system, or reasons other than sex (*Spaulding v. University of Washington*, 740 F.2d. 686 (1984)).[67] The court, however, is concerned with the actual job performance and content, not job description, titles or classifications, and the scrutiny is done on a case by case basis. If skill is irrelevant to job requirements, it is not considered. Therefore, a non-job related pretext can act as a shield for invidious discrimination.

Civil Rights Act

Important for minorities with a disability, the Civil Rights Act 1964 was implemented to safeguard important civil liberties. It serves to strengthen legislation, thereby helping the courts rule against discrimination. Section 703(a) of Title VII, the Civil Rights Act, states:

703(a) It shall be an unlawful employment practice for an employer, (1) to fail or refuse to hire or to discharge any individual, or otherwise to discriminate against any individual with respect to his compensation, terms, conditions, or privilege of employment, because of such individual's race, color, religion, sex, or national origin, or (2) to limit, segregate, or classify his employees or applicants for employment in any way which would deprive or tend to deprive any individual of employment opportunities or otherwise adversely affect his status as an employee, because of such individual's race, color, religion, sex, or national origin.[68]

Further, the Civil Rights Act incorporates some of the provisions of the earlier Equal Pay Act with the Bennett Act Amendment, which states:

> 703(h) Notwithstanding any other provision of this title, it shall be a lawful employment practice for an employer to apply different standards of compensation, or different terms, conditions, or privileges of employment pursuant to a bona fide seniority or merit system, or a system which measures earnings by quantity or quality of production or to employees who work different locations, provided that such are not the result of an intention to discriminate because of race, color, religion, sex, or national origin. It shall not be an unlawful employment practice under this title for any employer to differentiate upon the basis of sex in determining the amount of wages or compensation paid to employees of such employer if such differentiation is authorized by the provisions of Section 6(d) of the Fair Standards Act.[69]

Section 706(g) provides for adjudicative relief:

> 706(g) If the court finds that the respondent has intentionally engaged in or is intentionally engaging in an unlawful employment practice charged in the complaint, the court may enjoin the respondent from engaging in such unlawful employment practice, and order such affirmative action as may be appropriate, which may include, but is not limited to, reinstatement or hiring of employees, with or without back pay ..., or any other equitable relief as the court deems appropriate .... No order of the court shall require the admission or reinstatement of an individual as a member of a union, or the hiring, reinstatement, or promotion of an individual as an employee, or the payment to him of any back pay, if such individual was refused admission, suspended, or expelled, or was refused employment or advancement or was suspended or discharged for any reason other than discrimination on account of race, color, religion, sex, or national origin or in violation of section 704(a).[70]

Finally, Section 704(a) holds that it shall be an unlawful employment practice for an employer to discriminate against any of his employees or applicants for employment because he has made a charge, testified, assisted, or participated in any manner in an investigation, proceeding, or hearing under this title.[71]

The Civil Rights Act eliminates artificial, arbitrary and unnecessary barriers to employment in the form of invidious discrimination, unless there is a demonstrably reasonable measure of job performance (Griggs v. Duke Power Co., 401 US 424 (1971)).[72] Title VII prohibits discrimination allowing for compensation, thus recognizing equal pay as a legal right (*American Federation of State, County and Municipal Employees v. Washington*, 770 F.2d. 1401 (1985)).[73] In terms of the burden of proof, for cases brought under the Civil Rights Act, the Plaintiff has the burden to show he belongs to a group, has applied for a job, was qualified for the job that the employer tried to fill but was rejected, and the employer continued to seek applicants (*McDonnell Douglas Corp. v. Green*, 411 U.S. 792 (1973)).[74] Then, in rebutting a prima facie case, the defendant is required to show the absence of a discriminatory motive for his actions. However, this was later revised by the court, so that the defendant is not required to show the absence, but must merely articulate a legitimate non-discriminatory reason for the employee's rejection (*Board of Trustees of Keene State College v. Sweeney*, 439 US 24 (1978)).[75]

The Civil Rights Act is often used to fight discrimination in compensation, with a differentiation made between disparate treatment and impact. Disparate treatment is concerned with direct or circumstantial discriminatory motives, which lack well-defined criteria (*Spaulding v. University of Washington*, 740 F.2d. 686 (1984)).[76] It involves intent or motive as an essential element of liability concerning the effects of a chosen policy, with awareness alone of adverse consequences on a group being insufficient (*American Federation of State, County and Municipal Employees v. Washington*, 770 F.2d. 1401 (1985)).[77] In a disparate treatment approach, the plaintiff in a prima facie case is required to show by a preponderance of the evidence the overt motive. In turn, the Defendant must prove that it was non-discriminatory either by the four exceptions, by necessity or by a bona fide occupational qualification. On the other hand, disparate impact is more than an inference of discriminatory impact of outwardly neutral employment practices and adversity (*Spaulding v. University of Washington*, 740 F.2d. 686 (1984)).[78] It does not need a profession of intent by the employer to discriminate, only a clearly delineated employment practice (*American Federation of State, County and Municipal Employees v. Washington*, 770 F.2d. 1401 (1985)).[79] In a disparate impact approach, the plaintiff need only show the disproportionate impact, the burden then shifting to the defendant to show that it was non-discriminatory.

Americans with Disabilities Act (ADA)

The Americans with Disabilities Act was adopted on 23 January 1990 and is known as an Act to establish a clear and comprehensive prohibition of discrimination on the basis of disability. Disability law is largely regulated by the ADA, as it prohibits discrimination against individuals with disabilities in employment, housing, education, and access to public services. It further requires that reasonable accommodation be made so as to provide individuals with disabilities equal opportunities. Agencies and departments charged with enforcement of the ADA include the Equal Employment Opportunity Commission (EEOC) and the Department of Justice (DOJ). The ADA prohibits discrimination and ensures equal opportunity for persons with disabilities in employment, State and local government services, public accommodations, commercial facilities, and transportation. It also mandates the establishment of TDD/telephone relay services. It is a federal civil rights law designed to prevent discrimination and enable individuals with disabilities to participate fully in all aspects of society.

One fundamental principle of the ADA is that individuals with disabilities who want to work and are qualified to work must have an equal opportunity to work. A reasonable accommodation is any change or adjustment to a job, the work environment, or the way things usually are done that would allow one to apply for a job, perform job functions, or enjoy equal access to benefits available to other individuals in the workplace. There are many types of things that may help people with disabilities work successfully, such as installing a ramp or modifying a workspace or restroom; sign language interpreters for people who are deaf or readers for people who are blind; providing a quieter workspace or making other changes to reduce noisy distractions for someone with a mental disability; training and other written materials in an accessible format, such as in Braille, on audio tape, or on computer disk; TTYs for use with telephones by people who are deaf, and hardware and software that make computers accessible to people with vision impairments or who have difficulty using their hands; and time off for someone who needs treatment for a disability. To be protected by the ADA, one must have a disability or have a relationship or association with an individual with a disability.[80]

In terms of ADA Title I: Employment, it requires employers with 15 or more employees to provide qualified individuals with disabilities an equal opportunity to benefit from the full range of employment-related opportunities available to others. It prohibits discrimination in recruitment, hiring, promotions, training, pay, social activities, and other privileges of employment. As to what is a disability, the first part of the definition makes clear that the ADA applies to persons who have impairments and that these must substantially limit major life activities such as seeing, hearing, speaking, walking, breathing, performing manual tasks, learning, caring for oneself, and working. The second part of the definition protecting individuals with a record of a disability would cover a person who has recovered from cancer or mental illness. The third part of the definition protects individuals who are regarded as having a substantially limiting impairment, even though they may not have such an impairment. Requiring the ability to perform 'essential' functions assures that an individual with a disability will not be considered unqualified simply because of an inability to perform marginal or incidental job functions. Title I requires that employers make reasonable accommodation to the known physical or mental limitations of otherwise qualified individuals with disabilities, unless it results in undue hardship. In selecting the particular type of reasonable accommodation to provide, the principal test is that of effectiveness, that is whether the accommodation will provide an opportunity for a person with a disability to achieve the same level of performance and to enjoy benefits equal to those of an average, similarly situated person without a disability. However, the accommodation does not have to ensure equal results or provide exactly the same benefits. Religious entities with 15 or more employees are covered under title I. Title I complaints must be filed with the U.S. Equal Employment Opportunity Commission (EEOC) within 180 days of the date of discrimination, or 300 days if the charge is filed with a designated State or local fair employment practice agency. Individuals may file a lawsuit in Federal court only after they receive a 'right-to-sue' letter from the EEOC.

In terms of ADA Title II: State and Local Government Activities, it covers all activities of State and local governments regardless of the government entity's size or receipt of Federal funding. Title II requires that State and local governments give people with disabilities an equal opportunity to benefit from all of their programs, services, and activities, such as public education, employment, transportation, recreation, health care, social services, courts, voting, and town meetings. State and local governments are required to follow specific architectural standards in the new construction and alteration of their buildings. They also must relocate programs or otherwise provide access in inaccessible older buildings, and communicate effectively with people who have hearing, vision, or speech disabilities. Public entities are not required to take actions that would result in undue financial and administrative burdens. They are required to make reasonable modifications to policies, practices, and procedures where necessary to avoid discrimination, unless they can demonstrate that doing so would fundamentally alter the nature of the service, program, or activity being provided. Complaints of title II violations may be filed with the Department of Justice within 180 days of the date of discrimination. In certain situations, cases may be referred to a mediation program sponsored by the Department. The Department may bring a lawsuit where it has investigated a matter and has been unable to resolve violations. Title II may also be enforced through private lawsuits in Federal court.

In terms of ADA Title II: Public Transportation, it covers public transportation services, such as city buses and public rail transit, such as subways, commuter rails, Amtrak. Public transportation authorities may not discriminate against people with disabilities in the provision of their services. They must comply with requirements for accessibility in newly purchased vehicles, make good faith efforts to purchase or lease accessible used buses, remanufacture buses in an accessible manner, and, unless it would result in an undue burden, where they operate fixed-route bus or rail systems, provide paratransit which is a service where individuals who are unable to use the regular transit system independently, because of a physical or mental impairment, are picked up and dropped off at their destinations.

In terms of ADA Title III: Public Accommodations, it covers businesses and nonprofit service providers that are public accommodations, privately operated entities offering certain types of courses and examinations, privately operated transportation, and commercial facilities. Public accommodations are private entities who own, lease, lease to, or operate facilities such as restaurants, retail stores, hotels, movie theaters, private schools, convention centers, doctors' offices, homeless shelters, transportation depots, zoos, funeral homes, day care centers, and recreation facilities including sports stadiums and fitness clubs. Transportation services provided by private entities are also covered by title III. Public accommodations must comply with basic nondiscrimination requirements that prohibit exclusion, segregation, and unequal treatment. They also must comply with specific requirements related to architectural standards for new and altered buildings; reasonable modifications to policies, practices, and procedures; effective communication with people with hearing, vision, or speech disabilities; and other access requirements. Additionally, public accommodations must remove barriers in existing buildings where it is easy to do so without much difficulty or expense, given the public accommodation's resources. Courses and examinations related to professional, educational, or trade-related applications, licensing, certifications, or credentialing must be provided in a place and manner accessible to people with disabilities, or alternative accessible arrangements must be offered. Commercial facilities, must comply with the ADA's architectural standards for new construction and alterations. Complaints of title III violations may be filed with the Department of Justice. The Department is authorized to bring a lawsuit where there is a pattern or practice of discrimination in violation of title III, or where an act of discrimination raises an issue of general public importance. Title III may also be enforced through private lawsuits.

In terms of ADA Title IV: Telecommunications Relay Services, Title IV addresses telephone and television access for people with hearing and speech disabilities. It requires common carriers, that is telephone companies, to establish interstate and intrastate telecommunications relay services (TRS) 24 hours a day, 7 days a week. TRS enables callers with hearing and speech disabilities who use telecommunications devices for the deaf (TDDs), which are also known as teletypewriters (TTYs), and callers who use voice telephones to communicate with each other through a third party communications assistant. The Federal Communications Commission (FCC) has set minimum standards for TRS services. Title IV also requires closed captioning of federally funded public service announcements.

The Department of Justice established the ADA Mediation Program. In enacting the ADA, Congress specifically encouraged the use of alternative means of dispute resolution, including mediation, to resolve ADA disputes. Mediation is an informal process where an impartial third party helps disputing parties to find mutually satisfactory solutions to their differences. Mediation can resolve disputes quickly and satisfactorily, without the expense and delay of formal investigation and litigation. The proceedings are confidential and voluntary for all parties. It typically involves one or more meetings between the disputing parties and the mediator. It may also involve one or more confidential sessions between individual parties and the mediator. It provides a safe environment for the parties to air their differences and reach a mutually agreeable resolution. The mediator's role is to manage the process through which parties resolve their conflict, by facilitating communication, and maintaining the balance of power between the parties, not to decide how the conflict should be resolved. A successful mediation results in a binding agreement between the parties. If mediation is unsuccessful and an agreement cannot be reached, parties may still pursue all legal remedies provided under the ADA, including private lawsuits.[81]

Barriers to employment, transportation, public accommodations, public services, and telecommunications have imposed staggering economic and social costs on American society and have undermined well-intentioned efforts to educate, rehabilitate, and employ individuals with disabilities.[82] By breaking down these barriers, the Americans with Disabilities Act (ADA) will enable society to benefit from the skills and talents of individuals with disabilities, will allow us all to gain from their increased purchasing power and ability to use it, and will lead to fuller, more productive lives for all Americans.

In examining the Americans with Disabilities Act (ADA), Section 2(a) outlines general findings on disability:

2(a) Findings. The Congress finds that

    (1)   some 43,000,000 Americans have one or more physical or mental disabilities, and this number is increasing as the population as a whole is growing older;

    (2) historically, society has tended to isolate and segregate individuals with disabilities, and, despite some improvements, such forms of discrimination against individuals with disabilities continue to be a serious and pervasive social problem;

    (3)   discrimination against individuals with disabilities persists in such critical areas as employment, housing, public accommodations, education, transportation, communication, recreation, institutionalization, health services, voting, and access to public services;

    (4) unlike individuals who have experienced discrimination on the basis of race, color, sex, national origin, religion, or age, individuals who have experienced discrimination on the basis of disability have often had no legal recourse to redress such discrimination;

    (5)   individuals with disabilities continually encounter various forms of discrimination, including outright intentional exclusion, the discriminatory effects of architectural, transportation, and communication barriers, overprotective rules and policies, failure to make modifications to existing facilities and practices, exclusionary qualification standards and criteria, segregation, and relegation to lesser services, programs, activities, benefits, jobs, or other opportunities;

    (6)   census data, national polls, and other studies have documented that people with disabilities, as a group, occupy an inferior status in our society, and are severely disadvantaged socially, vocationally, economically, and educationally;

    (7)   individuals with disabilities are a discrete and insular minority who have been faced with restrictions and limitations, subjected to a history of purposeful unequal treatment, and relegated to a position of political powerlessness in our society, based on characteristics that are beyond the control of such individuals and resulting from stereotypic assumptions not truly indicative of the individual ability of such individuals to participate in, and contribute to, society;

    (8)   the Nation's proper goals regarding individuals with disabilities are to assure equality of opportunity, full participation, independent living, and economic self-sufficiency for such individuals; and

    (9)   the continuing existence of unfair and unnecessary discrimination and prejudice denies people with disabilities the opportunity to compete on an equal basis and to pursue those opportunities for which our free society is justifiably famous, and costs the United States billions of dollars in unnecessary expenses resulting from dependency and nonproductivity.[83]

Further, Section 2(b) outlines the purposes of the Act:

2(b) Purpose. It is the purpose of this Act
  (1) to provide a clear and comprehensive national mandate for the elimination of discrimination against individuals with disabilities;
  (2) to provide clear, strong, consistent, enforceable standards addressing discrimination against individuals with disabilities;
  (3) to ensure that the Federal Government plays a central role in enforcing the standards established in this Act on behalf of individuals with disabilities; and
  (4) to invoke the sweep of congressional authority, including the power to enforce the fourteenth amendment and to regulate commerce, in order to address the major areas of discrimination faced day-to-day by people with disabilities.[84]

The definition of disability is included in Section 3:

  3(2) Disability. The term 'disability' means, with respect to an individual
    (A) a physical or mental impairment that substantially limits one or more of the major life activities of such individual;
    (B) a record of such an impairment; or
    (C) being regarded as having such an impairment.[85]

In terms of employment, Section 101 outlines the various definitions:

  101(8) Qualified individual with a disability. The term 'qualified individual with a disability' means an individual with a disability who, with or without reasonable accommodation, can perform the essential functions of the employment position that such individual holds or desires. For the purposes of this title, consideration shall be given to the employer's judgment as to what functions of a job are essential, and if an employer has prepared a written description before advertising or interviewing applicants for the job, this description shall be considered evidence of the essential functions of the job.
  (9) Reasonable accommodation. The term 'reasonable accommodation' may include
    (A) making existing facilities used by employees readily accessible to and usable by individuals with disabilities; and
    (B) job restructuring, part-time or modified work schedules, reassignment to a vacant position, acquisition or modification of equipment or devices, appropriate adjustment or modifications of examinations, training materials or policies, the provision of qualified readers or interpreters, and other similar accommodations for individuals with disabilities.
  (10) Undue hardship.
    (A) In general. The term 'undue hardship' means an action requiring significant difficulty or expense, when considered in light of the factors set forth in subparagraph (B).
    (B) Factors to be considered. In determining whether an accommodation would impose an undue hardship on a covered entity, factors to be considered include
    (i) the nature and cost of the accommodation needed under this Act;

(ii) the overall financial resources of the facility or facilities involved in the provision of the reasonable accommodation; the number of persons employed at such facility; the effect on expenses and resources, or the impact otherwise of such accommodation upon the operation of the facility;

(iii) the overall financial resources of the covered entity; the overall size of the business of a covered entity with respect to the number of its employees; the number, type, and location of its facilities; and

(iv) the type of operation or operations of the covered entity, including the composition, structure, and functions of the workforce of such entity; the geographic separateness, administrative, or fiscal relationship of the facility or facilities in question to the covered entity.[86]

Section 102 deals with discrimination:

102(a) General Rule. No covered entity shall discriminate against a qualified individual with a disability because of the disability of such individual in regard to job application procedures, the hiring, advancement, or discharge of employees, employee compensation, job training, and other terms, conditions, and privileges of employment.

(b) Construction. As used in subsection (a), the term 'discriminate' includes

(1) limiting, segregating, or classifying a job applicant or employee in a way that adversely affects the opportunities or status of such applicant or employee because of the disability of such applicant or employee;

(2) participating in a contractual or other arrangement or relationship that has the effect of subjecting a covered entity's qualified applicant or employee with a disability to the discrimination prohibited by this title (such relationship includes a relationship with an employment or referral agency, labor union, an organization providing fringe benefits to an employee of the covered entity, or an organization providing training and apprenticeship programs);

(3) utilizing standards, criteria, or methods of administration

(A) that have the effect of discrimination on the basis of disability; or

(B) that perpetuate the discrimination of others who are subject to common administrative control;

(4) excluding or otherwise denying equal jobs or benefits to a qualified individual because of the known disability of an individual with whom the qualified individual is known to have a relationship or association;

(5)(A) not making reasonable accommodations to the known physical or mental limitations of an otherwise qualified individual with a disability who is an applicant or employee, unless such covered entity can demonstrate that the accommodation would impose an undue hardship on the operation of the business of such covered entity; or

(B) denying employment opportunities to a job applicant or employee who is an otherwise qualified individual with a disability, if such denial is based on the need of such covered entity to make reasonable accommodation to the physical or mental impairments of the employee or applicant;

(6)   using qualification standards, employment tests or other selection, criteria that screen out or tend to screen out an individual with a disability or a class of individuals with disabilities unless the standard, test or other selection criteria, as used by the covered entity, is shown to be job-related for the position in question and is consistent with business necessity; and

(7)   failing to select and administer tests concerning employment in the most effective manner to ensure that, when such test is administered to a job applicant or employee who has a disability that impairs sensory, manual, or speaking skills, such test results accurately reflect the skills, aptitude, or whatever other factor of such applicant or employee that such test purports to measure, rather than reflecting the impaired sensory, manual, or speaking skills of such employee or applicant (except where such skills are the factors that the test purports to measure).[87]

Further, Section 103 covers defenses:

103 (a) In General. It may be a defense to a charge of discrimination under this Act that an alleged application of qualification standards, tests, or selection criteria that screen out or tend to screen out or otherwise deny a job or benefit to an individual with a disability has been shown to be job-related and consistent with business necessity, and such performance cannot be accomplished by reasonable accommodation, as required under this title.

(b) Qualification Standards. The term 'qualification standards' may include a requirement that an individual shall not pose a direct threat to the health or safety of other individuals in the workplace.[88]

Finally, enforcement is outlined in Section 107:

107(a) Powers, Remedies, and Procedures. The powers, remedies, and procedures set forth in sections 705, 706, 707, 709, and 710 of the Civil Rights Act of 1964 (42 U.S.C. 2000e-4, 2000e-5, 2000e-6, 2000e-8, and 2000e-9) shall be the powers, remedies, and procedures this title provides to the Commission, to the Attorney General, or to any person alleging discrimination on the basis of disability in violation of any provision of this Act, or regulations promulgated under section 106, concerning employment.[89]

In terms of public services, Section 201 outlines definitions:

201(1) Public entity. The term 'public entity' means
(A) any State or local government;
(B) any department, agency, special purpose district, or other instrumentality of a State or States or local government; and
(C) the National Railroad Passenger Corporation, and any commuter authority (as defined in section 103(8) of the Rail Passenger Service Act).
(2)   Qualified individual with a disability. The term 'qualified individual with a disability' means an individual with a disability who, with or

without reasonable modifications to rules, policies, or practices, the removal of architectural, communication, or transportation barriers, or the provision of auxiliary aids and services, meets the essential eligibility requirements for the receipt of services or the participation in programs or activities provided by a public entity.[90]

Section 202 deals with discrimination:

202. Subject to the provisions of this title, no qualified individual with a disability shall, by reason of such disability, be excluded from participation in or be denied the benefits of the services, programs, or activities of a public entity, or be subjected to discrimination by any such entity.[91]

Section 223 covers paratransit as a complement to fixed route service for the disabled:

223 (a) General Rule. It shall be considered discrimination for purposes of section 202 of this Act and section 504 of the Rehabilitation Act of 1973 (29 U.S.C. 794) for a public entity which operates a fixed route system (other than a system which provides solely commuter bus service) to fail to provide with respect to the operations of its fixed route system, in accordance with this section, paratransit and other special transportation services to individuals with disabilities, including individuals who use wheelchairs, that are sufficient to provide to such individuals a level of service (1) which is comparable to the level of designated public transportation services provided to individuals without disabilities using such system; or (2) in the case of response time, which is comparable, to the extent practicable, to the level of designated public transportation services provided to individuals without disabilities using such system.

(c) Required Contents of Regulations.
(1) Eligible recipients of service. The regulations issued under this section shall require each public entity which operates a fixed route system to provide the paratransit and other special transportation services required under this section
(A)(i) to any individual with a disability who is unable, as a result of a physical or mental impairment (including a vision impairment) and without the assistance of another individual (except an operator of a wheelchair lift or other boarding assistance device), to board, ride, or disembark from any vehicle on the system which is readily accessible to and usable by individuals with disabilities;
(ii) to any individual with a disability who needs the assistance of a wheelchair lift or other boarding assistance device (and is able with such assistance) to board, ride, and disembark from any vehicle which is readily accessible to and usable by individuals with disabilities if the individual wants to travel on a route on the system during the hours of operation of the system at a time (or within a reasonable period of such time) when such a vehicle is not being used to provide designated public transportation on the route; and

(iii) to any individual with a disability who has a specific impairment-related condition which prevents such individual from traveling to a boarding location or from a disembarking location on such system;
(B) to one other individual accompanying the individual with the disability.

(4) Undue financial burden limitation. The regulations issued under this section shall provide that, if the public entity is able to demonstrate to the satisfaction of the Secretary that the provision of paratransit and other special transportation services otherwise required under this section would impose an undue financial burden on the public entity, the public entity, notwithstanding any other provision of this section (other than paragraph (5)), shall only be required to provide such services to the extent that providing such services would not impose such a burden.

(f) Statutory Construction. Nothing in this section shall be construed as preventing a public entity
(1) from providing paratransit or other special transportation services at a level which is greater than the level of such services which are required by this section,
(2) from providing paratransit or other special transportation services in addition to those paratransit and special transportation services required by this section, or
(3) from providing such services to individuals in addition to those individuals to whom such services are required to be provided by this section.[92]

Section 227 covers alterations of existing facilities:

227(a) General Rule. With respect to alterations of an existing facility or part thereof used in the provision of designated public transportation services that affect or could affect the usability of the facility or part thereof, it shall be considered discrimination, for purposes of section 202 of this Act and section 504 of the Rehabilitation Act of 1973 (29 U.S.C. 794), for a public entity to fail to make such alterations (or to ensure that the alterations are made) in such a manner that, to the maximum extent feasible, the altered portions of the facility are readily accessible to and usable by individuals with disabilities, including individuals who use wheelchairs, upon the completion of such alterations. Where the public entity is undertaking an alteration that affects or could affect usability of or access to an area of the facility containing a primary function, the entity shall also make the alterations in such a manner that, to the maximum extent feasible, the path of travel to the altered area and the bathrooms, telephones, and drinking fountains serving the altered area, are readily accessible to and usable by individuals with disabilities, including individuals who use wheelchairs, upon completion of such alterations, where such alterations to the path of travel or the bathrooms, telephones, and drinking fountains serving the altered area are not disproportionate to the overall alterations in terms of cost and scope (as determined under criteria established by the Attorney General).[93]

In terms of public accommodations and services operated by private entities, Section 301 outlines definitions:

> 301(1) Commerce. The term 'commerce' means travel, trade, traffic, commerce, transportation, or communication
>
> > (A) among the several States;
> >
> > (B) between any foreign country or any territory or possession and any State; or
> >
> > (C) between points in the same State but through another State or foreign country.
>
> (2) Commercial facilities. The term 'commercial facilities' means facilities
>
> > (A) that are intended for nonresidential use; and
> >
> > (B) whose operations will affect commerce.
>
> (7) Public accommodation. The following private entities are considered public accommodations for purposes of this title, if the operations of such entities affect commerce
>
> > (A) an inn, hotel, motel, or other place of lodging, except for an establishment located within a building that contains not more than five rooms for rent or hire and that is actually occupied by the proprietor of such establishment as the residence of such proprietor;
> >
> > (B) a restaurant, bar, or other establishment serving food or drink;
> >
> > (C) a motion picture house, theater, concert hall, stadium, or other place of exhibition or entertainment;
> >
> > (D) an auditorium, convention center, lecture hall, or other place of public gathering;
> >
> > (E) a bakery, grocery store, clothing store, hardware store, shopping center, or other sales or rental establishment;
> >
> > (F) a laundromat, dry-cleaner, bank, barber shop, beauty shop, travel service, shoe repair service, funeral parlor, gas station, office of an accountant or lawyer, pharmacy, insurance office, professional office of a health care provider, hospital, or other service establishment;
> >
> > (G) a terminal, depot, or other station used for specified public transportation;
> >
> > (H) a museum, library, gallery, or other place of public display or collection;
> >
> > (I) a park, zoo, amusement park, or other place of recreation;
> >
> > (J) a nursery, elementary, secondary, undergraduate, or postgraduate private school, or other place of education;
> >
> > (K) a day care center, senior citizen center, homeless shelter, food bank, adoption agency, or other social service center establishment; and
> >
> > (L) a gymnasium, health spa, bowling alley, golf course, or other place of exercise or recreation.[94]

Section 302 covers the prohibition of discrimination by public accommodations:

> 302(a) General Rule. No individual shall be discriminated against on the basis of disability in the full and equal enjoyment of the goods, services, facilities, privileges, advantages, or accommodations of any place of

public accommodation by any person who owns, leases (or leases to), or operates a place of public accommodation.

(b) Construction.

(1) General prohibition.

(A) Activities.

(i) Denial of participation. It shall be discriminatory to subject an individual or class of individuals on the basis of a disability or disabilities of such individual or class, directly, or through contractual, licensing, or other arrangements, to a denial of the opportunity of the individual or class to participate in or benefit from the goods, services, facilities, privileges, advantages, or accommodations of an entity.

(ii) Participation in unequal benefit. It shall be discriminatory to afford an individual or class of individuals, on the basis of a disability or disabilities of such individual or class, directly, or through contractual, licensing, or other arrangements with the opportunity to participate in or benefit from a good, service, facility, privilege, advantage, or accommodation that is not equal to that afforded to other individuals.

(iii) Separate benefit. It shall be discriminatory to provide an individual or class of individuals, on the basis of a disability or disabilities of such individual or class, directly, or through contractual, licensing, or other arrangements with a good, service, facility, privilege, advantage, or accommodation that is different or separate from that provided to other individuals, unless such action is necessary to provide the individual or class of individuals with a good, service, facility, privilege, advantage, or accommodation, or other opportunity that is as effective as that provided to others.

(B) Integrated settings. Goods, services, facilities, privileges, advantages, and accommodations shall be afforded to an individual with a disability in the most integrated setting appropriate to the needs of the individual.

(C) Opportunity to participate. Notwithstanding the existence of separate or different programs or activities provided in accordance with this section, an individual with a disability shall not be denied the opportunity to participate in such programs or activities that are not separate or different.

(D) Administrative methods. An individual or entity shall not, directly or through contractual or other arrangements, utilize standards or criteria or methods of administration

(i) that have the effect of discriminating on the basis of disability; or

(ii) that perpetuate the discrimination of others who are subject to common administrative control.

(E) Association. It shall be discriminatory to exclude or otherwise deny equal goods, services, facilities, privileges, advantages, accommodations, or other opportunities to an individual or entity because of the known disability of an individual with whom the individual or entity is known to have a relationship or association.

(2) Specific prohibitions.

(A) Discrimination. For purposes of subsection (a), discrimination includes

(i) the imposition or application of eligibility criteria that screen out or tend to screen out an individual with a disability or any class of individuals with disabilities from fully and equally enjoying any goods, services, facilities, privileges, advantages, or accommodations, unless such criteria can be shown to be necessary for the provision of the goods, services, facilities, privileges, advantages, or accommodations being offered;

(ii) a failure to make reasonable modifications in policies, practices, or procedures, when such modifications are necessary to afford such goods, services, facilities, privileges, advantages, or accommodations to individuals with disabilities, unless the entity can demonstrate that making such modifications would fundamentally alter the nature of such goods, services, facilities, privileges, advantages, or accommodations;

(iii) a failure to take such steps as may be necessary to ensure that no individual with a disability is excluded, denied services, segregated or otherwise treated differently than other individuals because of the absence of auxiliary aids and services, unless the entity can demonstrate that taking such steps would fundamentally alter the nature of the good, service, facility, privilege, advantage, or accommodation being offered or would result in an undue burden;

(iv) a failure to remove architectural barriers, and communication barriers that are structural in nature, in existing facilities, and transportation barriers in existing vehicles and rail passenger cars used by an establishment for transporting individuals (not including barriers that can only be removed through the retrofitting of vehicles or rail passenger cars by the installation of a hydraulic or other lift), where such removal is readily achievable; and

(v) where an entity can demonstrate that the removal of a barrier under clause (iv) is not readily achievable, a failure to make such goods, services, facilities, privileges, advantages, or accommodations available through alternative methods if such methods are readily achievable.[95]

Section 303 covers new construction and alterations in public accommodations and commercial facilities:

303(a) Application of Term. Except as provided in subsection (b), as applied to public accommodations and commercial facilities, discrimination for purposes of section 302(a) includes

(1) a failure to design and construct facilities for first occupancy later than 30 months after the date of enactment of this Act that are readily accessible to and usable by individuals with disabilities, except where an entity can demonstrate that it is structurally impracticable to meet the requirements of such subsection in accordance with standards set forth or incorporated by reference in regulations issued under this title; and

(2) with respect to a facility or part thereof that is altered by, on behalf of, or for the use of an establishment in a manner that affects or could affect the usability of the facility or part thereof, a failure to make alterations in such a manner that, to the maximum extent feasible, the altered portions of the facility are readily accessible to and usable by individuals with disabilities, including individuals who use wheelchairs. Where the entity is undertaking an alteration that affects or could affect usability of or access to an area of the facility containing a primary function, the entity shall also make the alterations in such a manner that,

to the maximum extent feasible, the path of travel to the altered area and the bathrooms, telephones, and drinking fountains serving the altered area, are readily accessible to and usable by individuals with disabilities where such alterations to the path of travel or the bathrooms, telephones, and drinking fountains serving the altered area are not disproportionate to the overall alterations in terms of cost and scope (as determined under criteria established by the Attorney General).

(b) Elevator. Subsection (a) shall not be construed to require the installation of an elevator for facilities that are less than three stories or have less than 3,000 square feet per story unless the building is a shopping center, a shopping mall, or the professional office of a health care provider or unless the Attorney General determines that a particular category of such facilities requires the installation of elevators based on the usage of such facilities.[96]

Further, enforcement is outlined in Section 308:

308(a) In General.

(2) Injunctive relief. In the case of violations of sections 302(b)(2)(A)(iv) and section 303(a), injunctive relief shall include an order to alter facilities to make such facilities readily accessible to and usable by individuals with disabilities to the extent required by this title. Where appropriate, injunctive relief shall also include requiring the provision of an auxiliary aid or service, modification of a policy, or provision of alternative methods, to the extent required by this title.

(b) Enforcement by the Attorney General.

(1) Denial of rights.

(A) Duty to investigate.

(i) In general. The Attorney General shall investigate alleged violations of this title, and shall undertake periodic reviews of compliance of covered entities under this title.

(B) Potential violation. If the Attorney General has reasonable cause to believe that

(i) any person or group of persons is engaged in a pattern or practice of discrimination under this title; or

(ii) any person or group of persons has been discriminated against under this title and such discrimination raises an issue of general public importance, the Attorney General may commence a civil action in any appropriate United States district court.

(2) Authority of court. In a civil action under paragraph (1)(B), the court

(A) may grant any equitable relief that such court considers to be appropriate, including, to the extent required by this title

(i) granting temporary, preliminary, or permanent relief;

(ii) providing an auxiliary aid or service, modification of policy, practice, or procedure, or alternative method; and

(iii) making facilities readily accessible to and usable by individuals with disabilities;

(B) may award such other relief as the court considers to be appropriate, including monetary damages to persons aggrieved when requested by the Attorney General; and

(C) may, to vindicate the public interest, assess a civil penalty against the entity in an amount
(i) not exceeding $50,000 for a first violation; and
(ii) not exceeding $100,000 for any subsequent violation.
(3) Single violation. For purposes of paragraph (2)(C), in determining whether a first or subsequent violation has occurred, a determination in a single action, by judgment or settlement, that the covered entity has engaged in more than one discriminatory act shall be counted as a single violation.
(4) Punitive damages. For purposes of subsection (b)(2)(B), the term 'monetary damages' and 'such other relief' does not include punitive damages.
(5) Judicial consideration. In a civil action under paragraph (1)(B), the court, when considering what amount of civil penalty, if any, is appropriate, shall give consideration to any good faith effort or attempt to comply with this Act by the entity. In evaluating good faith, the court shall consider, among other factors it deems relevant, whether the entity could have reasonably anticipated the need for an appropriate type of auxiliary aid needed to accommodate the unique needs of a particular individual with a disability.[97]

Importantly, Section 503 deals with the prohibition against retaliation and coercion:

503(a)   Retaliation. No person shall discriminate against any individual because such individual has opposed any act or practice made unlawful by this Act or because such individual made a charge, testified, assisted, or participated in any manner in an investigation, proceeding, or hearing under this Act.

(b)   Interference, Coercion, or Intimidation. It shall be unlawful to coerce, intimidate, threaten, or interfere with any individual in the exercise or enjoyment of, or on account of his or her having exercised or enjoyed, or on account of his or her having aided or encouraged any other individual in the exercise or enjoyment of, any right granted or protected by this Act.[98]

Interestingly, Section 513 provides for the alternative means of dispute resolution:

513.   Where appropriate and to the extent authorized by law, the use of alternative means of dispute resolution, including settlement negotiations, conciliation, facilitation, mediation, factfinding, minitrials, and arbitration, is encouraged to resolve disputes arising under this Act.[99]

In addition to the ADA, States may pass disability statutes so long as they are consistent with the ADA. Other statutes prohibiting discrimination against individuals with disabilities include the following.

Telecommunications Act

Section 255 and Section 251(a)(2) of the Communications Act of 1934, as amended by the Telecommunications Act of 1996, require manufacturers of telecommunications equipment and providers of telecommunications services to ensure that such equipment and services are accessible to and usable by persons with disabilities, if readily achievable. These amendments ensure that people with disabilities will have access to a broad range of products and services such as telephones, cell phones, pagers, call-waiting, and operator services, that were often inaccessible to many users with disabilities.[100]

Fair Housing Act

The Fair Housing Act, as amended in 1988, prohibits housing discrimination on the basis of race, color, religion, sex, disability, familial status, and national origin. Its coverage includes private housing, housing that receives Federal financial assistance, and State and local government housing. It is unlawful to discriminate in any aspect of selling or renting housing or to deny a dwelling to a buyer or renter because of the disability of that individual, an individual associated with the buyer or renter, or an individual who intends to live in the residence. Other covered activities include, financing, zoning practices, new construction design, and advertising. The Fair Housing Act requires owners of housing facilities to make reasonable exceptions in their policies and operations to afford people with disabilities equal housing opportunities. A landlord with a 'no pets' policy may be required to grant an exception to this rule and allow an individual who is blind to keep a guide dog in the residence. The Fair Housing Act also requires landlords to allow tenants with disabilities to make reasonable access-related modifications to their private living space, as well as to common use spaces, but the landlord is not required to pay for the changes. The Act further requires that new multifamily housing with four or more units be designed and built to allow access for persons with disabilities, which includes accessible common use areas, doors that are wide enough for wheelchairs, kitchens and bathrooms that allow a person using a wheelchair to maneuver, and other adaptable features within the units. Complaints of Fair Housing Act violations may be filed with the U.S. Department of Housing and Urban Development. Additionally, the Department of Justice can file cases involving a pattern or practice of discrimination. The Fair Housing Act may also be enforced through private lawsuits.[101]

Air Carrier Access Act

The Air Carrier Access Act prohibits discrimination in air transportation by domestic and foreign air carriers against qualified individuals with physical or mental impairments. It applies only to air carriers that provide regularly scheduled services for hire to the public. Requirements address a wide range of issues including boarding assistance and certain accessibility features in newly built aircraft and new or altered airport facilities. People may enforce rights under the

Air Carrier Access Act by filing a complaint with the U.S. Department of Transportation, or by bringing a lawsuit in Federal court.[102]

Voting Accessibility for the Elderly and Handicapped Act

The Voting Accessibility for the Elderly and Handicapped Act of 1984 generally requires polling places across the United States to be physically accessible to people with disabilities for federal elections. Where no accessible location is available to serve as a polling place, a political subdivision must provide an alternate means of casting a ballot on the day of the election. This law also requires states to make available registration and voting aids for disabled and elderly voters, including information by telecommunications devices for the deaf (TDDs) which are also known as teletypewriters (TTYs).[103]

National Voter Registration Act

The National Voter Registration Act of 1993, also known as the 'Motor Voter Act', makes it easier for all Americans to exercise their fundamental right to vote. One of the basic purposes of the Act is to increase the historically low registration rates of minorities and persons with disabilities that have resulted from discrimination. The Motor Voter Act requires all offices of State-funded programs that are primarily engaged in providing services to persons with disabilities to provide all program applicants with voter registration forms, to assist them in completing the forms, and to transmit completed forms to the appropriate State official.[104]

Civil Rights of Institutionalized Persons Act

The Civil Rights of Institutionalized Persons Act (CRIPA) authorizes the U.S. Attorney General to investigate conditions of confinement at State and local government institutions such as prisons, jails, pretrial detention centers, juvenile correctional facilities, publicly operated nursing homes, and institutions for people with psychiatric or developmental disabilities. Its purpose is to allow the Attorney General to uncover and correct widespread deficiencies that seriously jeopardize the health and safety of residents of institutions. The Attorney General does not have authority under CRIPA to investigate isolated incidents or to represent individual institutionalized persons. The Attorney General may initiate civil law suits where there is reasonable cause to believe that conditions are 'egregious or flagrant', that they are subjecting residents to 'grievous harm', and that they are part of a 'pattern or practice' of resistance to residents' full enjoyment of constitutional or Federal rights, including title II of the ADA and section 504 of the Rehabilitation Act.[105]

Individuals with Disabilities Education Act

The Individuals with Disabilities Education Act (IDEA) requires public schools to make available to all eligible children with disabilities a free appropriate public education in the least restrictive environment appropriate to their individual needs. IDEA requires public school systems to develop appropriate Individualized Education Programs (IEPs) for each child. The specific special education and related services outlined in each IEP reflect the individualized needs of each student. IDEA also mandates that particular procedures be followed in the development of the IEP. Each student's IEP must be developed by a team of knowledgeable persons and must be at least reviewed annually. The team includes the child's teacher; the parents, subject to certain limited exceptions; the child, if determined appropriate; an agency representative who is qualified to provide or supervise the provision of special education; and other individuals at the parents' or agency's discretion. If parents disagree with the proposed IEP, they can request a due process hearing and a review from the State educational agency if applicable in that state. They also can appeal the State agency's decision to State or Federal court.[106]

Rehabilitation Act

The Rehabilitation Act prohibits discrimination on the basis of disability in programs conducted by Federal agencies, in programs receiving Federal financial assistance, in Federal employment, and in the employment practices of Federal contractors.[107]

Architectural Barriers Act

The Architectural Barriers Act (ABA) requires that buildings and facilities that are designed, constructed, or altered with Federal funds, or leased by a Federal agency, comply with Federal standards for physical accessibility. ABA requirements are limited to architectural standards in new and altered buildings and in newly leased facilities.[108]

Conclusion

The keys to the future of this ability and human rights in North America are the implementation and development of the law, the deepening in understanding of specific legal issues relating to human rights in the courts, and the raising of the level of awareness of legal rights and obligations.

Martin Luther King Jr. in his struggle for civil rights stated:

> I have a dream that one day every valley shall be exalted, every hill and mountain shall be made plain, and the crooked places shall be made straight and the glory of the Lord will be revealed and all flesh shall see it together. This is our hope .... And when we allow freedom to ring, when we let it ring from every village and hamlet, from every state and city, we will be able to join hands and to sing in the words of the old Negro spiritual, 'Free at last, free at last; thank God Almighty, we are free at last'.[109]

Notes

1 Mandel, Michael, *The Charter of Rights and the Legalization of Politics in Canada*, Wall & Thompson, Toronto, 1989, p.4.

2 Canadian Constitution.

3 Canadian Constitution, the Canadian Charter of Rights and Freedoms, at Section 32.

4 Canadian Constitution, at Section 52(1).

5 Canadian Constitution, the Canadian Charter of Rights and Freedoms, at Section 32.

6 *Ibid.*, at Section 2.

7 *Ibid.*, at Section 27.

8 Canadian Constitution, at Section 35.

9 Canadian Constitution, the Canadian Charter of Rights and Freedoms, at Section 15.

10 *Ibid.*, at Section 28.

11 *Ibid.*, at Section 33.

12 *Ibid.*, at Section 1.

13 *Regina v. Oakes*, [1986] 1 SCR 103.

14 Canadian Bill of Rights, at Section 1.

15 *Ibid.*, at Section 25.

16 *Ibid.*, at Section 2.

17 Canadian Human Rights Act, at Section 3(1).

18 *Ibid.*, at Section 7.

19 *Ibid.*, at Section 10.

20 *Ibid.*, at Section 11.

21 *Ibid.*, at Section 15(1).

22 Canadian Human Rights Act, at Section 16.

23 *Ibid.*, at Section 17.

24 *Ibid.*, at Section 48(1).

25 Labor Canada, *Equal Pay for Work of Equal Value*, Ottawa, 1986, p.21.

26 *Basi v. Canadian National Railway* (1984), 9 CHRR 4. D/5029, 5037 (CHR Tribunal).

27 *Shakes v. Rex Pak Ltd.* (1982), 3 CHRR D/1001, 1002.

28 *Blake v. Ministry of Correctional Services and Mimico Correctional Institute* (1984), 5 CHRR D/2417 (Ontario).

29 *Ontario Human Rights Commission v. Simpsons-Sears Ltd.*, [1985] SCR 536, 547.

30 Canada Employment Equity Act, 1995, at Section 2.

31 *Ibid.*, at Section 5.

32 *Ibid.*, at Section 6.

33 *Ibid.*, at Section 10.

34 *Ibid.*, at Article 29.

35 Federal Task Force on Disability Issues, *Equal Citizenship for Canadians with Disabilities: The Will to Act*, 1996.

36 *Ibid.*

37 Constitución Política de los Estados Unidos Mexicanos.

38 *Ibid.*, at Article 1.

39 *Ibid.*, at Article 123(7).

40 Ley Federal de Trabajo, at Articles 3 and 164.

41 *Ibid.*, at Article 1.

42 *Ibid.*, at Article 86.

43 *Ibid.*, at Articles 50 and 52.

44 *Ibid.*, at Article 36.

45   United States Declaration of Independence.
46   Federalist Papers.
47   Coleman, Frank, *Hobbes and America*, University of Toronto, Toronto, 1977, p.3.
48   United States Constitution, at Amendment I.
49   *Ibid.*, at Amendment V.
50   *Ibid.*, at Amendment XIV.
51   Magna Carta.
52   United States Constitution, at Amendment XIII.
53   North, Arthur, *The Supreme Court, Judicial Process and Judicial Politics*, Appleton Century Crofts, New York, 1964, p.2.
54   *McCullough v. Maryland*, 4 Wheaton 415 (1819).
55   United States Constitution, Article 6(2).
56   *Marbury v. Madison*, 1 Cranch 137 (1803).
57   North, Arthur, *The Supreme Court, Judicial Process and Judicial Politics*, Appleton Century Crofts, New York, 1964, p.8.
58   Cox Archibald, *The Role of the Supreme Court in American Government*, Oxford University Press, New York, 1976, p.117.
59   Cox, Archibald, *Civil Rights, The Constitution and the Court*, Harvard University Press, Cambridge, 1967, p.21.
60   *Davis v. Passman*, 442 US 228 (1979).
61   United States Equal Pay Act.
62   *Ibid.*, at Section 16.
63   *Brennan v. City Stores*, 479 F.2d. 235 (1973).
64   *Murphy v. Miller Brewer Co.*, 307 F.Supp. 829 (1969).
65   *Corning Glass Works v. Brennan*, 417 US 188 (1974).
66   *American Nurses' Association v. State of Illinois*, 783 F.2d. 716 (1986).
67   *Spaulding v. University of Washington*, 740 F.2d. 686 (1984).
68   United States Civil Rights Act, Section 703(a).
69   *Ibid.*, at Section 703(h).
70   *Ibid.*, at Section 706(g).
71   *Ibid.*, at Section 704(a).
72   *Griggs v. Duke Power Co.*, 401 US 424 (1971).
73   *American Federation of State, County and Municipal Employees v. Washington*, 770 F.2d. 1401 (1985).
74   *McDonnell Douglas Corp. v. Green*, 411 US 792 (1973).
75   *Board of Trustees of Keene State College v. Sweeney*, 439 US 24 (1978).
76   *Spaulding v. University of Washington*, 740 F.2d. 686 (1984).
77   *American Federation of State, County and Municipal Employees v. Washington*, 770 F.2d. 1401 (1985).
78   *Spaulding v. University of Washington*, 740 F.2d. 686 (1984).
79   *American Federation of State, County and Municipal Employees v. Washington*, 770 F.2d. 1401 (1985).
80   U.S. Department of Justice, Civil Rights Division, *Disability Rights Section, A Guide to Disability Rights Laws*, 2004.
81   *Ibid.*
82   U.S. Equal Employment Opportunity Commission, U.S. Department of Justice Civil Rights Division, *The Americans with Disabilities Act*.
83   Americans with Disabilities Act, Section 2(a).
84   *Ibid.*, at Section 2(b).
85   *Ibid.*, at Section 3.

[86] *Ibid.*, at Section 101.
[87] *Ibid*, at Section 102.
[88] *Ibid.*, at Section 103.
[89] *Ibid.*, at Section 107.
[90] *Ibid.*, at Section 201.
[91] *Ibid.*, at Section 202.
[92] *Ibid.*, at Section 223.
[93] *Ibid.*, at Section 227.
[94] *Ibid.*, at Section 301.
[95] *Ibid.*, at Section 302.
[96] *Ibid.*, at Section 303.
[97] *Ibid.*, at Section 308.
[98] *Ibid.*, at Section 503.
[99] *Ibid.*, at Section 513.
[100] Telecommunications Act.
[101] Fair Housing Act.
[102] Air Carrier Access Act.
[103] Voting Accessibility for the Elderly and Handicapped Act.
[104] National Voter Registration Act.
[105] Civil Rights of Institutionalized Persons Act.
[106] Individuals with Disabilities Education Act.
[107] Rehabilitation Act.
[108] Architectural Barriers Act.
[109] Martin Luther King Jr., March on Washington, 28 August 1963.

References

Air Carrier Access Act.

American Federation of State, County and Municipal Employees v. Washington, 770 F.2d. 1401 (1985).

American Nurses Association v. State of Illinois, 783 F.2d. 716 (1985).

Americans with Disabilities Act.

Architectural Barriers Act.

Basi v. Canadian National Railway (1984), 9 CHRR 4. D/5029 (CHRTribunal).

Blake v. Ministry of Correctional Services and Mimico Correctional Institute (1984), 5 CHRR D/2417 (Ontario).

Board of Trustees of Keene State College v. Sweeney, 439 US 24 (1978).

Brennan v. City Stores, 479 F.2d. 235 (1973).

British North America Act, Canada, 1867.

Canada Employment Equity Act, 1995.

Canadian Bill of Rights, 1960.

Canadian Human Rights Act, 1978.

Canadian Constitution, 1982.

Canadian Constitution, Canadian Charter of Rights and Freedoms, 1982.

Civil Rights Act, United States, 1964.

Civil Rights of Institutionalized Persons Act.

Coleman, Frank (1977), *Hobbes and America*, University of Toronto, Toronto.

Constitución Política de los Estados Unidos Mexicanos.

Corning Glass Works v. Brennan, 417 US 188 (1974).

Cox, Archibald (1967), *Civil Rights, The Constitution and the Court*, Harvard University Press, Cambridge.

Cox, Archibald (1976), *The Role of the Supreme Court in American Government*, New York: Oxford University Press, New York.

Davis v. Passman, 442 US 228 (1979).

Declaration of Independence, United States, 1776.

Ely, J. (1980), *Democracy and Distrust*, Harvard University Press, Cambridge.

Equal Pay Act, United States, 1963.

Fair Housing Act.

Federalist Papers, United States, 1787-1788.

Federal Task Force on Disability Issues, *Equal Citizenship for Canadians with Disabilities: The Will to Act*, 1996.

Ford v. Quebec (Attorney General), [1988] 2 SCR 712.

Frontiero v. Richardson, 411 US 677 (1973).

Griggs v. Duke Power Co., 401 US 424 (1971).

Individuals with Disabilities Education Act.

King Jr., Martin Luther (1963), *March on Washington*.

Labor Canada (1986), *Equal Pay for Work of Equal Value*, Ottawa.

Ley del Seguro Social, Mexico.

Ley Federal de Trabajo, Mexico.

Magna Carta, 1215.

Mandel, Michael (1989), *The Charter of Rights and the Legalization of Politics in Canada*, Wall & Thompson, Toronto.

Marbury v. Madison, 1 Cranch 137 (1803).

McCullough v. Maryland, 4 Wheaton 415 (1819).

McDonnell Douglas Corp. v. Green, 411 US 792 (1973).

Murphy v. Miller Brewer Co., 307 F.Supp. 829 (1969).

National Voter Registration Act.

North, Arthur (1964), *The Supreme Court, Judicial Process and Judicial Politics*, Appleton Century Crofts, New York.

Ontario Human Rights Commission v. Simpsons-Sears Ltd., [1985] SCR 536.

Regina v. Oakes, [1986] 1 S.C.R. 103.

Rehabilitation Act.

San Antonio Independent School Division v. Rodriguez, 411 US 1 (1973).

Shakes v. Rex Pak Ltd. (1982), 3 CHRR D/1001.

Spaulding v. University of Washington, 740 F.2d. 686 (1984).

Statutes of Canada, 1869.

Telecommunications Act.

United States Constitution, 1776.

Universal Declaration of Human Rights, 1948.

U.S. Department of Justice, Civil Rights Division, *Disability Rights Section, A Guide to Disability Rights Laws*, 2004.

U.S. Equal Employment Opportunity Commission, U.S. Department of Justice Civil Rights Division, *The Americans with Disabilities Act*.

Voting Accessibility for the Elderly and Handicapped Act.

Chapter 7

This Ability in the
North American Free Trade Agreement

Introduction

This chapter will examine this ability in the area of the North American Free Trade Agreement (NAFTA), which was the largest economic and legal undertaking ever attempted, having an important impact on those with a disability and the labor force. It will look at NAFTA from its inception, examining first its benefits and then its drawbacks. It will also look at the North American Agreement on Labor Cooperation (NAALC) and the Free Trade Area of the Americas (FTAA); as well as other legislation, namely the American Declaration of the Rights and Duties of Man, the American Convention on Human Rights, the Statute of the Inter-American Court on Human Rights, and the Inter-American Democratic Charter.

Toward the North American Free Trade Agreement (NAFTA)

An economic association for 'free trade' was first brought about in North America in 1854. Prior to this, however, there were several developments in the relationship between the United States and British North America, what was to become Canada. The War of 1812 brought an end to the fear of US annexation of Canada, with rather a new view of commercial and economic rivalry between the two countries. The Canadian national sentiment favored trade with the United States through transportation via the railways and the waterways. With the industrial movement in the 1850s came the Grand Trunk Railway system, with an investment of $100 million in transportation and communication.[1] The construction of canals and railways were a move toward the avoidance of continental integration with the United States. The United States, with these developments, was not seen as the enemy but a concurrent competitor, with Canada furnishing natural resources. It was more economical for the United States to pass exports by Montreal through the St. Lawrence seaway in order to lower transportation costs. To assist them, the British, who controlled Canada at the time, would exempt the US traders from duties, treating them like Canadians. Among the market terminals of North America, Mississippi, the Hudson, New Orleans, New York and Montreal, the latter two were rivals, with New York prevailing. North American seaboard centres participated actively in the prosperity brought about by commercialism.

    The first major trade pact between the United States and Canada was the Elgin-Marcy Reciprocity Treaty of 1854. Reciprocity was an attempt to create, in

North America, a single market area covering several distinct political jurisdictions, where specified types of products were freely exchanged for a partial and limited economic union between British North America and the United States.[2] This was thought to be the only feasible alternative to annexation. However, the American Civil War influenced the economic development of British North America, with new markets in the United States opened for Canadian exports. At the end of the war, the removal of restraints on the expansion of US settlement west of the Mississippi jeopardized the security of the Canadian west and hastened Confederation.[3] However, the waterways were a uniting force. The businessmen from Upper Canada, what was to become the Canadian Province of Ontario, were the first to seize the idea of reciprocity. Nevertheless, immediate economic and political union with the United States would have sacrificed valued institutions, national identity and loyalty to Britain for Canada. In the United States, the South with its plantations wanted low tariffs to lower prices of imported goods and to reduce the costs of production for exports of raw materials. On the other hand, the North, with its small farms and factories, was protectionist. There was little enthusiasm for reciprocity in the United States. It was seen as simply a concession for the inclusion of fisheries, the immediate and urgent objective.

Thus, the Treaty was abrogated by the United States on 17 March 1866. British support for the Confederacy during the Civil War and new Canadian tariffs served to antagonize the United States.[4] Other factors played a role, namely the disastrous effects on timber- and grain-growing regions of the United States, the resentment by farming and lumber interests of Canadian competition, the jealousy by shipping and forwarding interests in Buffalo and Philadelphia of the St Lawrence Route and of the Grand Trunk Railway system (with the Victoria Bridge completion in Montreal in 1860 furthering competition), and the manufacturing interests blaming Canadian tariffs for the decline of certain exports. All were a rallying cry for its end. Canada's policy in economic relations was to favour east-west relations. However, the natural tendencies were the opposite, north-south. Shortly after the death of the Reciprocity Treaty until the advent of the 1911 'free trade' election in Canada, free trade with the United States had been the central issue in Canadian politics. Canadian Prime Minister Laurier was the first continentalist Prime Minister to appreciate that Canada shares North America with the United States, which shapes the national destiny.

With the 1911 Free Trade Agreement, Canada built up its own manufacturing protection tariff. In 1911, there was the sentiment in Canada of 'no truck or trade with the Yankees'.[5] However, with the exception of Britain, Canada was the chief trading partner of the United States. In 1910 alone, Canada bought $242 million and sold $97 million to the United States.[6] American President Taft negotiated for full-scale reciprocity for better trade relations between the United States and Canada. Common interests called for special arrangements. Canadians and the US were reminded that there were 3000 miles of joint border between the two countries. The 1911 free trade agreement was similar to the 1854 pact, but was not a treaty, and thus did not require the two-thirds approval of the US Senate. Most US tariffs on manufacturing goods were reduced, while most Canadian manufacturing tariffs remained. It was passed by Congress and signed by US

President Taft. However, Canadian Prime Minister Borden, who defeated Prime Minister Laurier in 1911, opposed the trade legislation and did not put the reciprocity agreement to a vote, with the United States rescinding its vote eight years later.

Other agreements were entered into over the years, and Canada wished for trade on a liberalized basis, the first Article of the General Agreement on Tariffs and Trade (GATT), as well as same treatment. GATT provided for an impressive reduction of tariffs, with some having impeded economic efficiency, production, competition and growth. GATT, through Article 24, permitted the United States and Canada to enter into free trade, with an agreement to remove customs duties and other restrictions on substantially all bilateral trade.[7] Over the last years of GATT and the World Trade Organization (WTO), Canadian exports have multiplied ten times, the national wealth has more than tripled and the number of jobs has doubled.[8] On the other hand, unemployment has also risen over this period, which raises important questions about the benefits of free trade. Wartime demands required greater cooperation on a continental basis, with Canada and Mexico being prime sources of raw materials for US factories.

Private negotiations on free trade once again took place in 1947 between American President Truman and Canadian Prime Minister King, in an era of the Marshall Plan, and of US economic assistance to Western Europe and Japan. King approved the agreement in October 1947, but it was later vetoed in May 1948, because he feared the Canadian public would label it continentalist and anti-British.[9] Overall, by examining the years leading to the advent of the Free Trade Agreement of the 1980s, we can observe a number of characteristics of the trade relationship between the two countries: (1) Canada has been the initiator in free trade on almost all the occasions; (2) the United States has been largely indifferent except for President Taft in 1911; (3) in the two most important negotiations of the twentieth century, 1911 and 1947, Canada had second thoughts and put an end to the agreement; (4) the United States is a formidable obstacle to closer economic ties between the two nations; (5) the 1911 and 1947 deals provided for more US concessions; (6) statements made by the United States were cannon fodder for groups in Canada which were opposed to annexation; (7) Canadian opponents that find economic costs to free trade outweigh economic benefits, and they react on an emotional, loyal, national, love of country level, branding those in favor as stooges of American financial interests; (8) while there is more emphasis today on business, commercial and economic issues, Canada on the other hand has cultural, regional economic development, social welfare and sovereignty concerns; and (9) when times are tough, Canada wants improved access to United States' markets while the United States turns inward toward protectionism.[10]

There is a regional aspect to the overall economic evolution of the North American continent. Canada's industrial development has been North American, with its development based on its natural resources, and its expansion characterized by large-scale monopolistic industries. Over time, Canada's dealings with Britain and the United States changed. Canada once had an autonomous relationship with Britain, producing an unAmerican sentiment. Britain was once the major investor in Canada. However, over the years, the United States has replaced it. Canada went from dependence on the British to dependence on the US, thus producing a foreign controlled economy. In addition, the nature of foreign investment had changed, since the British invested indirectly through obligations and finance, while US concerns invested directly, usually as proprietors funding production. Tariffs and natural resources attracted US enterprises, and Canada benefited from their capital, technological advancement and mass production. The United States invested $168 billion in 1900 and $881 billion in 1914. The Canadian policy was to increase tariffs and oblige US companies wishing to do business to build factories in Canada. The United States penetrated the Canadian economy by installing branch plants for US-made products. By 1932, the United States had dominated the industrial sector, accounting for 82 per cent of car production, 68 per cent of electricity, one third of pulp and paper, and was solidly ahead in petroleum, pharmaceuticals, rubber, machinery and non-metallic minerals. Of the US enterprises in Canada, 36 per cent of them were established in the period between 1920 to 1929. Today, Canada sends more than three-quarters of all its exports to the United States, accounting for 25 per cent of its annual gross national product.[11]

The policy process resulted in the overwhelming trade dependence of Canada on the United States over the years. US policies are destined to affect the policies of Canada and North America as a whole. Canada is carried into the whirlpool of common points of view, to the advantage of the United States, and its own point of view is easily overwhelmed. It is important to understand the way the biases of information would be used to control what individuals do and think. Approaches should be adopted by which cultural traits of civilization might persist, with the least possible depreciation of the national sensibility and dependence of Canadians upon the US. Canada's trade pattern from the outset was based on the importing of manufactured goods in return for the exporting of staples. This approach views staple exports to more advanced industrialized economies as the engine of growth of the Canadian economy.[12] The commercial rather than industrial bias of the Canadian capitalist class, along with dependent branch plant industrialization flowed from the unequal alliance with American foreign ownership and capital. Canada was within the tight embrace of the US empire, and occupied whatever room was left open by US capital. It became the exemplary client State. Today, the United States takes up 70 per cent of Canada's total exports. At the same time, Canada takes in over 20 per cent of United States' exports, and has a direct investment of roughly $20 billion.[13] It is not a zero sum gain with one benefiting at the expense of the other. Canada's prosperity depends on trade with other countries, with one third of its jobs and one quarter of its wealth tied to international trade.[14] From the outset, Canada was torn between republicanism and conservatism, trying to forge a national identity. Canada has wished to be more independent in its foreign policy. At the same time, it has had to guard against the departure of Canadian firms going south in search of cheaper labor and less regulation.

Free trade continentalism, according to its advocates, involves: (1) tariff liberalization; (2) a high volume of trade with the United States; (3) meagre diversification; (4) some protectionism by the United States; (5) restructuring of the Canadian economy for a more competitive industrial society; and (6) transborder transregionalism between provinces and states. Continentalism is a process of microregional (subcontinental) integration, which is transnational (multinational corporations, unions, economic elites) and transgovernmental (direct contacts between two central bureaucracies, relations between provinces and states), with closer Canada United States transactional ties (diplomatic, administrative, commercial, cultural) and structural interpenetration (economic).[15] Canada and the United States are similar as societies with transnational and transgovernmental relationships, attitudes and values, strong social factors and a deep-rooted structural economic interpenetration, in a widespread integration pattern. Canada is strategically situated, with its border close to US development centers.

The free trade zone has eliminated trade barriers as to goods. However, the movement of capital in production has caused negative integration generating disturbances and distortions in the economy. This occurs especially if there is asymmetry within the society, causing imbalances, both regionally and between partners in interactions. The freeing of circulation of goods creates initial imbalances and economic distortions. Before World War II, Canada's prosperity depended on resource industries, which required a high cost in order to protect the manufacturing sector serving the home market. However, in the 1980s, the prosperity of resource-based industries was seriously hurt by international development in the areas of new sources of supply and man-made substitutes for natural materials.[16] Export- and service-related products depended on hard pressed resource-based industries. This created uncertainties in business and job dislocations.[17] However, free trade advocates argued that it was important to secure continued access to the United States' market and to work against protectionism, for benefits to producers in sales and to consumers in prices.[18]

Overall, greater specialization in North America brings greater international competition, encouraging more rapid diffusion of new technology, new management and organizational production. Textile and clothing industries were vulnerable in trade liberalization. The clothing industry would be hard-pressed in lowering prices, except for high volume segments that are successful when moving into particular niches for export. Canada has specialized and expanded its primary and manufacturing sectors, which the proponents of free trade argue has afforded a net benefit through access to the vital US market that is less restrictive and more secure today. The tertiary service industries are more sharply differentiated among countries by the varied regulatory environments. In the goods-producing industries, tariffs or quotas have been the main barrier. The service industry has subtle impediments, with discrimination being a barrier because of immigration labor laws. National treatment calls for no regulatory distinction between foreign and domestic firms, which is good if there are similar industries for reciprocity and market access.[19] These laws restrict one country's firms transferring staff to the other country. Trade in services encompasses a large number of areas, having different characteristics of trade and efforts for international rule-making.

        Considering these factors, sectoral trade discussions in 1983 later gave
way to a comprehensive free trade approach in 1985. US President Reagan and
Canadian Prime Minister Mulroney launched an initiative for a bilateral trade
agreement, with its goal to remove all or most remaining barriers to cross-border
trade in goods and services, and to create an enlarged body of agreed rules to
govern trade, which produced the 1989 Canada United States Free Trade
Agreement (FTA). President Reagan called the document, signed on 2 January
1988, the most important bilateral trade negotiation ever undertaken by the United
States. It was horizontal not sectoral for market access, and called for mutual
restraint on unilateral commercial policies. It was believed that there would be a
direct link between productivity and jobs, with higher productivity and additional
spending power leading to higher incomes and more jobs.[20] Free trade is thought to
afford a longer cycle of production, investment and specialization. This Free Trade
Agreement was the biggest trade agreement ever reached between two countries, in
excess of $200 billion in trade of goods and services.[21] Canada exports more per
citizen than any counterpart in any other industrial power. Thirty per cent of its
national income is generated by exports, and more than three million jobs depend
on these exports. The United States absorbs 80 per cent of Canada's exports, in a
southward flow.[22]

        The Canada United States Free Trade Agreement involved a trading
relationship, which was the world's largest at the time, before NAFTA. The United
States has an economy ten times bigger than Canada's, affording the latter greater
access to opportunities. The relationship encourages lower-cost production in
factories, and more specialized and efficient industries, thereby strengthening the
capacity to compete in the global market. The goal is to generate growth and
production, in order to increase the standard of living for challenging and
rewarding careers. The United States, thereby, consolidates access to the biggest
export market.

North American Free Trade Agreement (NAFTA)

In June 1991, Canada, the United States and Mexico began negotiations in earnest
for the North American Free Trade Agreement (NAFTA). The free trade agenda
shifted from a sectoral approach to a comprehensive accord between the United
States, Canada and Mexico, because of a difficulty in matching sectors and in
accommodating regional concerns. The 1989 Canada United States Free Trade
Agreement laid the foundation for NAFTA, which secured Canada's economic
relationship with the United States.

        Prior to NAFTA coming into effect on 1 January 1994, trade between the
United States and Canada had never been larger and was growing faster than the
rest of the economy. In addition, the flow of trade and investment among the
United States, Canada and Mexico was $500 billion per year. Mexico has a rapidly
growing market of over 85 million people, which historically was hard to penetrate
because of strict Mexican barriers to trade. Before NAFTA, Mexico was restrictive
on foreign investment. However, with NAFTA, Mexican tariffs are phased out

over time. Mexico's border is aligned with the United States and its coastline faces Europe and Asia. It has a key global strategic advantage with its unique geographic position, and is considered the gateway to Latin America, being ranked twelfth in area among the world's nations.[23] Regulations give legal security to market transactions, protect consumers and the environment, and safeguard intellectual property rights. Free trade promotes competition and provides adequate incentives for private decision-making in a free market. However, the regulatory environment must ensure the rules of the game are clear and uniformly applied, subject to monitoring.

NAFTA was the biggest trade agreement ever reached. It covers 360 million consumers and is far-reaching, removing all tariffs and liberalizing non-tariff barriers to trade. NAFTA regulates trade in services, liberalizes investment, promotes specialization, and implements a mechanism for a binding resolution to disputes, which is unprecedented in free trade. The objectives of NAFTA are the removal of tariff and non-tariff barriers for goods and services, the neutralization of government policies, practices and procedures, and a consistency with the GATT agreement to cover all trade.[24] The long-term goals of free trade are the improvement of real income wages and production, an increase in the number of jobs, a reduction of protectionism, a decrease in competitive pressures from developing and newly industrialized countries, and the mitigation of pressures due to global imbalances.[25] The United States had several objectives of its own, namely the elimination of tariffs, the reduction of non-tariff barriers, the development of rules governing trade in services, trucking and insurance, the improvement of protection to intellectual property, greater discipline over subsidies, and an open and secure environment for foreign investment. Canada, for its part, had several goals as well, namely the improved access to the United States and Mexico for goods and services, the strengthening of the initial Canada United States Free Trade Agreement, and the guarantee of its position as a prime location for investors to serve all the North American Continent. Canada hopes that NAFTA will supply it with a sharper edge for international competitiveness, by widening trade horizons and providing a bigger stage on which to demonstrate and prove its economic expertize and leadership.

NAFTA provided that tariffs would be removed within 10 years in the traditional sectors, accounting for half of the trade, and removed either immediately, in five or exceptionally in twenty years for the remainder. It moves toward a harmonized system of tariff nomenclature. It has quantitative restrictions, which build on GATT, and has a sectoral perspective as to agriculture, foods, automotives and energy. There are new elements to the agreement, which include the restriction of investment, the freedom in the future to regulate in conformity with the basic principles of non-discrimination, and the principles of national treatment, right of establishment and right of commercial presence. NAFTA sets out strict rules of origin, requiring that products originate in North America to qualify for preferential duties. For those not meeting this, larger quotas for preferential access to the US market have been included, with these new levels helping textile and apparel manufacturers expand their exports of products to the lucrative US market. Canadian and Mexican tariffs on apparel were eliminated within 10 years, and tariffs on textiles within eight years. Mexico has concentrated on less expensive lower-quality items, while Canada is moving toward higher-value textiles and quality designer fashions. So too, the financial industry was first included in the Canadian United States Free Trade Agreement. It believed that freer market access for financial services would help trade flow more easily. The United States agreed to national treatment, market access and most favored nation status being applied to financial services, fully subjecting the sector to dispute settlement.

The NAFTA Secretariat, comprising the Canadian, US and Mexican Sections, is an organization established by the Free Trade Commission, pursuant to Article 2002, Chapter 20 of the North American Free Trade Agreement. It is responsible for the administration of the dispute settlement provisions of the Agreement, and its mandate includes the provision of assistance to the Commission, and support for various non-dispute-related committees and working groups. Each national Section maintains a court-like registry relating to panel, committee and tribunal proceedings. A similar administrative body, the Binational Secretariat, existed under the Canada United States Free Trade Agreement (FTA). The Parties have established permanent, national Section offices, which are 'mirror-images' of one another, and are located in Ottawa, Washington and Mexico City.

The principle dispute settlement mechanisms of NAFTA are found in Chapters 11, 14, 19 and 20 of the Agreement. NAFTA establishes a mechanism for the settlement of disputes that assures both equal treatment among Parties in accordance with the principle of international reciprocity and due process before an impartial tribunal. Alternatively, the investor may choose the remedies available in the host country's domestic courts. An important feature of the arbitral provisions is the enforceability in domestic courts of final awards by arbitration tribunals. NAFTA provides for a trade commission in charge of political management, which includes a dispute settlement mechanism in the form of a panel. An important role of the Commission is to consider matters relating to the Agreement which are under dispute. When general disputes concerning NAFTA are not resolved through consultation within a specified period of time, the matter may be referred at the request of either Party to a non-binding panel under Article 2008. Various third Party provisions are necessarily included in Chapter 20, as a third Party that considers it has a substantial interest in a disputed matter is entitled to join consultations or a proceeding as a complaining Party on written notice. If a third Party does not join as a complainant, upon written notice, it is entitled to attend hearings, make written and oral submissions and receive written submissions of the disputing Parties. Chapter 20 also provides for an advisory committee to be established to provide recommendations to the Commission on the use of arbitration and other procedures for the resolution of international private commercial disputes. If nothing results from the notification of a consultation action, then a panel review ensues with recommendations that are binding if both sides agree. The dispute settlement is also binding when one side believes that a surge of imports is damaging to it, thereby receiving compensation while the other side is snapped back to a most-favored nation tariff. This procedure was in effect for the first ten years of the agreement, providing steps for negotiation, legislation specificity and panel review. The settlement mechanism calls for compulsory consultation on changes of law, and an evaluation procedure by a panel, with the right to retaliate or withdraw if the panel so favors. NAFTA also provides, for the first time, a system of settling private investment disputes. Disputes between an investor from a NAFTA country and another NAFTA government can be settled at the investor's option by binding international arbitration, with all investors treated equally. The NAFTA dispute settlement provisions call for the rapid and fair settlement of disputes, including the use of impartial panels. There are three basic steps to the process, namely consultation among the three countries for a satisfactory settlement. If the first round fails, the NAFTA trade commission, which comprises cabinet-level representatives, will examine the case for interpretation of trade rules; and if this fails, in order to promote an impartial decision, the issue will be reviewed by a specially selected panel. This panel is composed of five members chosen from a trilaterally agreed roster, with two panellists from the complaining party selected by the defending party, two from the defending party nominated by the complainant and the panel's chair allowed to be a representative from the third NAFTA country or another neutral country chosen by mutual agreement or drawn by lot.

NAFTA has the first international code of binding rules and principles for services. The elimination of tariffs is important for a reduction of protectionism and a climate of open investment. Further, there is a provision for access for temporary personnel in the service and manufacturing sectors, and business recognition of professional and sales services in the spirit of freedom of movement. This latter aspect, however, has not yet been extended to blue-collar workers. NAFTA obliges one country's service providers to treat the other country's no less favorably than their own for domestic and cross-border sales, distribution, and the right of establishment of facilities, providing for mutually acceptable professional licensing standards. However, this equal employment provision in the Member States must go further to protect against any form of discrimination, including disability.

Cross-border trade in services was first included in the Canada United States Free Trade Agreement, and NAFTA has extended these provisions with procedures to encourage the recognition of licenses and certificates through mutually acceptable professional standards and criteria, such as education, experience and professional development. It opens up temporary entry across the border for over 60 professions. Canada's service industry is the fastest growing sector of the economy, accounting for the employment of roughly ten million Canadians, two thirds of the workforce. The service sector has provided 90 per cent of all new jobs in Canada in the last several years. More Canadians now work in software than in the auto industry. Canada's export of services around the world totals an average of $24 billion per year, with business and professional services accounting for 20 per cent of these exports.

While the Canada United States Free Trade Agreement established the first comprehensive set of principles governing services trade, NAFTA broadens these protections and extends them to Mexico. Virtually all services are covered by

NAFTA, with key sectors being: accounting, architecture, land transport, publishing, consulting, commercial education, environmental services, enhanced telecommunications, advertising, broadcasting, construction, tourism, engineering, health care, management, and legal services. Each country has also excluded certain sensitive sectors from coverage, such that Mexico will not liberalize services of public notaries, which are specifically reserved to Mexicans by the Mexican Constitution, and Canada has retained its cultural exclusion, which affects the entertainment and publishing industries. NAFTA does not remove or weaken licensing and certification requirements but, consistent with the NAFTA principle of non-discrimination, licensing of professionals, such as lawyers, doctors, and accountants, should be based on objective criteria aimed at ensuring competence, not on nationality. NAFTA does not permit US, Mexican or Canadian professionals to practice in the other Member countries, unless they have undergone the same licensing and certification procedures as a National professional.

The Preamble of the North American Free Trade Agreement, important for disability equality, states:

> The Government of Canada, the Government of the United Mexican States and the Government of the United States of America, resolved to:
>
> STRENGTHEN the special bonds of friendship and cooperation among their nations;
>
> CONTRIBUTE to the harmonious development and expansion of world trade and provide a catalyst to broader international cooperation;
>
> CREATE an expanded and secure market for the goods and services produced in their territories;
>
> REDUCE distortions to trade;
>
> ESTABLISH clear and mutually advantageous rules governing their trade;
>
> ENSURE a predictable commercial framework for business planning and investment;
>
> BUILD on their respective rights and obligations under the *General Agreement on Tariffs and Trade* and other multilateral and bilateral instruments of cooperation;
>
> ENHANCE the competitiveness of their firms in global markets;
>
> FOSTER creativity and innovation, and promote trade in goods and services that are the subject of intellectual property rights;
>
> CREATE new employment opportunities and improve working conditions and living standards in their respective territories;
>
> UNDERTAKE each of the preceding in a manner consistent with environmental protection and conservation;

PRESERVE their flexibility to safeguard the public welfare;

PROMOTE sustainable development;

STRENGTHEN the development and enforcement of environmental laws and regulations; and

PROTECT, enhance and enforce basic workers' rights.[26]

Specifically, under the agreement, in terms of service providers, Article 1201 applies to measures adopted or maintained by a Party relating to cross-border trade in services by service providers of another Party, including measures respecting the production, distribution, marketing, sale and delivery of a service; the purchase or use of, or payment for, a service; the access to and use of distribution and transportation systems in connection with the provision of a service; the presence in its territory of a service provider of another Party; and the provision of a bond or other form of financial security as a condition for the provision of a service. [27]

Articles 1202 and 1203 provide that each Party shall accord to service providers of another Party treatment no less favorable than that it accords, in like circumstances, to service providers of any other Party or of a non-Party.[28] Further, Article 1208 maintains that each Party shall set out in its Schedule to Annex VI its commitments to liberalize quantitative restrictions, licensing requirements, performance requirements or other non-discriminatory measures.[29]

Importantly, Article 1210 provides for licensing and certification requirements:

> 1210.1. With a view to ensuring that any measure adopted or maintained by a Party relating to the licensing or certification of nationals of another Party does not constitute an unnecessary barrier to trade, each Party shall endeavor to ensure that any such measure:
> (a) is based on objective and transparent criteria, such as competence and the ability to provide a service;
> (b) is not more burdensome than necessary to ensure the quality of a service; and
> (c) does not constitute a disguised restriction on the cross-border provision of a service.
> 2. ... a Party shall not be required to extend to a service provider of another Party the benefits of recognition of education, experience, licenses or certifications obtained in another country, whether such recognition was accorded unilaterally or by arrangement or agreement with that other country. The Party according such recognition shall afford any interested Party an adequate opportunity to demonstrate that education, experience, licenses or certifications obtained in that other Party's territory should also be recognized or to negotiate and enter into an agreement or arrangement of comparable effect.
> 3. ... a Party shall eliminate any citizenship or permanent residency requirement for the licensing and certification of professional service providers in its territory
> ....[30]

Professional services are defined in Article 1213 to mean services, the provision of which requires specialized post-secondary education, or equivalent training or experience, and for which the right to practice is granted or restricted by a Party, but does not include services provided by trades-persons or vessel and aircraft crew members.[31]

Licensing and certification standards for professionals are provided for in Annex 1210.A.2.:

> Annex 1210.A.2. The Parties shall encourage the relevant bodies in their respective territories to develop mutually acceptable standards and criteria for licensing and certification of professional service providers and to provide recommendations on mutual recognition to the Commission.[32]

Additionally, Annex 1210.A.3. provides for standards and criteria to be developed:

> Annex 1210.A.3. The standards and criteria referred to in paragraph 2 may be developed with regard to the following matters:
> (a) education: accreditation of schools or academic programs;
> (b) examinations: qualifying examinations for licensing, including alternative methods of assessment such as oral examinations and interviews;
> (c) experience: length and nature of experience required for licensing;
> (d) conduct and ethics: standards of professional conduct and the nature of disciplinary action for non-conformity with those standards;
> (e) professional development and re-certification: continuing education and ongoing requirements to maintain professional certification;
> (f) scope of practice: extent of, or limitations on, permissible activities;
> (g) local knowledge: requirements for knowledge of such matters as local laws, regulations, language, geography or climate; and
> (h) consumer protection: alternatives to residency requirements, including bonding, professional liability insurance and client restitution funds, to provide for the protection of consumers.[33]

Further, Annex 1210.B.1. provides that each Party shall, in implementing its obligations and commitments regarding foreign legal consultants as set out in its relevant Schedules and subject to any reservations therein, ensure that a national of another Party is permitted to practise or advise on the law of any country in which that national is authorized to practise as a lawyer.[34]

In terms of the temporary entry for business people, Chapter 16 and specifically Article 1601 specify:

> 1601. This Chapter reflects the preferential trading relationship between the Parties, the desirability of facilitating temporary entry on a reciprocal basis and of establishing transparent criteria and procedures for temporary entry, and the need to ensure border security and to protect the domestic labor force and permanent employment in their respective territories.[35]

Article 1602 outlines the general obligations:

1602. 1. Each Party shall apply its measures relating to the provisions of this Chapter in accordance with Article 1601 and, in particular, shall apply expeditiously those measures so as to avoid unduly impairing or delaying trade in goods or services or conduct of investment activities under this Agreement.
2. The Parties shall endeavor to develop and adopt common criteria, definitions and interpretations for the implementation of this Chapter.[36]

The dispute settlement procedure is included in Article 1606:

1606. 1. A Party may not initiate proceedings under Article 2007 (Commission - Good Offices, Conciliation and Mediation) regarding a refusal to grant temporary entry under this Chapter or a particular case arising under Article 1602(1) unless:
(a) the matter involves a pattern of practice; and
(b) the business person has exhausted the available administrative remedies regarding the particular matter.
2. The remedies referred to in paragraph (1) (b) shall be deemed to be exhausted if a final determination in the matter has not been issued by the competent authority within one year of the institution of an administrative proceeding, and the failure to issue a determination is not attributable to delay caused by the business person.[37]

Annex 1603 notes additional requirements in order to gain entry for different classes of individuals. Section A provides for business visitors:

Annex 1603.A.1. Each Party shall grant temporary entry to a business person seeking to engage in a business activity set out in Appendix 1603.A.1, without requiring that person to obtain an employment authorization, provided that the business person otherwise complies with existing immigration measures applicable to temporary entry, on presentation of:
(a) proof of citizenship of a Party;
(b) documentation demonstrating that the business person will be so engaged and describing the purpose of entry; and
(c) evidence demonstrating that the proposed business activity is international in scope and that the business person is not seeking to enter the local labor market.
2. Each Party shall provide that a business person may satisfy the requirements of paragraph 1(c) by demonstrating that:
(a) the primary source of remuneration for the proposed business activity is outside the territory of the Party granting temporary entry; and
(b) the business person's principal place of business and the actual place of accrual of profits, at least predominantly, remain outside such territory.
A Party shall normally accept an oral declaration as to the principal place of business and the actual place of accrual of profits. Where the Party requires further proof, it shall normally consider a letter from the employer attesting to these matters as sufficient proof.
3. Each Party shall grant temporary entry to a business person seeking to engage in a business activity other than those set out in Appendix 1603.A.1, without requiring that person to obtain an employment authorization, on a basis no less favorable than that provided under the existing provisions of the measures set out in Appendix 1603.A.3, provided that the business person otherwise complies with existing immigration measures applicable to temporary entry.

4. No Party may:

(a) as a condition for temporary entry under paragraph 1 or 3, require prior approval procedures, petitions, labor certification tests or other procedures of similar effect; or

(b) impose or maintain any numerical restriction relating to temporary entry under paragraph 1 or 3.

5. Notwithstanding paragraph 4, a Party may require a business person seeking temporary entry under this Section to obtain a visa or its equivalent prior to entry. Before imposing a visa requirement, the Party shall consult with a Party whose business persons would be affected with a view to avoiding the imposition of the requirement. With respect to an existing visa requirement, a Party shall consult, on request, with a Party whose business persons are subject to the requirement with a view to its removal.[38]

Section B provides for traders and investors:

Annex 1603.B.1. Each Party shall grant temporary entry and provide confirming documentation to a business person seeking to:

(a) carry on substantial trade in goods or services principally between the territory of the Party of which the business person is a citizen and the territory of the Party into which entry is sought, or

(b) establish, develop, administer or provide advice or key technical services to the operation of an investment to which the business person or the business person's enterprise has committed, or is in the process of committing, a substantial amount of capital, in a capacity that is supervisory, executive or involves essential skills, provided that the business person otherwise complies with existing immigration measures applicable to temporary entry.

2. No Party may:

(a) as a condition for temporary entry under paragraph 1, require labor certification tests or other procedures of similar effect; or

(b) impose or maintain any numerical restriction relating to temporary entry under paragraph 1.

3. Notwithstanding paragraph 2, a Party may require a business person seeking temporary entry under this Section to obtain a visa or its equivalent prior to entry.[39]

Section C provides for intra-company transferees:

Annex 1603.C.1. Each Party shall grant temporary entry and provide confirming documentation to a business person employed by an enterprise who seeks to render services to that enterprise or a subsidiary or affiliate thereof, in a capacity that is managerial, executive or involves specialized knowledge, provided that the business person otherwise complies with existing immigration measures applicable to temporary entry. A Party may require the business person to have been employed continuously by the enterprise for one year within the three-year period immediately preceding the date of the application for admission.

2. No Party may:

(a) as a condition for temporary entry under paragraph 1, require labor certification tests or other procedures of similar effect; or

(b) impose or maintain any numerical restriction relating to temporary entry under paragraph 1.

3. Notwithstanding paragraph 2, a Party may require a business person seeking temporary entry under this Section to obtain a visa or its equivalent prior to entry. Before imposing a visa requirement, the Party shall consult with a Party whose business persons would be affected with a view to avoiding the imposition of the requirement. With respect to an existing visa requirement, a Party shall consult, on request, with a Party whose business persons are subject to the requirement with a view to its removal.[40]

Section D provides for professionals:

> Annex 1603.D.1. Each Party shall grant temporary entry and provide confirming documentation to a business person seeking to engage in a business activity at a professional level in a profession set out in Appendix 1603.D.1, if the business person otherwise complies with existing immigration measures applicable to temporary entry, on presentation of:
> (a) proof of citizenship of a Party; and
> (b) documentation demonstrating that the business person will be so engaged and describing the purpose of entry.
> 2. No Party may:
> (a) as a condition for temporary entry under paragraph 1, require prior approval procedures, petitions, labor certification tests or other procedures of similar effect; or
> (b) impose or maintain any numerical restriction relating to temporary entry under paragraph 1.
> 3. Notwithstanding paragraph 2, a Party may require a business person seeking temporary entry under this Section to obtain a visa or its equivalent prior to entry. Before imposing a visa requirement, the Party shall consult with a Party whose business persons would be affected with a view to avoiding the imposition of the requirement. With respect to an existing visa requirement, a Party shall consult, on request, with a Party whose business persons are subject to the requirement with a view to its removal.
> 4. Notwithstanding paragraphs 1 and 2, a Party may establish an annual numerical limit, which shall be set out in Appendix 1603.D.4, regarding temporary entry of business persons of another Party seeking to engage in business activities at a professional level in a profession set out in Appendix 1603.D.1, if the Parties concerned have not agreed otherwise prior to the date of entry into force of this Agreement for those Parties. In establishing such a limit, the Party shall consult with the other Party concerned.
> 5. A Party establishing a numerical limit pursuant to paragraph 4, unless the Parties concerned agree otherwise:
> (a) shall, for each year after the first year after the date of entry into force of this Agreement, consider increasing the numerical limit set out in Appendix 1603.D.4 by an amount to be established in consultation with the other Party concerned, taking into account the demand for temporary entry under this Section;
> (b) shall not apply its procedures established pursuant to paragraph 1 to the temporary entry of a business person subject to the numerical limit, but may require the business person to comply with its other procedures applicable to the temporary entry of professionals; and
> (c) may, in consultation with the other Party concerned, grant temporary entry

under paragraph 1 to a business person who practices in a profession where accreditation, licensing, and certification requirements are mutually recognized by those Parties.

6. Nothing in paragraph 4 or 5 shall be construed to limit the ability of a business person to seek temporary entry under a Party's applicable immigration measures relating to the entry of professionals other than those adopted or maintained pursuant to paragraph 1.[41]

Appendix 1603.D.1 outlines the different professions provided for under NAFTA, along with the minimum educational requirements and alternative credentials.[42]

Further, there are a number of institutions that are part of NAFTA. Article 2001 provides for the Free Trade Commission:

> 2001. 1. The Parties hereby establish the Free Trade Commission, comprising cabinet-level representatives of the Parties or their designees.
> 2. The Commission shall:
> (a) supervise the implementation of this Agreement;
> (b) oversee its further elaboration;
> (c) resolve disputes that may arise regarding its interpretation or application;
> (d) supervise the work of all committees and working groups established under this Agreement, referred to in Annex 2001.2; and
> (e) consider any other matter that may affect the operation of this Agreement.
> 3. The Commission may:
> (a) establish, and delegate responsibilities to, ad hoc or standing committees, working groups or expert groups;
> (b) seek the advice of nongovernmental persons or groups; and
> (c) take such other action in the exercise of its functions as the Parties may agree.[43]

Further, Article 2002 provides for the Secretariat:

> 2002. 1. The Commission shall establish and oversee a Secretariat comprising national Sections.
> 2. Each Party shall:
> (a) establish a permanent office of its Section;
> (b) be responsible for
>   (i) the operation and costs of its Section, and
>   (ii) the remuneration and payment of expenses of panelists and members of committees and scientific review boards established under this Agreement, as set out in Annex 2002.2;
> (c) designate an individual to serve as Secretary for its Section, who shall be responsible for its administration and management; and
> (d) notify the Commission of the location of its Section's office.
> 3. The Secretariat shall:
> (a) provide assistance to the Commission;
> (b) provide administrative assistance to
>   (i) panels and committees established under Chapter Nineteen (Review and Dispute Settlement in Antidumping and Countervailing Duty Matters), in accordance with the procedures established pursuant to Article 1908, and
>   (ii) panels established under this Chapter, in accordance with procedures

established pursuant to Article 2012; and
(c) as the Commission may direct
(i) support the work of other committees and groups established under this Agreement, and
(ii) otherwise facilitate the operation of this Agreement.[44]

In terms of dispute settlement, cooperation is stressed under Article 2003:

2003. The Parties shall at all times endeavor to agree on the interpretation and application of this Agreement, and shall make every attempt through cooperation and consultations to arrive at a mutually satisfactory resolution of any matter that might affect its operation.[45]

Recourse to dispute settlement procedures is enunciated under Article 2004:

2004. Except for the matters covered in Chapter Nineteen (Review and Dispute Settlement in Antidumping and Countervailing Duty Matters) and as otherwise provided in this Agreement, the dispute settlement provisions of this Chapter shall apply with respect to the avoidance or settlement of all disputes between the Parties regarding the interpretation or application of this Agreement or wherever a Party considers that an actual or proposed measure of another Party is or would be inconsistent with the obligations of this Agreement or cause nullification or impairment in the sense of Annex 2004.[46]

In terms of panel proceedings, a request for an arbitral panel is contained in Article 2008:

2008. 1. If the Commission has convened pursuant to Article 2007(4), and the matter has not been resolved within:
(a) 30 days thereafter,
(b) 30 days after the Commission has convened in respect of the matter most recently referred to it, where proceedings have been consolidated pursuant to Article 2007(6), or
(c) such other period as the consulting Parties may agree,
any consulting Party may request in writing the establishment of an arbitral panel. The requesting Party shall deliver the request to the other Parties and to its Section of the Secretariat.
2. On delivery of the request, the Commission shall establish an arbitral panel.
3. A third Party that considers it has a substantial interest in the matter shall be entitled to join as a complaining Party on delivery of written notice of its intention to participate to the disputing Parties and its Section of the Secretariat. The notice shall be delivered at the earliest possible time, and in any event no later than seven days after the date of delivery of a request by a Party for the establishment of a panel.
4. If a third Party does not join as a complaining Party in accordance with paragraph 3, it normally shall refrain thereafter from initiating or continuing:
(a) a dispute settlement procedure under this Agreement, or
(b) a dispute settlement proceeding in the GATT on grounds that are substantially equivalent to those available to that Party under this Agreement,
regarding the same matter in the absence of a significant change in economic or

commercial circumstances.

5. Unless otherwise agreed by the disputing Parties, the panel shall be established and perform its functions in a manner consistent with the provisions of this Chapter.[47]

The rules of procedure are outlined in Article 2012:

2012. 1. The Commission shall establish by January 1, 1994, Model Rules of Procedure, in accordance with the following principles:
(a) the procedures shall assure a right to at least one hearing before the panel as well as the opportunity to provide initial and rebuttal written submissions; and
(b) the panel's hearings, deliberations and initial report, and all written submissions to and communications with the panel shall be confidential.
2. Unless the disputing Parties otherwise agree, the panel shall conduct its proceedings in accordance with the Model Rules of Procedure.
3. Unless the disputing Parties otherwise agree within 20 days from the date of the delivery of the request for the establishment of the panel, the terms of reference shall be:
'To examine, in the light of the relevant provisions of the Agreement, the matter referred to the Commission (as set out in the request for a Commission meeting) and to make findings, determinations and recommendations as provided in Article 2016(2)'.[48]

Third party participation is permitted under Article 2013:

2013. A Party that is not a disputing Party, on delivery of a written notice to the disputing Parties and to its Section of the Secretariat, shall be entitled to attend all hearings, to make written and oral submissions to the panel and to receive written submissions of the disputing Parties.

The panel's final report is contained in Article 2017:

2017. 1. The panel shall present to the disputing Parties a final report, including any separate opinions on matters not unanimously agreed, within 30 days of presentation of the initial report, unless the disputing Parties otherwise agree.[49]

Implementation of final report is stressed under Article 2018:

2018. 1. On receipt of the final report of a panel, the disputing Parties shall agree on the resolution of the dispute, which normally shall conform with the determinations and recommendations of the panel, and shall notify their Sections of the Secretariat of any agreed resolution of any dispute.[50]

Importantly, non-implementation and the suspension of benefits are provided for under Article 2019:

2019. 1. If in its final report a panel has determined that a measure is inconsistent with the obligations of this Agreement or causes nullification or impairment in the sense of Annex 2004 and the Party complained against has not reached agreement with any complaining Party on a mutually satisfactory resolution pursuant to

Article 2018(1) within 30 days of receiving the final report, such complaining Party may suspend the application to the Party complained against of benefits of equivalent effect until such time as they have reached agreement on a resolution of the dispute.

2. In considering what benefits to suspend pursuant to paragraph 1:

(a) a complaining Party should first seek to suspend benefits in the same sector or sectors as that affected by the measure or other matter that the panel has found to be inconsistent with the obligations of this Agreement or to have caused nullification or impairment in the sense of Annex 2004; and

(b) a complaining Party that considers it is not practicable or effective to suspend benefits in the same sector or sectors may suspend benefits in other sectors.[51]

In terms of domestic proceedings and private commercial dispute settlement, Article 2020 provides for referrals of matters from judicial or administrative proceedings:

2020. 1. If an issue of interpretation or application of this Agreement arises in any domestic judicial or administrative proceeding of a Party that any Party considers would merit its intervention, or if a court or administrative body solicits the views of a Party, that Party shall notify the other Parties and its Section of the Secretariat. The Commission shall endeavor to agree on an appropriate response as expeditiously as possible.

2. The Party in whose territory the court or administrative body is located shall submit any agreed interpretation of the Commission to the court or administrative body in accordance with the rules of that forum.

3. If the Commission is unable to agree, any Party may submit its own views to the court or administrative body in accordance with the rules of that forum.[52]

Further, private rights are guaranteed under Article 2021:

2021. No Party may provide for a right of action under its domestic law against any other Party on the ground that a measure of another Party is inconsistent with this Agreement.[53]

Finally, Article 2022 provides for alternative dispute resolution:

2022. 1. Each Party shall, to the maximum extent possible, encourage and facilitate the use of arbitration and other means of alternative dispute resolution for the settlement of international commercial disputes between private parties in the free trade area.

2. To this end, each Party shall provide appropriate procedures to ensure observance of agreements to arbitrate and for the recognition and enforcement of arbitral awards in such disputes.[54]

North American Agreement on Labor Cooperation (NAALC)

The North American Agreement on Labor Cooperation (NAALC) 1993, a side agreement to NAFTA, promotes the enforcement of national labor laws and transparency in their administration, important for disability equality. Through NAALC, the NAFTA partners seek to improve working conditions and living standards, and commit themselves to promoting principles that protect, enhance and enforce basic workers' rights. To accomplish these goals, the NAALC creates mechanisms for cooperative activities and intergovernmental consultations, as well as for independent evaluations and dispute settlement related to the enforcement of labor laws. Public submissions made under the NAALC have led to public hearings, ministerial consultations, and action plans to address concerns raised. In addition, NAFTA partners have established cooperative programs and technical exchanges on industrial relations, health and safety, child labor, gender equity and migrant worker issues.

The general obligation of each Party is to ensure the effective enforcement of its own labor law. Specific obligations refer to publication of labor laws and related regulations and procedures, and to promotion of awareness of and compliance with them. Parties will also ensure availability of public information related to its labor law, and enforcement and compliance procedures. Other obligations include government enforcement actions for promoting compliance and effective enforcement of its labor law, covering such matters as: appointing and training of inspectors, monitoring compliance and examining suspected violations; carrying out inspections, mandatory reporting and record keeping; encouraging worker-management committees; providing mediation, conciliation, or arbitration services; and initiating in a timely manner enforcement actions seeking appropriate remedies. Each Party is committed to ensuring access by persons with a legally recognized interest to administrative, judicial, and related tribunals, including recourse to procedures by which labor rights can be enforced in a binding fashion. The Agreement also provides that such tribunals and proceedings before them would be fair and comply with due process.

The intention of the Parties in the Agreement on Labor Cooperation is to pursue a set of general objectives, which aim at complementing NAFTA by promoting the improvement of working conditions and living standards in all three countries. The Commission for Labor Cooperation is trilateral and consists of a Ministerial Council and a Secretariat. The Council oversees the implementation of the agreement, promotes cooperative activities and directs the work of the Secretariat. The agreement reflects the shared recognition of the United States, Mexico, and Canada that their mutual prosperity depends on the promotion of fair and open competition based on innovation and rising levels of productivity and quality with due regard for the importance of labor laws and principles. The Agreement increases cooperation and promotes greater understanding among the Parties in a broad range of labor areas; establishes the obligation of each Party to ensure the enforcement of its domestic labor laws; provides mechanisms to permit problem-solving consultations; enables the Parties to initiate evaluations of patterns of practice by independent committees of experts; and allows for dispute settlement procedures.

A trinational Labor Commission is created to facilitate the achievement of the objectives of the Agreement and to deal with labor issues in a cooperative, and consultative manner that duly respects the three nations' sovereignty. The Labor Commission consists of a Ministerial Council, an International Coordinating Secretariat, and three National Administrative Offices (NAOs). The Ministerial Council consists of the labor Ministers from the three signatory countries, who supervise the implementation of the Agreement, including the work of the International Coordinating Secretariat (ICS). An ICS, under the direction of the Ministerial Council, carries out the day-to-day work of the Commission, and is responsible for assisting the Council in its work, for gathering and periodically publishing information on labor matters in Canada, the United States and Mexico, for planning and coordinating cooperative activities, and for supporting any working groups or evaluation committees established by the Ministerial Council. The NAOs, established by each Party, serve as a point of contact for and facilitate the provision of information to other Parties on domestic law and practice; receive public communications; conduct preliminary reviews; and promote the exchange of information relevant to the Agreement.

As to resolution of disputes, if the Council cannot resolve a dispute involving a Party's alleged persistent pattern of failure to effectively enforce labor laws with respect to health and safety, child labor and minimum wage, relating to a situation involving mutually recognized labor laws and the production of goods or services traded between the Parties, any Party may request an arbitral panel. A panel will be established on a two-thirds vote of the council, and panelists will normally be chosen from a previously agreed roster of experts, including experts on labor matters. With the approval of the disputing Parties, a panel may seek information and technical advice from any person or body that it deems appropriate, and the report of the panel will be made publicly available five days after it is transmitted to the Parties. If a panel makes a finding that a Party has engaged in a persistent pattern of failure to effectively enforce its labor laws, the Parties may, within 60 days, agree on a mutually satisfactory action plan to remedy the non-enforcement. If there is no agreed action plan, then between 60 and 120 days after the final panel report, the panel may be reconvened to evaluate an action plan proposed by the Party complained against or to set out an action plan in its stead. The panel would also make a determination on the imposition of monetary enforcement assessments on the alleged offending Party. The panel may be reconvened at any time to determine if an action plan is being fully implemented, and if not, the panel is to impose a monetary enforcement assessment on the alleged offending Party. In the event that a Party complained against fails to pay a monetary enforcement assessment or continues in its failure to enforce its labor law and minimum wage, the Party is liable to ongoing enforcement actions. In the case of Canada, the Commission, on the request of a complaining Party, collects the monetary enforcement assessment and enforces an action plan in summary proceedings before a Canadian court of competent jurisdiction. In the case of

Mexico and the United States, the complaining Party or Parties may suspend NAFTA benefits based on the amount of the assessment.

The Preamble to the North American Agreement on Labor Cooperation (NAALC) states that the Government of the United States of America, the Government of Canada and the Government of the United Mexican States undertake the agreement:

> RECALLING their resolve in the North American Free Trade Agreement (NAFTA) to:
> create an expanded and secure market for the goods and services produced in their territories,
> enhance the competitiveness of their firms in global markets,
> create new employment opportunities and improve working conditions and living standards in their respective territories, and
> protect, enhance and enforce basic workers' rights;
>
> AFFIRMING their continuing respect for each Party's constitution and law;
>
> DESIRING to build on their respective international commitments and to strengthen their cooperation on labor matters;
>
> RECOGNIZING that their mutual prosperity depends on the promotion of competition based on innovation and rising levels of productivity and quality;
>
> SEEKING to complement the economic opportunities created by the NAFTA with the human resource development, labor-management cooperation and continuous learning that characterize high-productivity economies;
>
> ACKNOWLEDGING that protecting basic workers' rights will encourage firms to adopt high-productivity competitive strategies;
>
> RESOLVED to promote, in accordance with their respective laws, high-skill, high-productivity economic development in North America by:
> investing in continuous human resource development, including for entry into the workforce and during periods of unemployment;
> promoting employment security and career opportunities for all workers through referral and other employment services;
> strengthening labor-management cooperation to promote greater dialogue between worker organizations and employers and to foster creativity and productivity in the workplace;
> promoting higher living standards as productivity increases;
> encouraging consultation and dialogue between labor, business and government both in each country and in North America;
> fostering investment with due regard for the importance of labor laws and principles;
> encouraging employers and employees in each country to comply with labor laws and to work together in maintaining a progressive, fair, safe and healthy working environment;

BUILDING on existing institutions and mechanisms in Canada, Mexico and the United States to achieve the preceding economic and social goals; and

CONVINCED of the benefits to be gained from further cooperation between them on labor matters.[55]

The objectives of the agreement are outlined in Article 1:

1(a) improve working conditions and living standards in each Party's territory;
(b) promote, to the maximum extent possible, the labor principles set out in Annex 1;
(c) encourage cooperation to promote innovation and rising levels of productivity and quality;
(d) encourage publication and exchange of information, data development and coordination, and joint studies to enhance mutually beneficial understanding of the laws and institutions governing labor in each Party's territory;
(e) pursue cooperative labor-related activities on the basis of mutual benefit;
(f) promote compliance with, and effective enforcement by each Party of, its labor law; and
(g) foster transparency in the administration of labor law.[56]

The Preamble to NAALC reaffirms relevant provisions of the Preamble to NAFTA and adds further shared goals related to labor matters. Importantly, each Party is committed, in accordance with its domestic laws, to promote equal pay and the elimination of employment discrimination, important for disability equality. Further, each is committed to the following labor principles: the freedom of association, the right to bargain collectively, the right to strike, prohibition of forced labor, restrictions on labor by children and young people, minimum employment standards, prevention of occupational accidents and diseases, compensation in cases of work accidents or occupational diseases, and protection of migrant workers. The Agreement sets forth the following general objectives: improving working conditions and living standards, promoting compliance with and effective enforcement of labor laws, promoting the Agreement's principles through cooperation and coordination, and promoting publication and exchange of information to enhance mutual understanding of Parties' laws, institutions and legal systems.

Specifically, in terms of Obligations of the Parties and the Levels of Protection, Article 2 holds that affirming full respect for each Party's constitution, and recognizing the right of each Party to establish its own domestic labor standards, and to adopt or modify accordingly its labor laws and regulations, each Party shall ensure that its labor laws and regulations provide for high labor standards, consistent with high quality and productivity workplaces, and shall continue to strive to improve those standards in that light.[57]

Government enforcement action is established under Article 3, which states that each Party shall promote compliance with and effectively enforce its labor law through appropriate government action, such as:

3(a) appointing and training inspectors;

(b) monitoring compliance and investigating suspected violations, including through on-site inspections;

(c) seeking assurances of voluntary compliance;

(d) requiring record keeping and reporting;

(e) encouraging the establishment of worker-management committees to address labor regulation of the workplace;

(f) providing or encouraging mediation, conciliation and arbitration services; or

(g) initiating, in a timely manner, proceedings to seek appropriate sanctions or remedies for violations of its labor law.[58]

The agreement safeguards private action in Article 4, which holds that each Party shall ensure that persons with a legally recognized interest under its law in a particular matter have appropriate access to administrative, quasi-judicial, judicial or labor tribunals for the enforcement of the Party's labor law. Further, each Party's law shall ensure that such persons may have recourse to, as appropriate, procedures by which rights arising under its labor law, including those in respect of occupational safety and health, employment standards, industrial relations and migrant workers, and collective agreements, can be enforced.[59]

Under procedural guarantees, Article 5 establishes that each Party shall ensure that its administrative, quasi-judicial, judicial and labor tribunal proceedings for the enforcement of its labor law are fair, equitable and transparent and, to this end, each Party shall provide that such proceedings comply with due process of law; any hearings in such proceedings are open to the public, except where the administration of justice otherwise requires; the parties to such proceedings are entitled to support or defend their respective positions and to present information or evidence; and such proceedings are not unnecessarily complicated and do not entail unreasonable charges or time limits or unwarranted delays. Further, each Party shall provide that final decisions on the merits of the case in such proceedings are in writing and preferably state the reasons on which the decisions are based; made available without undue delay to the parties to the proceedings and, consistent with its law, to the public; and based on information or evidence in respect of which the parties were offered the opportunity to be heard. Each Party shall provide, as appropriate, that parties to such proceedings have the right, in accordance with its law, to seek review and, where warranted, correction of final decisions issued in such proceedings. Additionally, each Party shall ensure that tribunals that conduct or review such proceedings are impartial and independent and do not have any substantial interest in the outcome of the matter. Each Party shall provide that the parties to administrative, quasi-judicial, judicial or labor tribunal proceedings may seek remedies to ensure the enforcement of their labor rights. Such remedies may include, as appropriate, orders, compliance agreements, fines, penalties, imprisonment, injunctions or emergency workplace closures. Each Party may, as appropriate, adopt or maintain labor defense offices to represent or advise workers or their organizations. Nothing in this Article shall be construed to require a Party to establish, or to prevent a Party from establishing, a judicial system for the enforcement of its labor law distinct from its system for the enforcement of laws in general. Finally, for greater certainty, decisions by each

Party's administrative, quasi-judicial, judicial or labor tribunals, or pending decisions, as well as related proceedings shall not be subject to revision or reopened under the provisions of this Agreement.[60]

In terms of cooperative activities, Article 11 underlines the importance of labor practices and cooperative activities for equality:

> 11.1. The Council shall promote cooperative activities between the Parties, as appropriate, regarding:
>   a.   occupational safety and health;
>   b.   child labor;
>   c.   migrant workers of the Parties;
>   d.   human resource development;
>   e.   labor statistics;
>   f.   work benefits;
>   g.   social programs for workers and their families;
>   h.   programs, methodologies and experiences regarding productivity improvement;
>   i.   labor-management relations and collective bargaining procedures;
>   j.   employment standards and their implementation;
>   k.   compensation for work-related injury or illness;
>   l.   legislation relating to the formation and operation of unions, collective bargaining and the resolution of labor disputes, and its implementation;
>   m.   the equality of women and men in the workplace;
>   n.   forms of cooperation among workers, management and government;
>   o.   the provision of technical assistance, at the request of a Party, for the development of its labor standards; and
>   p.   such other matters as the Parties may agree.
> 2. In carrying out the activities referred to in paragraph 1, the Parties may, commensurate with the availability of resources in each Party, cooperate through:
>   a.   seminars, training sessions, working groups and conferences;
>   b.   joint research projects, including sectoral studies;
>   c.   technical assistance; and
>   d.   such other means as the Parties may agree.
> 3. The Parties shall carry out the cooperative activities referred to in paragraph 1 with due regard for the economic, social, cultural and legislative differences between them.[61]

Article 49 defines labor law as laws and regulations, or provisions thereof, that are directly related to, among other things, the elimination of employment discrimination on the basis of grounds such as race, religion, age, sex, or other grounds, including disability, as determined by each Party's domestic laws; and equal pay.[62]

Annex 1 outlines guiding principles that the Parties are committed to promote, subject to each Party's domestic law but not establishing common minimum standards for their domestic law, and indicates broad areas of concern where the Parties have developed, each in its own way, laws, regulations, procedures and practices that protect the rights and interests of their respective workforces. These include the elimination of employment discrimination on such grounds as race, religion, age, sex or other grounds, including disability, subject to certain reasonable exceptions, such as, where applicable, bona fide occupational requirements or qualifications and established practices or rules governing retirement ages, and special measures of protection or assistance for particular groups designed to take into account the effects of discrimination; and equal wages for women and men, including those with a disability, by applying the principle of equal pay for equal work in the same establishment.[63]

North American Free Trade Agreement Benefits and Concerns

NAFTA, the advocates argue, provides several benefits: (1) improved access to the North American market of 360 million consumers, as to manufactured goods, and business and professional services; (2) opportunities to export more products and services to Mexico, which needs capital goods, services and investment; (3) new export and investment opportunities for companies in different markets; (4) a more equitable trading relationship through the elimination of almost all Mexican tariffs and imports, with Mexico being the largest trading partner in Latin America; (5) strengthened and precise North American rules of origin to determine which goods qualify for duty free treatment in North America; (6) Opportunities to bid on large government procurement contracts, with equal access to the bid process in some sectors; (7) improved methods to settle trade disputes among Canada, Mexico and the United States; (8) protection of key domestic interests, including culture, education, water, health and social services, such as childcare, the environment and aboriginal people; (9) increased market opportunities in Latin America; and (10) enhancement of the area as a foreign investment destination through secure access to the North American market for foreign investors, with key selling points of strong transportation and telecommunication infrastructures, abundant energy resources, a highly educated and skilled workforce, comprehensive social and health services, and a stable political and economic environment.[64] Further, the benefits of free trade, according to its advocates, are: (1) increased specialization; (2) rationalization, eliminating some production and expanding in others while introducing new production techniques; (3) longer production runs in larger specialized plants; and (4) easier transfer of technology. The costs of free trade are (1) transition; and (2) harmonization requirements.[65] Rationalization entails: (1) a reduction in the number of manufacturing plants; (2) an increase in production runs; (3) an increase in trade between the United States and Canada; and (4) a reduction in production costs.[66] Those in favor of the North American Free Trade Agreement argue that free trade improves efficiency and competition, stimulates production and economic growth, and opens new opportunities, supplementing and broadening GATT.[67]

NAFTA eliminates the majority of current tariffs and import licenses on all manufactured goods, provides greater access for service industries, permits more mobility for professional and business workers, and allows easier entry into the North American market of over 300 million consumers. By recognizing that we share a hemisphere, it sets an important precedent for north-south continental trade, and looks toward the future by allowing for participation by other countries, if they meet the membership criteria set by the three founding nations. Latin American countries have expressed an interest in becoming signatory members of the Free Trade Agreement. In addition, the Canadian Province of Quebec has already given thought to joining as a separate member in the event it becomes a separate nation. Quebec wishes to maintain the current division of legislative powers, respect fully its unique social policy, language and culture, maintain a leeway to modernize and develop its economy, provide for transitional periods for businesses in less competitive sectors, adopt a dispute settlement mechanism, maintain its special status for agriculture and fisheries, and protect its right to decide on the Agreement in light of its interests. By lowering trade barriers, the agreement has expanded trade in all three countries. This, some argue, has led to increased employment, more choices for consumers at competitive prices, and rising prosperity. From 1993, the year preceding the start of NAFTA implementation, to 2001, trade among the NAFTA nations climbed 109 per cent, from US\$297 billion to US\$622 billion. Each day the NAFTA parties conduct nearly US\$1.7 billion in trilateral trade. Because of NAFTA, North America is one of the most competitive, prosperous and economically integrated regions in the world. From 1993 to 2001, looking at the Canadian situation, Canada's merchandise exports to its NAFTA partners climbed 95 per cent, from US\$117 billion to US\$229 billion. By contrast, such exports to the rest of the world in the period increased only five per cent. In looking at the Mexican situation, Mexico exported US\$139 billion to its NAFTA partners, an increase of 225 per cent. By comparison, exports to the rest of the world increased 93 per cent, and growth in Mexican exports accounted for more than half of the increase in Mexico's real gross domestic product. In looking at the American situation, United States merchandise exports to NAFTA partners nearly doubled from US\$142 billion to US\$265 billion. This was significantly higher than the 44 per cent growth in exports to the rest of the world. [68]

An increasingly integrated North American market has stimulated capital flows, promoted the spread of technology, and contributed to increasing productivity and higher wages. Between 1994 and 2000, foreign direct investment (FDI) inflows in the NAFTA countries reached US\$1.3 trillion, or about 28 per cent of the world total, spurring economic development and growth throughout North America. Between 1994 and 2000, the United States received large flows of foreign capital, approximately US\$110.2 billion per year, and Mexico's annual average capital inflow reached US\$11.7 billion, three times the annual received in the seven years prior to the Agreement. The dynamic performance of exports and investment in North America has boosted economic activity and production in the region, and some argue has contributed to the creation of more and better paying jobs in all three countries. In Canada, the hourly wage rate in export-supported jobs is 35 per cent higher than in the non-export sector. In Mexico, the export sector is the country's leading job creation engine, accounting for more than half of Mexican manufacturing jobs gained between 1994 and 2000, with these jobs paying nearly 40 per cent more than those in the rest of the manufacturing sector. In the United States, employment supported by merchandise exports to NAFTA countries grew to an estimated 2.9 million jobs, with these jobs paying between 13 and 18 per cent more than the average American national wage.

Aside from a handful of tariffs, all NAFTA commitments have been fully implemented, including trade rules on services, investment, procurement, and standards. The NAFTA partners are committed to completing the full implementation of the Agreement according to the established schedule. Eight years of expanded trade, increased employment and investment, and enhanced opportunity for the citizens of all three countries have demonstrated that NAFTA works, and will continue to work.

NAFTA, according to its critics who paint a more realistic picture, is not free, since Canada has paid a high price to gain greater access to the American and Mexican markets. Canadian consumers have seen prices rise along with the advent of the Goods and Services Tax, and thousands of jobs have been lost, with unemployment hovering around the 9 per cent level.[69] The structural adjustment costs, such as a rise in unemployment, tend to be underestimated by free trade advocates. Further, the agreement is also not about trade, and is more about the creation of a new continental model of development for the regulation of capitalism.[70] It serves more as a corporate bill of rights entrenching deregulation and market orientation in an international treaty, while at the same time eroding national economic, social and political institutions. Neo-conservatives in Canada and the Unites States wanted a deregulated continental model of development to increase capital mobility in order to restore profitability. Corporate managers have worked in a continent-wide drive to bring down wages and welfare state spending, by playing communities off against one another. The goal is to harmonize and integrate Canadian standards and institutions with the United States. Canada's economy, political system and labor practices have been significantly altered as a result of closer ties with the United States' economy. Canada has been forced to acquiesce to the continental model of development by continental market forces and American geopolitical pressures. Free trade is designed to restructure society to suit corporate needs, causing a threat to communities, by capital-enhanced geographic mobility, which is not universally beneficial.

Many have benefitted, but in the eyes of the critics, many more have been hurt. Sovereignty has been compromised, and the three most important industries for Canada, wood exports, agriculture and automobile manufacturing, have been hurt. 'The burden of Free Trade driven restructuring was shared unequally on a national, regional, class and gender basis'.[71] The critics argue that the new capital labor accord relies on domination instead of negotiation. Canadian workers are suffering from a 'whiplash process', being forced-concessions on wage benefits and work rules. Mergers, temporary and part-time workers, and cheap labor increase competitiveness. Failure to acquiesce has resulted in relocation out of Canada. Free-trade-generated jobs have not materialized as promised by the advocates. The Continental Model has led to polarization and segmentation of the Canadian labor force. The discourse of universality has ended, so that there is more social inequality across Canada. The Welfare State is viewed as an impediment to profit in the eyes of business, which has chipped away at it, giving way to a 'policy of stealth'. With deregulation, budget cuts and privatization, importance is given to corporate profit at the expense of social equality.

'Continental free trade has helped to create a neo-conservative utopia where issues such as social justice and regional equality have become relics' of a bygone era.[72] Opponents of free trade are said to suffer from 'emporiophobia', a fear of free trade. Yet, the effects of free trade are something to fear, since hemispheric free trade is now a possibility. It was argued that there would be a 'sucking sound' of jobs going south of the border, ultimately to Mexico.[73] However, no tripartite treaty will disturb the overwhelming dominance that accrues to the United States, because of its geographic position, between Canada and Mexico. A borderland is a region jointly shared by two nations that houses people with common social characteristics in spite of the political boundaries between them, and thus the United States has a strong influence on the other two countries bordering it. The outflow of investment and the haemorrhaging of profits and service payments out of Canada is intrinsically intertwined with NAFTA.[74] According to the critics, the human and economic debris will be with us for as long as we can see into the future. The single most important impact of NAFTA is the decline in the standard of living of Canadians, which has coincided with the agreements. We need to reform democracy and political institutions so citizens and not just corporate business benefit from change. There is presently more foreign ownership and control, with fewer jobs and poorer jobs. More imports of goods and services should be sourced in Canada, but there is a failure to develop new competitive products while at the same time having less diversification of exports.

Northrop Frye pointed out long ago, 'Why go to the trouble of annexing a country that is so easy to exploit without taking any responsibility for it'.[75] Economic penetration has proven simpler than military force. NAFTA, according to its critics, is a neo-conservative Americanization of Canada.[76] The pre-agreement years saw trade on a multilateral level, without abandoning national control of the foreign market. The agreement is seen as a straightjacket, because it is difficult to introduce new measures to strengthen or expand national control of firms and industries. It can be argued that it is a dangerous and indefensible gamble for Canada to commit to a binding dispute settlement mechanism with a trading partner, the United States, which has such a disproportionate power. NAFTA has set up a trading bloc designed to fit Canada and Mexico into the US model of development, keeping Europe and Japan out. There is no willingness to share political powers in the European Community, but simply the use of US power. However, Mexico is an attractive site for low-wage production of standardized industrial goods, and with this comes Canadian and US job losses, with production shifts to Mexico and a downward pressure on wages. Workers have been displaced from industries and are vulnerable to competition from low-wage countries, with the loss especially to low-income jobs. NAFTA does nothing for basic labor. Obviously, the job crisis existed before free trade and was not confined to Canada. However, there is a conflict between the profitability of individual corporations and the pressures of global capabilities against human needs for high employment levels, decent pay, healthy working conditions and job security. What has occurred is a decrease in full-time employment and an increase in part-time and temporary employment, as well as an increase in unemployment and in welfare levels. This has been 'the longest and deepest unemployment crisis since the Great Depression', with inappropriate monetary policy playing a major role.[77]

There is a gap in the free trade effect between the top corporate executive and the average shop floor worker. Free trade encourages self-reinforcing cycles of destructive competition, exerting great pressure on the Continent. It has eliminated jobs, depressed incomes and standards, and aggregated demands. The effects of investment diversion and export harassment far outweigh the positive effects of tariff reductions. There is a one-sided advantage for a corporate elite that is globally competitive, increasing profits, surviving and growing unfettered by government controls, and securing the highest rate of return for the interests of financial capital. Decent jobs and decent living standards have become unimportant. Employment needs of society must be paramount, and therefore, corporate interests must yield to broader public interests. However, NAFTA is tilted in the wrong direction. Multilateral trading arrangements with the European Community and Japan would be alternatives to NAFTA and its shortfalls. Canada's social programs are a contrast to those of the United States. Americanization is balkanizing Canada. Regional equality is promised, but individuals, families, communities and regions are being abandoned. Canada was founded on the national principle of building strong communities and regions to serve the needs of their residents, not to deplete these areas in order to supply land and factories for economic interests. With lay-offs and closures, there is a bitter legacy of unemployment, poverty and inequality, with society becoming distinctly harsher. Those who are able to thrive are doing very well, but the societal gap is growing so that there is a chasm between rich and poor, non-disabled and disabled, young and old, black and white, men and women, with a disappearing middle class. There is a severe strain on the societal fabric, with a sacrificing of the needs of many for the demands of few.

Among those who were opposed to NAFTA, Canadian Mitchell Sharp, who has been a mentor to the current Prime Minister Jean Chrétien, stated it best:

> From the very beginnings of our country, we have sought to preserve a separate identity, to live in harmony with our next door neighbour but as an independent country. By entering into this ... preferential agreement, we would be deciding no longer to resist the continental pull. On the contrary, we would be accelerating the process of the Americanisation of Canada. [78]

Many believe that free trade challenges the fundamentals of Canada's nationhood, with its powers limited by interdependence and domination from foreign multinationals. The benefits of free trade do not fall equally. Free trade serves to undermine full employment.[79] The first essential ingredient for free trade should be a commitment to full employment. Sufficient independence for blueprint choices and for flexible alternatives for long-term planning is needed, looking away from integration.

By operating under the deceptive banner of 'free' trade, multinational corporations are working hard to expand their control over the international economy, and to dismantle vital health, safety and environmental protections, which in recent decades have been won by citizens' movements across the globe. According to consumer advocate Ralph Nader, this serves to devalue jobs, depress wage levels, make workplaces less safe, destroy family farms, and undermine consumer protections.[80] Because of NAFTA, large global companies have capitalized on poverty in the Third World, by lowering safety and wages in employment. As such, workers, consumers and communities will continue to lose, while short-term profits soar and big business wins, in a threat to move South. The centralization of commercial power is unsound. There is a need for community-oriented production in smaller-scale operations, along with more flexibility and adaptability to local needs for sustainable production methods and democratic controls. Thus, the allocation of power to lower levels of government bodies tends to increase citizen power. There is a race 'to the bottom', pitting State against State, for the lowest wage levels, lowest environmental policies and lowest consumer safety standards.[81]

NAFTA has forced Canada to harmonize its social and economic policies to conform to the United States. Free trade calls for privatization and deregulation, but policy intervention is needed to reduce unemployment and raise wage rates. There has been a shift away from service-type jobs, with pressure to decrease wages and provide fewer benefits. There has been major job loss by sourcing services outside Canada.[82] It is important to negotiate over the right of establishment and the right to national treatment. Manufacturing is vulnerable to trade liberalization, which will lead to an increase in unemployment, and adverse working conditions. The United States has an advantage over Canada, because of cheap material, capital intensiveness and technological advancement. Due to its size and climate, Canada is again at a disadvantage in the food industry. The United States is again favored in the electrical field, where there is a rationalization of production for specializations. There is a 'going South' policy. Firms want to locate elsewhere, while still having access to the Canadian market. At the same time, by phasing out import restrictions, the domestic sector is not protected.

US legislation for realignment, it is argued, will curtail equal rights legislation, since equal pay is too costly for the industry. Free trade will erode the domestic service economy.[83] Of the three major categories of sectors, the primary (agriculture and resource extracting), the secondary (construction and manufacturing) and the tertiary (service), the service sector accounts for two-thirds of the national income and 70 per cent of jobs in Canada. Foreign service industry activity is limited by non-tariff barriers, through control over investment, ownership and trade levels. The United States, however, believes that government intervention as a matter of security and sovereignty is an unfair practice. The United States accounts for roughly 80 per cent of Canada's trade. However, the Canadian market is vulnerable, because of the large percentage of US-owned businesses, which causes an indirect pressure to conform to United States policy. The United States has easier access to Canada than Canada to the United States. The US trade remedy legislation imposes pressure upon Canada to harmonize, which impacts social services, job loss, wages, working conditions and types of employment. It is found that trade-led growth is not always an adequate economic policy. Free trade is a means not an end.

Other Legislation

American Declaration of the Rights and Duties of Man

The Preamble of the American Declaration of the Rights and Duties of Man 1948, important for disability equality, states:

> All men are born free and equal, in dignity and in rights, and, being endowed by nature with reason and conscience, they should conduct themselves as brothers one to another.
>
> The fulfilment of duty by each individual is a prerequisite to the rights of all. Rights and duties are interrelated in every social and political activity of man. While rights exalt individual liberty, duties express the dignity of that liberty.
>
> Duties of a juridical nature presuppose others of a moral nature which support them in principle and constitute their basis.
>
> Inasmuch as spiritual development is the supreme end of human existence and the highest expression thereof, it is the duty of man to serve that end with all his strength and resources.
>
> Since culture is the highest social and historical expression of that spiritual development, it is the duty of man to preserve, practice and foster culture by every means within his power.
>
> And, since moral conduct constitutes the noblest flowering of culture, it is the duty of every man always to hold it in high respect.
>
> WHEREAS:
>
> The American peoples have acknowledged the dignity of the individual, and their national constitutions recognize that juridical and political institutions, which regulate life in human society, have as their principal aim the protection of the essential rights of man and the creation of circumstances that will permit him to achieve spiritual and material progress and attain happiness;
>
> The American States have on repeated occasions recognized that the essential rights of man are not derived from the fact that he is a national of a certain state, but are based upon attributes of his human personality;
>
> The international protection of the rights of man should be the principal guide of an evolving American law;
>
> The affirmation of essential human rights by the American States together with the guarantees given by the internal regimes of the states establish the initial system of protection considered by the American States as being suited to the present social and juridical conditions, not without a recognition on their part that they should increasingly strengthen that system in the international field as conditions become more favourable.[84]

In terms of rights, important for disability equality, the right to equality before the law is guaranteed under Article II:

> II. All persons are equal before the law and have the rights and duties established in this Declaration, without distinction as to race, sex, language, creed or any other factor.[85]

Further, important for advancement, the right to education is guaranteed under Article XII:

> XII. Every person has the right to an education, which should be based on the principles of liberty, morality and human solidarity.
> Likewise every person has the right to an education that will prepare him to attain a decent life, to raise his standard of living, and to be a useful member of society. The right to an education includes the right to equality of opportunity in every case, in accordance with natural talents, merit and the desire to utilize the resources that the state or the community is in a position to provide. Every person has the right to receive, free, at least a primary education.[86]

In addition, important in the fight against discrimination, the right to the benefits of culture is guaranteed under Article XIII:

> XIII. Every person has the right to take part in the cultural life of the community, to enjoy the arts, and to participate in the benefits that result from intellectual progress, especially scientific discoveries.
> He likewise has the right to the protection of his moral and material interests as regards his inventions or any literary, scientific or artistic works of which he is the author.[87]

The right to work and to fair remuneration are contained in Article XIV:

> XIV. Every person has the right to work, under proper conditions, and to follow his vocation freely, in so far as existing conditions of employment permit. Every person who works has the right to receive such remuneration as will, in proportion to his capacity and skill, assure him a standard of living suitable for himself and for his family.[88]

The scope of the rights of man is outlined in Article XXVIII:

> XXVIII. The rights of man are limited by the rights of others, by the security of all, and by the just demands of the general welfare and the advancement of democracy.[89]

In terms of duties, the duty to obey the law is contained in Article XXXIII:

> XXXIII. It is the duty of every person to obey the law and other legitimate commands of the authorities of his country and those of the country in which he may be.[90]

Further, the duty to work is contained in Article XXXVII:

> XXXVII. It is the duty of every person to work, as far as his capacity and possibilities permit, in order to obtain the means of livelihood or to benefit his community.[91]

American Convention on Human Rights

The Preamble of the American Convention on Human Rights 1978, which entered into force on 18 July 1978, states:

> The American states signatory to the present Convention,
> *Reaffirming* their intention to consolidate in this hemisphere, within the framework of democratic institutions, a system of personal liberty and social justice based on respect for the essential rights of man;
> *Recognizing* that the essential rights of man are not derived from one's being a national of a certain state, but are based upon attributes of the human personality, and that they therefore justify international protection in the form of a convention reinforcing or complementing the protection provided by the domestic law of the American states;
> *Considering* that these principles have been set forth in the Charter of the Organization of American States, in the American Declaration of the Rights and Duties of Man, and in the Universal Declaration of Human Rights, and that they have been reaffirmed and refined in other international instruments, worldwide as well as regional in scope;
> *Reiterating* that, in accordance with the Universal Declaration of Human Rights, the ideal of free men enjoying freedom from fear and want can be achieved only if conditions are created whereby everyone may enjoy his economic, social, and cultural rights, as well as his civil and political rights.[92]

The obligation to respect rights, important for disability equality, is contained in Article 1:

> 1. 1. The States Parties to this Convention undertake to respect the rights and freedoms recognized herein and to ensure to all persons subject to their jurisdiction the free and full exercise of those rights and freedoms, without any discrimination for reasons of race, color, sex, language, religion, political or other opinion, national or social origin, economic status, birth, or any other social condition.
> 2. For the purposes of this Convention, 'person' means every human being.[93]

Domestic legal effects are outlined in Article 2:

> 2. Where the exercise of any of the rights or freedoms referred to in Article 1 is not already ensured by legislative or other provisions, the States Parties undertake to adopt, in accordance with their constitutional processes and the provisions of this Convention, such legislative or other measures as may be necessary to give effect to those rights or freedoms.[94]

Further, in terms of civil and political rights, the right to Juridical Personality is contained in Article 3:

> 3. Every person has the right to recognition as a person before the law.[95]

Freedom of movement and residence is guaranteed under Article 22:

22. 1. Every person lawfully in the territory of a State Party has the right to move about in it, and to reside in it subject to the provisions of the law.

2. Every person has the right to leave any country freely, including his own.

3. The exercise of the foregoing rights may be restricted only pursuant to a law to the extent necessary in a democratic society to prevent crime or to protect national security, public safety, public order, public morals, public health, or the rights or freedoms of others.

4. The exercise of the rights recognized in paragraph 1 may also be restricted by law in designated zones for reasons of public interest.

5. No one can be expelled from the territory of the state of which he is a national or be deprived of the right to enter it.

6. An alien lawfully in the territory of a State Party to this Convention may be expelled from it only pursuant to a decision reached in accordance with law.

7. Every person has the right to seek and be granted asylum in a foreign territory, in accordance with the legislation of the state and international conventions, in the event he is being pursued for political offenses or related common crimes.

8. In no case may an alien be deported or returned to a country, regardless of whether or not it is his country of origin, if in that country his right to life or personal freedom is in danger of being violated because of his race, nationality, religion, social status, or political opinions.

9. The collective expulsion of aliens is prohibited.[96]

Importantly, the right to equal protection is guaranteed under Article 24:

24. All persons are equal before the law. Consequently, they are entitled, without discrimination, to equal protection of the law.[97]

Crucially, the right to judicial protection is guaranteed under Article 25:

25. 1. Everyone has the right to simple and prompt recourse, or any other effective recourse, to a competent court or tribunal for protection against acts that violate his fundamental rights recognized by the constitution or laws of the state concerned or by this Convention, even though such violation may have been committed by persons acting in the course of their official duties.

2. The States Parties undertake:

a. to ensure that any person claiming such remedy shall have his rights determined by the competent authority provided for by the legal system of the state;

b. to develop the possibilities of judicial remedy; and

c. to ensure that the competent authorities shall enforce such remedies when granted.[98]

In terms of economic, social and cultural Rights, Article 26 provides for progressive development:

26. The States Parties undertake to adopt measures, both internally and through international cooperation, especially those of an economic and technical nature, with a view to achieving progressively, by legislation or other appropriate means, the full realization of the rights implicit in the economic, social, educational, scientific, and cultural standards set forth in the Charter of the Organization of American States ....[99]

The suspension of guarantees is provided for in Article 27:

> 27. 1. In time of war, public danger, or other emergency that threatens the independence or security of a State Party, it may take measures derogating from its obligations under the present Convention to the extent and for the period of time strictly required by the exigencies of the situation, provided that such measures are not inconsistent with its other obligations under international law and do not involve discrimination on the ground of race, color, sex, language, religion, or social origin.[100]

Further, Article 28 contains a federal clause:

> 28. 1. Where a State Party is constituted as a federal state, the national government of such State Party shall implement all the provisions of the Convention over whose subject matter it exercises legislative and judicial jurisdiction.[101]

There are a number of competent organs involved as outlined in Article 33:

> 33. The following organs shall have competence with respect to matters relating to the fulfilment of the commitments made by the States Parties to this Convention:
> a. the Inter-American Commission on Human Rights, referred to as 'The Commission'; and
> b. the Inter-American Court of Human Rights, referred to as 'The Court'.[102]

In terms of the Inter-American Commission on Human Rights, Article 35 outlines the organization:

> 35. The Commission shall represent all the member countries of the Organization of American States.[103]

The functions of the Inter-American Commission on Human Rights are outlined in Article 41:

> 41. The main function of the Commission shall be to promote respect for and defense of human rights. In the exercise of its mandate, it shall have the following functions and powers:
> a. to develop an awareness of human rights among the peoples of America;
> b. to make recommendations to the governments of the member states, when it considers such action advisable, for the adoption of progressive measures in favor of human rights within the framework of their domestic law and constitutional provisions as well as appropriate measures to further the observance of those rights;
> c. to prepare such studies or reports as it considers advisable in the performance of its duties;
> d. to request the governments of the member states to supply it with information on the measures adopted by them in matters of human rights;
> e. to respond, through the General Secretariat of the Organization of American States, to inquiries made by the member states on matters related to human rights and, within the limits of its possibilities, to provide those states with the advisory

services they request;

f. to take action on petitions and other communications pursuant to its authority under the provisions of Articles 44 through 51 of this Convention; and

g. to submit an annual report to the General Assembly of the Organization of American States.[104]

The competency to lodge petitions is outlined in Article 44:

44. Any person or group of persons, or any nongovernmental entity legally recognized in one or more member states of the Organization, may lodge petitions with the Commission containing denunciations or complaints of violation of this Convention by a State Party.[105]

Admissibility of petitions is outlined in Article 46:

46. 1. Admission by the Commission of a petition or communication ... shall be subject to the following requirements:

a. that the remedies under domestic law have been pursued and exhausted in accordance with generally recognized principles of international law;

b. that the petition or communication is lodged within a period of six months from the date on which the party alleging violation of his rights was notified of the final judgment;

c. that the subject of the petition or communication is not pending in another international proceeding for settlement.

2. The provisions of paragraphs 1.a and 1.b of this article shall not be applicable when:

a. the domestic legislation of the state concerned does not afford due process of law for the protection of the right or rights that have allegedly been violated;

b. the party alleging violation of his rights has been denied access to the remedies under domestic law or has been prevented from exhausting them; or

c. there has been unwarranted delay in rendering a final judgment under the aforementioned remedies.[106]

The procedure is outlined in Article 48:

48. 1. When the Commission receives a petition or communication alleging violation of any of the rights protected by this Convention, it shall proceed as follows:

a. If it considers the petition or communication admissible, it shall request information from the government of the state indicated as being responsible for the alleged violations and shall furnish that government a transcript of the pertinent portions of the petition or communication. This information shall be submitted within a reasonable period to be determined by the Commission in accordance with the circumstances of each case.

b. After the information has been received, or after the period established has elapsed and the information has not been received, the Commission shall ascertain whether the grounds for the petition or communication still exist. If they do not, the Commission shall order the record to be closed.

c. The Commission may also declare the petition or communication inadmissible or out of order on the basis of information or evidence subsequently received.

d. If the record has not been closed, the Commission shall, with the knowledge of the parties, examine the matter set forth in the petition or communication in order to verify the facts. If necessary and advisable, the Commission shall carry out an investigation, for the effective conduct of which it shall request, and the states concerned shall furnish to it, all necessary facilities.

e. The Commission may request the states concerned to furnish any pertinent information and, if so requested, shall hear oral statements or receive written statements from the parties concerned.

f. The Commission shall place itself at the disposal of the parties concerned with a view to reaching a friendly settlement of the matter on the basis of respect for the human rights recognized in this Convention.

2. However, in serious and urgent cases, only the presentation of a petition or communication that fulfils all the formal requirements of admissibility shall be necessary in order for the Commission to conduct an investigation with the prior consent of the state in whose territory a violation has allegedly been committed.[107]

In terms of the Inter-American Court of Human Rights, the right of submission is outlined in Article 61:

61. 1. Only the States Parties and the Commission shall have the right to submit a case to the Court.[108]

The safeguarding of rights and the provision of measures are contained in Article 63:

63. 1. If the Court finds that there has been a violation of a right or freedom protected by this Convention, the Court shall rule that the injured party be ensured the enjoyment of his right or freedom that was violated. It shall also rule, if appropriate, that the consequences of the measure or situation that constituted the breach of such right or freedom be remedied and that fair compensation be paid to the injured party.

2. In cases of extreme gravity and urgency, and when necessary to avoid irreparable damage to persons, the Court shall adopt such provisional measures as it deems pertinent in matters it has under consideration. With respect to a case not yet submitted to the Court, it may act at the request of the Commission.[109]

In terms of procedure, Article 66 calls for reasons for judgments:

66. 1. Reasons shall be given for the judgment of the Court.[110]

Finality of judgment is contained in Article 67:

67. The judgment of the Court shall be final and not subject to appeal. In case of disagreement as to the meaning or scope of the judgment, the Court shall interpret it at the request of any of the parties, provided the request is made within ninety days from the date of notification of the judgment.[111]

Importantly, compliance with the judgment is underlined in Article 68:

68. 1. The States Parties to the Convention undertake to comply with the judgment

of the Court in any case to which they are parties.

2. That part of a judgment that stipulates compensatory damages may be executed in the country concerned in accordance with domestic procedure governing the execution of judgments against the state.[112]

Statute of the Inter-American Court on Human Rights

More specifically and carrying on from the American Convention on Human Rights, Article 1 of the Statute of the Inter-American Court on Human Rights 1980, which entered into force on 1 January 1980, outlines the nature of the legal organization:

> 1. The Inter-American Court of Human Rights is an autonomous judicial institution whose purpose is the application and interpretation of the American Convention on Human Rights. The Court exercises its functions in accordance with the provisions of the aforementioned Convention and the present Statute.[113]

The jurisdiction of the Court is contained in Article 2:

> 2. The Court shall exercise adjudicatory and advisory jurisdiction:
> 1. Its adjudicatory jurisdiction shall be governed by the provisions of Articles 61, 62 and 63 of the Convention, and
> 2. Its advisory jurisdiction shall be governed by the provisions of Article 64 of the Convention.[114]

The seat of the Court is contained in Article 3:

> 3. 1. The seat of the Court shall be San Jose, Costa Rica; however, the Court may convene in any member state of the Organization of American States (OAS) when a majority of the Court considers it desirable, and with the prior consent of the State concerned.[115]

Further, the composition of the Court is contained in Article 4:

> 4. 1. The Court shall consist of seven judges, nationals of the member states of the OAS, elected in an individual capacity from among jurists of the highest moral authority and of recognized competence in the field of human rights, who possess the qualifications required for the exercise of the highest judicial functions under the law of the State of which they are nationals or of the State that proposes them as candidates.
> 2. No two judges may be nationals of the same State.[116]

The structure of the Court includes the Presidency as outlined in Article 12 and the Secretariat as outlined in Article 14:

> 12. 1. The Court shall elect from among its members a President and Vice-President who shall serve for a period of two years; they may be reelected.
> 2. The President shall direct the work of the Court, represent it, regulate the disposition of matters brought before the Court, and preside over its sessions.[117]

14. 1. The Secretariat of the Court shall function under the immediate authority of the Secretary, in accordance with the administrative standards of the OAS General Secretariat, in all matters that are not incompatible with the independence of the Court.

2. The Secretary shall be appointed by the Court. He shall be a full-time employee serving in a position of trust to the Court, shall have his office at the seat of the Court and shall attend any meetings that the Court holds away from its seat.

3. There shall be an Assistant Secretary who shall assist the Secretary in his duties and shall replace him in his temporary absence.

4. The Staff of the Secretariat shall be appointed by the Secretary General of the OAS, in consultation with the Secretary of the Court. [118]

In terms of the workings of the Court, Article 24 outlines the hearings, deliberations and decisions:

24. 1. The hearings shall be public, unless the Court, in exceptional circumstances, decides otherwise.

2. The Court shall deliberate in private. Its deliberations shall remain secret, unless the Court decides otherwise.

3. The decisions, judgments and opinions of the Court shall be delivered in public session, and the parties shall be given written notification thereof. In addition, the decisions, judgments and opinions shall be published, along with judges' individual votes and opinions and with such other data or background information that the Court may deem appropriate. [119]

Article 27 stresses the importance of relations with the host country, governments and organizations:

27. 1. The relations of the Court with the host country shall be governed through a headquarters agreement. The seat of the Court shall be international in nature.

2. The relations of the Court with governments, with the OAS and its organs, agencies and entities and with other international governmental organizations involved in promoting and defending human rights shall be governed through special agreements. [120]

Finally, Article 28 stresses the importance of the relations with the Inter-American Commission on Human Rights:

28. The Inter-American Commission on Human Rights shall appear as a party before the Court in all cases within the adjudicatory jurisdiction of the Court, pursuant to Article 2(1) of the present Statute. [121]

Inter-American Democratic Charter

The Preamble of the Inter-American Democratic Charter 2001, which came into force on 11 September 2001, states:

THE GENERAL ASSEMBLY,

CONSIDERING that the Charter of the Organization of American States recognizes that representative democracy is indispensable for the stability, peace, and development of the region, and that one of the purposes of the OAS is to promote and consolidate representative democracy, with due respect for the principle of nonintervention;

RECALLING that the Heads of State and Government of the Americas, gathered at the Third Summit of the Americas, held from April 20 to 22, 2001 in Quebec City, adopted a democracy clause which establishes that any unconstitutional alteration or interruption of the democratic order in a state of the Hemisphere constitutes an insurmountable obstacle to the participation of that state's government in the Summits of the Americas process;

REAFFIRMING that the participatory nature of democracy in our countries in different aspects of public life contributes to the consolidation of democratic values and to freedom and solidarity in the Hemisphere;

CONSIDERING that solidarity among and cooperation between American states require the political organization of those states based on the effective exercise of representative democracy, and that economic growth and social development based on justice and equity, and democracy are interdependent and mutually reinforcing;

BEARING IN MIND that the American Declaration on the Rights and Duties of Man and the American Convention on Human Rights contain the values and principles of liberty, equality, and social justice that are intrinsic to democracy;

REAFFIRMING that the promotion and protection of human rights is a basic prerequisite for the existence of a democratic society, and recognizing the importance of the continuous development and strengthening of the inter-American human rights system for the consolidation of democracy;

CONSIDERING that education is an effective way to promote citizens' awareness concerning their own countries and thereby achieve meaningful participation in the decision-making process, and reaffirming the importance of human resource development for a sound democratic system;

RECOGNIZING that the right of workers to associate themselves freely for the defense and promotion of their interests is fundamental to the fulfillment of democratic ideals.[122]

The anti-discrimination provision, important for disability equality, is contained in Article 9:

The elimination of all forms of discrimination, especially gender, ethnic and race discrimination, as well as diverse forms of intolerance, the promotion and protection of human rights of indigenous peoples and migrants, and respect for ethnic, cultural and religious diversity in the Americas contribute to strengthening democracy and citizen participation.[123]

Workers' rights and labor standards are emphasized in Article 10:

The promotion and strengthening of democracy requires the full and effective exercise of workers' rights and the application of core labor standards, as recognized in the International Labour Organization (ILO) Declaration on Fundamental Principles and Rights at Work ..., adopted in 1998, as well as other related fundamental ILO conventions. Democracy is strengthened by improving standards in the workplace and enhancing the quality of life for workers in the Hemisphere.[124]

The importance of claims and redress for grievances is outlined in Article 8:

Any person or group of persons who consider that their human rights have been violated may present claims or petitions to the inter-American system for the promotion and protection of human rights in accordance with its established procedures.
Member states reaffirm their intention to strengthen the inter-American system for the protection of human rights for the consolidation of democracy in the Hemisphere.[125]

Further, in terms of democracy and the inter-American system, Article 4 espouses the importance of transparency:

Transparency in government activities, probity, responsible public administration on the part of governments, respect for social rights, and freedom of expression and of the press are essential components of the exercise of democracy.
The constitutional subordination of all state institutions to the legally constituted civilian authority and respect for the rule of law on the part of all institutions and sectors of society are equally essential to democracy.[126]

Finally, in terms of democracy and human rights, Article 7 stresses the importance of democracy:

Democracy is indispensable for the effective exercise of fundamental freedoms and human rights in their universality, indivisibility and interdependence, embodied in the respective constitutions of states and in inter-American and international human rights instruments.[127]

Conclusion

The North American Free Trade Agreement (NAFTA) partners are cooperating to advance trade liberalization not only within North America, but also in the negotiations for the Free Trade Area of the Americas (FTAA). Recognizing their shared interests, the NAFTA partners have worked together to advance trade liberalization. In 2001, Canada hosted the Summit of the Americas, a gathering of the 34 democratically elected Heads of State of the Western Hemisphere. As one of the key elements of the Summit Agenda, NAFTA partners are working together to ensure that the Free Trade Area of the Americas (FTAA) negotiations continue to progress toward the goal of conclusion of an agreement by 2005. The FTAA would eliminate trade and investment barriers on virtually all goods and services traded by member countries, reducing prices for consumers and creating new markets for producers throughout the hemisphere. However, more needs to be done to legislate for disability rights. President John F. Kennedy's statement concerning the relationship between Canada and the United States is still applicable today and can even be further extended to North America: 'Geography has made us neighbors, history has made us friends, the economy has made us partners and necessity has made us allies'.[128] In this spirit, important for this ability, we need to work together to bring about full equality in the Americas.

Notes

[1]   Hamelin, Jean, *Histoire du Québec*, Edisem, St. Hyacinthe, 1976, p.371.

[2]   Easterbrook, W.T. and Aitken, Hugh, *Canadian Economic History*, Macmillan, Toronto, 1976, p.362.

[3]   *Ibid.*, at p.361.

[4]   Fry, Earl, 'Trends in Canada-U.S. Free Trade Discussions', in A. R. Riggs and Tom Welk, *Canadian-American Free Trade: Historical, Political and Economic Dimensions*, The Institute for Research in Public Policy, Montreal, 1987, p.28.

[5]   d'Aquino, Thomas, 'Truck and Trade with the Yankees, The Case for a Canada-U.S. Comprehensive Trade Agreement', in A.R. Riggs and Tom Velk, *Canadian-American Free Trade: Historical, Political and Economic Dimensions*, The Institute for Research on Public Policy, Montreal, 1987, p.74.

[6]   Velk, Tom, and Riggs, A.R., 'The Ongoing Debate Over Free Trade', in A.R. Riggs and Tom Velk, *Canadian-American Free Trade: (The Sequel) Historical, Political and Economic Dimensions*, The Institute for Research on Public Policy, Montreal, 1988, p.93.

[7]   General Agreement on Tariffs and Trade, at Article 24.

[8]   Laun, Louis, 'U.S.-Canada Free Trade Negotiations: Historical Opportunities', in A.R. Riggs and Tom Velk, *Canadian-American Free Trade: Historical, Political and Economic Dimensions*, The Institute for Research in Public Policy, Montreal, 1987, p.205.

[9]   Fry, Earl, 'Trends in Canada-U.S. Free Trade Discussions', in A. R., Riggs and Tom Welk, *Canadian-American Free Trade: Historical, Political and Economic Dimensions*, The Institute for Research in Public Policy, Montreal, 1987, p.9.

[10]   *Ibid.*, at p.34.

[11]   *Ibid.*, at p. 27.

[12]   Watkins, Mel, 'The Political Economy of Growth', in Wallace Clement and Glen Williams, *The New Canadian Political Economy*, McGill-Queen's University Press, Kingston, 1989, p.17.

[13]   Laun, Louis, 'U.S.-Canada Free Trade Negotiations: Historical Opportunities', in A.R. Riggs and Tom Velk, *Canadian-American Free Trade: Historical, Political and Economic Dimensions*, The Institute for Research in Public Policy, Montreal, 1987, p.205.

[14]   Government of Canada, *The North American Free Trade Agreement At A Glance*, Ottawa, p.1.

15 Soldatos, P., 'Canada's Foreign Policy in Search of a Fourth Option: Continuity and Change in Orientation Towards the U.S.', in A.R. Riggs and Tom Velk, *Canadian-American Free Trade: (The Sequel) Historical, Political and Economic Dimensions*, The Institute for Research on Public Policy, Montreal, 1988, p.41.

16 Lipsey, Richard, 'Canada's Trade Options', in A.R. Riggs and TomVelk, *Canadian-American Free Trade: Historical, Political and Economic Dimensions*, The Institute for Research on Public Policy, Montreal, 1987, p.59.

17 Brecher, Irving, 'The Free Trade Initiative, On Course or Off', in A. R. Riggs and Tom Velk, *Canadian-American Free Trade: Historical, Political and Economic Dimensions*, The Institute for Research in Public Policy, Montreal, 1987, p.67.

18 Neufeld, E.P, 'Financial and Economic Dimensions of Free Trade', in A.R. Riggs and Tom Velk, *Canadian-American Free Trade: Historical, Political and Economic Dimensions*, The Institute for Research on Public Policy, Montreal, 1987, p.152.

19 *Ibid.*, at p.155.

20 Layton, Robert, 'Why Canada Needs Free Trade', in A. R. Riggs and Tom Velk, *Canadian-American Free Trade: Historical, Political and Economic Dimensions*, The Institute for Research in Public Policy, Montreal, 1987, p.200.

21 Velk, Tom, and Riggs, A.R., 'The Ongoing Debate Over Free Trade', in A.R. Riggs and Tom Velk, *Canadian-American Free Trade: (The Sequel) Historical, Political and Economic Dimensions*, The Institute for Research on Public Policy, Montreal, 1988, p.3.

22 d'Aquino, Thomas, 'Truck and Trade with the Yankees, The Case for a Canada-U.S. Comprehensive Trade Agreement', in A.R. Riggs and Tom Velk, *Canadian-American Free Trade: Historical, Political and Economic Dimensions*, The Institute for Research on Public Policy, Montreal, 1987, p.74.

23 Mexican Investment Board, *Mexico Your Partner for Growth, Regulatory Reform and Competition Policy, Setting the Incentives for an Efficient Economy*, Mexico, 1994, p.1.

24 Laun, Louis, 'U.S.-Canada Free Trade Negotiations: Historical Opportunities', in A.R. Riggs and Tom Velk, *Canadian-American Free Trade: Historical, Political and Economic Dimensions*, The Institute for Research in Public Policy, Montreal, 1987, p.208.

25 Harris, Richard, 'Some Observations on the Canada-U.S. Free Trade Deal', in A.R. Riggs and Tom Velk, *Canadian-American Free Trade: (The Sequel) Historical, Political and Economic Dimensions*, The Institute for Research on Public Policy, Montreal 1988, p.52.

26 North American Free Trade Agreement, at the Preamble.

27 *Ibid.*, at Article 1201.

28 *Ibid.*, at Article 1202, 1203.

29 *Ibid.*, at Article 1208.

30 *Ibid.*, at Article 1210.

31 *Ibid.*, at Article 1213.

32 *Ibid.*, at Annex 1210.A.2.

33 *Ibid.*, at Annex 1210.A.3.

34 *Ibid.*, at Annex 1210.B.1.

35 *Ibid.*, at Article 1601.

36 *Ibid.*, at Article 1602.

37 *Ibid.*, at Article 1606.

38 *Ibid.*, at Annex 1603.A.

39 *Ibid.*, at Annex 1603.B.

40 *Ibid.*, at Annex 1603.C.
41 *Ibid.*, at Annex 1603.D.
42 *Ibid.*, at Appendix 1603.D.1.
43 *Ibid.*, at Article 2001.
44 *Ibid.*, at Article 2002.
45 *Ibid.*, at Article 2003.
46 *Ibid.*, at Article 2004.
47 *Ibid.*, at Article 2008.
48 *Ibid.*, at Article 2012.
49 *Ibid.*, at Article 2017.
50 *Ibid.*, at Article 2018.
51 *Ibid.*, at Article 2019.
52 *Ibid.*, at Article 2020.
53 *Ibid.*, at Article 2021.
54 *Ibid.*, at Article 2022.
55 North American Agreement on Labor Cooperation (NAALC), at the Preamble.
56 *Ibid.*, at Article 1.
57 *Ibid.*, at Article 2.
58 *Ibid.*, at Article 3.
59 *Ibid.*, at Article 4.
60 *Ibid.*, at Article 5.
61 *Ibid.*, at Article 11.
62 *Ibid.*, at Article 49.
63 *Ibid.*, at Annex 1.
64 Government of Canada, *The North American Free Trade Agreement At A Glance*, Ottawa, p.3.
65 Raynauld, Andre, 'Looking Outward Again', in A.R. Riggs and Tom Velk, *Canadian American Free Trade: Historical, Political and Economic Dimensions*, The Institute for Research on Public Policy, Montreal, 1987, p.86.
66 Wigle, Randall, 'The Received Wisdom of the Canada-U.S. Free Trade Qualifications', in A. R. Riggs and Tom Velk, *Canadian-American Free Trade: Historical, Political and Economic Dimensions*, The Institute for Research in Public Policy, Montreal, 1987, p.92.
67 Stone, Frank, 'Removing Barriers to Canada', in A. R. Riggs and Tom Velk, *Canadian-American Free Trade: Historical, Political and Economic Dimensions*, The Institute for Research in Public Policy, Montreal, 1987, p.183.
68 Government of Canada, *NAFTA at Eight*, Ottawa, 2002.
69 Merrett, Christopher, *Free Trade, Neither Free Nor About Trade*, Black Rose Books, New York, 1996, p.270.
70 *Ibid.*, at p.95.
71 *Ibid.*, at p.271.
72 *Ibid.*, at p.279.
73 McPhail, Brenda, *NAFTA Now,* University Press of America, Lanham, 1985, p.44.
74 Hurtig, Mel, *The Betrayal of Canada*, Stoddart Publishing, Toronto, 1991, p.303.
75 *Ibid.*, at p.89.
76 Watkins, Mel, 'The Political Economy of Growth', in Wallace Clement and Glen Williams, *The New Canadian Political Economy*, McGill-Queen's University Press, Kingston, 1989, p.3.
77 Campbell, Bruce, *Free Trade, Destroyer of Jobs*, Canadian Centre for Policy Alternatives, Ottawa. 1993, p.2.

[78] Axworthy, Lloyd, 'Free Trade, The Costs for Canada', in A.R. Riggs and Tom Velk, *Canadian-American Free Trade: (The Sequel) Historical, Political and Economic Dimensions*, The Institute for Research on Public Policy, Montreal, 1988, p.38.

[79] *Ibid.*, at p.39.

[80] Nader, Ralph, *The Case Against Free Trade*, Earth Island Press, San Francisco, 1993, p.1.

[81] *Ibid.*, at p.6.

[82] Griffin Cohen, Marjorie, *Free Trade and the Future of Women's Work, Manufacturing and Service Industries*, Garamond Press, Toronto, 1987, p.16.

[83] *Ibid.*, at p.49.

[84] American Declaration of the Rights and Duties of Man, at the Preamble.

[85] *Ibid.*, at Article II.

[86] *Ibid.*, at Article XII.

[87] *Ibid.*, at Article XIII.

[88] *Ibid.*, at Article XIV.

[89] *Ibid.*, at Article XXVIII.

[90] *Ibid.*, at Article XXXIII.

[91] *Ibid.*, at Article XXXVII.

[92] American Convention on Human Rights, at the Preamble.

[93] *Ibid.*, at Article 1.

[94] *Ibid.*, at Article 2.

[95] *Ibid.*, at Article 3.

[96] *Ibid.*, at Article 22.

[97] *Ibid.*, at Article 24.

[98] *Ibid.*, at Article 25.

[99] *Ibid.*, at Article 26.

[100] *Ibid.*, at Article 27.

[101] *Ibid.*, at Article 28.

[102] *Ibid.*, at Article 33.

[103] *Ibid.*, at Article 35.

[104] *Ibid.*, at Article 41.

[105] *Ibid.*, at Article 44.

[106] *Ibid.*, at Article 46.

[107] *Ibid.*, at Article 48.

[108] *Ibid.*, at Article 61.

[109] *Ibid.*, at Article 63.

[110] *Ibid.*, at Article 66.

[111] *Ibid.*, at Article 67.

[112] *Ibid.*, at Article 68.

[113] Statute of the Inter-American Court on Human Rights, at Article 1.

[114] *Ibid.*, at Article 2.

[115] *Ibid.*, at Article 3.

[116] *Ibid.*, at Article 4.

[117] *Ibid.*, at Article 12.

[118] *Ibid.*, at Article 14.

[119] *Ibid.*, at Article 24.

[120] *Ibid.*, at Article 27.

[121] *Ibid.*, at Article 28.

[122] Inter-American Democratic Charter, at the Preamble.

[123] *Ibid.*, at Article 9.

[124] *Ibid.*, at Article 10.
[125] *Ibid.*, at Article 8.
[126] *Ibid.*, at Article 4.
[127] *Ibid.*, at Article 7.
[128] President John F. Kennedy.

References

American Convention on Human Rights.

American Declaration of the Rights and Duties of Man.

Axworthy, Lloyd (1988), 'Free Trade, The Costs for Canada', in A.R. Riggs and Tom Velk, *Canadian-American Free Trade: (The Sequel) Historical, Political and Economic Dimensions*, The Institute for Research on Public Policy, Montreal.

Brecher, Irving (1987), 'The Free Trade Initiative, On Course or Off', in A. R. Riggs and Tom Velk, *Canadian-American Free Trade: Historical, Political and Economic Dimensions*, The Institute for Research in Public Policy, Montreal.

Campbell, Bruce (1993), *Free Trade, Destroyer of Jobs*, Canadian Centre for Policy Alternatives, Ottawa.

Canada–United States Free Trade Agreement.

d'Aquino, Thomas (1987), 'Truck and Trade with the Yankees, The Case for a Canada-U.S. Comprehensive Trade Agreement', in A.R. Riggs and Tom Velk, *Canadian-American Free Trade: Historical, Political and Economic Dimensions*, The Institute for Research on Public Policy, Montreal.

Easterbrook, W.T. and Aitken, Hugh (1976), *Canadian Economic History*, Macmillan, Toronto.

Fry, Earl (1987), 'Trends in Canada-U.S. Free Trade Discussions', in A. R. Riggs and Tom Welk, *Canadian-American Free Trade: Historical, Political and Economic Dimensions*, The Institute for Research in Public Policy, Montreal.

General Agreement on Tariffs and Trade.

Government of Canada (2002), *NAFTA at Eight*, Ottawa.

Government of Canada (1993), *The North American Free Trade Agreement At A Glance*, Ottawa.

Griffin Cohen, Marjorie (1987), *Free Trade and the Future of Women's Work, Manufacturing and Service Industries*, Garamond Press, Toronto.

Hamelin, Jean (1976), *Histoire du Québec*, Edisem, St. Hyacinthe.

Harris, Richard (1988), 'Some Observations on the Canada-U.S. Free Trade Deal', in A.R. Riggs and Tom Velk, *Canadian-American Free Trade: (The Sequel) Historical, Political and Economic Dimensions*, The Institute for Research on Public Policy, Montreal.

Hurtig, Mel (1991), *The Betrayal of Canada*, Stoddart Publishing, Toronto.

Inter-American Democratic Charter.

Laun, Louis (1987), 'U.S.-Canada Free Trade Negotiations: Historical Opportunities', in A.R. Riggs and Tom Velk, *Canadian-American Free Trade: Historical, Political and Economic Dimensions*, The Institute for Research in Public Policy, Montreal.

Layton, Robert (1987), 'Why Canada Needs Free Trade', in A. R. Riggs and Tom Velk, *Canadian-American Free Trade: Historical, Political and Economic Dimensions*, The Institute for Research in Public Policy, Montreal.

Lipsey, Richard (1987), 'Canada's Trade Options', in A. R. Riggs and Tom Velk, *Canadian-American Free Trade: Historical, Political and Economic Dimensions*, The Institute for Research in Public Policy, Montreal.

McPhail, Brenda (1985), *NAFTA Now*, University Press of America, Lanham.

Merrett, Christopher (1996), *Free Trade, Neither Free Nor About Trade*, Black Rose Books, New York.

Mexican Investment Board (1994), *Mexico Your Partner for Growth, Regulatory Reform and Competition Policy, Setting the Incentives for an Efficient Economy*, Mexico.

Nader, Ralph (1993), *The Case Against Free Trade*, Earth Island Press, San Francisco.

Neufeld, E.P. (1987), 'Financial and Economic Dimensions of Free Trade', in A.R. Riggs and Tom Velk, *Canadian-American Free Trade: Historical, Political and Economic Dimensions*, The Institute for Research on Public Policy, Montreal.

North American Agreement on Labor Cooperation.

North American Free Trade Agreement.

Raynauld, Andre (1987), 'Looking Outward Again', in A.R. Riggs and Tom Velk, *Canadian-American Free Trade: Historical, Political and Economic Dimensions*, The Institute for Research on Public Policy, Montreal.

Soldatos, P (1988), 'Canada's Foreign Policy in Search of a Fourth Option: Continuity and Change in Orientation Towards the U.S.', in A.R. Riggs and Tom Velk, *Canadian-American Free Trade: (The Sequel) Historical, Political and Economic Dimensions*, The Institute for Research on Public Policy, Montreal.

Statute of the Inter-American Court on Human Rights.

Stone, Frank (1987), 'Removing Barriers to Canada', in A.R. Riggs and Tom Velk, *Canadian-American Free Trade: Historical, Political and Economic Dimensions*, The Institute for Research on Public Policy, Montreal.

Velk, Tom and Riggs, A.R. (1987), 'The Ongoing Debate Over Free Trade', in A.R. Riggs and Tom Velk, *Canadian-American Free Trade: Historical, Political and Economic Dimensions*, The Institute for Research on Public Policy, Montreal.

Watkins, Mel (1989), 'The Political Economy of Growth', in Wallace Clement and Glen Williams, *The New Canadian Political Economy*, McGill-Queen's University Press, Kingston.

Wigle, Randall (1987), 'The Received Wisdom of the Canada-U.S. Free Trade Qualifications', in A. R. Riggs and Tom Welk, *Canadian-American Free Trade: Historical, Political and Economic Dimensions*, The Institute for Research in Public Policy, Montreal.

Chapter 8

This Ability in
the United Kingdom and Ireland

Introduction

This chapter will examine this ability in the United Kingdom and Ireland. It will initially look at the United Kingdom, which encompasses England, Scotland, Wales and Northern Ireland, examining such legislation as the Disability Discrimination Act, the Disability Rights Commission Act, the Human Rights Act and the Equal Pay Act, as well as for minorities with a disability the Racial Relations Act and for women with a disability the Sexual Discrimination Act. It will then go on to look at the Republic of Ireland, examining such legislation as the Employment Equality Act, the Equal Status Act and the Disability Bill. There is a need for intervention in the application of human rights law to disability rights.

United Kingdom

Disability Discrimination Act 1995 (DDA 1995) and the Disability Discrimination Act 2005 (DDA 2005)

The Disability Discrimination Act 1995 (DDA) deals with discrimination against disabled people in the areas of employment, the provision of goods, facilities and services and premises, education and public transport.[1] It aims to end the discrimination that many disabled people face. This Act gives disabled people rights in the areas of employment, education, access to goods, facilities and services, and buying or renting land or property. The Act also allows the government to set minimum standards so that disabled people can use public transport easily. The development of legislation to improve the rights of disabled people is an ongoing process. From 1 October 2004, Part 3 of the DDA 1995 has required businesses and other organisations to take reasonable steps to tackle physical features that act as a barrier to disabled people who want to access their services. This means to remove, alter or provide a reasonable means of avoiding physical features of a building which make access impossible or unreasonably difficult for disabled people, such as putting in a ramp to replace steps, providing larger well-defined signs for people with a visual impairment, and improving access to toilet or washing facilities. Businesses and organisations are called 'service providers' and include shops, restaurants, leisure centres and places of worship.

Under the DDA, it is unlawful for employers to discriminate against disabled people for a reason related to their disability, in all aspects of employment, unless this can be justified. The Act covers application forms, interview arrangements, proficiency tests, job offers, terms of employment, promotion, transfer or training opportunities, work-related benefits such as access to recreation or refreshment facilities, dismissal or redundancy. Under the DDA, the employer has a duty to consider making 'reasonable adjustments' to make sure no one with a disability is put at a substantial disadvantage by employment arrangements or any physical feature of the workplace. Adjustments the employer should consider are set out in the DDA and include allocating some of the work to someone else, transferring one to another post or another place of work, making adjustments to the buildings, being flexible about hours, allowing different core working hours and to be away from the office for assessment, treatment or rehabilitation, providing training, modified equipment, and a reader or interpreter, and making instructions and manuals more accessible. Before 2005, the DDA only applied to employers with 15 or more staff, but now employers with fewer than 15 staff are now included. The DDA also covers work-based training opportunities for employees.

In April 2005, a new Disability Discrimination Act (DDA) was passed by Parliament, which amends or extends existing provisions in the DDA 1995, including making it unlawful for operators of transport vehicles to discriminate against disabled people; making it easier for disabled people to rent property and for tenants to make disability-related adaptations; making sure that private clubs with 25 or more members cannot keep disabled people out, because they have a disability; extending protection to cover people who have cancer and multiple sclerosis from the moment they are diagnosed; and ensuring that discrimination law covers all the activities of the public sector; requiring public bodies to promote equality of opportunity for disabled people.

The Disability Rights Commission (DRC) was set up by the government to help secure civil rights for disabled people and produces guidance and further information on which aspects of life are covered by anti-discrimination law for disabled people. The DRC is the statutory body set up by the government to help secure civil rights for disabled people. It was established by an act of parliament under the Disability Rights Commission Act 1999 (DRCA) to work towards ending discrimination against disabled people, promote equal opportunities for disabled people, encourage good practice in the treatment of disabled people, and keep under review the working of the Disability Discrimination Act and the DRCA. The DRC is an executive Non-Departmental Public Body. It operates independently of the government and provides information and advice to disabled people, businesses and education providers, supports disabled people in securing their rights under the Disability Discrimination Act (DDA), offers a conciliation service for disabled people and service providers including education providers, develops statutory codes of practice, conducts research, advises the government on the operation of existing legislation and whether changes need to be made to it.

In bringing a DDA case, the requirement that a person be 'substantially' adversely affected points towards a 'protected group' philosophy and is consistent with an element of redistribution and positive action in favour of disabled people.

Tribunal cases suggest that employers should expect to have to demonstrate that they have investigated the possibilities for accommodation before dismissing a worker. The case law also establishes that reasonable accommodation may involve physical adjustments to the workplace, but may also involve changes to a person's job description, redeployment, or changes to the work time pattern, such as time off for medical treatment. While the restrictive definition of disability and the reasonable accommodation clause might suggest that the DDA is founded on an 'equality of results' conception, many cases are actually based on individual merit. DDA cases are heard by specialist Employment Tribunals, which are experienced in unfair dismissal cases and other aspects of employee rights. The Tribunals are accustomed to looking critically at employers' actions and balancing the employer's right to manage against the interests of workers. This leans towards an 'equality as fairness' approach to discrimination, whereas ordinary courts may be more inclined to restrict themselves to the firmer judicial territory of 'equality as rationality'. It is also significant that there are many DDA cases where the issue of the definition of disability does not arise. Very often the employee has a case under the law relating to unfair dismissal alongside the DDA claim, and is thereby able to utilise the general rights of employees in establishing the claim. Of the DDA cases that had reached an outcome, some 40 per cent were settled through conciliation and arbitration, while 20 per cent had gone to an employment tribunal hearing.[2]

The Act provides that it is unlawful to discriminate under Section 4:

> 4. (1) It is unlawful for an employer to discriminate against a disabled person (a) in the arrangements which he makes for the purpose of determining to whom he should offer employment; (b) in the terms on which he offers that person employment; or   (c) by refusing to offer, or deliberately not offering, him employment.
>
> (2) It is unlawful for an employer to discriminate against a disabled person whom he employs
>
> > (a) in the terms of employment which he affords him;
> >
> > (b) in the opportunities which he affords him for promotion, a transfer, training or receiving any other benefit;
> >
> > (c) by refusing to afford him, or deliberately not affording him, any such opportunity; or
> >
> > (d) by dismissing him, or subjecting him to any other detriment.
>
> (3) Subsection (2) does not apply to benefits of any description if the employer is concerned with the provision (whether or not for payment) of benefits of that description to the public, or to a section of the public which includes the employee in question, unless
>
> > (a) that provision differs in a material respect from the provision of the benefits by the employer to his employees; or

(b) the provision of the benefits to the employee in question is regulated by his contract of employment; or

(c) the benefits relate to training.[3]

The definition of 'discrimination' is found under Section 5:

5.(1) For the purposes of this Part, an employer discriminates against a disabled person if

(a) for a reason which relates to the disabled person's disability, he treats him less favourably than he treats or would treat others to whom that reason does not or would not apply; and

(b) he cannot show that the treatment in question is justified.

(6) Regulations may make provision, for purposes of this section, as to circumstances in which

(a) treatment is to be taken to be justified;

(b) failure to comply with a section 6 duty is to be taken to be justified;

(c) treatment is to be taken not to be justified;

(d) failure to comply with a section 6 duty is to be taken not to be justified.

(7) Regulations under subsection (6) may, in particular

(a) make provision by reference to the cost of affording any benefit; and

(b) in relation to benefits under occupational pension schemes, make provision with a view to enabling uniform rates of contributions to be maintained.[4]

In terms of employment, Section 6 notes the duty of employers to make adjustments:

6.(1)Where

(a) any arrangements made by or on behalf of an employer, or

(b) any physical feature of premises occupied by the employer,

place the disabled person concerned at a substantial disadvantage in comparison with persons who are not disabled, it is the duty of the employer to take such steps as it is reasonable, in all the circumstances of the case, for him to have to take in order to prevent the arrangements or feature having that effect.

(3) The following are examples of steps which an employer may have to take in relation to a disabled person in order to comply with subsection (1)

(a) making adjustments to premises;

(b) allocating some of the disabled person's duties to another person;

(c) transferring him to fill an existing vacancy;

(d) altering his working hours;

(e) assigning him to a different place of work;

(f) allowing him to be absent during working hours for rehabilitation, assessment or treatment;

(g) giving him, or arranging for him to be given, training;

(h) acquiring or modifying equipment;

(i) modifying instructions or reference manuals;

(j) modifying procedures for testing or assessment;

(k) providing a reader or interpreter;

(l) providing supervision.

(4) In determining whether it is reasonable for an employer to have to take a particular step in order to comply with subsection (1), regard shall be had, in particular, to

(a) the extent to which taking the step would prevent the effect in question;

(b) the extent to which it is practicable for the employer to take the step;

(c) the financial and other costs which would be incurred by the employer in taking the step and the extent to which taking it would disrupt any of his activities;

(d) the extent of the employer's financial and other resources;

(e) the availability to the employer of financial or other assistance with respect to taking the step.

(6) Nothing in this section imposes any duty on an employer in relation to a disabled person if the employer does not know, and could not reasonably be expected to know

(a) in the case of an applicant or potential applicant, that the disabled person concerned is, or may be, an applicant for the employment; or

(b) in any case, that that person has a disability and is likely to be affected in the way mentioned in subsection (1).

(7) Subject to the provisions of this section, nothing in this Part is to be taken to require an employer to treat disabled person more favourably than he treats or would treat others.

(8) Regulations may make provision, for the purposes of subsection (1)

(a) as to circumstances in which arrangements are, or a physical feature is, to be taken to have the effect mentioned in that subsection;

(b) as to circumstances in which arrangements are not, or a physical feature is not, to be taken to have that effect;

(c) as to circumstances in which it is reasonable for an employer to have to take steps of a prescribed description;

(d) as to steps which it is always reasonable for an employer to have to take;

(e) as to circumstances in which it is not reasonable for an employer to have to take steps of a prescribed description;

(f) as to steps which it is never reasonable for an employer to have to take;

(g) as to things which are to be treated as physical features;

(h) as to things which are not to be treated as such features.

(11) This section does not apply in relation to any benefit under an occupational pension scheme or any other benefit payable in money or money's worth under a scheme or arrangement for the benefit of employees in respect of

(a) termination of service;

(b) retirement, old age or death;

(c) accident, injury, sickness or invalidity; or

(d) any other prescribed matter.[5]

Section 8 outlines enforcement, remedies and procedure:

8.(1) A complaint by any person that another person

(a) has discriminated against him in a way which is unlawful under this Part, or

(b) is ... to be treated as having discriminated against him in such a way,

may be presented to an industrial tribunal.

(2) Where an industrial tribunal finds that a complaint presented to it under this section is well-founded, it shall take such of the following steps as it considers just and equitable

(a) making a declaration as to the rights of the complainant and the respondent in relation to the matters to which the complaint relates;

(b) ordering the respondent to pay compensation to the complainant;

(c) recommending that the respondent take, within a specified period, action appearing to the tribunal to be reasonable, in all the circumstances of the case, for the purpose of obviating or reducing the adverse effect on the complainant of any matter to which the complaint relates.[6]

Section 9 notes the validity of certain agreements:

9.(1) Any term in a contract of employment or other agreement is void so far as it purports to

(a) require a person to do anything which would contravene any provision of, or made under, this Part;

(b) exclude or limit the operation of any provision of this Part; or

(c) prevent any person from presenting a complaint to an industrial tribunal under this Part.[7]

Support for particular groups of persons has special recognition under Section 10:

10. (2) Nothing in this Part prevents

(a) a person who provides supported employment from treating members of a particular group of disabled persons more favourably than other persons in providing such employment; or

(b) the Secretary of State from agreeing to arrangements for the provision of supported employment which will, or may, have that effect.[8]

The Act is especially watchful of advertisements suggesting that employers will discriminate against disabled persons, as noted in Section 11:

11. (1) This section applies where

(a) a disabled person has applied for employment with an employer;

(b) the employer has refused to offer, or has deliberately not offered, him the employment;

(c) the disabled person has presented a complaint under section 8 against the employer;

(d) the employer has advertised the employment (whether before or after the disabled person applied for it); and

(e) the advertisement indicated, or might reasonably be understood to have indicated, that any application for the advertised employment would, or might, be determined to any extent by reference to-

> (i) the successful applicant not having any disability or any category of disability which includes the disabled person's disability; or

> (ii) the employer's reluctance to take any action of a kind mentioned in section 6.

(2) The tribunal hearing the complaint shall assume, unless the contrary is shown, that the employer's reason for refusing to offer, or deliberately not offering, the employment to the complainant was related to the complainant's disability.[9]

Section 12 outlaws discrimination against contract workers:

12.(1) It is unlawful for a principal, in relation to contract work, to discriminate against a disabled person

(a) in the terms on which he allows him to do that work;

(b) by not allowing him to do it or continue to do it;

(c) in the way he affords him access to any benefits or by refusing or deliberately omitting to afford him access to them; or

(d) by subjecting him to any other detriment.[10]

In terms of the provision of services, discrimination is outlawed under Section 19:

19.(1) It is unlawful for a provider of services to discriminate against a disabled person

(a) in refusing to provide, or deliberately not providing, to the disabled person any service which he provides, or is prepared to provide, to members of the public;

(b) in failing to comply with any duty imposed on him by section 21 in circumstances in which the effect of that failure is to make it impossible or unreasonably difficult for the disabled person to make use of any such service;

(c) in the standard of service which he provides to the disabled person or the manner in which he provides it to him; or

(d) in the terms on which he provides a service to the disabled person.

(2) For the purposes of this section and sections 20 and 21

(a) the provision of services includes the provision of any goods or facilities;

(3) The following are examples of services to which this section and sections 20 and 21 apply

(a) access to and use of any place which members of the public are permitted to enter;

(b) access to and use of means of communication;

(c) access to and use of information services;

(d) accommodation in a hotel, boarding house or other similar establishment;

(e) facilities by way of banking or insurance or for grants, loans, credit or finance;

(f) facilities for entertainment, recreation or refreshment;

(g) facilities provided by employment agencies or under section 2 of the Employment and Training Act 1973;

(h) the services of any profession or trade, or any local or other public authority.[11]

The definition of 'discrimination' is noted under Section 20:

20.(1) For the purposes of section 19, a provider of services discriminates against a disabled person if

(a) for a reason which relates to the disabled person's disability, he treats him less favourably than he treats or would treat others to whom that reason does not or would not apply; and

(b) he cannot show that the treatment in question is justified.

(3) For the purposes of this section, treatment is justified only if

> (a) in the opinion of the provider of services, one or more of the conditions mentioned in subsection (4) are satisfied; and

> (b) it is reasonable, in all the circumstances of the case, for him to hold that opinion.

(4) The conditions are that

> (a) in any case, the treatment is necessary in order not to endanger the health or safety of any person (which may include that of the disabled person);

> (b) in any case, the disabled person is incapable of entering into an enforceable agreement, or of giving an informed consent, and for that reason the treatment is reasonable in that case;

> (c) in a case falling within section 19(1)(a), the treatment is necessary because the provider of services would otherwise be unable to provide the service to members of the public;

> (d) in a case falling within section 19(1)(c) or (d), the treatment is necessary in order for the provider of services to be able to provide the service to the disabled person or to other members of the public;

> (e) in a case falling within section 19(1)(d), the difference in the terms on which the service is provided to the disabled person and those on which it is provided to other members of the public reflects the greater cost to the provider of services in providing the service to the disabled person.[12]

Section 21 provides for the duty of providers of services to make adjustments:

> 21.(1) Where a provider of services has a practice, policy or procedure which makes it impossible or unreasonably difficult for disabled persons to make use of a service which he provides, or is prepared to provide, to other members of the public, it is his duty to take such steps as it is reasonable, in all the circumstances of the case, for him to have to take in order to change that practice, policy or procedure so that it no longer has that effect.

> (2) Where a physical feature (for example, one arising from the design or construction of a building or the approach or access to premises) makes it impossible or unreasonably difficult for disabled persons to make use of such a service, it is the duty of the provider of that service to take such steps as it is reasonable, in all the circumstances of the case, for him to have to take in order to

> > (a) remove the feature;

> > (b) alter it so that it no longer has that effect;

> > (c) provide a reasonable means of avoiding the feature; or

(d) provide a reasonable alternative method of making the service in question available to disabled persons.

(6) Nothing in this section requires a provider of services to take any steps which would fundamentally alter the nature of the service in question or the nature of his trade, profession or business.

(7) Nothing in this section requires a provider of services to take any steps which would cause him to incur expenditure exceeding the prescribed maximum.[13]

In terms of transportation, taxi accessibility regulations are provided for under Section 32:

32.(1) The Secretary of State may make regulations ('taxi accessibility regulations') for the purpose of securing that it is possible

(a) for disabled persons-

(i) to get into and out of taxis in safety;

(ii) to be carried in taxis in safety and in reasonable comfort; and

(b) for disabled persons in wheelchairs

(i) to be conveyed in safety into and out of taxis while remaining in their wheelchairs; and

(ii) to be carried in taxis in safety and in reasonable comfort while remaining in their wheelchairs.

(2) Taxi accessibility regulations may, in particular

(a) require any regulated taxi to conform with provisions of the regulations as to-

(i) the size of any door opening which is for the use of passengers;

(ii) the floor area of the passenger compartment;

(iii) the amount of headroom in the passenger compartment;

(iv) the fitting of restraining devices designed to ensure the stability of a wheelchair while the taxi is moving;

(b) require the driver of any regulated taxi which is plying for hire, or which has been hired, to comply with provisions of the regulations as to the carrying of ramps or other devices designed to facilitate the loading and unloading of wheelchairs;

(c) require the driver of any regulated taxi in which a disabled person who is in a wheelchair is being carried (while remaining in his wheelchair) to comply with provisions of the regulations as to the position in which the wheelchair is to be secured.

(3) The driver of a regulated taxi which is plying for hire, or which has been hired, is guilty of an offence if

(a) he fails to comply with any requirement imposed on him by the regulations; or

(b) the taxi fails to conform with any provision of the regulations with which it is required to conform.

(4) A person who is guilty of such an offence is liable, on summary conviction, to a fine not exceeding level 3 on the standard scale.[14]

Under Section 34, new licences are conditional on compliance with taxi accessibility regulations:

34.(1) No licensing authority shall grant a licence for a taxi to ply for hire unless the vehicle conforms with those provisions of the taxi accessibility regulations with which it will be required to conform if licensed.[15]

The carrying of passengers in wheelchairs is provided for under Section 36:

36.(1) This section imposes duties on the driver of a regulated taxi which has been hired

(a) by or for a disabled person who is in a wheelchair; or

(b) by a person who wishes such a disabled person to accompany him in the taxi.

(3) The duties are

(a) to carry the passenger while he remains in his wheelchair;

(b) not to make any additional charge for doing so;

(c) if the passenger chooses to sit in a passenger seat, to carry the wheelchair;

(d) to take such steps as are necessary to ensure that the passenger is carried in safety and in reasonable comfort;

(e) to give such assistance as may be reasonably required

(i) to enable the passenger to get into or out of the taxi;

(ii) if the passenger wishes to remain in his wheelchair, to enable him to be conveyed into and out of the taxi while in his wheelchair;

(iii) to load the passenger's luggage into or out of the taxi;

(iv) if the passenger does not wish to remain in his wheelchair, to load the wheelchair into or out of the taxi.

(4) Nothing in this section is to be taken to require the driver of any taxi

(a) except in the case of a taxi of a prescribed description, to carry more than one person in a wheelchair, or more than one wheelchair, on any one journey; or

(b) to carry any person in circumstances in which it would otherwise be lawful for him to refuse to carry that person.

(5) A driver of a regulated taxi who fails to comply with any duty imposed on him by this section is guilty of an offence and liable, on summary conviction, to a fine not exceeding level 3 on the standard scale.

(6) In any proceedings for an offence under this section, it is a defence for the accused to show that, even though at the time of the alleged offence the taxi conformed with those provisions of the taxi accessibility regulations with which it was required to conform, it would not have been possible for the wheelchair in question to be carried in safety in the taxi.

(7) If the licensing authority is satisfied that it is appropriate to exempt a person from the duties imposed by this section

(a) on medical grounds, or

(b) on the ground that his physical condition makes it impossible or unreasonably difficult for him to comply with the duties imposed on drivers by this section,

it shall issue him with a certificate of exemption.

(8) A certificate of exemption shall be issued for such period as may be specified in the certificate.

(9) The driver of a regulated taxi is exempt from the duties imposed by this section if

(a) a certificate of exemption issued to him under this section is in force; and

(b) the prescribed notice of his exemption is exhibited on the taxi in the prescribed manner.[16]

Disability Rights Commission Act 1999

Section 1 notes the creation of the Disability Rights Commission (DRC):

> 1.(1) There shall be a body known as the Disability Rights Commission (referred to in this Act as 'the Commission').[17]

The general functions of the Commission are outlined in Section 2:

> 2.(1) The Commission shall have the following duties
>
> > (a) to work towards the elimination of discrimination against disabled persons;
> >
> > (b) to promote the equalisation of opportunities for disabled persons;
> >
> > (c) to take such steps as it considers appropriate with a view to encouraging good practice in the treatment of disabled persons; and
> >
> > (d) to keep under review the working of the Disability Discrimination Act 1995 ('the 1995 Act') and this Act.
>
> (2) The Commission may, for any purpose connected with the performance of its functions
>
> > (a) make proposals or give other advice to any Minister of the Crown as to any aspect of the law or a proposed change to the law;
> >
> > (b) make proposals or give other advice to any Government agency or other public authority as to the practical application of any law;
> >
> > (c) undertake, or arrange for or support (whether financially or otherwise), the carrying out of research or the provision of advice or information.
> >
> > Nothing in this subsection is to be regarded as limiting the Commission's powers.[18]

A formal investigation is provided for under Section 3:

> 3.(1) The Commission may decide to conduct a formal investigation for any purpose connected with the performance of its duties under section 2(1).
>
> (2) The Commission shall conduct a formal investigation if directed to do so by the Secretary of State for any such purpose.
>
> (3) The Commission may at any time decide to stop or to suspend the conduct of a formal investigation; but any such decision requires the approval of the Secretary of State if the investigation is being conducted in pursuance of a direction under subsection (2).

(4) The Commission may, as respects any formal investigation which it has decided or been directed to conduct

> (a) nominate one or more commissioners, with or without one or more additional commissioners appointed for the purposes of the investigation, to conduct the investigation on its behalf; and

> (b) authorise those persons to exercise such of its functions in relation to the investigation (which may include drawing up or revising terms of reference) as it may determine.[19]

Non-discrimination notices are mentioned in Section 4:

4.(1) If in the course of a formal investigation the Commission is satisfied that a person has committed or is committing an unlawful act, it may serve on him a notice (referred to in this Act as a non-discrimination notice) which

> (a) gives details of the unlawful act which the Commission has found that he has committed or is committing; and

> (b) requires him not to commit any further unlawful acts of the same kind (and, if the finding is that he is committing an unlawful act, to cease doing so).

(2) The notice may include recommendations to the person concerned as to action which the Commission considers he could reasonably be expected to take with a view to complying with the requirement mentioned in subsection (1)(b).

(3) The notice may require the person concerned

> (a) to propose an adequate action plan … with a view to securing compliance with the requirement mentioned in subsection (1)(b); and

> (b) once an action plan proposed by him has become final, to take any action which-

>> (i) is specified in the plan; and

>> (ii) he has not already taken,

> at the time or times specified in the plan.

(4) For the purposes of subsection (3)

> (a) an action plan is a document drawn up by the person concerned specifying action (including action he has already taken) intended to change anything in his practices, policies, procedures or other arrangements which

>> (i) caused or contributed to the commission of the unlawful act concerned; or

(ii) is liable to cause or contribute to a failure to comply with the requirement mentioned in subsection (1)(b); and

(b) an action plan is adequate if the action specified in it would be sufficient to ensure, within a reasonable time, that he is not prevented from complying with that requirement by anything in his practices, policies, procedures or other arrangements;

and the action specified in an action plan may include ceasing an activity or taking continuing action over a period.[20]

Section 6 guarantees against persistent discrimination:

6.(1) This section applies during the period of five years beginning on the date on which

(a) a non-discrimination notice served on a person,

(b) a finding by a court or tribunal in proceedings under section 8 or 25 of the 1995 Act that a person has committed an act which is unlawful discrimination for the purposes of any provision of Part II or Part III of that Act, or

(c) a finding by a court or tribunal in any other proceedings that a person has committed an act of a description prescribed under subsection (4)(b),

has become final.

(2) If during that period it appears to the Commission that unless restrained the person concerned is likely to do one or more unlawful acts, the Commission may apply to a county court for an injunction, or to the sheriff for interdict, restraining him from doing so.

(3) The court, if satisfied that the application is well-founded, may grant the injunction or interdict in the terms applied for or in more limited terms.

(5) A finding of a court or tribunal becomes final for the purposes of this section when an appeal against it is dismissed, withdrawn or abandoned or when the time for appealing expires without an appeal having been brought.[21]

In terms of codes of practice, Section 9 notes:

9. (1) The Disability Rights Commission may prepare and issue codes of practice giving practical guidance

(a) to employers, service providers or other persons to whom provisions of Part II or Part III apply on how to avoid discrimination or on any other matter relating to the operation of those provisions in relation to them; or

(b) to any persons on any other matter, with a view to

> (i) promoting the equalisation of opportunities for disabled persons and persons who have had a disability, or

> (ii) encouraging good practice regarding the treatment of such persons,

in any field of activity regulated by any provision of Part II or Part III.

(2) The Commission shall, when requested to do so by the Secretary of State, prepare a code of practice dealing with the matters specified in the request.

(3) In preparing a code of practice the Commission shall carry out such consultations as it considers appropriate (which shall include the publication for public consultation of proposals relating to the code).[22]

In terms of conciliation of disputes, Section 10 notes:

> 10. (1) The Commission may make arrangements with any other person for the provision of conciliation services by, or by persons appointed by, that person in relation to disputes arising under this Part.

> (2) In deciding what arrangements (if any) to make, the Commission shall have regard to the desirability of securing, so far as reasonably practicable, that conciliation services are available for all disputes arising under this Part which the parties may wish to refer to conciliation.[23]

The following legislative instruments may be relevant to cases of disability discrimination.

Human Rights Act 1998 (HRA)

Important for disability rights, the Human Rights Act came into force on 2 October 2000. The scope of the non-discrimination Section is wider than current anti-discrimination legislation, because it includes a greater range of criteria in respect of which discrimination is prohibited but it is not a freestanding provision.
Section 14 prohibits discrimination:

> 14. The enjoyment of the rights and freedoms set forth in this convention shall be secured without discrimination on any ground such as sex, race, color, language, religion, political or other opinion, national or social origin, association with a national minority, property, birth or other status.[24]

Prohibition of abuse of rights is provided for in Section 17:

> 17. Nothing in this Convention may be interpreted as implying for any State, group or person any right to engage in any activity or perform any act aimed at the destruction of any of the rights and freedoms set forth herein or at their limitation to a greater extent than is provided for in the Convention.[25]

The HRA incorporates most of the substantive provisions of the European Convention of Human Rights (ECHR) into the law of the United Kingdom. Individuals can bring claims under the HRA against public authorities for breaches of Convention rights, which include a right not to be discriminated against on non-exhaustive grounds.

Equal Pay Act (EPA)

Important for disability rights, under the Equal Pay Act 1970 (EPA), genuine occupational qualification is recognized in Section 1(3):

> 1(3) An equality clause shall not operate in relation to a variation between the woman's contract and the man's contract if the employer proves that the variation is genuinely due to a material factor which is not the difference of sex ....[26]

Section 2(1) guarantees the important right of tribunal recourse for redress:

> 2(1) Any claim in respect of the contravention of a term modified or included by virtue of an equality clause, including a claim for arrears of remuneration or damages in respect of the contravention, may be presented by way of a complaint to an employment tribunal.[27]

The Equal Pay Act covers all contractual terms and not simply those relating to pay, with claims taken initially to an Industrial Tribunal.

Equal Opportunities Commission (EOC) and the Code of Practice on Equal Pay

The Code of Practice on Equal Pay is the main source of advice on implementing equal pay in the workplace and was issued by the Equal Opportunities Commission (EOC) in 1997. Employers must include an equality clause into individual contracts of employment. The EOC issued a Code of Practice for the purposes of the elimination of discrimination in employment; for guidance as to what steps it is reasonably practicable for employers to take to ensure that their employees do not in the course of their employment act contrary to the law; and for the promotion of equality of opportunity in employment. The Code gives guidance to employers, trade unions and employment agencies on measures that can he taken to achieve equality. The primary responsibility at law rests with each employer to ensure that there is no unlawful discrimination. The Code recommends the establishment and use of consistent criteria for selection, training, promotion, redundancy and dismissal that are made known to all employees, as part of good employment practices in eliminating disability discrimination. It is recommended that each individual should be assessed according to his personal capability to carry out a given job.

The EOC recommends that a pay systems review should involve the following stages. Stage 1: undertake a thorough analysis of the pay system to produce a breakdown of all employees, which covers job title, grade, whether part-time or full-time, with basic pay, performance ratings and all other elements of remuneration; stage 2: examine each element of the pay system against the data obtained in stage 1; stage 3: identify any elements of the pay system that the review indicates may be the source of any discrimination; stage 4: change any rules or practices, including those in collective agreements, which stages 1 to 3 have identified as likely to give rise to discrimination in pay, in consultation with employees, trade unions or staff representatives where appropriate. Stages 1 to 3 may reveal that practices and procedures in relation to recruitment, selection and access to training have contributed to discrimination in pay, and these should be addressed. There follow stage 5: analyze the likely effects of any proposed changes in practice to the pay system before implementation, to identify and rectify any discrimination that could be caused; stage 6: give equal pay to current employees. Where the review shows that some employees are not receiving equal pay for equal work and the reasons cannot be shown to be free of bias, then a plan must be developed for dealing with this; stage 7: set up a system of regular monitoring to allow checks to be made to pay practices; and stage 8: draw up and publish an equal pay policy with provision for assessing the new pay system or modification to a system in terms of discrimination.[28]

Race Relations Act

Important for disability rights, the Race Relations Act 1976 defines direct and indirect discrimination, and victimization. The Act outlaws racial discrimination in employment, training, education, housing, public appointments, and the provision of goods, facilities and services. The Commission for Racial Equality (CRE) has the power to enforce the duties specified in the Act. The CRE will issue a compliance notice and if necessary seek a court order to enforce the notice. The Act defines 'public authorities' widely, for the purposes of outlawing discrimination, so that it includes public functions carried out by private sector organizations and has only limited exemption. The general duty of the Act also expects public authorities to take the lead in eliminating racial discrimination, and promoting equality of opportunity and good relations between people of different racial groups. The new public duty requires public bodies to implement race equality in all aspects of employment matters, such as recruitment and selection, training, promotion, discipline and dismissal.

The Act places a general duty on a wide range of public authorities to promote race equality, with the duty's aim to make the promotion of race equality central to the work of the listed public authorities. This duty means that authorities must have due regard to the need to eliminate unlawful racial discrimination; promote equality of opportunity; and promote good relations between people of different racial groups. In relation to policy development and service delivery, the duty will encourage policy-makers to be more aware of possible problems; contribute to more informed decision-making; make sure that policies are properly targeted; improve the authority's ability to deliver suitable and accessible services that meet varied needs; encourage greater openness about policy making; increase confidence in public services, especially among ethnic minority communities; help to develop good practice; and help to avoid claims of unlawful racial discrimination. Four principles should govern public authorities' efforts to meet their duty to promote race equality: promoting race equality is obligatory for all public authorities listed; public authorities must meet the duty to promote race equality in all relevant functions; the weight given to race equality should be proportionate to its relevance; and the elements of the duty are complementary, which means they are all necessary to meet the whole duty. The general duty has three parts: eliminating unlawful racial discrimination; promoting equality of opportunity; and promoting good relations between people of different racial groups.[29]

In terms of a General Statutory duty, Section 71(1) of the Race Relations Act states:

> 71(1) Every body or other person specified in Schedule 1A or a description falling within that Schedule shall, in carrying out its functions, have due regard to the need
> a)   to eliminate unlawful racial discrimination; and
> b)   to promote equality of opportunity and good relations between persons of different racial groups.[30]

In terms of the Employment Duty, Section 5 of the Race Relations Act 1976 (Statutory Duties) Order 2001 or Section 4 of the Race Relations Act 1976 (Statutory Duties) Order 2003 state:

> a)   A person…shall:
> (i)   Before 31 May 2002 (2001 Order) or 31 May 2004 (2003 Order) or 31 May 2005 (2004 Order) …, have in place arrangements for fulfilling, as soon as is reasonably practicable, its duties …, and fulfil those duties in accordance with such arrangements.
>
> (ii)   It shall be the duty of such a person to monitor, by reference to the racial groups to which they belong, the numbers of:
> Staff in post.
> Applicants for employment, training and promotion from each such group, and where that person has 150 or more full-time staff, the numbers of staff from each such group who:
> -   Receive training.
> -   Benefit or suffer detriment as a result of its performance assessment procedures.
> -   Are involved in grievance procedures.
> -   Are the subject of disciplinary procedures.
> -   Cease employment with that person. [31]

Sex Discrimination Act (SDA)

Important for women with a disability, according to the Sex Discrimination Act 1975, direct and indirect discrimination is defined in Section 1:

1(1) In any circumstances relevant for the purposes of any provision of this Act
..., a person discriminates against a woman if:

(a) on the ground of her sex he treats her less favourably than he treats or would
treat a man, or

(b) he applies to her a requirement or condition which he applies or would apply
equally to a man but:

(i) which is such that the proportion of women who can comply with it is
considerably smaller than the proportion of men who can comply with it, and

(ii) which he cannot show to be justifiable irrespective of the sex of the person to
whom it is applied, and

1(1)(b)(iii) which is to her detriment because she cannot comply with it.[32]

In looking at discrimination in the employment stage, Section 6(2) states:

6(2) It is unlawful for a person, in the case of a woman employed by him at an
establishment in Great Britain, to discriminate against her:

(a) in the way he affords her access to opportunities for promotion, transfer or
training, or to any other benefits, facilities or services, or by refusing or
deliberately omitting to afford her access to them, or

(b) by dismissing her, or subjecting her to any other detriment.[33]

There is an exception to the rule where sex is a genuine occupational
qualification, which is contained in Section 7:

7(1) In relation to sex discrimination:

(a) section 6(1)(a) or (c) does not apply to any employment where being a man is a
genuine occupational qualification for the job.

7(2) Being a man is a genuine occupational qualification for a job only where:

(a) the essential nature of the job calls for a man for reasons of physiology
(excluding physical strength or stamina) or, in dramatic performances or other
entertainment, for reasons of authenticity, so that the essential nature of the job
would be materially different if carried out by a woman; or

(b) the job needs to be held by a man to preserve decency or privacy ...; or

(c) the nature or location of the establishment makes it impracticable for the
holder of the job to live elsewhere than in premises provided by the employer ...;

(d) the nature of the establishment, or of the part of it within which the work is
done, requires it to be held by a man ...; or

(e) the job needs to be held by a man because of restrictions imposed by
the laws regulating the employment of women, or

(f) the holder of the job provides individuals with personal services promoting
their welfare or education, or similar personal services, and those services can
most effectively be provided by a man, or

(g) the job needs to be held by a man because it is likely to involve the
performance of duties outside the United Kingdom in a country whose laws or
customs are such that the duties could not, or could not effectively, be performed
by a woman, or

(h) the job is one of two to be held by a married couple.[34]

In a claim of sex discrimination presented to an employment tribunal, it is first up to the applicant to establish facts, which constitute a 'prima facie' case of discrimination. The burden of proof is initially on the employee to show on the balance of probabilities that her male comparator is doing the same or broadly similar work, or that her work has been rated as equivalent to his, or that her work is of equal value, and that his contract contains a more favorable term. The burden of proof then shifts from the applicant to the employer to show that there is a nondiscriminatory reason for their actions, that is the difference between the contracts is genuinely due to a material factor which is not the difference of gender. The material factor defence is the reason put forward by the employer to explain why the comparator, although doing equal work, is paid more than the applicant. To be successful, this factor must be significant and relevant; that is, it must be an important cause of the difference and apply to the jobs in question. The difference in pay must be genuinely due to the material factor which must not be tainted by gender discrimination. If the reason given for paying the comparator more is that he has certain skills which the applicant does not have, then the employer would have to demonstrate that these skills are necessary for the job, and genuinely applied during the performance of the job, and are not simply rewarded because past pay agreements recognized and rewarded skills which are no longer applicable. To succeed in a defence, the employer needs to show that the material factor accounts for the whole of the difference in pay.

Ireland

In looking at disability discrimination in the Republic of Ireland, the two main pieces of legislation are the Employment Equality Act and the Equal Status Act.

Employment Equality Act

In Ireland, the Employment Equality Act (1998) prohibits discrimination in employment and in other spheres of life on a number of grounds, including disability. A definition of disability is provided in the Act, which states that disability means: (a) the total or partial absence of a person's bodily or mental functions, including the absence of a part of a person's body; (b) the presence in the body of organisms causing, or likely to cause, chronic disease or illness; (c) the malfunction, malformation or disfigurement of a part of a person's body; (d) a condition or malfunction which results in a person learning differently from a person without the condition or malfunction, or (e) a condition, illness or disease which affects a person's thought processes, perception of reality, emotions or judgement, which results in disturbed behaviour; and shall be taken to include a disability which presently exists, or which previously existed but no longer exists, or which may exist in the future or which is imputed to a person. Thus, the Irish definition encompasses minor and perceived impairments, and does not require that a person's limitations be substantial.[35]

The original Employment Equality Bill (1996) was declared unconstitutional by the Supreme Court (Judgement 118/97, 15 May 1997). It found that the requirement to accommodate disabled workers unless this caused the employer 'undue hardship' did not strike an appropriate balance between the employer's constitutional right to property and the principles of social justice which could regulate that right. The Court accepted that it was in accordance with social justice that society should ensure the provision of accommodation for disabled people. However, it argued that to place the cost of accommodation on individual employers was not appropriate, in that the cost of the social obligation to accommodate should be distributed across society. The Court drew attention to the vagueness and uncertainty of the obligations on employers: 'the financial circumstances of the employer' could be taken into account in determining the duty to accommodate, but this was not within the framework of a proper system for the disclosure of financial circumstances. The Court also noted the wide definition of disability in the Irish Act, which covers even minor impairments and future disabilities, which, it argued, introduced an unacceptable level of uncertainty into the costs which might be faced by an employer.

The new Act as passed in 1998 incorporated amendments reflecting the Supreme Court's decision, and requires employers to accommodate only if the cost is 'nominal'. This suggests that the conception of equality in the EEA is based on individual merit, and moves towards the 'equality as rationality' end of the spectrum, addressing discrimination based on prejudice or stereotypes but not requiring an employer to take significant steps to accommodate a disabled person. However, it is possible that the authorities will implement an 'equality as fairness' conception despite the constraints of the nominal cost restriction.

Furthermore, the Act creates some positive duties to promote equality, despite the limits to positive action in favour of individuals. The Act established an Equality Authority with powers to develop codes of practice that have enhanced legal standing. The Equality Authority has powers to promote equality through Equality Reviews and Action Plans. However, these powers do not create individual rights of litigation for disabled people. Positive measures in favour of disabled people are permitted under the Employment Equality Act, where the measures are 'intended to reduce or eliminate the effects of discrimination'. Various provisions prevent challenges to measures targeted to disadvantaged groups; for example, the provision of special treatment or facilities for a disabled person does not create a right to the same facilities for a person without a disability, or a person with a different disability.

Important for disability rights, the Employment Equality Act 1998 outlines the concept of discrimination in Section 6:

> 6.(1) For the purposes of this Act, discrimination shall be taken to occur where, on any of the grounds in *subsection (2)* (in this Act referred to as 'the discriminatory grounds'), one person is treated less favorably than another is, has been or would be treated.

(2) As between any 2 persons, the discriminatory grounds (and the descriptions of those grounds for the purposes of this Act) are:

(*a*) that one is a woman and the other is a man (in this Act referred to as 'the gender ground'),

(*b*) that they are of different marital status (in this Act referred to as 'the marital status ground'),

(*c*) that one has family status and the other does not (in this Act referred to as 'the family status ground'),

(*d*) that they are of different sexual orientation (in this Act referred to as 'the sexual orientation ground'),

(*e*) that one has a different religious belief from the other, or that one has a religious belief and the other has not (in this Act referred to as 'the religion ground'),

(*f*) that they are of different ages, but subject to *subsection (3)* (in this Act referred to as 'the age ground'),

(*g*) that one is a person with a disability and the other either is not or is a person with a different disability (in this Act referred to as 'the disability ground'),

(*h*) that they are of different race, color, nationality or ethnic or national origins (in this Act referred to as 'the ground of race'),

(*i*) that one is a member of the traveller community and the other is not (in this Act referred to as 'the traveller community ground').

(3) Where:

(*a*) a person has attained the age of 65 years, or

(*b*) a person has not attained the age of 18 years,

then … treating that person more favorably or less favorably than another (whatever that other person's age) shall not be regarded as discrimination on the age ground.

(4) The Minister shall review the operation of this Act, within 2 years of the date of the coming into operation of this section, with a view to assessing whether there is a need to add to the discriminatory grounds set out in this section.[36]

Section 7(1) establishes like work:

7.(1) Subject to *subsection (2)*, for the purposes of this Act, in relation to the work which one person is employed to do, another person shall be regarded as employed to do like work if:

(*a*) both perform the same work under the same or similar conditions, or each is interchangeable with the other in relation to the work,

(*b*) the work performed by one is of a similar nature to that performed by the other and any differences between the work performed or the conditions under which it is performed by each either are of small importance in relation to the work as a whole or occur with such irregularity as not to be significant to the work as a whole, or

(*c*) the work performed by one is equal in value to the work performed by the other, having regard to such matters as skill, physical or mental requirements, responsibility and working conditions.

(3) In any case where:

> (*a*) the remuneration received by one person ('the primary worker') is less than the remuneration received by another ('the comparator'), and
>
> (*b*) the work performed by the primary worker is greater in value than the work performed by the comparator, having regard to the matters mentioned in *subsection (1)(c)*,

then, for the purposes of *subsection (1)(c)*, the work performed by the primary worker shall be regarded as equal in value to the work performed by the comparator.[37]

Discrimination by employers is covered under Section 8:

8.(1) In relation to:

> (*a*) access to employment,
>
> (*b*) conditions of employment,
>
> (*c*) training or experience for or in relation to employment,
>
> (*d*) promotion or re-grading, or
>
> (*e*) classification of posts,

an employer shall not discriminate against an employee or prospective employee and a provider of agency work shall not discriminate against an agency worker.

(5) Without prejudice to the generality of *subsection (1)*, an employer shall be taken to discriminate against an employee or prospective employee in relation to access to employment if the employer discriminates against the employee or prospective employee:

> (*a*) in any arrangements the employer makes for the purpose of deciding to whom employment should be offered, or
>
> (*b*) by specifying, in respect of one person or class of persons, entry requirements for employment which are not specified in respect of other persons or classes of persons, where the circumstances in which both such persons or classes would be employed are not materially different.

(6) Without prejudice to the generality of *subsection (1)*, an employer shall be taken to discriminate against an employee or prospective employee in relation to conditions of employment if, on any of the discriminatory grounds, the employer does not offer or afford to that employee or prospective employee or to a class of persons of whom he or she is one:

> (*a*) the same terms of employment (other than remuneration and pension rights),
>
> (*b*) the same working conditions, and
>
> (*c*) the same treatment in relation to overtime, shift work, short time, transfers, lay-offs, redundancies, dismissals and disciplinary measures,

as the employer offers or affords to another person or class of persons, where the circumstances in which both such persons or classes are or would be employed are not materially different.

(7) Without prejudice to the generality of *subsection (1)*, an employer shall be taken to discriminate against an employee in relation to training or experience for, or in relation to, employment if, on any of the discriminatory grounds, the employer refuses to offer or afford to that employee the same opportunities or

facilities for employment counseling, training (whether on or off the job) and work experience as the employer offers or affords to other employees, where the circumstances in which that employee and those other employees are employed are not materially different.

(8) Without prejudice to the generality of *subsection (1)*, an employer shall be taken to discriminate against an employee in relation to promotion if, on any of the discriminatory grounds:

> (*a*) the employer refuses or deliberately omits to offer or afford the employee access to opportunities for promotion in circumstances in which another eligible and qualified person is offered or afforded such access, or
>
> (*b*) the employer does not in those circumstances offer or afford the employee access in the same way to those opportunities.[38]

The Employment Equality Act makes the principle of 'equal pay for like work' a term of every employment contract. Proving 'like work' means showing that the work of the person claiming equal pay, the claimant, is the same, similar or equal in value to the work of the appropriate comparator, the person with whom the claimant is comparing themselves. The comparator must, among other things, be employed by the same or an associated employer, at the same time or during the previous or following three years. In guarding against discrimination, comparators in general are necessary as outlined under Section 28:

> 28.(1) For the purpose of this Part, 'C' and 'D' represent 2 persons who differ as follows:
>
> > (*g*) in relation to the ground of race, C and D differ as to race, colour, nationality or ethnic or national origins or any combination of those factors;
> >
> > (*h*) in relation to the traveller community ground, C is a member of the traveller community and D is not, or *vice versa*.
>
> (2) In the following provisions of this Part, any reference to C and D which does not apply to a specific discriminatory ground shall be treated as a reference to C and D in the context of each of the discriminatory grounds (other than the gender ground) considered separately.[39]

Entitlement to equal remuneration is covered under Section 29:

> 29.(1) It shall be a term of the contract under which C is employed that, subject to this Act, C shall at any time be entitled to the same rate of remuneration for the work which C is employed to do as D who, at that or any other relevant time, is employed to do like work by the same or an associated employer.
>
> (3) For the purposes of this Part, where D's employer is an associated employer of C's employer, C and D shall not be regarded as employed to do like work unless they both have the same or reasonably comparable terms and conditions of employment.

(4) Where a term of a contract of employment or a criterion applied to employees (including C and D):

> (*a*) applies to all employees of a particular employer or to a particular class of such employees (including C and D),
> (*b*) is such that the remuneration of those who fulfil the term or criterion is different from that of those who do not,
> (*c*) is such that the proportion of employees who can fulfil the term or criterion is substantially smaller in the case of the employees having the same relevant characteristic as C when compared with the employees having the same relevant characteristic as D, and
> (*d*) cannot be justified as being reasonable in all the circumstances of the case,

then, for the purposes of *subsection (1)*, C and D shall each be treated as fulfilling or, as the case may be, as not fulfilling the term or criterion, whichever results in the higher remuneration.

(5) Subject to *subsection (4)*, nothing in this Part shall prevent an employer from paying, on grounds other than the discriminatory grounds, different rates of remuneration to different employees.[40]

Important for disability rights, an equality clause is outlined under Section 30:

30.(1) If and so far as the terms of a contract of employment do not include (expressly or by reference to a collective agreement or otherwise) a non-discriminatory equality clause, they shall be taken to include one.

(2) A non-discriminatory equality clause is a provision relating to the terms of a contract of employment, other than a term relating to remuneration or pension rights, which has the effect that if:

(*a*) C is employed in circumstances where the work done by C is not materially different from that done by D in the same employment, and

(*b*) at any time C's contract of employment would (but for the non-discriminatory equality clause):

> (i) contain a term which is or becomes less favorable to C than a term of a similar kind in D's contract of employment, or
> (ii) not include a term corresponding to a term in D's contract of employment which benefits D,
> then the terms of C's contract of employment shall be treated as modified so that the term in question is not less favorable to C or, as the case may be, so that they include a similar term benefiting C.

(3) A non-discriminatory equality clause shall not operate in relation to a difference between C's contract of employment and D's contract of employment if the employer proves that the difference is genuinely based on grounds which are not among those specified in *paragraphs (a) to (h) of section 28(1)*.[41]

Indirect discrimination is covered in Section 31:

31.(1) Where a provision (whether in the nature of a requirement, practice or otherwise) relating to employment:

(*a*) applies to all the employees or prospective employees of a particular employer who include C and D or, as the case may be, to a particular class of those employees or prospective employees which includes C and D,

(*b*) operates to the disadvantage of C, as compared with D, in relation to any of the matters specified in *paragraphs (a)* to *(e)* of *section 8(1)*,

(*c*) in practice can be complied with by a substantially smaller proportion of the employees or prospective employees having the same relevant characteristic as C when compared with the employees or prospective employees having the same relevant characteristic as D, and

(*d*) cannot be justified as being reasonable in all the circumstances of the case,

then ... for the purposes of this Act the employer shall be regarded as discriminating against C, contrary to *section 8,* on whichever of the discriminatory grounds gives rise to the relevant characteristics referred to in *paragraph (c).*[42]

Further, harassment in the workplace is covered under Section 32:

32.(1) If, at a place where C is employed (in this section referred to as 'the workplace'), or otherwise in the course of C's employment, another individual ('E') harasses C by reference to the relevant characteristic of C and:

(*a*) C and E are both employed at that place or by the same employer,

(*b*) E is C's employer, or

(*c*) E is a client, customer or other business contact of C's employer and the circumstances of the harassment are such that C's employer ought reasonably to have taken steps to prevent it,

then, for the purposes of this Act, the harassment constitutes discrimination by C's employer, in relation to C's conditions of employment, on whichever discriminatory ground is relevant to persons having the same relevant characteristic as C.

(6) If, as a result of any act or conduct of E another person ('F') who is C's employer would, apart from this subsection, be regarded...as discriminating against C, it shall be a defence for F to prove that F took such steps as are reasonably practicable:

(*a*) ... to prevent C being treated differently in the workplace or otherwise in the course of C's employment and, if and so far as any such treatment has occurred, to reverse the effects of it, and

(*b*) ... to prevent E from harassing C (or any class of persons of whom C is one).[43]

Positive action for those with a disability is permitted as contained in Section 33:

33.(1) Nothing in this Part or *Part II* shall prevent the taking of such measures as are specified in *subsection (2)* in order to facilitate the integration into employment, either generally or in particular areas or a particular workplace, of:

(*a*) persons who have attained the age of 50 years,

(*b*) persons with a disability or any class or description of such persons, or (*c*) members of the traveler community.

(2) The measures mentioned in *subsection (1)* are those intended to reduce or eliminate the effects of discrimination against any of the persons referred to in *paragraphs (a)* to *(c)* of that subsection.

(3) Nothing in this Part or *Part II* shall render unlawful the provision, by or on behalf of the State, of training or work experience for a disadvantaged group of persons if the Minister certifies that, in the absence of the provision in question, it is unlikely that that disadvantaged group would receive similar training or work experience.[44]

The Equality Authority has important legal powers, not to decide on disputes but to work generally for the elimination of discrimination and the promotion of equal opportunities. It can develop Codes of Practice, carry out equality reviews in particular employment, draw up Equality Action Plans, and serve Substantive Notices. The Authority has broad powers to ensure the development of a proactive, equality-conscious approach to equal opportunities in the workplace. The functions of the Equality Authority are outlined under Section 39:

> 39. The Authority shall have, in addition to the functions assigned to it by any other provision of this Act or of any other Act, the following general functions:
> > (*a*) to work towards the elimination of discrimination in relation to employment;
> > (*b*) to promote equality of opportunity in relation to the matters to which this Act applies.[45]

The forum for seeking redress is covered under Section 77:

> 77.(1) A person who claims:
> > (*a*) to have been discriminated against by another in contravention of this Act,
> > (*b*) not to be receiving remuneration in accordance with an equal remuneration term,
> > (*c*) not to be receiving a benefit under an equality clause, or
> > (*d*) to have been penalized in circumstances amounting to victimization,
> may, subject to *subsections (2)* to *(8)*, seek redress by referring the case to the Director.
>
> (2) If a person claims to have been dismissed:
> > (*a*) in circumstances amounting to discrimination by another in contravention of this Act, or
> > (*b*) in circumstances amounting to victimization,
> then, subject to *subsection (3)*, a claim for redress for the dismissal may be brought to the Labor Court and shall not be brought to the Director.
>
> (3) If the grounds for such a claim as is referred to in *subsection (1)* or *(2)* arise:
> > (*a*) under *Part III*, or

    (*b*) in any other circumstances (including circumstances amounting to victimization) to which the Equal Pay Directive or the Equal Treatment Directive is relevant,

then ... the person making the claim may seek redress by referring the case to the Circuit Court, instead of referring it to the Director under *subsection (1)* or, as the case may be, to the Labor Court under *subsection (2)*.

(4) In this Part, in relation to a case referred under any provision of this section:

(*a*) 'the complainant' means the person by whom it is referred, and

(*b*) 'the respondent' means the person who is alleged to have discriminated against the complainant or, as the case may be, who is responsible for providing the remuneration to which the equal remuneration term relates or who is responsible for providing the benefit under the equality clause or who is alleged to be responsible for the victimization.[46]

Enforcement of determinations, decisions and mediated settlements is outlined under Section 91:

91.(1) If an employer or any other person who is bound by the terms of:
    (*a*) a final determination of the Labor Court under this Part, or
    (*b*) a final decision of the Director under this Part,

fails to comply with the terms of the determination or decision then, on an application under this section, the Circuit Court shall make, subject to *section 93,* an order directing the person affected (that is to say, the employer or other person concerned) to carry out the determination or decision in accordance with its terms.

(2) If an employer or the person who is a party to a settlement ... fails to give effect, in whole or in part, to the terms of the settlement, then, on an application under this section, the Circuit Court may make an order directing the person affected (that is to say, the employer or the person who is a party to the settlement) to carry out those terms or, as the case may be, the part of those terms to which the application relates; but the Circuit Court shall not, by virtue of this subsection, direct any person to pay any sum or do any other thing which (had the matter been dealt with otherwise than by mediation) could not have been provided for by way of redress ....

(3) An application under this section may not be made before the expiry of:
    (*a*) in the case of a determination or decision, the period within which an appeal might be brought against the determination or decision, and
    (*b*) in the case of a settlement reached as a result of mediation, 42 days from the date of the written record of the settlement.

(4) An application under this section may be made:
    (*a*) by the complainant, or
    (*b*) in a case where the Authority is not the complainant, then, by the Authority with the consent of the complainant if the Authority considers that the determination, decision or settlement is unlikely to be implemented without its intervention.

(5) On an application under this section, the Circuit Court shall exercise its functions under *subsection (1)* or *(2)* on being satisfied:

(*a*) of the existence and terms of the determination, decision or settlement, and

(*b*) of the failure by the person affected to comply with those terms.

(6) For the purposes of this section, a determination or decision is final if no appeal lies from it under this Part or if the time for bringing an appeal has expired and either:

(*a*) no appeal has been brought, or

(*b*) any appeal which was brought has been abandoned.

(7) Without prejudice to the power of the Circuit Court to make an order for costs in favor of the complainant or the person affected, where an application is made by the Authority by virtue of *subsection (4)(b),* the costs of the Authority may be awarded by the Circuit Court.

(8) The jurisdiction conferred on the Circuit Court by this section shall be exercised by the judge for the time being assigned to the circuit where the respondent ordinarily resides or carries on any profession, business or occupation.[47]

Equal Status Act

Important for disability rights, under the Equal Status Act 2000, discrimination in general is outlined in Section 3:

3.(1) For the purposes of this Act, discrimination shall be taken to occur where:

(*a*) on any of the grounds specified in *subsection (2)* (in this Act referred to as 'the discriminatory grounds') which exists at present or previously existed but no longer exists or may exist in the future, or which is imputed to the person concerned, a person is treated less favorably than another person is, has been or would be treated,

(*b*) (i) a person who is associated with another person is treated, by virtue of that association, less favorably than a person who is not so associated is, has been or would be treated, and

(ii) similar treatment of that person on any of the discriminatory grounds would, by virtue of *paragraph (a),* constitute discrimination,

or

(*c*) (i) a person is in a category of persons who share a common characteristic by reason of which discrimination may, by virtue of *paragraph (a),* occur in respect of those persons,

(ii) the person is obliged by the provider of a service … to comply with a condition (whether in the nature of a requirement, practice or otherwise) but is unable to do so,

(iii) substantially more people outside the category than within it are able to comply with the condition, and

(iv) the obligation to comply with the condition cannot be justified as being reasonable in all the circumstances of the case.

(2) As between any two persons, the discriminatory grounds (and the descriptions of those grounds for the purposes of this Act) are:

(*a*) that one is male and the other is female (the 'gender ground'),

(*b*) that they are of different marital status (the 'marital status ground'),

(*c*) that one has family status and the other does not or that one has a different family status from the other (the 'family status ground'),

(*d*) that they are of different sexual orientation (the 'sexual orientation ground'),

(*e*) that one has a different religious belief from the other, or that one has a religious belief and the other has not (the 'religion ground'),

(*f*) … that they are of different ages (the 'age ground'),

(*g*) that one is a person with a disability and the other either is not or is a person with a different disability (the 'disability ground'),

(*h*) that they are of different race, color, nationality or ethnic or national origins (the 'ground of race'),

(*i*) that one is a member of the Traveller community and the other is not (the 'Traveller community ground'),

(*j*) that one:

(i) has in good faith applied for any determination or redress provided for in *Part II* or *III*,

(ii) has attended as a witness before the Authority, the Director or a court in connection with any inquiry or proceedings under this Act,

(iii) has given evidence in any criminal proceedings under this Act,

(iv) has opposed by lawful means an act which is unlawful under this Act, or

(v) has given notice of an intention to take any of the actions specified in *subparagraphs (i)* to *(iv)*,

and the other has not (the 'victimization ground').[48]

Section 5 provides for non-discrimination including for those with a disability in the disposal of goods and provision of services:

5.(1) A person shall not discriminate in disposing of goods to the public generally or a section of the public or in providing a service, whether the disposal or provision is for consideration or otherwise and whether the service provided can be availed of only by a section of the public.

(2) *Subsection (1)* does not apply in respect of:

(*c*) differences in the treatment of persons on the gender ground in relation to services of an aesthetic, cosmetic or similar nature, where the services require physical contact between the service provider and the recipient,

(*d*) differences in the treatment of persons in relation to annuities, pensions, insurance policies or any other matters related to the assessment of risk where the treatment:

(i) is effected by reference to:

(I) actuarial or statistical data obtained from a source on which it is reasonable to rely, or

(II) other relevant underwriting or commercial factors,

and

(ii) is reasonable having regard to the data or other relevant factors,

(*e*) differences in the treatment of person on the religion ground in relation to goods or services provided for a religious purpose, (*f*) differences in the treatment of persons on the gender, age or disability ground or on the basis of nationality or national origin in relation to the provision or organization of a sporting facility or sporting event to the extent that the differences are reasonably necessary having regard to the nature of the facility or event and are relevant to the purpose of the facility or event,

(*h*) differences in the treatment of persons in a category of persons in respect of services that are provided for the principal purpose of promoting, for a *bona fide* purpose and in a *bona fide* manner, the special interests of persons in that category to the extent that the differences in treatment are reasonably necessary to promote those special interests,

(*i*) differences in the treatment of persons on the gender, age or disability ground or on the ground of race, reasonably required for reasons of authenticity, aesthetics, tradition or custom in connection with a dramatic performance or other entertainment, or

(*l*) differences, not otherwise specifically provided for in this section, in the treatment of persons in respect of the disposal of goods, or the provision of a service, which can reasonably be regarded as goods or a service suitable only to the needs of certain persons.[49]

Certain measures or activities are not prohibited under Section 14:

14. Nothing in this Act shall be construed as prohibiting:
(*a*) the taking of any action that is required by or under:
(i) any enactment or order of a court,
(ii) any act done or measure adopted by the European Union, by the European Communities or institutions thereof or by bodies competent under the Treaties establishing the European Communities, or
(iii) any convention or other instrument imposing an international obligation on the State,
    or
(*b*) preferential treatment or the taking of positive measures which are *bona fide* intended to:
(i) promote equality of opportunity for persons who are, in relation to other persons, disadvantaged or who have been or are likely to be unable to avail themselves of the same opportunities as those other persons, or
(ii) cater for the special needs of persons, or a category of persons, who, because of their circumstances, may require facilities, arrangements, services or assistance not required by persons who do not have those special needs. [50]

Certain activities are not considered discrimination under Section 15:

15.(1) For greater certainty, nothing in this Act prohibiting discrimination shall be construed as requiring a person to dispose of goods or premises, or to provide services or accommodation or services and amenities related to accommodation, to another person ('the customer') in circumstances which would lead a reasonable individual having the responsibility, knowledge and experience of the person to the belief, on grounds other than discriminatory grounds, that the disposal of the goods or premises or the provision of the services or accommodation or the services and amenities related to accommodation, as the case may be, to the customer would produce a substantial risk of criminal or disorderly conduct or behavior or damage to property at or in the vicinity of the place in which the goods or services are sought or the premises or accommodation are located.[51]

Redress in respect of prohibited grounds is covered under Section 21:

21.(1) A person who claims that prohibited conduct has been directed against him or her may, subject to this section, seek redress by referring the case to the Director.

(2) Before seeking redress under this section the complainant:
    (*a*) shall, within 2 months after the prohibited conducted is alleged to have occurred, or, where more than one incident of prohibited conduct is alleged to have occurred, within 2 months after the last such occurrence, notify the respondent in writing of:
(i) the nature of the allegation,
(ii) the complainant's intention, if not satisfied with the respondent's response to the allegation, to seek redress by referring the case to the Director,
    and
    (*b*) may in that notification, with a view to assisting the complainant in deciding whether to refer the case to the Director, question the respondent in writing so as to obtain material information and the respondent may, if the respondent so wishes, reply to any such questions.

(3) If, on application by the complainant, the Director is satisfied:
    (*a*) that exceptional circumstances prevented the complainant from notifying the respondent in accordance with *subsection (2)*, and
    (*b*) that it is just and equitable, having regard to the nature of the alleged conduct and to any other relevant circumstances, that the period for doing so should be extended beyond the period of 2 months provided for in that subsection,
the Director may direct that, in relation to that case, *subsection (2)* shall have effect as if for the reference to 2 months there were substituted a reference to such period not exceeding 4 months as is specified in the direction; and where such a direction is given, this Part shall have effect accordingly.

(4) The Director shall not investigate a case unless he or she is satisfied either that the respondent has replied to the notification or that at least one month has elapsed after it was sent to the respondent.

(5) The Minister may by regulations prescribe the form to be used by a complainant and respondent for the purposes of *subsection (2)*.

(6) Subject to *subsection (7)*, a claim for redress in respect of prohibited conduct may not be referred under this section after the end of the period of 6 months from the date of the occurrence of the prohibited conduct to which the case relates or, as the case may be, the date of its most recent occurrence.

(7) If, on application by the complainant, the Director is satisfied that exceptional circumstances prevented the complainant's case from being referred within the time limit specified in *subsection (6)*:
    (*a*) the Director may direct that, in relation to that case, *subsection (6)* shall have effect as if for the reference to a period of 6 months there were substituted a

reference to such period not exceeding 12 months as is specified in the direction, and

(*b*) where such a direction is given, this Part shall have effect accordingly.[52]

Disability Bill 2004

The National Disability Strategy was launched by the Government on 21 September 2004 and comprises four elements.

1. The Disability Bill 2004 is a positive action measure designed to support the provision of disability-specific services to people with disabilities and to improve access to mainstream public services for people with disabilities. The Bill provides an individual right to an independent assessment of need, to a related Service Statement and to independent redress and enforcement. It provides a statutory basis for accessible public buildings and services, six Sectoral Plans, positive action for employment in the public service, restrictions on the use of genetic information and the establishment of a Centre for Excellence in Universal Design to support the design of buildings, products and systems which are usable by all;
2. The Comhairle (Amendment) Bill 2004, published by the Department of Social and Family Affairs, provides for the establishment of a Personal Advocacy Service. The Comhairle (Amendment) Bill 2004 introduces personal advocacy services specifically for people with disabilities. The new service will be administered by Comhairle and envisages the provision of a personal advocate to persons with a disability who have difficulty in obtaining, without assistance or support, a social service;
3. Six Outline Sectoral Plans published by six Government Departments as provided in the Disability Bill 2004 set out programs for action to improve service provision and access to infrastructure by people with disabilities. Under the legislation six Ministers (Minister for Health and Children, Minister for Social and Family Affairs, Minister for Transport, Minister for Environment, Heritage and Local Government, Minister for Communications, Marine and Natural Resources and the Minister for Enterprise, Trade and Employment) are required to draw up Sectoral Plans. The six plans were published in outline form on 21 September 2004;
4. A multi-annual Investment Program for high priority disability support services, the details of which were announced in Budget 2005. A Multi-annual Investment Program will apply to a number of priority disability specific services. Details were announced in the 2005 Estimates and Budget 2005 of the multi-annual Programme, which will have both a Capital and revenue element starting in 2005.

Importantly, the Disability Bill is mainly concerned with placing duties on public bodies in relation to services for people with disabilities. It would 'oblige public bodies to provide services' not currently available such as health needs assessments and advocacy services. It would also require that public bodies make their services and buildings accessible so far as is possible. A major criticism is that the bill adopts a 'duties of public bodies' approach rather than a 'rights of individuals approach'. An individual with a disability would have no right to take legal action against a public body for failure to comply with the act. Another serious objection concerned the implementation dates for the bill, since trains would not have to be accessible until 2015, and the railway platforms would not have to be made accessible until 2020. The bill's health care provisions have also been widely criticized. While the bill would require a health care assessment for individuals with disabilities, it also indicates that a 'health board may dispense with an assessment of need if, in its opinion ... such an assessment is otherwise inappropriate in the circumstances of the particular case'. Even when a person with disability got a health needs assessment, the health board need only 'take such steps as are reasonable to provide the service as soon as practicable and to the greatest practicable extent'.

The Disability Bill 2004, dated 21 September 2004, is known as the Disability Act 2004, and is entitled 'An Act to enable provision to be made for the assessment of health and education needs occasioned to persons with disabilities, to enable ministers of the government to make provision, consistent with the resources available to them and their obligations in relation to their allocation, for services to meet those needs, to provide for the preparation of plans by the appropriate ministers of government in relation to the provision of certain of those, and certain other services, to provide for appeals by those persons in relation to the non-provision of those services, to make further and better provision in respect of the use by those persons of public buildings and their employment in the public service and thereby to facilitate generally access by such persons to certain such services and employment and to promote equality and social inclusion and to provide for related matters'.

Definitions are included in Section 2 including:

> 2. 'disability', in relation to a person, means a substantial restriction in the capacity of the person to carry on a profession, business or occupation in the State or to participate in social or cultural life in the State by reason of an enduring physical, sensory, mental health or intellectual impairment;
>
> 'service' means a service or facility of any kind provided by a public body which is available to or accessible by the public generally or a section of the public and, without prejudice to the generality of the foregoing, includes
>
> (*a*) the use of any place or amenity owned, managed or controlled by a public body,
>
> (*b*) the provision of information or an information resource or a scheme or an allowance or other benefit administered by a public body,
>
> (*c*) any cultural or heritage services provided by such a body, and
>
> (*d*) any service provided by a court or other tribunal.[53]

In terms of assessment of needs, service statements and redress, Section 6 defines assessment:

> 6. 'assessment' means an assessment undertaken or arranged by a health board to determine, in respect of a person with a disability, the health and education needs (if any) occasioned by the disability and the health services or education services (if any) required to meet those needs.[54]

Complaints in relation to assessments or service statements are provided for under Section 13:

> 13.(1) An applicant may, either by himself or herself or through a person referred to in *section 8(2)*, make a complaint to the chief executive officer of the health board concerned in relation to one or more of the following:
>
> (*a*) a determination by the assessment officer concerned that he or she does not have a disability;
>
> (*b*) the fact, if it be the case, that the assessment … was not conducted in a manner that conforms to the standards determined … ;
>
> (*c*) the contents of the service statement provided to the applicant;
>
> (*d*) the fact, if it be the case, that the board or the education service provider, as the case may be, failed to provide or to fully provide a service specified in the service statement.[55]

Appeals officer are provided for under Section 15:

> 15.(1) (*a*) There shall be a person, who shall be appointed by the Minister, and who shall be known, and is referred to in this Act, as 'the appeals officer', to consider and determine appeals under this Part.
>
> (*b*) The appeals officer shall perform the functions conferred on him or her by this Act.
>
> (2) The appeals officer shall be independent in the performance of his or her functions under this Act.
>
> (3) The provisions of the Schedule shall have effect in relation to the appeals officer.[56]

Important for disability rights, mediation is contained in Section 18:

> 18.(1) The appeals officer may authorise such and so many members of his or her staff as he or she may determine (referred to in this Act as 'mediation officers') to perform the functions conferred on mediation officers by this section.

(2) If at any time after an appeal has been initiated under *section 17*, the appeals officer is of opinion that the appeal could be resolved by mediation, he or she shall inform the applicant concerned of that opinion and, subject to *subsection (3)*, refer the matter for mediation to a mediation officer.

(3) If an applicant objects to his or her appeal being dealt with by mediation, the appeals officer shall deal with the matter under *section 17*.

(4) Mediation shall be conducted otherwise than in public.

(5) Where an appeal is resolved by mediation

(*a*) the mediation officer concerned shall prepare a written record of the resolution arrived at, and

(*b*) the record aforesaid shall be signed by the applicant and the chief executive officer of the health board concerned and, if appropriate, the head of the education service provider concerned, or both of them, and a copy thereof shall be retained by the appeals officer and shall be sent to the applicant concerned and the chief executive officer of the health board concerned and, if appropriate, the assessment officer concerned, the liaison officer concerned and the head of the education service provider concerned.

Further, appeal to the High Court is contained in Section 19:

19.An appeal to a court shall not lie against a determination of the appeals officer other than an appeal on a point of law to the High Court.

In addition, enforcement of determinations is provided for under Section 21:

21.(1) (*a*) If the chief executive officer of the health board concerned or the head of the education service provider concerned fails

(i)   to implement in accordance with its terms a determination of the appeals officer in relation to an appeal under *section 17*, or
(ii) to give effect to a resolution arrived at under *section 18*, or
(iii) to implement in full a recommendation of a complaints officer,

within 3 months from the date on which the determination, resolution or recommendation is communicated to him or her or, where the determination, resolution or recommendation specifies a date for the provision of a service, within 3 months from the date specified in the determination, resolution or recommendation for such provision, then, the applicant concerned ... may apply to the Circuit Court on notice to the chief executive officer concerned or the head of the education service provider concerned for an order directing him or her to implement the determination or recommendation in accordance with its terms or to give effect to the resolution, as the case may be.[57]

Important for disability rights, Section 23 provides for access to public buildings:

23.(1) Subject to *subsection (4)* and *section 27*, a public body shall ensure that its public buildings are, as far as practicable, accessible to persons with disabilities.

(2) (*a*) The Minister may request the National Disability Authority ('the Authority') to prepare and submit to him or her a draft code of practice ('a draft code of practice') relating to the accessibility of public buildings to persons with disabilities for the purpose of giving guidance to public bodies.[58]

Importantly, access to services is provided under Section 24:

24.(1) Where a service is provided by a public body, the head of the body shall

(*a*) where practicable and appropriate, ensure that the provision of access to the service by persons with and persons without disabilities is integrated,

(*b*) where practicable and appropriate, provide for assistance, if requested, to persons with disabilities in accessing the service if the head is satisfied that such provision is necessary in order to ensure compliance with *paragraph (a)*, and

(*c*) where appropriate, ensure the availability of persons with appropriate expertise and skills to give advice to the body about the means of ensuring that the service provided by the body is accessible to persons with disabilities.

(2) Each head of a public body referred to in *subsection (1)* shall authorise at least one of his or her officers (referred to in this Act as 'access officers') to provide or arrange for and co-ordinate the provision of assistance and guidance to persons with disabilities in accessing its services.[59]

Further, Section 29 provides for sectoral plans:

29.(1) Each of the following Ministers of the Government

(*a*) the Minister for Health and Children,

(*b*) the Minister for Social and Family Affairs,

(*c*) the Minister for Transport,

(*d*) the Minister for Communications, Marine and Natural Resources,

(*e*) the Minister for the Environment, Heritage and Local Government, and

(*f*) the Minister for Enterprise, Trade and Employment,

shall prepare and publish a plan (referred to in this Act as a 'sectoral plan') … outlining the program of the measures proposed to be taken by or on behalf of the Minister of the Government concerned for and in relation to those matters as they relate to the provision of services to persons with specified disabilities by him or her or by public bodies or other persons in relation to which he or she performs functions or allocates moneys....

(4) A sectoral plan shall contain

(*a*) appropriate information concerning codes of practice (if any) and regulations (if any) relating to the subject matter of the plan,

(*b*) the complaints procedure to be provided by a public body or by other persons in relation to any matters which are the subject of the plan,

(*c*) monitoring and review procedures in relation to the subject matter of the plan,

(*d*) if appropriate, the level of access relating to the services specified in the plan, and

(*e*) such other matters (if any) as the Minister of the Government concerned considers appropriate.[60]

In particular, employment in the public service is covered under Section 45:

45.(1) A public body shall

(*a*) in so far as practicable take all reasonable measures to promote and support the employment by it of persons with disabilities,

(*b*) have regard to any relevant codes of practice approved under *section 48* and section 10A of the 1999 Act by the relevant Minister.

(2) A public body shall ensure, unless there is good reason to the contrary for not doing so, that it reaches any compliance targets prescribed....[61]

Further, monitoring of compliance is covered under Section 46:

46.(1) A Minister of the Government shall establish a committee (which shall be known as 'a monitoring committee') in respect of the public bodies in relation to which he or she is the relevant Minister.

(2) ... a public body shall, not later than 31 March in each year, draw up a report in writing in relation to its compliance, with this Part during the preceding year and submit it to the relevant monitoring committee.[62]

In addition, action to achieve compliance is included in Section 47:

47.(1) A public body, shall, at the request of the relevant Minister or of the Authority, following consultation with that Minister, furnish not more than 3 months after the making of the request, that Minister or the Authority, as the case may be, with any information that that Minister or the Authority requires in order to determine whether the body is complying with this Part.

(2) Where, either

    (*a*) at the end of any 2 successive years a public body is, in the opinion of the Authority, not complying with this Part, or

    (*b*) (i) a public body has not complied with *subsection (1)*, and

        (ii) the relevant Minister or the Authority is of opinion that the body may not be complying with another provision of this Part,

the Authority may, with the consent of the relevant Minister, request the body to take such measures as it may specify to ensure such compliance and the public body shall comply with such request.

(3) The measures referred to in *subsection (2)* may include

    (*a*) the provision by or on behalf of the body concerned of the training or education of persons with disabilities who are employed by the body, either in or outside it for the purpose of qualifying them for specific posts or employments in the body,

    (*b*) the amendment of the requirements for particular posts or employments in the body to enable persons with disabilities to compete for posts or employments in the body in relation to which the work is similar or of equal value,

    (*c*) measures for the filling, by suitably qualified such persons, of employment vacancies or specified such vacancies or of categories of such vacancies in the body, either for a specified period or until the provisions of this Part have been complied with,

    (*d*) the holding of competitions for recruitment to specific posts or employments which are confined to such persons,

    (*e*) the making of reasonable alterations to the work premises or environment of the body concerned and the provision of suitable technical or organisational supports so as to reasonably facilitate the employment by the body of persons with disabilities and to support existing employees of the body who are persons with disabilities in the performance of their duties,

    (*f*) the provision of information to employees of the body to increase their awareness and understanding of the contribution that persons with disabilities may make to the work of the body.

Finally, positive action measures are provided for under Section 49:

49.Nothing in this Part precludes the taking of measures referred to in section 33 of the Employment Equality Act 1998 that are intended to reduce or eliminate the effects of discrimination (within the meaning of that Act) against persons with a disability or the provision, by or on behalf of the State, of training or work experience for groups of such persons in accordance with that section.[63]

Conclusion

Overall, more emphasis needs to be given to encouraging career development and to 'disability proofing' systems of promotion and higher-level recruitment in the United Kingdom and Ireland. As disability monitoring of posts, recruitment and promotion would be useful, action is needed both to encourage all humans, including those with a disability to develop their careers and to remove obstacles in their paths. The principle is that redressing this inequality is a shared responsibility by all aspects of government stakeholders in disability analysis, planning and training. The State's accountability for violations committed by private actors has long been an important debate. This will be of critical relevance to Commonwealth governments and the Secretariat as part of their continuing priority work in the area of democracy, rule of law, and human rights. The increased participation of all humans, especially those with a disability at decision-making levels in conflict prevention, mediation and resolution is vital to achieving this ability.

Notes

[1]   Disability Discrimination Act, UK.
[2]   *Ibid.*
[3]   *Ibid.*, at Section 4.
[4]   *Ibid.*, at Section 5.
[5]   *Ibid.*, at Section 6.
[6]   *Ibid.*, at Section 9.
[7]   *Ibid.*, at Section 9.
[8]   *Ibid.*, at Section 10.
[9]   *Ibid.*, at Section 11.
[10] *Ibid.*, at Section 12.
[11] *Ibid.*, at Section 19.
[12] *Ibid.*, at Section 20.
[13] *Ibid.*, at Section 21.
[14] *Ibid.*, at Section 32.
[15] *Ibid.*, at Section 34.
[16] *Ibid.*, at Section 36.
[17] Disability Rights Commission Act, UK, at Section 1.
[18] *Ibid.*, at Section 2.
[19] *Ibid.*, at Section 3.
[20] *Ibid.*, at Section 4.
[21] *Ibid.*, at Section 6.
[22] *Ibid.*, at Section 9.

23 *Ibid.*, at Section 10.
24 Human Rights Act, UK, at Section 14.
25 *Ibid.*, at Section 17.
26 *Ibid.*, at Section 1(3).
27 *Ibid.*, at Section 2(1).
28 Equal Opportunities Commission, *Code of Practice on Equal Pay*, UK.
29 Commission for Racial Equality, *Code of Practice on the Duty to Promote Race Equality*, UK, 2002.
30 Race Relations Act, UK, at Section 71(1).
31 Race Relations Act (Statutory Duties) Order 2001, UK, at Section 5; Race Relations Act (Statutory Duties) Order 2003, UK, at Section 4.
32 Sex Discrimination Act, UK, at Section 1.
33 *Ibid.*, at Section 6(2).
34 *Ibid.*, at Section 7.
35 European Union Commission, Directorate-General for Employment and Social Affairs, *Definition of Disability in Europe, A Comparative Analysis, Social Security and Social Integration*, 2002.
36 Employment Equality Act, Ireland, at Section 6.
37 *Ibid.*, at Section 7.
38 *Ibid.*, at Section 8.
39 *Ibid.*, at Section 28.
40 *Ibid.*, at Section 29.
41 *Ibid.*, at Section 30.
42 *Ibid.*, at Section 31.
43 *Ibid.*, at Section 32.
44 *Ibid.*, at Section 33.
45 *Ibid.*, at Section 39.
46 *Ibid.*, at Section 77.
47 *Ibid.*, at Section 91.
48 Equal Status Act, Ireland, at Section 3.
49 *Ibid.*, at Section 5.
50 *Ibid.*, at Section 14.
51 *Ibid.*, at Section 15.
52 *Ibid.*, at Section 21.
53 Disability Bill, Ireland, at Section 2.
54 *Ibid.*, at Section 6.
55 *Ibid.*, at Section 13.
56 *Ibid.*, at Section 15.
57 *Ibid.*, at Section 21.
58 *Ibid.*, at Section 23.
59 *Ibid.*, at Section 24.
60 *Ibid.*, at Section 29.
61 *Ibid.*, at Section 45.
62 *Ibid.*, at Section 46.
63 *Ibid.*, at Section 49.

References

Commission for Racial Equality (2002), *Code of Practice on the Duty to Promote Race Equality*, UK.

Disability Bill, Ireland.

Disability Discrimination Act, UK.

Disability Rights Commission Act, UK.

Employment Equality Act, Ireland.

Employment Rights Act, UK.

Equal Opportunities Commission, *Code of Practice on Equal Pay*, UK.

Equal Status Act, Ireland.

European Union Commission, Directorate-General for Employment and Social Affairs (2002), *Definition of Disability in Europe, A Comparative Analysis, Social Security and Social Integration.*

Human Rights Act, UK.

Race Relations Act, UK.

Race Relations Act (Statutory Duties) Orders, UK.

Sex Discrimination Act, UK.

Chapter 9

This Ability in the European Union

Introduction

This chapter will examine this ability in the European Union (EU). It will examine the European Union treaties from their inception, and will then look at the European Court of Justice (ECJ), the European Convention for the Protection of Human Rights and Fundamental Freedoms (ECHR) and the European Social Charter and their impact on equality. Finally, important European legislation affecting disability will be analyzed, namely Council Resolution 1999/C 186/02 on equal employment opportunities for people with disabilities, Council Directive 2000/78/EC Establishing a General Framework for Equal Treatment in Employment and Occupation, Council Decision 2000/750/EC establishing a Community Action Program to Combat Discrimination (2001 to 2006), and Council Resolution 2003/C 175/01 on promoting the employment and social integration of people with disabilities. The European Union has provided important contributions to the ending of disability discrimination in the coming together of people of different nations, and equal pay and equal treatment are real commitments for the Member States.

Toward the European Union

The European Union's share of the world population is falling, and as such, the EU ranks third in the world population behind China and India. If current trends for fertility, mortality and migration continue, the European Union population will peak in the year 2025 and revert to its current level in the year 2050. Education is proven to help overcome some discrimination. Further, Europe has experienced an increased divorce rate, a falling birth rate, a longer life expectancy and a positive net balance of migration.

There have been several important legislative instruments in Europe. The Treaty of Paris (1951) created the European Steel and Coal Community (ESCC). The Treaties of Rome (1957) established the European Economic Community (EEC) and the European Atomic Energy Community (EAEC). The Single European Act (1986) introduced measures aimed at achieving an internal market and greater political cooperation. The Maastricht Treaty (1992) established EU citizenship and the European Monetary Union (EMU). The Treaty of Amsterdam (1997) introduced measures to reinforce political union and prepare for enlargement towards the East. The Nice Treaty (2001) defined the institutional changes necessary for enlargement. And finally, the Treaty Establishing a Constitution for Europe seeks to simplify and synthesize previous treaties within a single, clear, foundational document for the European Union.

Initially, many centuries ago, Europe was united within the Roman Empire. Throughout its history, the European continent has naturally been restless, fragile, contradictory, competitive and pluralistic, divided by language and religion. National ambitions and self-interest have been the predominant political forces throughout the twentieth century. However, with the two World Wars and the threat of the Cold War, European integration by peaceful methods was seriously reconsidered as an alternative to the independent and aggressive nation state. With democratic governments reinstated in liberated Europe in the post-war era, the restructuring of the region was begun. A Congress of Europe was held in the Hague in May 1948, bringing together leading figures from France, Britain, the Netherlands, Belgium, Germany, Italy and elsewhere. Britain's Prime Minister Churchill referred to the idea of a setting up of 'a kind of United States of Europe', which made a powerful impact.[1] Political integration is the peaceful creation of a larger political unit out of several separate ones, which voluntarily give up some powers to a central authority and renounce the use of force toward the other units.[2] In Europe, a political structure at a supranational level exists. Only continental-wide superpowers can think of solving their major problems at the national level, but for smaller powers like Western Europe, it requires wider alliance decisions. It is a multitiered approach to government and decision-making.

Treaty of Paris

The advocates of integration sought to escape from national rivalries. Thus came the flagship of European integration, the European Communities. The first of these was the Coal and Steel Community, also known as the Treaty of Paris signed on 18 April 1951, which entered into force on 23 July 1952, and expired on 23 July 2002. It removed the coal and steel industries from full national control to a supranational stewardship. The High Authority, which it created, was presided over by Jean Monnet and comprised delegates from the Member States, making decisions in consultation with the Assembly. The Treaty of Paris was regarded only as a starting point, with the success foreseen in this sector expected to spread to others. The preamble of the Treaty wrote of safeguarding world peace, establishing an economic community, and substituting essential interests for age-old rivalries and conflicts.[3] Monnet, the most influential of the founding fathers of the European Economic Community, insisted on cooperation across national frontiers in a sector by sector approach. He persuaded the foreign ministers of the six countries involved to meet at Messina on 1 June 1955. They resolved that the moment had come to go a step further towards the construction of Europe. The Messina Conference set up a committee of government representatives, who wanted to proceed to a customs union with no internal tariff barriers, but only a common external tariff.

Treaty of Rome

The Treaty of Rome was signed by France, Italy, West Germany, Luxembourg, the Netherlands and Belgium on 25 March 1957, and entered into force on 1 January 1958, creating the European Economic Community (EEC). The European Community was set up by the Treaty of Rome to maintain peace in Europe and to foster prosperity through cooperation. With the Treaty of Rome, the European Economic Community States transferred to the Community the power to conclude treaties with international organizations and with non-member countries.[4] Lord Denning, a leading constitutional expert, stated 'the Treaty of Rome is like an incoming tide. It flows into the estuaries and up the rivers. It cannot be held back'.[5] The Member States agreed to work together for an integrated multinational economy for the free movement of labor and capital in the Community, while having joint institutions and common policies toward underdeveloped regions of the Community and toward those outside the Community. The Treaty gave the community institutions power to take the necessary steps to adjust national legal rules through harmonization procedures. This was required in order to remove national, technical or legal arrangements inhibiting the free movement of products, people and resources. The larger market allowed for a more rational use of resources and provided for higher productivity. By 1 July 1968, all internal tariffs had been abolished among the Member States for a community-wide production and distribution of products and services.[6] The abolition of tariffs encouraged mutual trade so that by 1969, intraCommunity trade in manufactured products was about 50 per cent higher than previously. The long-term implications of the Treaty of Rome were a system of majority voting among the representatives of the national governments in the Council, a supranational bureaucracy over which national governments would have little control, a directly elected European Parliament, and a commitment by the Member States to work for a closer union.

In accordance with Article 3, the activities of the Community include:

> 3(a) the elimination as between Member States, of customs duties and quantitative restrictions on the import and export of goods, and of all other measures having equivalent effect;
> (b) a common commercial policy;
> (c) an internal market characterized by the abolition, as between Member States, of obstacles to the free movement of goods, persons, services and capital;
> (d) measures concerning the entry and movement of persons in the internal market ...;
> (e) a common policy in the sphere of agriculture and fisheries;
> (f) a common policy in the sphere of transport;
> (g) a system ensuring that competition in the common market is not distorted;
> (h) the approximation of the laws of the Member States to the extent required for the functioning of the common market;
> (i) a policy in the social sphere comprising a European Social Fund;
> (j) the strengthening of economic and social cohesion;
> (k) a policy in the sphere of the environment;
> (l) the strengthening of the competitiveness of Community industry;

(m) the promotion of research and technological development;

(n) encouragement for the establishment and development of trans-European networks;

(o) a contribution to the attainment of a high level of health protection;

(p) a contribution to education and training of quality and to the flowering of the cultures of the Member States;

(q) a policy in the sphere of development cooperation;

(r) the association of the overseas countries and territories in order to increase trade and promote jointly economic and social development;

(s) a contribution to the strengthening of consumer protection;

(t) measures in the spheres of energy, civil protection and tourism.[7]

Important for disability rights, Article 6(a) prohibits discrimination:

6(a) Within the scope of application of this Treaty, and without prejudice to any special provisions contained therein, any discrimination on grounds of nationality shall be prohibited.[8]

Further, in terms of the free movement of persons, services and capital, in particular workers, Article 48 provides:

48. 1. Freedom of movement for workers shall be secured within the Community by the end of the transitional period at the latest.

2. Such freedom of movement shall entail the abolition of any discrimination based on nationality between workers of the Member States as regards employment, remuneration and other conditions of work and employment.

3. It shall entail the right, subject to limitations justified on grounds of public policy, public security or public health:

   a.   to accept offers of employment actually made;

   b.   to move freely within the territory of Member States for this purpose;

   c.   to stay in a Member State for the purpose of employment in accordance with the provisions governing the employment of nationals of that State laid down by law, regulation or administrative action;

   d.   to remain in the territory of a Member State after having been employed in that State, subject to conditions which shall be embodied in implementing regulations to be drawn up by the Commission.

4. The provisions of this Article shall not apply to employment in the public service.[9]

Important for women with a disability, in terms of equal pay, Article 119 states:

119. Each Member State shall during the first stage ensure and subsequently maintain the application of the principle that men and women should receive equal pay for equal work.

For the purpose of this Article, 'pay' means the ordinary basic or minimum wage or salary and any other consideration, whether in cash or in kind, which the worker receives, directly or indirectly, in respect of his employment from his employer.

Equal pay without discrimination based on sex means:

(a) that pay for the same work at piece rates shall be calculated on the basis of the same unit of measurement;

(b) that pay for work at time rates shall be the same for the same job.[10]

Maastricht Treaty

The Maastricht Treaty was signed on 7 February 1992 and entered into force on 1 November 1993, creating the European Union (EU). The EU became an internal market of over 340 million people providing for the free movement of goods, capital, services and citizens of Member States. The Maastricht Treaty affirms that it marks a new stage in the process of European integration undertaken with the establishment of the European Communities. The Treaty was designed to create a firm basis for the construction of the future of Europe, by deepening the solidarity between peoples while respecting the different histories, cultures and traditions. Further, the Maastricht Treaty espoused the desire to enhance the democracy and efficient functioning of the institutions so as to enable them better to carry out, within a single institutional framework, the tasks entrusted to them. The foundations for a united Europe were laid on fundamental values including peace, unity, equality, freedom, solidarity and security, through intergovernmental cooperation and the creation of the three pillars of EC society. By the Maastricht Treaty, the European Union confirms its 'attachment to the principles of liberty, democracy and respect for human rights and fundamental freedoms and of the rule of law'.

According to Article A, the Treaty 'marks a new stage in the process of creating an ever closer union among the peoples of Europe, in which decisions are taken as closely as possible to the citizen'.[11] Further, Article B states:

> B.The Union shall set itself the following objectives:
> to promote economic and social progress which is balanced and sustainable, in particular through the creation of an area without internal frontiers, through the strengthening of economic and social cohesion and through the establishment of economic and monetary union, ultimately including a single currency in accordance with the provisions of this Treaty;
> to assert its identity on the international scene, in particular through the implementation of a common foreign and security policy including the eventual framing of a common defence policy, which might in time lead to a common defence;
> to strengthen the protection of the rights and interests of the nationals of its Member States through the introduction of a citizenship of the Union;
> to develop close cooperation on justice and home affairs;

to maintain in full the 'acquis communautaire' and build on it with … the aim of ensuring the effectiveness of the mechanisms and the institutions of the Community.[12]

Treaty of Amsterdam

The Treaty of Amsterdam, amending the Treaty on European Union, the Treaties establishing the European Communities and Related Acts, amending and renumbering the EU and EC treaties, was signed on 2 October 1997 and entered into force on 1 May 1999.[13]

Important for those with a disability, in order to combat disability discrimination, Article 13, amending Article 6(a) of the Treaty of Rome for specificity, provides:

> 13. Without prejudice to the other provisions of this Treaty and within the limits of the powers conferred by it upon the Community, the Council, acting unanimously on a proposal from the Commission and after consulting the European Parliament, may take appropriate action to combat discrimination based on sex, racial or ethnic origin, religion or belief, disability, age or sexual orientation.[14]

Further, in terms of the free movement of persons, services and capital, in particular workers, Article 39, amending Article 48 of the Treaty of Rome, states:

> 39. 1. Freedom of movement for workers shall be secured within the Community.
> 2. Such freedom of movement shall entail the abolition of any discrimination based on nationality between workers of the Member States as regards employment, remuneration and other conditions of work and employment.
> 3. It shall entail the right, subject to limitations justified on grounds of public policy, public security or public health:
> (a) to accept offers of employment actually made;
> (b) to move freely within the territory of Member States for this purpose;
> (c) to stay in a Member State for the purpose of employment in accordance with the provisions governing the employment of nationals of that State laid down by law, regulation or administrative action;
> (d) to remain in the territory of a Member State after having been employed in that State, subject to conditions which shall be embodied in implementing regulations to be drawn up by the Commission.
> 4. The provisions of this Article shall not apply to employment in the public service.[15]

Important for women with a disability, in terms of equal pay, Article 141, amending Article 119 of the Treaty of Rome, states:

> 141. 1. Each Member State shall ensure that the principle of equal pay for male and female workers for equal work or work of equal value is applied.
> 2. For the purpose of this Article, 'pay' means the ordinary basic or minimum wage or salary and any other consideration, whether in cash or in kind, which the

worker receives directly or indirectly, in respect of his employment, from his employer.

Equal pay without discrimination based on sex means:

(a) that pay for the same work at piece rates shall be calculated on the basis of the same unit of measurement;

(b) that pay for work at time rates shall be the same for the same job.

3. The Council, acting in accordance with the procedure referred to in Article 251, and after consulting the Economic and Social Committee, shall adopt measures to ensure the application of the principle of equal opportunities and equal treatment of men and women in matters of employment and occupation, including the principle of equal pay for equal work or work of equal value.

4. With a view to ensuring full equality in practice between men and women in working life, the principle of equal treatment shall not prevent any Member State from maintaining or adopting measures providing for specific advantages in order to make it easier for the under-represented sex to pursue a vocational activity or to prevent or compensate for disadvantages in professional careers.[16]

The extension of civil rights is a step toward European integration. The concept of citizenship is based on the principle that nationals of Member States have certain rights to move freely across national borders in the common market. Freedom of movement, under the Treaty of Rome, applied only to certain economic categories of workers, the self-employed and service providers. This, however, was expanded by the Treaty of Amsterdam and the European Court of Justice, which had a profound impact on employment. Where European Union law has direct effect, it will take precedence over domestic law in such cases as equal pay.

Under national law, the national court of the Member State is within its limits of discretion, when interpreting domestic law. However, domestic law must be in accord with the requirements of community law, and if this is not possible, then domestic law is inapplicable. This, therefore, is a strong incentive for national courts to rule against disability discrimination. Community legislation establishes that a citizen of the European Union should not be discriminated against in the workplace on the basis of disability. In employment, discrimination can occur in two ways: direct discrimination occurs when people are treated differently, solely on the basis of their disability; and indirect discrimination occurs when people are treated differently because an apparently neutral provision, criterion or practice determining recruitment, pay, working conditions, dismissal, and social security in practice disadvantages a substantially higher proportion of the members of one group, the disabled. Such provisions, criteria or practices are prohibited under Community law, unless it is proven that they are justified by objective reasons in no way related to disability discrimination. In examining positive action, community law allows European Union countries and companies to undertake several initiatives to counter disability discrimination. While there is no official definition of positive action, it does include all measures which are designed to counter the effects of past disadvantages and existing discrimination, and to promote equality of opportunity in the field of employment. Historically, there have been discriminatory policies directly, that is on their face, or indirectly, applied to different groups. Positive action is needed not only to help guarantee equality, but also to combat the perpetuation of traditional discriminatory attitudes so as to ensure access to equal opportunities for all.

In terms of the burden of proof, in the European Court of Justice, the plaintiff has the burden of showing, in indirect cases, that a neutral policy has a disproportionate impact (*Teuling v. Bredrijfsvereniging*, [1987] ECR 2497).[17] The burden is then shifted to the defendant who must justify this by objective reasons other than discrimination. The plaintiff must then show that the explanation is not effective for the purpose, or that there is an alternative provision to accomplish it in a manner that has a less discriminatory impact. Otherwise, if there is a difference in treatment, it must be justified by objective factors other than discrimination. If a provision is neutral on its terms, but factually disadvantages a particular group, the disabled, an employer bears the burden of justification. The European Court of Justice requires a showing of objective justification as a defense to discrimination.

European Union and the European Court of Justice (ECJ)

There are five European Union (EU) institutions, each playing a specific role, namely the European Parliament, which is elected by the citizens of the Member States; the Council of the European Union, which represents the governments of the Member States; the European Commission, which is the driving force and is the executive body; the European Court of Justice, which ensures compliance with the law; and the Court of Auditors, which controls sound and lawful management of the European Union budget. There are five other important bodies, namely the European Economic and Social Committee, which expresses the opinions of organized civil society on economic and social issues; the Committee of the Regions, which expresses the opinions of regional and local authorities; the European Central Bank, which is responsible for monetary policy and managing the euro; the European Ombudsman, who deals with citizens' complaints about maladministration by any European Union institution or body; and the European Investment Bank, which helps achieve European Union objectives by financing investment projects. A number of agencies and other bodies complete the system.

The Commission is responsible for making legislative proposals, executing policies and monitoring the compliance of Member States with their obligations. It is the driving force behind European integration by its right of initiative. It is also the guardian of the treaties by its right to intervene with Member States and to demand compliance with their obligations. If Member States breach their treaty obligations, they will face Commission action, and possible legal proceedings in the European Court of Justice. As assistance to the European Court of Justice, the Commission is the Community watchdog for the observance of the treaties. It originates and administers Community law. The Council of Ministers is composed of representatives of Member State governments, and decides on Commission proposals. It is the Union's legislator, with all decisions involving new policies requiring unanimity. The Assembly is charged with proposing, to the Council, arrangements for universal direct elections. The Council, in turn, commends them to the Member States for adoption under constitutional procedures. The Assembly is consultative and can, if it has a sufficient majority, express its non-confidence in the commission by dismissing it.

The Community can legislate directly through regulations, which are binding in law and are automatically incorporated into the national legal systems of Member States, without the need for specific individual ratification. The Community can also work through the legal systems of the Member States, by the use of the Commission, which implements directives with broad objectives. Although directives require some legal action, such as legislation, by the Member States before they become national law, they are laws transposed into Member States' legislation to enforce treaty principles. Decisions by the European Court of Justice are binding as force of law, whereas recommendations and opinions by the Council of Ministers or the Commission are not.

The European Court of Justice (ECJ) is the European Union's supreme constitutional authority. It renders judgments on the obligations of the institutions, Member States and citizens. The very existence of the European Union is conditional on the recognition of the binding nature of its rules, by the Member States, by the institutions, and by individuals. Community law has successfully embedded itself thoroughly in the legal life of the Member States through the supervision of the European Court of Justice. The founding European Treaties are the primary source of Community law, and therein is found the central jurisdiction of the European Court of Justice. Community law involves primary law, namely treaties, and secondary law, namely legislative acts, both of which are binding on national governments, and take precedence over national law. The nature of the EU, its existence and its functions, demand a consistent application of Community law between Member States.

The European Court of Justice was to provide the legal sanctions for the carrying out of the Treaties. Before the European Community and the European Union, courts operating beyond national boundaries were set up by international agreement, such as the International Court of Justice. In essence, European Union citizens are affected by two legal systems, national and Community law. The courts of law must apply both systems of law where relevant, and if there is a conflict, the Community law takes precedence. The supremacy of Community law is implicit in the nature of the Communities, since their existence and functioning require its application. This surrender of sovereignty cannot be reversed by measures taken by national authorities in conflict with Community law. Community law is directly applicable to Member States, and there is no requirement that it be passed into national law for its validity, since the rights and obligations accrue directly to European Union citizens.[18]

The primacy of Community law and its direct applicability are distinctive features of the European Union, turning freedoms into rights. European Community law is a system of laws, which is directly applicable to people and institutions in Member States, and is invoked in national courts. Community law touches on many aspects of national life, including immigration, control of foreign workers, and matters relating to equality. National law has been challenged or influenced by Community law, which is enforced and overseen by the European

Court of Justice. This is a loss of sovereignty by the Member States, surrendering far-reaching powers to an independent legal order, which binds Member States. Points of law and the interpretation of treaties are decided by the European Court of Justice, the community's judicial institution having jurisdiction over disputes concerning the Member States. Often, the national court is faced with issues, such as the interpretation of a treaty, the validity of acts, or the lack of a judicial remedy under national law. If a nation state's court decides that a question of community law needs to be answered before it can render a judgment, it can go before the European Court of Justice for the ruling. The European Union Treaties are part of the domestic law of the State. As such, they impinge on the finality of national court decisions.

Two types of cases may be brought before the European Court of Justice, namely direct actions, brought directly before the Court by the Commission, other Community institutions or a Member State, or preliminary rulings, requested by courts or tribunals in the Member States on a question of Community law. The European Court of Justice may hear a variety of cases involving: annulment of binding legal acts; failure to act; infringement of the European Union treaties, under Article 33, in order to have Commission decisions or recommendations declared void for lack of competence, infringement of an essential procedural requirement, the treaty or any rule of law relating to its application, or misuse of powers; preliminary rulings, in which national courts petition the Court of Justice for a ruling on a point of Community law, binding in the case; damages; and application of staff regulations. The Treaties state that the Community's legal system, which must not be impeded by any State, applies throughout the European Union.

The European Court of Justice is at the heart of the legal system, and ensures that Community law is observed in the interpretation and application of the treaties. Its judgments are binding on Member States. The court reviews the lawfulness of acts of Council, the Commission, the Member State's governments and citizens. National laws in conflict with Community law may be declared invalid by the European Court of Justice. Appeals against acts of an institution or a Member State can be lodged by any other institution, government, firm or individual citizen directly affected.

The legal order is called the 'originality' of the European Union, which is the jurisdiction of the constitutional court, the European Court of Justice. The Court's decisions are made by majority vote, presented in open court. The judgments are directly applicable to Member States and are enforceable through the national courts. The Court of Justice located in Luxembourg may sit in plenary session, when a Member State or an European Union institution is a party to the proceeding and so requests or when a case is considered complex and important, or may sit in chamber. Since all the official languages of the European Union are used at some point, the Court provides for a large translation and interpretation service. The Court is also assisted by an Advocate General, as amicus curiae acting as an independent judicial observer representing the public interest, who makes a reasoned presentation of the case before the Court, gives a summary of the submissions of the parties, puts forth observations of oral hearings, statute law and previous cases, and offers an opinion, which although published is not binding on the Court. In order to enable the Court of Justice to concentrate its activities on the fundamental task of ensuring uniform interpretation of Community law, a Court of First Instance was established in 1989, which has jurisdiction over actions brought by individuals and companies against decisions of the European Union institutions and agencies, and these judgments are in turn subject to appeal before the Court of Justice on a point of law.

As the arbiter of Community law, the European Court of Justice, with its power, has strengthened the European Union as a political system. Defiance of its rulings has been exceptional. By creating a body of independent Community law, the European Union has promoted its survival, by requiring harmonization of the laws of the Member States. The national courts are, therefore, responsible for aligning national law with Community law. The treaties are a comprehensive code of law, which set out the rights and duties of governments and individuals, and from which rights and remedies can be deduced. For the European Court of Justice, the European Union's common aims count more than a literal construction of legal texts. The legal character of the European Union is also concerned with influencing, shaping and controlling the legislative output of the Community.

Fundamental rights are part of the bedrock of the Community's legal order. The European Court of Justice held that the protection of such rights, while inspired by the constitutional traditions common to Member States, must be ensured within the framework of the structure and objectives of the Community (*Internationale Handelsgesellschaft* [1970] ECR 1125, [1972] CMLR 255).[19] Importantly, in a seminal case, the European Court of Justice stated:

> The integration into the laws of each Member State of provisions which derive from the Community, and more generally the terms and the spirit of the Treaty, make it impossible for the States, as a corollary, to accord precedence to a unilateral and subsequent measure over a legal system accepted by them on a basis of reciprocity .... The executive force of Community law cannot vary from one State to another ... without jeopardising the attainment of the object of the Treaty....It follows from all these observations that the law stemming from the treaty, an independent source of law, could not, because of its special and original nature, be overridden by domestic legal provisions, however framed, without being deprived of its character as Community law and without the legal basis of the Community itself being called into question (*Costa v. ENEL* [1964] CMLR 425).[20]

European Convention for the Protection of Human Rights and Fundamental Freedoms (ECHR) and the European Social Charter

European Convention for the Protection of Human Rights and Fundamental Freedoms (ECHR)

The European Convention for the Protection of Human Rights and Fundamental Freedoms came into being on 4 November 1950, which afforded protection against discrimination. In the Preamble, the Governments signatory hereto, being Members of the Council of Europe, undertake the agreement:

> Considering the Universal Declaration of Human Rights proclaimed by the General Assembly of the United Nations on 10th December 1948;
>
> Considering that this Declaration aims at securing the universal and effective recognition and observance of the Rights therein declared;
>
> Considering that the aim of the Council of Europe is the achievement of greater unity between its Members and that one of the methods by which the aim is to be pursued is the maintenance and further realisation of Human Rights and Fundamental Freedoms;
>
> Reaffirming their profound belief in those Fundamental Freedoms which are the foundation of justice and peace in the world and are best maintained on the one hand by an effective political democracy and on the other by a common understanding and observance of the Human Rights upon which they depend;
>
> Being resolved, as the Governments of European countries which are like-minded and have a common heritage of political traditions, ideals, freedom and the rule of law to take the first steps for the collective enforcement of certain of the Rights stated in the Universal Declaration.[21]

> Article 1 guarantees:

> 1. The High Contracting Parties shall secure to everyone within their jurisdiction the rights and freedoms defined.[22]

The right to an effective remedy is secured by Article 13:

> 13. Everyone whose rights and freedoms as set forth in this Convention are violated shall have an effective remedy before a national authority notwithstanding that the violation has been committed by persons acting in an official capacity.[23]

> Important for disability rights, the prohibition of discrimination is guaranteed under Article 14:

> 14. The enjoyment of the rights and freedoms set forth in this Convention shall be secured without discrimination on any ground such as sex, race, color, language, religion, political or other opinion, national or social origin, association with a national minority, property, birth or other status.[24]

Further, Article 17 provides for the prohibition of abuse of rights:

> 17. Nothing in this Convention may be interpreted as implying for any State, group or person any right to engage in any activity or perform any act aimed at the destruction of any of the rights and freedoms set forth herein or at their limitation to a greater extent than is provided for in the Convention.[25]

The European Court of Human Rights is established under Article 19:

19. To ensure the observance of the engagements undertaken by the High Contracting Parties in the Convention and the Protocols thereto, there shall be set up a European Court of Human Rights, hereinafter referred to as 'the Court'. It shall function on a permanent basis.[26]

Article 27 outlines the structure of Committees, Chambers and Grand Chamber:

27. 1. To consider cases brought before it, the Court shall sit in committees of three judges, in Chambers of seven judges and in a Grand Chamber of seventeen judges. The Court's Chambers shall set up committees for a fixed period of time.
2. There shall sit as an ex officio member of the Chamber and the Grand Chamber the judge elected in respect of the State Party concerned or, if there is none or if he is unable to sit, a person of its choice who shall sit in the capacity of judge.
3. The Grand Chamber shall also include the President of the Court, the Vice-Presidents, the Presidents of the Chambers and other judges chosen in accordance with the rules of the Court. When a case is referred to the Grand Chamber under Article 43, no judge from the Chamber which rendered the judgment shall sit in the Grand Chamber, with the exception of the President of the Chamber and the judge who sat in respect of the State Party concerned.[27]

Article 32 outlines the jurisdiction of the Court:

32. 1. The jurisdiction of the Court shall extend to all matters concerning the interpretation and application of the Convention and the protocols thereto which are referred to it as provided in Articles 33, 34 and 47.
2. In the event of dispute as to whether the Court has jurisdiction, the Court shall decide.[28]

Inter-State cases are provided for under Article 33:

33. Any High Contracting Party may refer to the Court any alleged breach of the provisions of the Convention and the protocols thereto by another High Contracting Party.[29]

Further, individual applications are provided for under Article 34:

34. The Court may receive applications from any person, non-governmental organization or group of individuals claiming to be the victim of a violation by one of the High Contracting Parties of the rights set forth in the Convention or the protocols thereto. The High Contracting Parties undertake not to hinder in any way the effective exercise of this right.[30]

Additionally, third party intervention is provided for under Article 36:

36. 1. In all cases before a Chamber or the Grand Chamber, a High Contracting Party one of whose nationals is an applicant shall have the right to submit written comments and to take part in hearings.

2. The President of the Court may, in the interest of the proper administration of justice, invite any High Contracting Party which is not a party to the proceedings or any person concerned who is not the applicant to submit written comments or take part in hearings.[31]

Article 35 contains the admissibility criteria:

35. 1. The Court may only deal with the matter after all domestic remedies have been exhausted, according to the generally recognized rules of international law, and within a period of six months from the date on which the final decision was taken.

2. The Court shall not deal with any application submitted under Article 34 that:

(a) is anonymous; or

(b) is substantially the same as a matter that has already been examined by the Court or has already been submitted to another procedure of international investigation or settlement and contains no relevant new information.

3. The Court shall declare inadmissible any individual application submitted under Article 34 which it considers incompatible with the provisions of the Convention or the protocols thereto, manifestly ill-founded, or an abuse of the right of application.

4. The Court shall reject any application which it considers inadmissible under this Article. It may do so at any stage of the proceedings.[32]

Further, Article 37 contains the striking out applications:

37. 1. The Court may at any stage of the proceedings decide to strike an application out of its list of cases where the circumstances lead to the conclusion that:

(a) the applicant does not intend to pursue his application; or

(b) the matter has been resolved; or

(c) for any other reason established by the Court, it is no longer justified to continue the examination of the application.

However, the Court shall continue the examination of the application if respect for human rights as defined in the Convention and the protocols thereto so requires.

2. The Court may decide to restore an application to its list of cases if it considers that the circumstances justify such a course.[33]

Article 38 outlines the examination of the case and friendly settlement proceedings:

38. 1. If the Court declares the application admissible, it shall:

(a) pursue the examination of the case, together with the representatives of the parties, and if need be, undertake an investigation, for the effective conduct of which the States concerned shall furnish all necessary facilities;

(b) place itself at the disposal of the parties concerned with a view to securing a friendly settlement of the matter on the basis of respect for human rights as defined in the Convention and the protocols thereto.

2. Proceedings conducted under paragraph 1.b shall be confidential.[34]

Further, Article 39 outlines the finding of a friendly settlement:

39. If a friendly settlement is effected, the Court shall strike the case out of its list by means of a decision which shall be confined to a brief statement of the facts and of the solution reached.[35]

Public hearings and access to documents are provided for under Article 40:

40. 1. Hearings shall be in public unless the Court in exceptional circumstances decides otherwise.
2. Documents deposited with the Registrar shall be accessible to the public unless the President of the Court decides otherwise.[36]

Further, Article 41 provides for just satisfaction:

41. If the Court finds that there has been a violation of the Convention or the protocols thereto, and if the internal law of the High Contracting Party concerned allows only partial reparation to be made, the Court shall, if necessary, afford just satisfaction to the injured party.[37]

Final judgments are contained in Article 44:

44. 1. The judgment of the Grand Chamber shall be final.
2. The judgment of a Chamber shall become final:
(a) when the parties declare that they will not request that the case be referred to the Grand Chamber; or
(b) three months after the date of the judgment, if reference of the case to the Grand Chamber has not been requested; or
(c) when the panel of the Grand Chamber rejects the request to refer under Article 43.
3. The final judgment shall be published.[38]

Reasons for judgments and decisions are contained in Article 45:

45. 1. Reasons shall be given for judgments as well as for decisions declaring applications admissible or inadmissible.
2. If a judgment does not represent, in whole or in part, the unanimous opinion of the judges, any judge shall be entitled to deliver a separate opinion.[39]

Binding force and execution of judgments are contained in Article 46:

46. 1. The High Contracting Parties undertake to abide by the final judgment of the Court in any case to which they are parties.
2. The final judgment of the Court shall be transmitted to the Committee of Ministers, which shall supervise its execution.[40]

Finally, Article 47 provides for advisory opinions:

47. 1. The Court may, at the request of the Committee of Ministers, give advisory opinions on legal questions concerning the interpretation of the Convention and

the protocols thereto.

2. Such opinions shall not deal with any question relating to the content or scope of the rights or freedoms defined in Section I of the Convention and the protocols thereto, or with any other question which the Court or the Committee of Ministers might have to consider in consequence of any such proceedings as could be instituted in accordance with the Convention.

3. Decisions of the Committee of Ministers to request an advisory opinion of the Court shall require a majority vote of the representatives entitled to sit on the Committee.[41]

Further, important for disability rights, in the Preamble of the Protocol No. 12 to the European Convention for the Protection of Human Rights and Fundamental Freedoms, opened for signature on 11 April 2000, the Member States of the Council of Europe signatory hereto, undertake the agreement:

Having regard to the fundamental principle according to which all persons are equal before the law and are entitled to the equal protection of the law;

Being resolved to take further steps to promote the equality of all persons through the collective enforcement of a general prohibition of discrimination by means of the Convention for the Protection of Human Rights and Fundamental Freedoms signed at Rome on 4 November 1950 (hereinafter referred to as 'the Convention');

Reaffirming that the principle of non-discrimination does not prevent States Parties from taking measures in order to promote full and effective equality, provided that there is an objective and reasonable justification for those measures.[42]

Article 1 outlines the general prohibition against discrimination:

1(1) The enjoyment of any right set forth by law shall be secured without discrimination on any ground such as sex, race, color, language, religion, political or other opinion, national or social origin, association with a national minority, property, birth or other status.

(2) No one shall be discriminated against by any public authority on any ground such as those mentioned in paragraph 1.[43]

It is important to note the words 'other status' includes disability, and such a specific inclusion was considered unnecessary from a legal point of view, since the list of non-discrimination grounds is not exhaustive, and because inclusion of any particular additional ground might give rise to unwarranted a contrario interpretations as regards discrimination based on grounds not so included.

European Social Charter

The European Social Charter promotes the right for workers to equal opportunities and equal treatment in matters of employment and occupation without discrimination. The Charter espouses the notion of 'equal pay for work of equal value', and also provides for the equal treatment with regard to access to employment, vocational training, promotion and working conditions, aimed at eliminating all discrimination, both direct and indirect, in the world of work, and provides for opportunities for positive measures.

In the Preamble to the European Social Charter of 18 October 1961, the governments signatory hereto, being members of the Council of Europe, undertake the agreement:

> Considering that the aim of the Council of Europe is the achievement of greater unity between its members for the purpose of safeguarding and realising the ideals and principles which are their common heritage and of facilitating their economic and social progress, in particular by the maintenance and further realisation of human rights and fundamental freedoms;
>
> Considering that in the Convention for the Protection of Human Rights and Fundamental Freedoms signed at Rome on 4th November 1950, and the Protocol thereto signed at Paris on 20th March 1952, the member States of the Council of Europe agreed to secure to their populations the civil and political rights and freedoms therein specified;
>
> Considering that the enjoyment of social rights should be secured without discrimination on grounds of race, color, sex, religion, political opinion, national extraction or social origin;
>
> Being resolved to make every effort in common to improve the standard of living and to promote the social well-being of both their urban and rural populations by means of appropriate institutions and action.[44]

In the Preamble to the European Social Charter (revised) of 3 May 1996, the governments signatory thereto, being members of the Council of Europe, undertake the agreement:

> ...Considering that in the European Social Charter opened for signature in Turin on 18 October 1961 and the Protocols thereto, the member States of the Council of Europe agreed to secure to their populations the social rights specified therein in order to improve their standard of living and their social well-being;
>
> Recalling that the Ministerial Conference on Human Rights held in Rome on 5 November 1990 stressed the need, on the one hand, to preserve the indivisible nature of all human rights, be they civil, political, economic, social or cultural and, on the other hand, to give the European Social Charter fresh impetus.[45]

Important for disability rights, Article E defines non-discrimination:

> E. The enjoyment of the rights set forth in this Charter shall be secured without discrimination on any ground such as race, color, sex, language, religion, political or other opinion, national extraction or social origin, health, association with a national minority, birth or other status. [46]

Important for disability rights, under Part I, several rights and principles are espoused:

> The Parties accept as the aim of their policy, to be pursued by all appropriate means both national and international in character, the attainment of conditions in which the following rights and principles may be effectively realized:

1. Everyone shall have the opportunity to earn his living in an occupation freely entered upon.
2. All workers have the right to just conditions of work.
3. All workers have the right to safe and healthy working conditions.
4. All workers have the right to a fair remuneration sufficient for a decent standard of living for themselves and their families.
5. All workers and employers have the right to freedom of association in national or international organizations for the protection of their economic and social interests.
6. All workers and employers have the right to bargain collectively.
7. Children and young persons have the right to a special protection against the physical and moral hazards to which they are exposed.
8. Employed women, in case of maternity, have the right to a special protection.
9. Everyone has the right to appropriate facilities for vocational guidance with a view to helping him choose an occupation suited to his personal aptitude and interests.
10. Everyone has the right to appropriate facilities for vocational training.
11. Everyone has the right to benefit from any measures enabling him to enjoy the highest possible standard of health attainable.
12. All workers and their dependents have the right to social security.
13. Anyone without adequate resources has the right to social and medical assistance.
14. Everyone has the right to benefit from social welfare services.
15. Disabled persons have the right to independence, social integration and participation in the life of the community.
16. The family as a fundamental unit of society has the right to appropriate social, legal and economic protection to ensure its full development.
17. Children and young persons have the right to appropriate social, legal and economic protection.
18. The nationals of any one of the Parties have the right to engage in any gainful occupation in the territory of any one of the others on a footing of equality with the nationals of the latter, subject to restrictions based on cogent economic or social reasons.
19. Migrant workers who are nationals of a Party and their families have the right to protection and assistance in the territory of any other Party.
20. All workers have the right to equal opportunities and equal treatment in matters of employment and occupation without discrimination on the grounds of sex.
21. Workers have the right to be informed and to be consulted within the undertaking.
22. Workers have the right to take part in the determination and improvement of the working conditions and working environment in the undertaking.

23. Every elderly person has the right to social protection.
24. All workers have the right to protection in cases of termination of employment.
25. All workers have the right to protection of their claims in the event of the insolvency of their employer.
26. All workers have the right to dignity at work.
27. All persons with family responsibilities and who are engaged or wish to engage in employment have a right to do so without being subject to discrimination and as far as possible without conflict between their employment and family responsibilities.
28. Workers' representatives in undertakings have the right to protection against acts prejudicial to them and should be afforded appropriate facilities to carry out their functions.
29. All workers have the right to be informed and consulted in collective redundancy procedures.
30. Everyone has the right to protection against poverty and social exclusion.
31. Everyone has the right to housing.[47]

In Part II, the right to work is provided for in Article 1:

1. With a view to ensuring the effective exercise of the right to work, the Parties undertake:

1. to accept as one of their primary aims and responsibilities the achievement and maintenance of as high and stable a level of employment as possible, with a view to the attainment of full employment;
2. to protect effectively the right of the worker to earn his living in an occupation freely entered upon;
3. to establish or maintain free employment services for all workers;
4. to provide or promote appropriate vocational guidance, training and rehabilitation.[48]

Further, Article 4 guarantees the right to a fair remuneration and equal pay:

4. With a view to ensuring the effective exercise of the right to a fair remuneration, the Parties undertake:

1. to recognize the right of workers to a remuneration such as will give them and their families a decent standard of living;
2. to recognize the right of workers to an increased rate of remuneration for overtime work, subject to exceptions in particular cases;
3. to recognize the right of men and women workers to equal pay for work of equal value;
4. to recognize the right of all workers to a reasonable period of notice for termination of employment;
5. to permit deductions from wages only under conditions and to the extent prescribed by national laws or regulations or fixed by collective agreements or arbitration awards. The exercise of these rights shall be achieved by

freely concluded collective agreements, by statutory wage-fixing machinery, or by other means appropriate to national conditions.[49]

In addition, Article 24 provides for termination of employment under appropriate means:

> 24. It is understood that for the purposes of this article the terms 'termination of employment' and 'terminated' mean termination of employment at the initiative of the employer.
>
> 1. It is understood that this article covers all workers but that a Party may exclude from some or all of its protection the following categories of employed persons:
>   a. workers engaged under a contract of employment for a specified period of time or a specified task;
>   b. workers undergoing a period of probation or a qualifying period of employment, provided that this is determined in advance and is of a reasonable duration;
>   c. workers engaged on a casual basis for a short period.
>
> 2. For the purpose of this article the following, in particular, shall not constitute valid reasons for termination of employment:
>   a. trade union membership or participation in union activities outside working hours, or, with the consent of the employer, within working hours;
>   b. seeking office as, acting or having acted in the capacity of a workers' representative;
>   c. the filing of a complaint or the participation in proceedings against an employer involving alleged violation of laws or regulations or recourse to competent administrative authorities;
>   d. race, color, sex, marital status, family responsibilities, pregnancy, religion, political opinion, national extraction or social origin;
>   e. maternity or parental leave;
>   f. temporary absence from work due to illness or injury.
>
> 3. It is understood that compensation or other appropriate relief in case of termination of employment without valid reasons shall be determined by national laws or regulations, collective agreements or other means appropriate to national conditions.[50]

Pursuant to Article 22, the Parties undertake to adopt or encourage measures enabling workers or their representatives, in accordance with national legislation and practice, to contribute to the determination and the improvement of the working conditions, work organization and working environment; to the protection of health and safety within the undertaking; to the organization of social and sociocultural services and facilities within the undertaking; and to the supervision of the observance of regulations on these matters.[51]

European Legislation

Council Resolution 1999/C 186/02 on Equal Employment Opportunities for People with Disabilities

The Preamble of Council Resolution 1999/C 186/02 of 17 June 1999 on Equal Employment Opportunities for People with Disabilities states:

> THE COUNCIL OF THE EUROPEAN UNION,
> Having regard to the Treaty establishing the European Community,
> (1) an essential objective of the Community, as identified in the coordinated European employment strategy, is to promote a high level of employment;
> (2) in the 1999 employment guidelines (1), guideline 9 acknowledges the need for the Member States to give special attention to the needs of the disabled, ethnic minorities and other groups and individuals who may be disadvantaged, and develop appropriate forms of preventive and active policies to promote their integration into the labor market.;
> (3) in its recommendation of 24 July 1986 (2), the Council recognised the key issues of the integration of people with disabilities in vocational training and employment;
> (4) the Community Charter on the fundamental social rights of workers of 9 December 1989 stipulates in point 26: .All disabled persons, whatever the origin and nature of their disability, must be entitled to additional concrete measures aimed at improving their social and professional integration. These measures must concern, in particular, according to the capacities of the beneficiaries, vocational training, ergonomics, accessibility, mobility, means of transport and housing;
> (5) in their resolution of 20 December 1996 on equality of opportunity for people with disabilities (3), the Council and the representatives of the Governments of the Member States meeting within the Council reaffirmed their commitment to the principle of equality of opportunity in the development of comprehensive policies in the field of disability;
> (6) the Commission of the European Communities formulated fundamental policy issues concerning the disabled and employment in a document of 22 September 1998 entitled Raising employment levels of people with disabilities the common challenge, taking into account the European employment strategy and the analysis of some key elements of the 1998 national action plans; the Commission also concluded that there must be a move away from piecemeal initiatives and that a coordinated strategy must be established;
> (7) in order to establish equal opportunities for people with disabilities with regard to securing, retaining and advancing in employment, Convention 159 and Recommendation 168 of the International Labor Organisation concerning vocational rehabilitation and employment (disabled persons) of 20 June 1983, the Council of Europe Recommendation No R(92) 6 of 9 April 1992 for a coherent policy for disabled people, and the standard rules on the equalisation of opportunities for persons with disabilities which were adopted in a United Nations General Assembly resolution on 20 December 1993, call upon the Member States to develop, evaluate and review support programmes for the integration of people with disabilities in various ways, in particular in the field of employment;
> (8) people with disabilities, despite individual successes and improvements, are still more likely to face barriers and disadvantages in finding and maintaining

suitable employment and in fully participating in the economic and social life of their communities,
HEREBY ADOPTS THIS RESOLUTION.[52]

The Resolution goes on to state:

1. The Council acknowledges and welcomes the serious efforts made and planned by the Member States to develop and implement policies aimed at integrating people with disabilities into the labor market, in particular within the EN 2.7.1999 Official Journal of the European Union Communities C 186/3 (1) OJ C 69, 12.3.1999, p. 2. (2) OJ L 225, 12.8.1986, p. 43. (3) OJ C 12, 13.1.1997, p. 1. framework of the European employment strategy; it welcomes equally the new impetus by the annual employment guidelines.
2. The Council underlines that the national action plans for employment provide a comprehensive platform within which the abovementioned policies should be strengthened.
Member States are therefore called upon:

(a) within the framework of their national employment policies, and in cooperation with the social partners and non-governmental organisations for people with disabilities, to place particular emphasis on the promotion of employment opportunities for people with disabilities and to develop suitable preventive and active policies for the specific promotion of their integration into the labor market in the private sector, including self-employment, and in the public sector,

(b) to make full use of the existing and future possibilities of the European Structural Funds, in particular the European Social Fund, and relevant Community initiatives, to promote equal employment opportunities for people with disabilities,

(c) also in the above context, to attach particular attention to the possibilities offered by the development of the information society for opening new employment opportunities but also challenges for people with disabilities.

3. The Council welcomes the initiative of the social partners at European level to identify good practices and invites the social partners at all levels to play an increasing role in creating improved employment opportunities and negotiated work organisation changes in cooperation with people with disabilities.
4. The Council invites people with disabilities themselves and their organisations to make their contribution towards the goal of equal employment opportunities by sharing and exchanging their experience with all those involved in the labor market.
5. The Council encourages the Community Institutions to promote equal employment opportunities for people with disabilities within their own services, by enacting rules while taking full advantage of existing legal instruments and practices.
6. The Council calls upon the Commission to work together with the Member States, in particular within the framework of the European employment guidelines and in accordance with the mainstreaming principle, to monitor and analyse the development of the employment of people with disabilities on the basis of comparable data and to develop new strategies and campaigns, taking into consideration national, regional and local differences.

7. The Council affirms that, in the framework of a coherent global policy, equal employment opportunities for people with disabilities will be enhanced if specific attention is given to recruitment and retention of employees, promotion, training, life-long learning and development, and protection against unfair dismissal, and appropriate support provided in areas such as:
. workplace accommodation, such as technical equipment including access to new information and communication technologies,
. access to the place of work,
. qualifications and skills required at work, and
. access to vocational guidance and placement services.
8. The Council notes the Commission's intention to make a proposal for a legal instrument covering equal employment opportunities for people with disabilities.[53]

Council Directive 2000/78/EC Establishing a General Framework for Equal Treatment in Employment and Occupation

Important for disability rights, the Preamble of Council Directive 2000/78/EC of 27 November 2000 Establishing a General Framework for Equal Treatment in Employment and Occupation states:

THE COUNCIL OF THE EUROPEAN UNION,

Having regard to the Treaty establishing the European Community, and in particular Article 13 thereof,

Having regard to the proposal from the Commission,

Having regard to the Opinion of the European Parliament,

Having regard to the Opinion of the Economic and Social Committee,

Having regard to the Opinion of the Committee of the Regions,

Whereas:

1.In accordance with Article 6 of the Treaty on European Union, the European Union is founded on the principles of liberty, democracy, respect for human rights and fundamental freedoms, and the rule of law, principles which are common to all Member States and it respects fundamental rights, as guaranteed by the European Convention for the Protection of Human Rights and Fundamental Freedoms and as they result from the constitutional traditions common to the Member States, as general principles of Community law.

4.The right of all persons to equality before the law and protection against discrimination constitutes a universal right recognised by the Universal Declaration of Human Rights, the United Nations Convention on the Elimination of All Forms of Discrimination against Women, United Nations Covenants on Civil and Political Rights and on Economic, Social and Cultural Rights and by the European Convention for the Protection of Human Rights and Fundamental Freedoms, to which all Member States are signatories. Convention No 111 of the

International Labor Organisation (ILO) prohibits discrimination in the field of employment and occupation.

6.The Community Charter of the Fundamental Social Rights of Workers recognises the importance of combating every form of discrimination, including the need to take appropriate action for the social and economic integration of elderly and disabled people.

7.The EC Treaty includes among its objectives the promotion of coordination between employment policies of the Member States. To this end, a new employment chapter was incorporated in the EC Treaty as a means of developing a coordinated European strategy for employment to promote a skilled, trained and adaptable workforce.

8.The Employment Guidelines for 2000 agreed by the European Council at Helsinki on 10 and 11 December 1999 stress the need to foster a labor market favourable to social integration by formulating a coherent set of policies aimed at combating discrimination against groups such as persons with disability. They also emphasise the need to pay particular attention to supporting older workers, in order to increase their participation in the labor force.

9.Employment and occupation are key elements in guaranteeing equal opportunities for all and contribute strongly to the full participation of citizens in economic, cultural and social life and to realising their potential.

11.Discrimination based on religion or belief, disability, age or sexual orientation may undermine the achievement of the objectives of the EC Treaty, in particular the attainment of a high level of employment and social protection, raising the standard of living and the quality of life, economic and social cohesion and solidarity, and the free movement of persons.

12.To this end, any direct or indirect discrimination based on religion or belief, disability, age or sexual orientation as regards the areas covered by this Directive should be prohibited throughout the Community. This prohibition of discrimination should also apply to nationals of third countries but does not cover differences of treatment based on nationality and is without prejudice to provisions governing the entry and residence of third-country nationals and their access to employment and occupation.

15.The appreciation of the facts from which it may be inferred that there has been direct or indirect discrimination is a matter for national judicial or other competent bodies, in accordance with rules of national law or practice. Such rules may provide, in particular, for indirect discrimination to be established by any means including on the basis of statistical evidence.

16.The provision of measures to accommodate the needs of disabled people at the workplace plays an important role in combating discrimination on grounds of disability.

17.This Directive does not require the recruitment, promotion, maintenance in employment or training of an individual who is not competent, capable and available to perform the essential functions of the post concerned or to undergo the relevant training, without prejudice to the obligation to provide reasonable accommodation for people with disabilities.

20.Appropriate measures should be provided, i.e. effective and practical measures to adapt the workplace to the disability, for example adapting premises and equipment, patterns of working time, the distribution of tasks or the provision of training or integration resources.

21.To determine whether the measures in question give rise to a disproportionate burden, account should be taken in particular of the financial and other costs entailed, the scale and financial resources of the organisation or undertaking and the possibility of obtaining public funding or any other assistance.

23.In very limited circumstances, a difference of treatment may be justified where a characteristic related to religion or belief, disability, age or sexual orientation constitutes a genuine and determining occupational requirement, when the objective is legitimate and the requirement is proportionate. Such circumstances should be included in the information provided by the Member States to the Commission.

25.The prohibition of age discrimination is an essential part of meeting the aims set out in the Employment Guidelines and encouraging diversity in the workforce .... It is therefore essential to distinguish between differences in treatment which are justified, in particular by legitimate employment policy, labor market and vocational training objectives, and discrimination which must be prohibited.

26.The prohibition of discrimination should be without prejudice to the maintenance or adoption of measures intended to prevent or compensate for disadvantages suffered by a group of persons of a particular religion or belief, disability, age or sexual orientation, and such measures may permit organisations of persons of a particular religion or belief, disability, age or sexual orientation where their main object is the promotion of the special needs of those persons.

27.In its Recommendation 86/379/EEC of 24 July 1986 on the employment of disabled people in the Community, the Council established a guideline framework setting out examples of positive action to promote the employment and training of disabled people, and in its Resolution of 17 June 1999 on equal employment opportunities for people with disabilities, affirmed the importance of giving specific attention inter alia to recruitment, retention, training and lifelong learning with regard to disabled persons.

28.This Directive lays down minimum requirements, thus giving the Member States the option of introducing or maintaining more favourable provisions. The implementation of this Directive should not serve to justify any regression in relation to the situation which already prevails in each Member State.

29.Persons who have been subject to discrimination based on religion or belief, disability, age or sexual orientation should have adequate means of legal protection. To provide a more effective level of protection, associations or legal entities should also be empowered to engage in proceedings, as the Member States so determine, either on behalf or in support of any victim, without prejudice to national rules of procedure concerning representation and defence before the courts.

30.The effective implementation of the principle of equality requires adequate judicial protection against victimisation.

31.The rules on the burden of proof must be adapted when there is a prima facie case of discrimination and, for the principle of equal treatment to be applied effectively, the burden of proof must shift back to the respondent when evidence of such discrimination is brought. However, it is not for the respondent to prove that the plaintiff adheres to a particular religion or belief, has a particular disability, is of a particular age or has a particular sexual orientation.

32.Member States need not apply the rules on the burden of proof to proceedings in which it is for the court or other competent body to investigate the facts of the case. The procedures thus referred to are those in which the plaintiff is not required to prove the facts, which it is for the court or competent body to investigate.

33.Member States should promote dialogue between the social partners and, within the framework of national practice, with non-governmental organisations to address different forms of discrimination at the workplace and to combat them.

35.Member States should provide for effective, proportionate and dissuasive sanctions in case of breaches of the obligations under this Directive.

36.Member States may entrust the social partners, at their joint request, with the implementation of this Directive, as regards the provisions concerning collective agreements, provided they take any necessary steps to ensure that they are at all times able to guarantee the results required by this Directive.

37.In accordance with the principle of subsidiarity set out in Article 5 of the EC Treaty, the objective of this Directive, namely the creation within the Community of a level playing-field as regards equality in employment and occupation, cannot be sufficiently achieved by the Member States and can therefore, by reason of the scale and impact of the action, be better achieved at Community level. In accordance with the principle of proportionality, as set out in that Article, this Directive does not go beyond what is necessary in order to achieve that objective,

HAS ADOPTED THIS DIRECTIVE.[54]

Article 1 outlines the Purpose:

1. The purpose of this Directive is to lay down a general framework for combating discrimination on the grounds of religion or belief, disability, age or sexual orientation as regards employment and occupation, with a view to putting into effect in the Member States the principle of equal treatment.[55]

Importantly, the concept of discrimination is defined under Article 2:

2(1)For the purposes of this Directive, the 'principle of equal treatment' shall mean that there shall be no direct or indirect discrimination whatsoever on any of the grounds referred to in Article 1.

(2)For the purposes of paragraph 1:

    a.   direct discrimination shall be taken to occur where one person is treated less favourably than another is, has been or would be treated in a comparable situation, on any of the grounds referred to in Article 1;

    b.   indirect discrimination shall be taken to occur where an apparently neutral provision, criterion or practice would put persons having a particular religion or belief, a particular disability, a particular age, or a particular sexual orientation at a particular disadvantage compared with other persons unless:

        i.   that provision, criterion or practice is objectively justified by a legitimate aim and the means of achieving that aim are appropriate and necessary, or

        ii.   as regards persons with a particular disability, the employer or any person or organisation to whom this Directive applies, is obliged, under national legislation, to take appropriate measures in line with the principles contained in Article 5 in order to eliminate disadvantages entailed by such provision, criterion or practice.

(3)Harassment shall be deemed to be a form of discrimination within the meaning of paragraph 1, when unwanted conduct related to any of the grounds referred to in Article 1 takes place with the purpose or effect of violating the dignity of a person and of creating an intimidating, hostile, degrading, humiliating or offensive environment. In this context, the concept of harassment may be defined in accordance with the national laws and practice of the Member States.

(4)An instruction to discriminate against persons on any of the grounds referred to in Article 1 shall be deemed to be discrimination within the meaning of paragraph 1.

(5)This Directive shall be without prejudice to measures laid down by national law which, in a democratic society, are necessary for public security, for the maintenance of public order and the prevention of criminal offences, for the protection of health and for the protection of the rights and freedoms of others.[56]

The scope of the Directive is outlined in Article 3:

3(1)Within the limits of the areas of competence conferred on the Community, this Directive shall apply to all persons, as regards both the public and private sectors, including public bodies, in relation to:

a. conditions for access to employment, to self-employment or to occupation, including selection criteria and recruitment conditions, whatever the branch of activity and at all levels of the professional hierarchy, including promotion;

b. access to all types and to all levels of vocational guidance, vocational training, advanced vocational training and retraining, including practical work experience;

c. employment and working conditions, including dismissals and pay;

d. membership of, and involvement in, an organisation of workers or employers, or any organisation whose members carry on a particular profession, including the benefits provided for by such organisations.

(2) This Directive does not cover differences of treatment based on nationality and is without prejudice to provisions and conditions relating to the entry into and residence of third-country nationals and stateless persons in the territory of Member States, and to any treatment which arises from the legal status of the third-country nationals and stateless persons concerned.

(3)This Directive does not apply to payments of any kind made by state schemes or similar, including state social security or social protection schemes.

(4)Member States may provide that this Directive, in so far as it relates to discrimination on the grounds of disability and age, shall not apply to the armed forces.[57]

Article 4 contains occupational requirements:

4(1)Notwithstanding Article 2(1) and (2), Member States may provide that a difference of treatment which is based on a characteristic related to any of the grounds referred to in Article 1 shall not constitute discrimination where, by reason of the nature of the particular occupational activities concerned or of the context in which they are carried out, such a characteristic constitutes a genuine and determining occupational requirement, provided that the objective is legitimate and the requirement is proportionate.

(2)Member States may maintain national legislation in force at the date of adoption of this Directive or provide for future legislation incorporating national practices existing at the date of adoption of this Directive pursuant to which, in the case of occupational activities within churches and other public or private organisations the ethos of which is based on religion or belief, a difference of treatment based on a person's religion or belief shall not constitute discrimination where, by reason of the nature of these activities or of the context in which they are carried out, a person's religion or belief constitute a genuine, legitimate and justified occupational requirement, having regard to the organisation's ethos. This difference of treatment shall be implemented taking account of Member States' constitutional provisions and principles, as well as the general principles of Community law, and should not justify discrimination on another ground....[58]

Reasonable accommodation for disabled persons is guaranteed under Article 5:

> 5. In order to guarantee compliance with the principle of equal treatment in relation to persons with disabilities, reasonable accommodation shall be provided. This means that employers shall take appropriate measures, where needed in a particular case, to enable a person with a disability to have access to, participate in, or advance in employment, or to undergo training, unless such measures would impose a disproportionate burden on the employer. This burden shall not be disproportionate when it is sufficiently remedied by measures existing within the framework of the disability policy of the Member State concerned.[59]

Positive action is provided for under Article 7:

> 7(1)With a view to ensuring full equality in practice, the principle of equal treatment shall not prevent any Member State from maintaining or adopting specific measures to prevent or compensate for disadvantages linked to any of the grounds referred to in Article 1.

> (2)With regard to disabled persons, the principle of equal treatment shall be without prejudice to the right of Member States to maintain or adopt provisions on the protection of health and safety at work or to measures aimed at creating or maintaining provisions or facilities for safeguarding or promoting their integration into the working environment.[60]

Further, Article 8 provides for minimum requirements:

> 8(1)Member States may introduce or maintain provisions which are more favourable to the protection of the principle of equal treatment than those laid down in this Directive.

> (2)The implementation of this Directive shall under no circumstances constitute grounds for a reduction in the level of protection against discrimination already afforded by Member States in the fields covered by this Directive.[61]

In terms of remedies and enforcement, Article 9 provides for defence of rights:

> 9(1)Member States shall ensure that judicial and/or administrative procedures, including where they deem it appropriate conciliation procedures, for the enforcement of obligations under this Directive are available to all persons who consider themselves wronged by failure to apply the principle of equal treatment to them, even after the relationship in which the discrimination is alleged to have occurred has ended.

> (2)Member States shall ensure that associations, organisations or other legal entities which have, in accordance with the criteria laid down by their national law, a legitimate interest in ensuring that the provisions of this Directive are complied with, may engage, either on behalf or in support of the complainant,

with his or her approval, in any judicial and/or administrative procedure provided for the enforcement of obligations under this Directive.[62]

The burden of proof is detailed in Article 10:

> 10(1)Member States shall take such measures as are necessary, in accordance with their national judicial systems, to ensure that, when persons who consider themselves wronged because the principle of equal treatment has not been applied to them establish, before a court or other competent authority, facts from which it may be presumed that there has been direct or indirect discrimination, it shall be for the respondent to prove that there has been no breach of the principle of equal treatment.[63]

Article 11 guards against victimization:

> 11. Member States shall introduce into their national legal systems such measures as are necessary to protect employees against dismissal or other adverse treatment by the employer as a reaction to a complaint within the undertaking or to any legal proceedings aimed at enforcing compliance with the principle of equal treatment.[64]

Article 16 provides for compliance:

> 16. Member States shall take the necessary measures to ensure that:
>
> a.   any laws, regulations and administrative provisions contrary to the principle of equal treatment are abolished;
>
> b.   any provisions contrary to the principle of equal treatment which are included in contracts or collective agreements, internal rules of undertakings or rules governing the independent occupations and professions and workers' and employers' organisations are, or may be, declared null and void or are amended.[65]

Further, Article 17 deals with sanctions:

> 17.Member States shall lay down the rules on sanctions applicable to infringements of the national provisions adopted pursuant to this Directive and shall take all measures necessary to ensure that they are applied. The sanctions, which may comprise the payment of compensation to the victim, must be effective, proportionate and dissuasive. Member States shall notify those provisions to the Commission by 2 December 2003 at the latest and shall notify it without delay of any subsequent amendment affecting them.[66]

Finally, Article 18 provides for implementation:

> 18. Member States shall adopt the laws, regulations and administrative provisions necessary to comply with this Directive by 2 December 2003 at the latest or may entrust the social partners, at their joint request, with the implementation of this Directive as regards provisions concerning collective agreements. In such cases,

Member States shall ensure that, no later than 2 December 2003, the social partners introduce the necessary measures by agreement, the Member States concerned being required to take any necessary measures to enable them at any time to be in a position to guarantee the results imposed by this Directive. They shall forthwith inform the Commission thereof.

In order to take account of particular conditions, Member States may, if necessary, have an additional period of 3 years from 2 December 2003, that is to say a total of 6 years, to implement the provisions of this Directive on age and disability discrimination. In that event they shall inform the Commission forthwith. Any Member State which chooses to use this additional period shall report annually to the Commission on the steps it is taking to tackle age and disability discrimination and on the progress it is making towards implementation. The Commission shall report annually to the Council.

When Member States adopt these measures, they shall contain a reference to this Directive or be accompanied by such reference on the occasion of their official publication. The methods of making such reference shall be laid down by Member States.[67]

Council Decision 2000/750/EC Establishing a Community Action Program to Combat Discrimination (2001 to 2006)

The Preamble of Council Decision 2000/750/EC of 27 November 2000, establishing a community action program to combat discrimination states:

(1) The European Union is founded on the principles of liberty, democracy, respect for human rights and fundamental freedoms, and the rule of law, principles which are common to all Member States. In accordance with Article 6(2) of the Treaty on European Union, the Union should respect fundamental rights as guaranteed by the European Convention for the Protection of Human Rights and Fundamental Freedoms and as derived from the shared constitutional traditions common to the Member States, as general principles of Community law.

(2) The European Parliament has strongly and repeatedly urged the European Union to develop and strengthen its policy in the field of equal treatment and equal opportunities across all grounds of discrimination.

(5) The different forms of discrimination cannot be ranked: all are equally intolerable. The program is intended both to exchange existing good practice in the Member States and to develop new practice and policy for combating discrimination, including multiple discrimination. This Decision may help to put in place a comprehensive strategy for combating all forms of discrimination on different grounds, a strategy which should henceforward be developed in parallel.

(8) Access to the program should be open to all public and/or private bodies and institutions involved in the fight against discrimination. In this connection account must be taken of the experience and abilities of both local and national non-governmental organizations.

(9) Many non-governmental organizations at European level have experience and

expertise in fighting discrimination, as well as acting at European level as the advocates of people who are exposed to discrimination. They can therefore make an important contribution towards a better understanding of the diverse forms and effects of discrimination and to ensuring that the design, implementation and follow-up of the program take account of the experience of people exposed to discrimination.

(11) It is necessary, in order to reinforce the added value of Community action, that the Commission, in cooperation with the Member States, should ensure, at all levels, the coherence and complementarity of actions implemented in the framework of this Decision and other relevant Community policies, instruments and actions, in particular those in the fields of education and training and equal opportunities between men and women under the European Social Fund and those to promote social inclusion. Consistency and complementarity with the relevant activities of the European Monitoring Centre on Racism and Xenophobia should also be ensured.[68]

Important for disability rights, Article 1 enunciates the establishment of the program:

1. This Decision establishes a Community action program, hereinafter referred to as 'the program', to promote measures to combat direct or indirect discrimination based on racial or ethnic origin, religion or belief, disability, age or sexual orientation, for the period from 1 January 2001 to 31 December 2006.[69]

Objectives are outlined in Article 2:

2. Within the limits of the Community's powers, the program shall support and supplement the efforts at Community level and in the Member States to promote measures to prevent and combat discrimination whether based on one or on multiple factors, taking account, where appropriate, of future legislative developments. It shall have the following objectives:
(a) to improve the understanding of issues related to discrimination through improved knowledge of this phenomenon and through evaluation of the effectiveness of policies and practice;
(b) to develop the capacity to prevent and address discrimination effectively, in particular by strengthening organizations' means of action and through support for the exchange of information and good practice and networking at European level, while taking into account the specific characteristics of the different forms of discrimination;
(c) to promote and disseminate the values and practices underlying the fight against discrimination, including through the use of awareness-raising campaigns.[70]

Article 3 stipulates the Community actions to be undertaken:

3. 1. With a view to achieving the objectives set out in Article 2, the following actions may be implemented within a transnational framework:
(a) analysis of factors related to discrimination, including through studies and the development of qualitative and quantitative indicators and benchmarks, in

accordance with national law and practices, and the evaluation of anti-discrimination legislation and practice, with a view to assessing its effectiveness and impact, with effective dissemination of the results;
(b) transnational cooperation and the promotion of networking at European level between partners active in the prevention of, and the fight against, discrimination, including non-governmental organizations;
(c) awareness-raising, in particular to emphasize the European dimension of the fight against discrimination and to publicize the results of the program, in particular through communications, publications, campaigns and events.[71]

In terms of the implementation of the program and cooperation with the Member States, Article 4 states:

4. 1. The Commission shall:
(a) ensure the implementation of the Community actions covered by the program in conformity with the Annex;
(b) have a regular exchange of views with representatives of non-governmental organizations and the social partners at European level on the design, implementation and follow-up of the program and on related policy orientations. To that end the Commission shall make the relevant information available to the non-governmental organizations and the social partners. The Commission shall inform the committee established under Article 6 of their exchange of views.

2. The Commission, in cooperation with the Member States, shall take the necessary steps to:
(a) promote the involvement in the program of all the parties concerned, including non-governmental organizations of all sizes;
(b) promote active partnership and dialogue between all the partners involved in the program, inter alia to encourage an integrated and coordinated approach to the fight against discrimination;
(c) ensure the dissemination of the results of the actions undertaken within the framework of the program;
(d) provide accessible information and appropriate publicity and follow-up with regard to actions supported by the program.[72]

Council Resolution 2003/C 175/01 on Promoting the Employment and Social Integration of People with Disabilities

The Preamble of Council Resolution 2003/C 175/01 of 15 July 2003 on Promoting the Employment and Social Integration of People with Disabilities states:

THE COUNCIL OF THE EUOPEAN UNION,
(1) STRESSING that the European Union has a substantial number of people with disabilities who face a variety of difficulties in their daily lives and cannot always exercise their rights;
(2) NOTING that the Treaty establishing the European Community enables the Community to take appropriate action to combat discrimination based on sex, racial or ethnic origin, religion or belief, disability, age or sexual orientation;
(3) RECALLING in particular that acting on the basis of Article 13 of the Treaty establishing the European Community, which enables the Council to take

appropriate action to combat discrimination based on sex, racial or ethnic origin, religion or belief, disability, age or sexual orientation, the Council adopted Directive 2000/78/EC of 27 November 2000 establishing a general framework for equal treatment in employment and occupation;

(4) RECALLING that Article 21 of the Charter of Fundamental Rights recognises the importance of combating every form of discrimination and Article 26 of that Charter states that the Union recognises and respects the right of persons with disabilities to benefit from measures designed to ensure their independence, social and occupational integration and participation in the life of the Community;

(5) CONSIDERING that the European Employment Strategy is a key instrument for underpinning the integration of people with disabilities into the mainstream labor market;

(8) RECALLING the political declaration of Ministers responsible for Integration Policies for People with Disabilities (Malaga, 8 May 2003), which affirms that one of the main aims of the next decade is to improve the quality of life of people with disabilities and their families;

(10) BEARING IN MIND that people with disabilities still face a variety of barriers to full participation in society, often leading to social exclusion and poverty;

(11) BEARING IN MIND the discussions of the informal Council meeting in Nafplion, on 23 and 24 January 2003, which emphasised the need for more extensive inclusion of disability issues in employment and social protection policies;

(12) NOTING the process related to the preparation of a United Nations legally binding instrument to promote and protect the rights and dignity of persons with disabilities and the EU contribution thereto (May 2003) and taking note of the Commission communication entitled 'Towards a United Nations legally binding instrument to promote and protect the rights and dignity of persons with disabilities' (January 2003).[73]

The Resolution goes on to establish certain responsibilities for Member States and:

CALLS ON THE MEMBER STATES AND THE COMMISSION, WITHIN THE FRAMEWORK OF THEIR RESPECTIVE POWERS, TO:
(i) promote greater cooperation with all bodies concerned with people with disabilities at national and European Union level, including civil society;
(ii) promote the full integration and participation of people with disabilities in all aspects of society, recognising that they have equal rights with other citizens;
(iii) continue efforts to remove barriers to the integration and participation of people with disabilities in the labor market, by enforcing equal treatment measures and improving integration and participation at all levels of the educational and training system;
(iv) pursue efforts to make lifelong learning more accessible to people with disabilities and, within this context, give particular attention to the barrier-free use of new information and communication technologies and the Internet to improve the quality of learning, vocational training and access to employment;
(v) remove barriers impeding the participation of people with disabilities in social life and, in particular, in working life, and prevent the setting up of new barriers through the promotion of design for all;

(vi) ensure the transposition and implementation of the Directive on establishing a general framework for equal treatment in employment and occupation before the deadlines agreed;

(vii) reflect on the need for further measures to promote the employment and social integration of people with disabilities into society;

(viii) consider the possibility of taking measures at national and European level, consistent with the objectives of the European Employment Strategy, to promote the employment of people with disabilities;

(ix) mainstream disability issues when drafting future national action plans relating to social exclusion and poverty;

(x) continue the exchange of information and experience at European level with regard to these issues, with the participation, as appropriate, of the European Union bodies and networks with relevant experience in this area;

(xi) collect statistical material on the situation of people with disabilities, paying particular attention to gender specific data, including on the development of services and benefits for this group;

(xii) support the work of the EU Group of High Level Officials on Disability Questions;

(xiii) reinforce the mainstreaming of the disability perspective into all relevant policies at the stages of policy formulation, implementation, monitoring and evaluation;

(xiv) pay due attention to issues of concern to women with disabilities when adopting, designing and evaluating policies for people with disabilities so as to secure equal treatment for women.

ENCOURAGES THE SOCIAL PARTNERS:

(xv) in the spirit of their Declaration of 20 January 2003 entitled 'Promoting equal opportunities and access to employment for people with disabilities' to promote the integration of people with disabilities, in particular on the mainstream labor market, through their actions and their collective agreements at all the relevant levels of social dialogue.[74]

European Union Disability Strategy

All States maintain disability definitions that are more or less restrictive in social policy.[75] The main idea motivating the use of a restrictive definition was that the potential cost for employers of complying with disability law had to be controlled by limiting the size of the protected group. The European Union social model is one of extensive employee rights. Most European Union States accord employees an extensive set of rights against the employer after a minimum period of employment. These rights include the right to sick pay and paid parental leave, various protections in circumstances of individual and mass redundancy, and protection against unfair dismissal. In some States, limited rights to request part-time work have been introduced. These rights can be exercised by any employee who is in a relevant situation. Several States provide financial support to employers to pay for accommodations for disabled employees, which serve to facilitate acceptance of anti-discrimination legislation by employers.

Council Directive 2000/78/EC on Establishing a General Framework for Equal Treatment in Employment and Occupation is intended to implement an 'individual merit' approach to equality lies at the 'equality as fairness' end of the spectrum, and does not require Member States to introduce measures to achieve equality of results. An 'individual merit' approach is consistent with a broad definition of disability. Some rights to accommodation may be encompassed within the general regime of employee rights. The general regime of employee rights differs across Member States, as does the availability of public funding for costly accommodations. The Directive allows that norms as to reasonable accommodation may vary across Member States in the light of each State's social policy. In terms of the 'radical equality of opportunity', States' policies indicate that there is the creation of positive duties on employers to promote equality. However, these duties are enforced through the activities of authorities and commissions charged with promoting equality, rather than through the creation of individual rights of litigation. In several States, duties to promote equality coexist with individual rights to litigate. The Directive does not contain explicit provisions creating positive duties to promote equality, but it does urge Member States to step in this direction through the promotion of social dialogue and dialogue with non-governmental organisations. It can be seen as a measure that does not rely entirely on individual litigation for its effectiveness. Its value might come from its contribution to the framing and visibility of particular issues in social policy as well as from the strict requirements of transposition. Anti-discrimination law provides an alternative set of principles through which the principles and assumptions governing policies towards disabled people can be opened up for fresh debate.

There was initially a lack of mutual recognition of national decisions on disability and the impact of this on disabled people moving within the Union. Free movement in the European Union is governed by two main sets of provisions, namely provisions on the right to take up residence in another State and be treated without discrimination on grounds of nationality, and provisions on the exportability of certain social security benefits. One concept is based on non-discrimination, whereby a European Union citizen is treated as a host State national wherever he is resident. On this concept, there would be free movement for European Union citizens if they could take up residence wherever they chose and claim benefits as if they had always lived where they now resided, with periods of residence in other States treated as residence in the host State, such that events which occurred in other States are treated as having occurred in the host State. The legislation of Member States guarantees different and unequal social security advantages, and under the non-discrimination concept, people would find that, when they moved between the States, they would encounter different levels of social provision, along with different organisational structures, mixes of cash and benefits in kind, so that the mover can expect to be better off in some ways and worse off in others. The other concept of free movement, from which exportability is derived, is based on security of property rather than non-discrimination, that is the protection of rights derived from having contributed to social security. Contributions are seen as giving the mover a property right which can be made private, in the sense of being attached to the person and moving with him, rather than having to be exercised in a particular social setting. If a person takes out an insurance contract with a private company, the scope of the contract should not be bounded territorially, and with the development of European Union as a unified economic space, territorial boundaries in private insurance coverage are increasingly being eliminated. In terms of the rights of residence, the current position in European Union law is that the right of residence is broadly operational for workers, who have the right to take up residence in any State where they obtain work, and must be treated without discrimination in the allocation of social benefits and advantages in the host State, as established in Regulation EEC N° 1612/68. Disabled people who are unable to work are excluded from the personal coverage of these provisions, although they may utilize the provisions on family unification. For non-workers, the right to take up residence in another Member State is highly constrained. Under Directive EC 90/364, a State may refuse residence to a non-working migrant who does not have sufficient resources to ensure that he will not be a burden on the host State's social assistance system.

States differ in the extent to which they aim to identify medical causes of a person's problems in the work environment. If governments take the view that their own assessment system is best tailored to achieve legitimacy in their State, then some degree of 'administrative nationalism' is inevitable. It is well-established that the pattern of receipt of work incapacity benefits has been strongly influenced by labor market conditions. Different States have adopted different approaches to the permeable boundary between incapacity, unemployment, early retirement and old age pension receipt. Some States have maintained a high normal retirement age with a high rate of incapacity benefit awards for older workers, while others have permitted more early retirement, with or without medical indications. These labor market policy decisions are also reflected in differences in the way labor market conditions are 'modelled' in the disability assessment process, and differences in the way that education, skills and other social factors influence the assessment. However, it is unlikely that free movement for disabled people will be achieved without greater convergence of economic conditions generally, and social provisions in particular, across the Member States.[76]

A society open and accessible to all is the goal of the European Union Disability Strategy. The barriers need to be identified and removed. This approach has been stimulated by the United Nations Standard Rules on Equalization of Opportunities for Persons with Disabilities. The Commission's major goal in the years to come will be to boost equal opportunities for people with disabilities. In this way a lasting dynamic will be created for the full inclusion of people with disabilities into society while shaping the European Union social construct in such a way that it will provide real equality of opportunities. Most actions in the field of disability are principally a matter of Member State responsibility and most effectively dealt with at national level. Therefore, the Commission's strategic goal is to be achieved by three complementary and mutually supportive operational objectives, making full use of the Commission's ability to act so as to maximize the European Union contribution. These operational objectives are:

1. Achieving full application of the Equal Treatment in Employment and Occupation Directive (2000/78/EC), and launching the debate on the future strategy to combat discrimination: The Commission will monitor the transposition

of the legislative provisions on discrimination in the Member States and in the acceding countries within the deadlines agreed by the Council. The Directive is set to become a major element in achieving equality of opportunities for people with disabilities. As such, the Directive will also challenge the misconception that disability is equal to inability or lack of ability, and over time, if applied properly, should therefore contribute towards removing the prejudice, fear and ignorance which surrounds disability.

2. Successful mainstreaming of disability issues in relevant Community policies and existing processes: Modern developments in disability policies show an increasing tendency towards mainstreaming to better incorporate the rights of people with disabilities and to promote equal opportunities for people with disabilities. The mainstreaming strategy implies the integration of the disability perspective into every stage of policy processes, from design and implementation to monitoring and evaluation, with a view to promoting equal opportunities for people with disabilities. In parallel to mainstreaming disability, persistent inequalities require the implementation of specific actions in favour of people with disabilities. Even if considerable progress has been made regarding the situation of people with disabilities, much remains to be done and renewed efforts are needed. As employment remains the primary and most effective way of creating lasting improvements for people with disabilities and of achieving their full social inclusion, special attention will be given to the mainstreaming of disability issues in employment related policies, especially in education and lifelong learning, using all means through which the Commission has the possibility to act.

3. Accessibility for All: In terms of improving 'Accessibility for all', mainstreaming should focus in particular on the area of accessibility and should be clearly linked with the principle of Design For All. Accessibility to goods, services and the built environment is a central issue for people with disabilities and is also of concern to all European Union citizens. The Commission intends to promote the elaboration of European Union technical standards, standardization documents and other more general guidelines giving technical expression to the concept of 'Accessibility for all', which is crucial for the further integration of people with disabilities into the economy and society. It will also encourage efforts to raise awareness among standardization stakeholders on the concept of 'Accessibility for all' and the corresponding market opportunities. Equipping people with disabilities with all available knowledge and competencies is a key element for improving access to employment, combating exclusion and improving social cohesion.[77]

The goal of the Action Plan is to mainstream disability issues into relevant Community policies and develop concrete actions in crucial areas to enhance the integration of people with disabilities. The Commission proposes to reinforce the involvement of stakeholders and key players in the policy dialogue in order to bring about far reaching and lasting changes within the economy and society as a whole. The European Union's long-standing commitment towards its disabled citizens goes hand in hand with a new approach to disability. From seeing people with disabilities as the passive recipients of compensation, society has come to recognize their legitimate demands for equal rights and to realize that participation relates directly to insertion. Contributing to shaping society in a fully inclusive way is therefore the overall European Union objective. The fight against discrimination and the promotion of the participation of people with disabilities into the economy and society play a fundamental role. In the context of rapid economic and social restructuring, the Commission is particularly committed to making full use of voluntary cooperation methods that provide for adequate participation of all stakeholders, Member States, social partners, civil society in an open method of coordination in the areas of employment, social inclusion and lifelong learning, which are crucial to people with disabilities and where common objectives can be translated into national policies and good practices. In order to enhance respect for diversity through individual rights, recognizing and protecting the rights of people with disabilities is at the core of European Union actions.

In making the environment more accessible through elimination of barriers, the European Union sees disability as a social construct. The European Union social model of disability stresses the environmental barriers in society which prevent the full participation of people with disabilities in society. These barriers must be removed on the basis of the Commission communication of May 2000 'Towards a barrier free European Union for people with disabilities' which has important implications for the way in which policies and law in relation to disability are now developed. Accessibility and mobility issues are now dealt with in the light of equal opportunities and the right to participate. In particular, it has become crucial to ensure the removal of technical and legal barriers to the effective participation of people with disabilities in the knowledge-based economy and society to empower them to tap the information society potential. As employment remains the most critical factor for social inclusion, the first phase of implementation of the European Union Disability Action Plan focuses on creating the conditions necessary to promote the employment of people with disabilities, while making the mainstream labor market more accessible to them across the enlarged Union. Accordingly, it concentrates on four concrete employment-related priority actions: access to, and retention in, employment including the fight against discrimination; lifelong learning to support and increase employability, adaptability, personal development and active citizenship; new technologies to empower people with disabilities and therefore facilitate access to employment; and accessibility to the public built environment to improve participation in the work place and integration into the economy and society.

In terms of the European Union Employment Strategy with regard to structural funds and the modernization of social protection encouraging inclusion through employment, entry into employment is crucial for the integration of people with disabilities in the economy and society at large. Participating in the labor market allows people to earn a living and to participate more fully. It also gives individuals additional dignity and a greater degree of independence. The European Union Employment Strategy is contributing to a general shift in emphasis away from disability-specific programmes towards a more mainstreamed approach. Most Member States' active policies designed to combat massive unemployment have moved towards more personalized policies tailored to addressing the needs of individuals, including those of particularly vulnerable groups such as people with disabilities.

Modern social protection systems are essential to provide adequate support to disabled persons who are unable to get sufficient income from work, and to promote access to employment for those who are excluded from the labor market but have the capacity to earn their living. Thus, greater attention is being paid to the provision of work-related benefit incentives to make work pay and to overcome the effects of 'benefit traps'. Such a shift from long-term dependency on passive welfare benefits to active labor market measures will have a positive effect on the economic situation of the beneficiaries as well as on their self-esteem. It may also improve the structure and quality of public expenditure and contribute to making it more sustainable in the medium-long term. In this respect, the corporate sector plays an important role in promoting better integration, to the benefit of both the companies themselves and disabled employees and customers. Progressive integration strategies are now being developed, companies considering that costs incurred in adaptations to the workplace and to goods and services are by nature transitory. In terms of empowering and enhancing structures in society which sustain participation and the mainstreaming of the disability perspective into relevant sectors of policy, supporting citizens with disabilities to become an effective part of the economy and society as a whole means participation in the mainstream for everyone for whom this is possible and in every area where this is possible, rather than segregation into disability-specific arrangements. Mainstreaming requires well-informed policy-making and wide participation in the policy process to ensure that disabled people, and their diverse needs and experiences, are at the heart of policy-making each time it has an impact, directly or indirectly, on their lives. The issue of inclusion of people with disabilities is to be seen as an issue of concern to the whole of society and which requires the contribution of all, since roughly 15 per cent of the population report either a moderate or severe disability. There is an important untapped potential for the development of economic growth, since roughly 40 per cent of people with disabilities are employed. By eliminating barriers to the labor market, it will be possible to create opportunities.

Further, in terms of promoting the rights of people with disabilities at the United Nations level and through European Community development co-operation, the Commission supports global efforts to secure the full and equal enjoyment of human rights for disabled persons, notably by means of a United Nations Convention to promote and protect the human rights of people with disabilities. Recognizing that international human rights should be tailored to the circumstances faced by people with disabilities, this initiative is in line with the Community rights-based approach to disability. Finally, to strengthen its commitment and raise awareness of disability issues more generally, the European Union decided to adopt 2003 as the European Union Year of People with Disabilities (EYPD). The concept developed by the Commission and the Member States for the European Union Year offered disabled people at national, regional and local level a unique opportunity to bring to the fore issues of concern to them and to contribute to focusing policy priorities and encouraging specific actions. The Year was set up as a people's campaign, built on a strong alliance of nongovernmental organizations representative of people with disabilities, such as the European Union Disability

Forum and disability organizations at national level; public administration commitment; social partners, corporate support and organizations of service providers. The EYPD thus has had the capacity to mobilize European Union society as a whole.[78]

Toward a European Constitution

Towards the end of the twentieth century, it became clear for a large number of European leaders that the European Union required a refoundation and renovation. From an initial agenda that included the distribution of competencies, simplification and the incorporation of the Charter of Fundamental Rights, the Convention on the Future of Europe produced a fully-fledged proposal for a Constitution or Constitutional Treaty for Europe. On 29 October 2004, the Heads of State or Government of the 25 Member States and the three candidate countries signed the Treaty establishing a Constitution for Europe. This will then need to be ratified by all 25 member states of the enlarged Union, in order for it to come into effect, and in order to enable the European Union to ensure the well-being of citizens, the defence of values and interests, and to assume responsibilities as a leading international player, and to fight unemployment and social exclusion more effectively, to promote sustainable economic growth, to respond to the challenges of globalization, to safeguard internal and external security, and to protect the environment.

The European Union has always stated its commitment to human rights and fundamental freedoms and has explicitly confirmed its attachment to fundamental social rights. The Charter of Fundamental Rights of the European Union, part of the intended Constitution of Europe, has to be seen in the wider context of the European Union's long-lasting commitment to human rights and fundamental freedoms and of its policy in the areas of justice, freedom and security.

The Preamble of the Treaty 2004/C 310/01 establishing a Constitution for Europe states:

> DRAWING INSPIRATION from the cultural, religious and humanist inheritance of Europe, from which have developed the universal values of the inviolable and inalienable rights of the human person, freedom, democracy, equality and the rule of law,
>
> CONVINCED that, while remaining proud of their own national identities and history, the peoples of Europe are determined to transcend their former divisions and, united ever more closely, to forge a common destiny,
>
> CONVINCED that, thus 'United in diversity', Europe offers them the best chance of pursuing, with due regard for the rights of each individual and in awareness of their responsibilities towards future generations and the Earth, the great venture which makes of it a special area of human hope,

DETERMINED to continue the work accomplished within the framework of the Treaties establishing the European Communities and the Treaty on European Union, by ensuring the continuity of the Community *acquis*,

WHO, having exchanged their full powers, found in good and due form. [79]

Article I-1 on the establishment of the Union states:

I-1. 1. Reflecting the will of the citizens and States of Europe to build a common future, this Constitution establishes the European Union, on which the Member States confer competences to attain objectives they have in common. The Union shall coordinate the policies by which the Member States aim to achieve these objectives, and shall exercise in the Community way the competences they confer on it.
2. The Union shall be open to all European States which respect its values and are committed to promoting them together.[80]

Important for disability rights, the Union's values are outlined in Article I-2:

I-2. The Union is founded on the values of respect for human dignity, liberty, democracy, equality, the rule of law and respect for human rights, including the rights of persons belonging to minorities. These values are common to the Member States in a society in which pluralism, non-discrimination, tolerance, justice, solidarity and equality between women and men prevail.[81]

Further, the Union's objectives are outlined in Article I-3:

I-3. 1. The Union's aim is to promote peace, its values and the well-being of its peoples.
2. The Union shall offer its citizens an area of freedom, security and justice without internal frontiers, and an internal market where competition is free and undistorted.
3. The Union shall work for the sustainable development of Europe based on balanced economic growth and price stability, a highly competitive social market economy, aiming at full employment and social progress, and a high level of protection and improvement of the quality of the environment. It shall promote scientific and technological advance.
It shall combat social exclusion and discrimination, and shall promote social justice and protection, equality between women and men, solidarity between generations and protection of the rights of the child.
It shall promote economic, social and territorial cohesion, and solidarity among Member States.
It shall respect its rich cultural and linguistic diversity, and shall ensure that Europe's cultural heritage is safeguarded and enhanced.
4. In its relations with the wider world, the Union shall uphold and promote its values and interests. It shall contribute to peace, security, the sustainable development of the Earth, solidarity and mutual respect among peoples, free and fair trade, eradication of poverty and the protection of human rights, in particular the rights of the child, as well as to the strict observance and the development of

international law, including respect for the principles of the United Nations Charter.

5. The Union shall pursue its objectives by appropriate means commensurate with the competences which are conferred upon it in the Constitution.[82]

Important for disability rights, fundamental freedoms and non-discrimination are upheld in Article I-4:

I-4. 1. The free movement of persons, services, goods and capital, and freedom of establishment shall be guaranteed within and by the Union, in accordance with the Constitution.

2. Within the scope of the Constitution, and without prejudice to any of its specific provisions, any discrimination on grounds of nationality shall be prohibited.[83]

The primacy of Union law is emphasized in Article I-6:

I-6. The Constitution and law adopted by the institutions of the Union in exercising competences conferred on it shall have primacy over the law of the Member States.[84]

Further, relations between the Union and Member States are contained in Article I-5:

I-5. 1. The Union shall respect the equality of Member States before the Constitution as well as their national identities, inherent in their fundamental structures, political and constitutional, inclusive of regional and local self-government. It shall respect their essential State functions, including ensuring the territorial integrity of the State, maintaining law and order and safeguarding national security.

2. Pursuant to the principle of sincere cooperation, the Union and the Member States shall, in full mutual respect, assist each other in carrying out tasks which flow from the Constitution.

The Member States shall take any appropriate measure, general or particular, to ensure fulfillment of the obligations arising out of the Constitution or resulting from the acts of the institutions of the Union.

The Member States shall facilitate the achievement of the Union's tasks and refrain from any measure which could jeopardize the attainment of the Union's objectives.[85]

The Preamble of the Charter of Fundamental Rights, part of the Constitution of Europe, states:

The peoples of Europe, in creating an ever closer union among them, are resolved to share a peaceful future based on common values.

Conscious of its spiritual and moral heritage, the Union is founded on the indivisible, universal values of human dignity, freedom, equality and solidarity; it is based on the principles of democracy and the rule of law. It places the individual at the heart of its activities, by establishing the citizenship of the Union and by creating an area of freedom, security and justice.

The Union contributes to the preservation and to the development of these common values while respecting the diversity of the cultures and traditions of the peoples of Europe as well as the national identities of the Member States and the organization of their public authorities at national, regional and local levels; it seeks to promote balanced and sustainable development and ensures free movement of persons, goods, services and capital, and the freedom of establishment.

To this end, it is necessary to strengthen the protection of fundamental rights in the light of changes in society, social progress and scientific and technological developments by making those rights more visible in a Charter.

This Charter reaffirms, with due regard for the powers and tasks of the Community and the Union and the principle of subsidiarity, the rights as they result, in particular, from the constitutional traditions and international obligations common to the Member States, the Treaty on European Union, the Community Treaties, the European Convention for the Protection of Human Rights and Fundamental Freedoms, the Social Charters adopted by the Community and by the Council of Europe and the case law of the Court of Justice of the European Communities and of the European Court of Human Rights.

Enjoyment of these rights entails responsibilities and duties with regard to other persons, to the human community and to future generations.

The Union therefore recognizes the rights, freedoms and principles set out hereafter.[86]

Equality before the law is contained in Article II-80:

II-80. Everyone is equal before the law.[87]

Important for disability rights, Article II-81 deals with non-discrimination:

II-81. 1. Any discrimination based on any ground such as sex, race, color, ethnic or social origin, genetic features, language, religion or belief, political or any other opinion, membership of a national minority, property, birth, disability, age or sexual orientation shall be prohibited.

2. Within the scope of application of the Treaty establishing the European Community and of the Treaty on European Union, and without prejudice to the special provisions of those Treaties, any discrimination on grounds of nationality shall be prohibited.[88]

Further, Article III-118 states:

III-118. In defining and implementing the policies and activities referred to in this Part, the Union shall aim to combat discrimination based on sex, racial or ethnic origin, religion or belief, disability, age or sexual orientation.[89]

Finally, Article III-124 provides for measures for combating discrimination:

III-124. 1. Without prejudice to the other provisions of the Constitution and within the limits of the powers assigned by it to the Union, a European law or framework law of the Council may establish the measures needed to combat discrimination based on sex, racial or ethnic origin, religion or belief, disability, age or sexual orientation. The Council shall act unanimously after obtaining the consent of the European Parliament.

2. By way of derogation from paragraph 1, European laws or framework laws may establish basic principles for Union incentive measures and define such measures, to support action taken by Member States in order to contribute to the achievement of the objectives referred to in paragraph 1, excluding any harmonisation of their laws and regulations.[90]

Currently, the Member States of the European Union are: Austria, Belgium, Denmark, Finland, France, Germany, Greece, Ireland, Italy, Luxembourg, the Netherlands, Portugal, Spain, Sweden and the United Kingdom, and since 1 May 2004, Cyprus (Greek part), the Czech Republic, Estonia, Hungary, Latvia, Lithuania, Malta, Poland, Slovakia and Slovenia, expanded it from 15 to 25 Member States. The European Union Member States are still looking to formulate a Constitution for Europe. The EU is at a crossroads challenged to adapt the vision of the 'founding fathers' that was first designed for six Member States to a future union of over twenty States. In essence, Europe is now the biggest frontier-free market in the world. The single market removed three types of barriers to free movement, namely physical, technical and fiscal. The four freedoms of the Union, for goods, services, people and capital, have become a reality. Further, the new single currency, the euro was introduced as legal tender on 1 January 1999, and replaced the currencies of those Member States in agreement on 1 January 2002. The criteria used for a nation to secure membership in the ever-growing European Union are: (1) democratic institutions and the rule of law, with respect for human rights and minorities within the borders; (2) a functioning market economy capable of competing within the union's single market; and (3) the acceptance of obligations of membership, signing onto the union's body of rules. The latter is perhaps the most important criterion for equal rights and their enforcement.

Conclusion

It is important that this ability and equality be achieved in securing access to jobs, which are commensurate with skill levels. Some groups, namely the disabled, are still lagging behind due to horizontal segregation, and vertical segregation, with difficulty acceding to higher positions in the occupational hierarchy. The system has failed to reward skills, and even provides guises for discrimination. The demographic changes on the horizon will bring about a further need for qualified workers. However, some remain under-utilized, considered as reserve labor. This attitude is a barrier to progressive legislation. Although European laws have gone a long way to improving the plight of many in the European Union, in reality, some have yet to enjoy the equality they are entitled to in theory. The European Union is a political structure, which emerged out of a general act of will of heterogeneous States. It is ultimately dependent on statements of general principle. Therefore, Community law is the motor to enable the European Union to move toward its ultimate aim, the 'ever closer union'. The European Union's action programme has several main components, namely a fair deal in rights at work involving equality legislation and court cases; better opportunities to earn a living involving the promotion of jobs, education and entrepreneurship; getting minorities in positions of power involving equal opportunities in employment; and community-wide networks involving training, expanding subjects in school and reinforcing a positive image of those with a disability.[91] Relations between the institutions of the European Union are based on partnership, cooperation and mutual dependence. All Member States within the European Union have legislation prohibiting direct or indirect pay discrimination on the grounds of disability. The concern is to enhance the social, economic and cultural welfare of all citizens in an atmosphere of peace. This, thereby, advances the cause for disability equality in stamping out discrimination of any kind, including disability discrimination, through the effective use of laws and the courts.

Notes

[1]   Nicoll, William and Salmon, Trevor, *Understanding the New European Community*, Prentice Hall, Exeter, 1994, p.11.

[2]   Daltrop, Anne (1982), *Political Realities, Politics and the European Community*, Longman, London, 1982, p.2.

[3]   Nicoll, William and Salmon, Trevor, *Understanding the New European Community*, Prentice Hall, Exeter, 1994, at p.13.

[4]   *Ibid.*, at p.20.

[5]   *Ibid.*, at p.99.

[6]   Daltrop, Anne (1982), *Political Realities, Politics and the European Community*, Longman, London, 1982, p.18.

[7]   Treaty of Rome, at Article 3.

[8]   *Ibid.*, at Article 6(a).

[9]   *Ibid.*, at Article 48.

[10]   *Ibid.*, at Article 119.

[11]   Maastricht Treaty, at Article A.

[12]   *Ibid.*, at Article B.

[13]   Treaty of Amsterdam, at Article 141.

[14]   *Ibid.*, at Article 13.

[15]   *Ibid.*, at Article 39.

[16]   *Ibid.*, at Article 141.

17 *Teuling v. Bredrijfsvereniging* [1987] ECR 2497.
18 Nicoll, William and Salmon, Trevor, *Understanding the New European Community*, Prentice Hall, Exeter, 1994, p.97.
19 *Internationale Handelsgesellschaft* [1970] ECR 1125, [1972] CMLR 255.
20 *Costa v. ENEL* [1964] CMLR 425.
21 European Convention for the Protection of Human Rights and Fundamental Freedoms (ECHR), at the Preamble.
22 *Ibid.*, at Article 1.
23 *Ibid.*, at Article 13.
24 *Ibid.*, at Article 14.
25 *Ibid.*, at Article 17.
26 *Ibid.*, at Article 19.
27 *Ibid.*, at Article 27.
28 *Ibid.*, at Article 32.
29 *Ibid.*, at Article 3.
30 *Ibid.*, at Article 34.
31 *Ibid.*, at Article 36.
32 *Ibid.*, at Article 35.
33 *Ibid.*, at Article 37.
34 *Ibid.*, at Article 38.
35 *Ibid.*, at Article 39.
36 *Ibid.*, at Article 40.
37 *Ibid.*, at Article 41.
38 *Ibid.*, at Article 44.
39 *Ibid.*, at Article 45.
40 *Ibid.*, at Article 46.
41 *Ibid.*, at Article 47.
42 European Convention for the Protection of Human Rights and Fundamental Freedoms as amended by Protocol No. 12, at the Preamble.
43 *Ibid.*, at Article 1.
44 European Social Charter, 1961, at the Preamble.
45 European Social Charter (revised), 1996, at the Preamble.
46 *Ibid.*, at Article E.
47 *Ibid.*, at Part I.
48 *Ibid*, at Part II, Article 1.
49 *Ibid.*, at Article 4.
50 *Ibid.*, at Article 24.
51 *Ibid.*, at Article 22.
52 Council Resolution on Equal Employment Opportunities for People with Disabilities, at the Preamble.
53 Council Resolution on Equal Employment Opportunities for People with Disabilities.
54 Council Directive 2000/78/EC Establishing a General Framework for Equal Treatment in Employment and Occupation, at the Preamble.
55 *Ibid.*, at Article 1.
56 *Ibid.*, at Article 2.
57 *Ibid.*, at Article 3.
58 *Ibid.*, at Article 4.
59 *Ibid.*, at Article 5.
60 *Ibid.*, at Article 7.

[61] *Ibid.*, at Article 8.
[62] *Ibid.*, at Article 9.
[63] *Ibid.*, at Article 10.
[64] *Ibid.*, at Article 11.
[65] *Ibid.*, at Article 16.
[66] *Ibid.*, at Article 17.
[67] *Ibid.*, at Article 18.
[68] Council Decision 2000/750/EC of 27 November 2000 establishing a Community Action Program to Combat Discrimination (2001 to 2006) [OJ L 303, 02/12/2000 P. 0023 – 0028], at the Preamble.
[69] *Ibid.*, at Article 1.
[70] *Ibid.*, at Article 2.
[71] *Ibid.*, at Article 3.
[72] *Ibid.*, at Article 4.
[73] Council Resolution on Promoting the Employment and Social Integration of People with Disabilities, at the Preamble.
[74] Council Resolution on Promoting the Employment and Social Integration of People with Disabilities.
[75] European Commission, Directorate-General for Employment and Social Affairs, *Definition of Disability in Europe, A Comparative Analysis, Social Security and Social Integration*, 2002.
[76] *Ibid.*
[77] Commission of the European Communities, Communication from the Commission to the Council, the European Parliament, the European Economic and Social Committee, and the Committee of the Regions, *Equal Opportunities for People with Disabilities: A European Action Plan,* Brussels, 2003.
[78] *Ibid.*
[79] Treaty establishing a Constitution for Europe, at the Preamble.
[80] *Ibid.*, at Article I-1.
[81] *Ibid.*, at Article I-2.
[82] *Ibid.*, at Article I-3.
[83] *Ibid.*, at Article I-4.
[84] *Ibid.*, at Article I-6.
[85] *Ibid.*, at Article I-5.
[86] Treaty establishing a Constitution for Europe, the Charter of Fundamental Rights, at the Preamble.
[87] *Ibid.*, at Article II-20.
[88] *Ibid.*, at Article II-21.
[89] *Ibid.*, at Article III-118.
[90] *Ibid.*, at Article III-124.
[91] Commission of the European Communities, *Equal Opportunity for Women and Men*, Brussels, p.5.

References

Commission of the European Communities, Communication from the Commission to the Council, the European Parliament, the European Economic and Social Committee and the Committee of the Regions, *Equal Opportunities for People with Disabilities: A European Action Plan,* Brussels, 2003.

Commission of the European Communities (1993), *Equal Opportunities for Women in the Community,* Brussels.

Costa v. ENEL [1964] CMLR 425.

Council Decision 2000/750/EC of 27 November 2000 establishing a Community Action Program to Combat Discrimination (2001 to 2006) [OJ L 303, 02/12/2000 P. 0023 – 0028].

Council Directive 2000/78/EC Establishing a General Framework for Equal Treatment in Employment and Occupation.

Council Resolution of 15 July 2003 on Promoting the Employment and Social Integration of People with Disabilities, (2003/C 175/01).

Council Resolution of 17 June 1999 on Equal Employment Opportunities for People with Disabilities (1999/C 186/02).

Daltrop, Anne (1982), *Political Realities, Politics and the European Community,* Longman, London.

European Commission, Directorate-General for Employment and Social Affairs, *Definition of Disability in Europe, A Comparative Analysis, Social Security and Social Integration,* 2002.

European Convention for the Protection of Human Rights and Fundamental Freedoms.

European Convention for the Protection of Human Rights and Fundamental Freedoms as amended by Protocol No. 12.

European Social Charter.

European Social Charter (revised).

Internationale Handelsgesellschaft, [1970] ECR 1125, [1972] CMLR 255.

Maastricht Treaty.

Nicoll, William and Salmon, Trevor (1994), *Understanding the New European Community,* Prentice Hall, Exeter.

Teuling v. Bredrijfsvereniging [1987] ECR 2497.

Treaty establishing a Constitution for Europe.

Treaty of Amsterdam.

Treaty of Paris.

Treaty of Rome.

Chapter 10

Conclusion to This Ability

A deep embedded patriarchal authority is still keeping society on the designated track, as *de jure* discrimination has given way to *de facto* discrimination, and in essence, inequality, once obvious and accepted, is now hidden and protected in a most dangerous way. Since within society there is an a-priori assumption of freedom and impartiality, the burden is high on the attackers of this universal opinion. Human inequality both encompasses disability inequality and conceals it, and although other types of discrimination exist apart from disability inequality, discrimination which is so blatant and open as to focus on one's physical and mental incapacities is most persistent and threatening to society. Therefore, seeking out disability inequality and bringing it to the forefront of microscopic debate can only serve to advance all quests for equality toward this ability.

Both legislation and the court system have made inroads into disability inequality. It is important to have adequate legislation to influence conduct and outcomes, as well as an appropriate legal system to achieve favorable and enforceable results. By cooperating and learning from other similarly disadvantaged groups in the fight for equality of opportunity, more advances can be made in the fight for disability equality. We will never totally correct the injustices of the past or of the present. However, with a greater appreciation of disability, as well as a better understanding of the importance of adequate legislation, future endeavors in the field will help to improve the situation, but for all people.

Countries around the world have made important progress in the development of equal rights. Equality rights legislation and court challenges are required, in order to improve the situation of all in the workplace. The desire is for equal social rights for all. Therefore, the law needs to be enforced by way of the courts to achieve greater equality in an effort to modify historical attitudes, so that nations conform to certain standards. There should be real freedom to choose one's amount of participation in the work force, in the pursuit of flexibility as to a just remuneration and access to employment.

Further, taking into account the fact that continuing inequalities and noticeable progress coexist, rethinking employment policies is necessary in order to integrate the disability perspective, not only to address any negative implications of current patterns of work and employment, but also to draw attention to a wider range of opportunities. Governments and other actors need to promote an active and visible policy of mainstreaming an 'Ability' perspective into all policies and programs.

The central importance of equality legislation in order to bring about change is evident and indeed critical. Our very rights as human beings emanate from the word of the law and the interpretation given by the highest courts in the

land. Therefore, it is imperative that the struggle for disability equality encompass
the legal system. The concept of total equality has never truly existed, nor was it
ever meant to be anything more than empty promises of change. Absolute equality
is not sought in this book, nor is it realistic. However, in a feeling of mutual respect
for individual differences, a better equality among the humans is possible and
desirable through society's laws and legal institutions.

The keys to the future are the implementation and development of the
law, the deepening in understanding of specific legal issues relating to employment
discrimination, and the raising of the level of awareness of legal rights and
obligations. In addition, a continuing exchange of experience and expertise needs
to occur on the international front for mutual benefit among all groups in order to
best serve the fight for disability equality. We must all strive to promote and
improve the situation of all humans through networks of awareness, in the raising
of initiatives, the dissemination of information and the provision of support for
equality. In addition, there needs to be a full employment policy for the integration
of all humans into the labor market, the reduction of barriers to access and
participation in employment, the improvement in the quality of employment
through education, training and management of resources, and the improvement in
the status of all races in society for a change of attitudes and a lasting progress.[1]

Further, we must learn from other groups' experiences in the fight for
equality. As such, like the civil rights' movement and the women's liberation
movement, in examining legislation, we should take into account the disability
movement, and specifically its advancements in disability rights and tolerance for
those with a disability. Therefore, in the struggle to secure equal rights for all, the
consultation process must include input from other groups for strategic purposes in
order to strengthen the cause. The process must be one of inclusion not exclusion.

It is realistic to say that inequality in general exists, but especially
inequality of opportunity within the labor force. This is to be expected, since not all
humans have occupied a major role in the employment sphere. In addition to this,
laws have been enacted and courts have enforced them in a traditionally white
male non-disability dominant way. However, all humans too need to be a rallying
symbol of political and economic force, so that equality can become a reality. The
impact of equality legislation will depend on the legislative provisions as well as
the effectiveness of the legislation's enforcement.

The full and equal enjoyment of all human rights and fundamental
freedoms should be a priority for all and is essential for the advancement of all.
Equal rights are explicitly mentioned in the Preamble to the Charter of the United
Nations, and all the major international human rights instruments include or should
include disability as one of the grounds upon which States may not discriminate.
Unless the human rights of all, as defined by international human rights
instruments, are fully recognized and effectively protected, applied, implemented
and enforced in national law as well as in national practice in family, civil, penal,
labor and commercial codes and administrative rules and regulations, they will
exist in name only.[2]

It is evident that we are moving in the right direction, since some change
has taken place. However, further change is necessary and plausible. Only by

working on the very thing that controls and defines all of our lives, the law, can further progress be made.

Once again, the memorable words of the Rev. Martin Luther King Jr. in his struggle for civil rights are most relevant today in the struggle for equality for those with a disability in achieving equal rights toward this ability recognition for all:

> I have a dream that one day every valley shall be exalted, every hill and mountain shall be made low, the rough places shall be made plain, and the crooked places shall be made straight and the glory of the Lord will be revealed and all flesh shall see it together. This is our hope .... And when we allow freedom to ring, when we let it ring from every village and hamlet, from every state and city, we will be able to speed up that day when all of God's children ... will be able to join hands and to sing in the words of the old Negro spiritual, 'Free at last, free at last; thank God Almighty, we are free at last'.[3]

Notes

[1] Commission of the European Communities, *Promotion of Positive Action*, Brussels, p.4.
[2] United Nations, *Beijing Declaration and Platform for Action*.
[3] King Jr., Martin Luther, *March on Washington*, 1963.

References

Commission of the European Communities, *Promotion of Positive Action*, Brussels.
King Jr., Martin Luther (1963), *March on Washington*.
United Nations, *Beijing Declaration and Platform for Action*.

Bibliography

African Charter on Human and Peoples' Rights.

African Court on Human and Peoples' Rights.

Air Carrier Access Act.

American Convention on Human Rights.

American Declaration of the Rights and Duties of Man.

American Federation of State, County and Municipal Employees v. Washington, 770 F.2d. 1401 (1985).

American Nurses Association v. State of Illinois, 783 F.2d. 716 (1985).

Americans with Disabilities Act.

Architectural Barriers Act.

Axworthy, Lloyd (1988), 'Free Trade, The Costs for Canada', in A.R. Riggs and Tom Velk, *Canadian-American Free Trade: (The Sequel) Historical, Political and Economic Dimensions*, The Institute for Research on Public Policy, Montreal.

Basi v. Canadian National Railway (1984), 9 CHRR 4. D/5029 (CHRTribunal).

Bill of Rights Act, New Zealand, 1990.

Blake v. Ministry of Correctional Services and Mimico Correctional Institute (1984), 5 CHRR D/2417 (Ontario).

Board of Trustees of Keene State College v. Sweeney, 439 US 24 (1978).

Brecher, Irving (1987), 'The Free Trade Initiative, On Course or Off', in A. R. Riggs and Tom Velk, *Canadian-American Free Trade: Historical, Political and Economic Dimensions*, The Institute for Research in Public Policy, Montreal.

Brennan v. City Stores, 479 F.2d. 235 (1973).

British North America Act, Canada, 1867.

Canada Employment Equity Act, 1995.

Campbell, Bruce (1993), *Free Trade, Destroyer of Jobs*, Canadian Centre for Policy Alternatives, Ottawa.

Canada–United States Free Trade Agreement.

Canadian Advisory Council on the Status of Women (1992), *Feminist Guide to the Canadian Constitution*, Ottawa.

Canadian Bill of Rights, 1960.

Canadian Constitution, 1982.

Canadian Constitution, Canadian Charter of Rights and Freedoms, 1982.

Canadian Human Rights Act, 1978.

Cassin, René (1969), *From the Ten Commandments to the Rights of Man*, France.

Charter of the Organization of African Unity.

Civil Rights Act, United States, 1964.

Civil Rights of Institutionalized Persons Act.

Coleman, Frank (1977), *Hobbes and America*, University of Toronto, Toronto.

Constitución Política de los Estados Unidos Mexicanos.

Commission for Racial Equality (2002), *Code of Practice on the Duty to Promote Race Equality*, UK.

Commission of the European Communities (1993), *Equal Opportunities for Women in the Community*, Brussels.

Commission of the European Communities, Communication from the Commission to the Council, the European Parliament, the European Economic and Social Committee and the Committee of the Regions, *Equal Opportunities for People with Disabilities: A European Action Plan,* Brussels, 2003.

Commission of the European Communities, *Promotion of Positive Action*, Brussels.

Constitution of South Africa.

Corning Glass Works v. Brennan, 417 US 188 (1974).

Costa v. ENEL [1964] CMLR 425.

Council Decision 2000/750/EC of 27 November 2000 establishing a Community Action Program to Combat Discrimination (2001 to 2006) [OJ L 303, 02/12/2000 P. 0023 – 0028].

Council Directive 2000/78/EC Establishing a General Framework for Equal Treatment in Employment and Occupation.

Council Resolution of 15 July 2003 on Promoting the Employment and Social Integration of People with Disabilities (2003/C 175/01).

Council Resolution of 17 June 1999 on Equal Employment Opportunities for People with Disabilities (1999/C 186/02).

Cox, Archibald (1967), *Civil Rights, The Constitution and the Court*, Harvard University Press, Cambridge.

Cox, Archibald (1976), *The Role of the Supreme Court in American Government*, New York: Oxford University Press, New York.

d'Aquino, Thomas (1987), 'Truck and Trade with the Yankees, The Case for a Canada-U.S. Comprehensive Trade Agreement', in A.R. Riggs and Tom Velk, *Canadian-American Free Trade: Historical, Political and Economic Dimensions*, The Institute for Research on Public Policy, Montreal.

Daltrop, Anne (1982), *Political Realities, Politics and the European Community*, Longman, London.

Davis v. Passman, 442 US 228 (1979).

Declaration of Independence, United States, 1776.

Ely, J. (1980), *Democracy and Distrust*, Harvard University Press, Cambridge.

Equal Pay Act, United States, 1963.

Disability Bill, Ireland.

Disability Discrimination Act, Australia, 1992.

Disability Discrimination Act, UK.

Disability Rights Commission Act, UK.

Easterbrook, W.T. and Aitken, Hugh (1976), *Canadian Economic History*, Macmillan, Toronto.

Economic Commission for Africa (2002), *Economic Report on Africa*.

Employment Contracts Act, New Zealand.

Employment Equality Act, Ireland.

Employment Equity Act, South Africa.

Employment Rights Act, UK.

Equal Opportunities Commission, *Code of Practice on Equal Pay*, UK.

Equal Status Act, Ireland.

European Commission, Directorate-General for Employment and Social Affairs, *Definition of Disability in Europe, A Comparative Analysis, Social Security and Social Integration*, 2002.

European Convention for the Protection of Human Rights and Fundamental Freedoms.

European Convention for the Protection of Human Rights and Fundamental Freedoms as amended by Protocol No. 12.

European Social Charter.

European Social Charter (revised).

European Union Commission, Directorate-General for Employment and Social Affairs, *Definition of Disability in Europe, A Comparative Analysis, Social Security and Social Integration*, 2002.

European Union Commission, Directorate-General for Employment and Social Affairs (2002), *Definition of Disability in Europe, A Comparative Analysis, Social Security and Social Integration*.

Fair Housing Act.

Federal Task Force on Disability Issues, *Equal Citizenship for Canadians with Disabilities: The Will to Act*, 1996.

Federalist Papers, United States, 1787-1788.

Ford v. Quebec (Attorney General), [1988] 2 SCR 712.

Fried, Morton (1967), *The Evolution of Political Society*, Random House, New York.

Frontiero v. Richardson, 411 US 677 (1973).

Fry, Earl (1987), 'Trends in Canada-U.S. Free Trade Discussions', in A. R. Riggs and Tom Welk, *Canadian-American Free Trade: Historical, Political and Economic Dimensions*, The Institute for Research in Public Policy, Montreal.

General Agreement on Tariffs and Trade.

Government of Australia, *Australia's Beijing Plus Five Action Plan 2001~2005*.

Government of Canada (1993), *The North American Free Trade Agreement At A Glance*, Ottawa.

Government of Canada (2002), *NAFTA at Eight*, Ottawa.

Griffin Cohen, Marjorie (1987), *Free Trade and the Future of Women's Work, Manufacturing and Service Industries*, Garamond Press, Toronto.

Griggs v. Duke Power Co., 401 US 424 (1971).

Habermas, Jurgen (1998), *Between Facts and Norms*, MIT Press, Massachusetts.

Hamelin, Jean (1976), *Histoire du Québec*, Edisem, St. Hyacinthe.

Harris, Richard (1988), 'Some Observations on the Canada-U.S. Free Trade Deal', in A.R. Riggs and Tom Velk, *Canadian-American Free Trade: (The Sequel) Historical, Political and Economic Dimensions*, The Institute for Research on Public Policy, Montreal.

Health and Disability Commissioner Act 1994 and Code of Health & Disability Services Consumers' Rights, New Zealand.

Human Rights Act, New Zealand.

Human Rights Act, UK.

Hurtig, Mel (1991), *The Betrayal of Canada*, Stoddart Publishing, Toronto.

Individuals with Disabilities Education Act.

Inter-American Democratic Charter.

Interim Constitution of South Africa, Schedule 4.

Internationale Handelsgesellschaft, [1970] ECR 1125, [1972] CMLR 255.

King Jr., Dr. Martin Luther (1963), *March on Washington*.

Labor Canada (1986), *Equal Pay for Work of Equal Value*, Ottawa.

Laun, Louis (1987), 'U.S.-Canada Free Trade Negotiations: Historical Opportunities', in A.R. Riggs and Tom Velk, *Canadian-American Free Trade: Historical, Political and Economic Dimensions*, The Institute for Research in Public Policy, Montreal.

Layton, Robert (1987), 'Why Canada Needs Free Trade', in A. R. Riggs and Tom Velk, *Canadian-American Free Trade: Historical, Political and Economic Dimensions*, The Institute for Research in Public Policy, Montreal.

Ley del Seguro Social, Mexico.

Ley Federal de Trabajo, Mexico.

Lipsey, Richard (1987), 'Canada's Trade Options', in A. R. Riggs and Tom Velk, *Canadian-American Free Trade: Historical, Political and Economic Dimensions*, The Institute for Research in Public Policy, Montreal.

Maastricht Treaty.

Magna Carta, 1215.

Mandel, Michael (1989), *The Charter of Rights and the Legalization of Politics in Canada*, Wall & Thompson, Toronto.

Marbury v. Madison, 1 Cranch 137 (1803).

McCullough v. Maryland, 4 Wheaton 415 (1819).

McDonnell Douglas Corp. v. Green, 411 US 792 (1973).

McPhail, Brenda (1985), *NAFTA Now*, University Press of America, Lanham.

Merrett, Christopher (1996), *Free Trade, Neither Free Nor About Trade*, Black Rose Books, New York.

Mexican Investment Board (1994), *Mexico Your Partner for Growth, Regulatory Reform and Competition Policy, Setting the Incentives for an Efficient Economy*, Mexico.

Miles, M., *History of Educational & Social Responses to Disability in Anglophone Eastern & Southern Africa*, 2001.

Ministry of Health, New Zealand, Making a World of Difference, Whakanui Oranga, Minister for Disability Issues, 2001.

Murphy v. Miller Brewer Co., 307 F.Supp. 829 (1969).

Nader, Ralph (1993), *The Case Against Free Trade*, Earth Island Press, San Francisco.

National Voter Registration Act.

Neufeld, E.P. (1987), 'Financial and Economic Dimensions of Free Trade', in A.R. Riggs and Tom Velk, *Canadian-American Free Trade: Historical, Political and Economic Dimensions*, The Institute for Research on Public Policy, Montreal.

Nicoll, William and Salmon, Trevor (1994), *Understanding the New European Community*, Prentice Hall, Exeter.

North American Agreement on Labor Cooperation.

North American Free Trade Agreement.

North, Arthur (1964), *The Supreme Court, Judicial Process and Judicial Politics*, Appleton Century Crofts, New York.

Ontario Human Rights Commission v. Simpsons-Sears Ltd., [1985] SCR 536.

Pope John Paul II (1981), *Laborem Exercens*, Rome.

Pope John XXIII (1963), *Pacem in Terris*, Rome.

Promotion of Equality and Prevention of Unfair Discrimination Act, South Africa, South Africa, 2000.

Protocol on the Rights of Women in Africa.

Protocol to the African Charter on Human and Peoples' Rights on the Establishment of an

Race Relations Act (Statutory Duties) Orders, UK.

Race Relations Act, New Zealand.

Race Relations Act, UK.

Racial Discrimination Act, Australia.

Raynauld, Andre (1987), 'Looking Outward Again', in A.R. Riggs and Tom Velk, *Canadian-American Free Trade: Historical, Political and Economic Dimensions*, The Institute for Research on Public Policy, Montreal.

Regina v. Oakes, [1986] 1 S.C.R. 103.

Rehabilitation Act.

San Antonio Independent School Division v. Rodriguez, 411 US 1 (1973).

Sex Discrimination Act, Australia.

Sex Discrimination Act, UK.

Shakes v. Rex Pak Ltd. (1982), 3 CHRR D/1001.

Soldatos, P (1988), 'Canada's Foreign Policy in Search of a Fourth Option: Continuity and Change in Orientation Towards the U.S.', in A.R. Riggs and Tom Velk, *Canadian-American Free Trade: (The Sequel) Historical, Political and Economic Dimensions*, The Institute for Research on Public Policy, Montreal.

South Africa, *White Paper on Integrated National Disability Strategy*, 1997.

Spaulding v. University of Washington, 740 F.2d. 686 (1984).

Statutes of Canada, 1869.

Statistics South Africa.

Statute of the Inter-American Court on Human Rights.

Stone, Frank (1987), 'Removing Barriers to Canada', in A.R. Riggs and Tom Velk, *Canadian-American Free Trade: Historical, Political and Economic Dimensions*, The Institute for Research on Public Policy, Montreal.

Telecommunications Act.

Teuling v. Bredrijfsvereniging [1987] ECR 2497.

Treaty establishing a Constitution for Europe.

Treaty of Amsterdam.

Treaty of Paris.

Treaty of Rome.

Treaty of Waitangi, New Zealand,

U.S. Department of Justice, Civil Rights Division, *Disability Rights Section, A Guide to Disability Rights Laws*, 2004.

U.S. Equal Employment Opportunity Commission, U.S. Department of Justice Civil Rights Division, *The Americans with Disabilities Act*.

United Nations Development Program (1994), *Human Development Report*, Oxford University Press, Oxford.

United Nations Standard Rules on the Equalization of Opportunities for Persons with Disabilities, Adopted by General Assembly Resolution 48/96.

United Nations, *Beijing Declaration and Platform for Action*.

United Nations, Charter of the United Nations, 1945.

United Nations, Convention on the Elimination of all Forms of Discrimination Against Women, 1979.

United Nations, Declaration on the Rights of Disabled Persons, 1975.

United Nations, Declaration on the Rights of Mentally Retarded Persons, 1971.

United Nations, Discrimination (Employment and Occupation) Convention (ILO No. 111), 1958.

United Nations, Employment Policy Convention (ILO No. 122), 1964.

United Nations, Equal Remuneration Convention (ILO No. 100), 1951.

United Nations, International Convention on the Elimination of All Forms of Racial Discrimination, 1965.

United Nations, International Covenant on Civil and Political Rights, 1966.

United Nations, International Covenant on Economic, Social and Cultural Rights, 1966.

United Nations, Optional Protocol to the Convention on the Elimination of All Forms of Discrimination against Women, 1999.

United Nations, Optional Protocol to the International Covenant on Civil and Political Rights, 1966.

United Nations, Principles for the Protection of Persons with Mental Illness and the Improvement of Mental Health Care, 1991.

United Nations, Statute of the International Court of Justice, 1945.

United Nations, Universal Declaration of Human Rights, 1948.

United Nations, World Program of Action Concerning Disabled Persons.

United States Constitution, 1776.

Universal Declaration of Human Rights, 1948.

Velk, Tom and Riggs, A.R. (1987), 'The Ongoing Debate Over Free Trade', in A.R. Riggs and Tom Velk, *Canadian-American Free Trade: Historical, Political and Economic Dimensions*, The Institute for Research on Public Policy, Montreal.

Voting Accessibility for the Elderly and Handicapped Act.

Vuyiswa McClain, Charlotte, *Democracy & Disability in South Africa: Still Three Nations*.

Watkins, Mel (1989), 'The Political Economy of Growth', in Wallace Clement and Glen Williams, *The New Canadian Political Economy*, McGill-Queen's University Press, Kingston.

Wigle, Randall (1987), 'The Received Wisdom of the Canada-U.S. Free Trade Qualifications', in A. R. Riggs and Tom Welk, *Canadian-American Free Trade: Historical, Political and Economic Dimensions*, The Institute for Research in Public Policy, Montreal.

Workplace Relations Act, Australia.

Index